Politics of Post-Civil Society

Bulk Sales

SAGE India offers special discounts
for purchase of books in bulk.
We also make available special imprints
and excerpts from our books on demand.

For orders and enquiries, write to us at

Marketing Department
SAGE Publications India Pvt Ltd
B1/I-1, Mohan Cooperative Industrial Area
Mathura Road, Post Bag 7
New Delhi 110044, India

E-mail us at **marketing@sagepub.in**

Get to know more about SAGE

Be invited to SAGE events, get on our mailing list.
Write today to **marketing@sagepub.in**

This book is also available as an e-book.

Politics of Post-Civil Society

Contemporary History of Political Movements in India

Ajay Gudavarthy

Los Angeles I London I New Delhi
Singapore I Washington DC I Melbourne

First published in 2013 by

 SAGE Publications India Pvt Ltd
B1/I-1 Mohan Cooperative Industrial Area
Mathura Road, New Delhi 110 044, India
www.sagepub.in

SAGE Publications Inc
2455 Teller Road
Thousand Oaks, California 91320, USA

SAGE Publications Ltd
1 Oliver's Yard, 55 City Road
London EC1Y 1SP, United Kingdom

SAGE Publications Asia-Pacific Pte Ltd
3 Church Street
#10-04 Samsung Hub
Singapore 049483

Published by Vivek Mehra for SAGE Publications India Pvt Ltd, Phototypeset in 10/12 Minion by Diligent Typesetter, Delhi.

Library of Congress Cataloging-in-Publication Data

Gudavarthy, Ajay.
   Politics of post-civil society: contemporary history of political movements in India/Ajay Gudavarthy.
      p. cm.
   Includes bibliographical references and index.
   1. Social movements—India. 2. Civil society—India. I. Title.
HM881.G83   303.48'4—dc23   2012   2012045159

ISBN: 978-81-321-1041-5 (HB)

The SAGE Team: Rudra Narayan, Rohini Rangachari Karnik, and Nand Kumar Jha

Contents

Preface and Acknowledgements

This book is a result of my past and current engagement with the contemporary political movements in India. While these movements face what seem like insurmountable problems, they still manage to hold a promise and a hope. It is through my keen interest to understand these subtle and yet formidable transformative processes that I have attempted to think along with them. In thinking with political movements in India, I seem to discover and come to believe that there is something new beyond the known ways of conceptualizing them, which is what I refer to here as the emerging *Politics of Post-Civil Society*. This work, undoubtedly, would not have been possible without my everyday interactions and discussions with scores of activists and intellectuals associated with various political movements; to all of them I owe my gratitude. I thank specially those who helped in collection of material, offered to give interviews, and shared the organizational documents they had. I wish to specially mention Dr K. Balagopal, who has been a constant source of inspiration, defining, in said and unsaid ways, the purpose, intent and content of much of what I have thought and written, over the last decade or so. His loss continues to hurt.

I am thankful to all my colleagues at the Centre for Political Studies. Without the daily interactions and academic exchanges with them, it would have been a much tougher and a lonelier journey. In particular, I remain thankful to Gurpreet Mahajan who has, as always, taken a keen interest in this work, in the past as the supervisor of my Ph.D. thesis and lately as a colleague, with whom discussing issues has been as much of a learning process as was in being her student. I am thankful to Maninder, for the academic conversations, as much as for the fun-filled gossip as and for the sheer pleasure of talking to a colleague without having to think of consequences in the near and far-off future! I am grateful to B. S. Chimni, for his indulgence, and for all those wonderful evening walks and sane advice.

Most of the chapters have been presented at many national and international seminars, workshops and conferences. From the interactions in these events, I immensely benefitted, and in fact gained the confidence to put it together as a book. These would not have been possible without friends, colleagues and well wishers in the academic world. I presented the introduction as a special talk at the Centre for Citizenship, Civil society and Rule of Law (CISRUL), University of Aberdeen. Thanks are due to all those who offered useful comments, especially to Matyas Bodig and Andrea Teti. The second chapter on human rights was presented at Roskilde University, Denmark; my heartfelt thanks to Preben and Bodil with CIPACI, Punjab University, Chandigarh; Harvard Law School, Boston; LASSNET, Pune; DCRC and APISA, Delhi and the Centre for Human Rights (CHR), University of Hyderabad; I owe special thanks to Prof. Sudershanam at CHR for his efforts to organize and initiate discussion on this paper, and for inviting me as visiting faculty to the centre, where I completed some of the work related to the manuscript. An earlier version of the third chapter was presented at Queen's University, Belfast; ISEC, Bangalore; CESS, Hyderabad; Dr Ambedkar Centre, Madras University, Madras; and Tubingen University, Stuttgart, Germany; thanks are due to Divyaraj Amiya, for organizing this talk and many rounds of interesting discussions. The fourth chapter was presented at Global Cooperation Centre, EWHA Women's University, Seoul, South Korea; King's College, University of Aberdeen; NEHU, Shillong and NUJS, Kolkata. The fifth chapter was presented with CLACSO at San Jose, Costa Rica; Centre for Political Studies, Jawaharlal Nehru University, New Delhi; Centre for Civil Society, London School of Economics, London; CISRUL, University of Aberdeen; The sixth chapter was presented at the Department of Politics and International Relations, University of Aberdeen; Centre for Political Studies, Jawaharlal Nehru University, New Delhi. I am thankful to all the organizers and participants at these various events. I take this occasion to also thank the trustees of the Charles Wallace Trust, and the staff and faculty at the Centre for South Asian Studies, SOAS, for the three-month fellowship, where I completed the current version of the second chapter on the human rights movement. I am deeply grateful to the staff at the British Library, London, without whose efficiency this book would have been much poorer. I am also thankful to the British Academy for the grant as Visiting Fellow with Goldsmiths College, London, during which I completed much of the reading in plugging the gaps of the first draft of the manuscript.

I am ever thankful to all my friends who have steadfastly remained pillars of support. Kailash has been more than a friend, and like an antioxidant always held out prudent suggestions against my free-radicalism; Prashant, whose honest and simple ways have always come as a relief in cluttered times. Burra Srinivas always extended inexhaustible friendship, scotch and scorching debates. I am much obliged to my friend Trevor Stack, with whom I probably discussed all of the chapters and the nitty-gritty of many of the arguments presented here. I am also thankful to him for his timely invite as a visiting fellow to the Centre for Citizenship, Civil Society and Rule of Law, University of Aberdeen, where I completed the final draft of this manuscript, and for many rounds at the pubs in chilly summer evenings. Seetharam Kakarala, who has been supportive on more than one occasion, and has always been someone with whom I shared a lot of common concerns; I thank him for the support and encouragement; Govindraj Hegde, for his friendship and fond memories of Bangalore. I fondly remember Ram and Shiju, for Beef and Beefeaters, and for their constant support, and much needed breaks. Vishnu Dev, alias Lama, has been a constant factor in life for as long as I can remember. His friendship, great culinary skills and debates on his encounters with the everyday aspects of caste have been a source of great joy. This book hopefully will bring him back to academics! I wish to also thank Prof. Ravindra Sastry, Dr Ram Reddy and Dr Krishna Reddy, for their many invites to Osmania, and great many discussions on current developments in Andhra Pradesh. I owe special thanks to Krishna for helping me with material regarding the sub-caste movement. Finally, to John Game, for many spirited discussions on 'political society', and the disappearing breed of Socialists in Britain! I am thankful to Nivedita Menon for accepting to read earlier versions of the manuscript and Nandini Sundar for asking me to write for the Contributions to Indian Sociology.

I am grateful to my relations, without whose interruptions I cannot ever imagine writing. My uncles have been more in the order of friends, than relations. I got the best of the spirit of kinship and friendship; Bhakthavatsal, for his confidence in himself and me! Sujanvatshal for his daily calls, which had to be taken with a sense of urgency, more than even nature calls, to talk of nothingness and becoming, but those became an addiction for my being. Narender, Radha and Sreenivas, whose tough ways of life, and smooth ways of thinking, always kept company. Our family friends in Hyderabad, whose support and encouragement, since my childhood, in many silent ways added to the academic spirit. In particular, I am thankful to Prof. DNR and Prof. V. S. Prasad.

I wish to thank my brother Vijay, whose spirited ways more than made up for his being a teetotaller. I specially thank him for the fifth chapter of this book, the earlier version of which was jointly written. His knowledge of Kazipally was indispensable for that chapter. Hopefully, there will be more to come, and Krishna, for her silent ways and putting up with acrimonious debates at home, without giving up on us. Finally, I thank my parents, without whom this book simply would not have been possible. Both extended unflinching support through the thick and thin of my life, and it is to them that I dedicate this book.

I wish to acknowledge that some of the chapters in this book have been published, in earlier versions, though they have been substantially revised and read very different now. The second chapter, titled 'Human Rights Movements in India: State, Civil Society and Beyond', was published in the Contributions to Indian Sociology (April 2008); an earlier version of the third chapter was published titled 'Dalit and Naxalite Movements in Andhra Pradesh: Hegemony or Solidarity?' in the *Economic and Political Weekly* (December, 2005); and the fifth chapter was published titled as 'Antinomies of Political Society: Implications of Uncivil Development' (co-authored with G. Vijay) in the *Economic and Political Weekly* (July 2007). I duly acknowledge the journals.

Finally, I wish to thank the staff at SAGE Publications, who were not only professional but also warm and friendly, which made my task all the more enjoyable. In particular, I thank Rudra Narayan and Rohini Ranagachari Karnik for their help and cooperation all through the publication of this book.

1

Why Beyond Civil Society?

Civil Society has emerged as the most celebrated concept of the twentieth and also the twenty-first centuries. It has set parameters in offering practices that are the means and also certain normative ideals that are the ends to be achieved to preserve democracy and expand the process of democratization. However, whenever civil society has failed in actualizing these ideals, it has managed to obfuscate its failures. Whenever available practices have failed, reasons have been sought in the ideals being too lofty, and when the ideals have looked minimalist, the blame has been shifted to the nature of practices being free-floating and bereft of definitive borders. In this slip between means and ends, what has not diminished, however, is the hope that civil society will deliver, and is the *most desirable* way to achieve both democracy and democratization in contemporary times. The hope in civil society continues because it manages to project potently magical value in reinventing itself to hold the best of socialist ideals and the best of capitalist means.[1] It continues to have an uncanny ability of holding a promise to rejuvenate itself and reframe its ideals depending on who the actors are and what the ideals they wish to achieve are. Further, when these projects in reinventing and promising to rejuvenate fail to contain growing discontent and fail to translate into better living conditions for scores of peoples, it once again shifts the terrain to project itself as a neutral realm, where the rulers and the governed, capital and workers can not only peacefully cohabit but equally claim civil society for their own purposes—whatever they be.

This 'success' story of civil society in not actualizing the processes of democratization and yet continuing to remain our best hope is, perhaps, a comment on the ultra-flexibility of the concept itself, which is often seen as a mark of its democratic potential, but it could as well be a consequence of, what increasingly look and feel like 'politically disorienting times' we seem to collectively inhabit. Scholars and commentators of civil society have therefore, notwithstanding their own critique, despair and impatience, often sought to reimpose their faith in civil society and dithered away from writing its obituary. They have taken even the most scathing of arguments regarding the power dynamics, oppressions and structural inequalities that civil society is fraught with, to only read them back as a mark of the very spirit—manifested in its deliberative processes—in which civil society functions. Scholars who have been critical of the limitations of civil society, have continued in the spirit that they expose the 'conceits of civil society' '...not because I wish to discard the concept but precisely because I regard it as valuable' (Chandhoke 2003: 30). Much of the scholarship today has taken shelter in and sought the safety of reconciled—*fait accompli*—frames, where being resigned to the critique comes in lieu of looking for alternatives: Why should we move beyond a concept that celebrates the most bitter of its critiques as an evidence of its democratic spirit and draws strength in constantly adjusting the equation between means and ends so that we achieve democratization without sacrificing democracy itself?

Part of the reason for this 'refusal' to look beyond seems to emerge not so much because there is no critique, or acknowledgement by the scholars of civil society in place, as for the utter lack of clarity in envisaging the alternative. The unpredictability in envisaging the alternative and mapping its consequences look far more ominous, especially in the contemporary 'Risk Society' that we all inhabit, which is fraught with generic uncertainty as Ulrich Beck had argued. It is therefore felt and perceived to be more prudent to live with the familiar—the way we 'know' and understand freedoms, even if that means acknowledging no radical change and imposing debilitating limitations on the processes of democratization. Predictability is comforting, as against the 'homelessness' of the unknown, when we seem to have little choice in living as the 'Nomads of the Present'. With the stamp of the 'predictable-unpredictable dilemma', *on* and *in* democracy, civil society emerges as a zone of bounded anarchy, or predictable (read simulated) unpredictability.[2] Therefore, while there is no dearth of creative experiments—best represented by contemporary political movements—in negotiating the limitations of the processes of democratization within the contours of civil society, there however seem to be anxious attempts (as part of overcoming the discomfort with the unpredictable—the 'not-yet-known') to read and mould these creative experiments back into the safe haven and familiar categories that civil society offers. As Neera Chandhoke, representative of much of the recent scholarship on civil society remarks, with optimism:

> Having said that, let me also suggest that social movements can, through struggle, expand, and even transform, the sphere of civil society. They can do this by demanding that civil society deliver what it promises in theory— freedom from domination, freedom to achieve self-realization, freedom to assert selfhood. But this would mean that civil society possesses *but* the

potential for the self-actualisation of its inhabitants. Far from being a given, civil society is a project whereby individuals can realize their self through engagement, contestation and affirmation. (Chandhoke 2003: 27–28)

It is the argument that political movements can 'expand and transform the sphere of civil society' and the emphasis that it 'possesses but the potential' and the reaffirmation that 'individuals can realize their self', which are questioned and interrogated in this book. Much to the contrary, the arguments presented here make a case for the impossibility of negotiating structured power relations—of the rulers over the governed, of capital over workers, of various social hierarchies, including those of caste and gender—within the limits and through the kind of practices, institutions and ideas that civil society privileges. The impossibility (of achieving 'freedom from domination, freedom to achieve self-realization, freedom to assert selfhood') is created, as it will be argued in this book, due to two closely inter-related processes.

At one level, the different practices of civil society, such as constitutionalism, citizenship, legality, rights, autonomous intermediary institutions, voluntary spirit, diversity, cultural plurality, secular-associational values, among many others, interact and mutually condition each other in such a way that far from *progressively and cumulatively* leading to expanding free spaces, as scholars of civil society have been claiming, they in fact delimit, regulate and impose restrictions on the fuller articulation of 'contradictions', leading to a 'blocked dialectics'. As Gramsci had enunciated, 'blocked dialectics' is a situation where the anti-thesis (in this case the contemporary political movements) is itself appropriated to create a surrogate or a false synthesis (Gramsci 1971). The multiplicity and the tension *between* the practices of civil society that express themselves as '*the ambiguities of civil society*', as Chandhoke refers to, are not contextual or contingent in the sense of being neutral vis-à-vis dominant power relations, but constitutive in the sense that the very processes that they seem to inaugurate, in the name of democracy and democratization, become hegemonic—in actively replicating and reproducing dominant and structured power relations. It is therefore argued that *ambiguities are a modality of power in civil society* and the disparate looking practices of civil society *intersect*—reinforce—one another in reproducing power relations: economic, political and cultural. In other words, what are projected as the 'ambiguities of civil society' are neither open-ended and neutral, nor do they mutually or progressively check each other's excesses/democratic transgressions, but congeal democratic space (essentially but not exclusively for oppositional movements) to produce *points of intersection*—nodal points that reproduce, replicate and reinforce power relations.

At another level, it is argued that the lack or absence of progressive and cumulative 'direction' of these stated ambiguities in creating free spaces, have to and can be made sense of in the context of the *convergence* between the ostensibly autonomous realms or domains of State, market and civil society. Here again, *autonomy or separation of domains is a modality of power and power relations,* in the sense of consolidation and condensation of structured power relations in society at large. In other words, the *claims* of civil society to be autonomous of the dominant interests in state and market, allow for increasing convergence, in the sense of replication and reproduction, of such interests. Thus, ambiguities within or of civil society, and the purported autonomy or separation between different domains operate or fructify in a cohesive logic—as necessary and integral to the process of reproducing power relations; and therefore the consequences of 'the ambiguities of civil society' and the logic of separation of civil society from other domains are not contingent or open-ended, in the sense of being neutral to the existent power equations, as they are often made to be by the scholars and theorists of civil society. In an obverse way, the emergence of civil society as a neutralized site and as a consensual concept is *but* an indomitable evidence of this.

The constitutive nature of power relations have often been obscured in 'the ambiguities of civil society' being made to look contingent and open-ended; this in turn was made possible since its various practices— legal, moral, associational and institutional—have been studied either as independent and disconnected or if connected as necessarily complementary to each other in expanding freedoms, if not always as actively reinforcing each other but certainly as passively maintaining 'checks and balances' that are indispensable in producing an alliteration between democracy and democratization. David Beetham, in his article titled 'Liberal Democracy and Limits of Democratization' precisely makes this point affirming that certain limits in achieving democratization—primarily meaning overcoming injustices related to structured inequalities—are necessary to maintain the basic edifice of democracy, representative processes, privileging individual rights and autonomy, among other things, and therefore, according to him, liberal democracy is necessarily a 'paradoxical conjunction' (Beetham 1993). Similarly, with reference to civil society, it has been visualized that the limitations and tensions integral *to* and *between* various practices, institutions and processes in civil society are cumulatively made good, evened out, and counter-balanced, and thereby thought to also produce their own 'counter-hegemonic' discourses and politics. This ability to produce their own counter-hegemonic processes in itself accounts for and moderates the limits imposed on democratization, and therefore *gradually,* it is claimed, they open up free spaces that can be occupied by social actors struggling against dominant power relations.

However, if we were to approach these very practices and institutions that are privileged in the site we refer to as civil society at the point of their mutual interconnection in their concrete and operative dimensions, and study the consequences of such an *intersection* for radical-democratic political movements in India, the script and story seem to look very different. *Thinking with political movements in India,* it can be argued that increasingly the *constitutive ambiguities* of civil society have lead to a *mutual interconnection* of practices in such a way that they reaffirm and rein*force* the structural arrangements in society at large, including those in the state and the market. The ambiguities look and produce less of free spaces and more of providing a play for dominant structures to discipline those who attempt to escape its constraints. Civil society studied not merely or exclusively in theory or through the ideals it professes, but in its 'real-concrete' interaction with political movements and the way these movements have, especially in the last three decades, attempted to negotiate, engage and transform power relations, allows us to observe the way practices of civil society have repeatedly congealed to disallow and block this process; allowing us to then rewrite the script of the 'drama of history' and in the process might contribute to its obituary. It is therefore not the question of the slip between theory and practice that can be corrected by making amendments to either, but it is about the fit between them that makes civil society a formidable site of power and domination with dynamics that can be mapped in their moment of delimiting, overpowering and nudging-out those political expressions that have attempted to invoke an 'alternative' set of practices and ideals that hold a better promise of substantive justice, in the sense of overcoming power relations in their economic, cultural and political dimensions through the inter-linked processes of 'redistribution, recognition and representation'. In other words, we need to look at civil society through its dark side to properly appreciate, and in that process moderate our hope of what is really possible within the limits of this site.

The conflict of political movements with civil society and their attempts to innovate practices that might be in a fundamental conflict with the permissible—civil—limits of civil society, has often been missed by scholars in India, since political movements have been considered more as representative of this site rather than those contesting against civil society. While it is true that civil society provides them with space to mobilize and practices to work with, institutions to sustain them and ideals to achieve, it is also true that political movements have entered into irreducible conflict with the dominant and the most legitimate practices of civil society. The nature of this conflict is not *within* but *with* civil society, since the tension occurs at the *point of intersection* of several of its practices and not merely by the interaction between and through various practices of civil society. Ironically, this intersection is created in and through the very ambiguities of civil society. These ambiguities, far from creating open-ended and ever-expanding free spaces, congeal around political movements to block their political action, if not to suspend it. It is therefore sought to be argued here that *constitutive ambiguities* are a modality of the way power is structured and operates in civil society, rather than representing free spaces for political movements to work their way through. While they have overwhelmingly given a play to dominant structures and actors, they have predominantly blocked the 'dialectics of struggle'.

Ambiguities and Intersection

What, then, are these *constitutive ambiguities* of civil society and how have they entailed increasing and multiplying *points of intersection* that congeal 'democratic space' for political movements in mobilizing and resisting power relations? How are these *points of intersection* connected to the larger process of *convergence* between state, market and civil society? Since a wide range of practices, institutions, processes and ideals has been included in the ambit of civil society (one of the reasons, perhaps, why we remained oblivious to its structured operations), I will attempt here, and in the course of other chapters in the book, to trace and focus on those ambiguities and their links with the ensuing convergence between different realms that political movements in India themselves confronted, through a close study of their emerging discourse and politics.[3]

I will focus on five such contemporary political movements in India: the human rights, Dalit, Naxalite and feminist movements, and those emergent collectives against pollution and industrialization.[4] These movements are of significance since, as I argue, they have not only been in perpetual tension with the dominant site of civil society but also have attempted in the course of their struggles to inaugurate a new set of terms or politics that is beyond or *post-civil society*. In the course of building the trajectories of these political movements we find that these practices, ideas and institutions—in necessary tension and thereby in the projected ambiguous relation with each other—congeal by cancelling out each other and thereby their potential for democracy and democratization that they purportedly hold, to remerge in 'real-concrete' as practices that effectively block the ideals and goals that radical-democratic political movements espouse. The practices have an impact other than what they promise, since these practices do not operate in a vacuum but in relation to other practices within civil society, as well as those in the state and the market, and in course of this interaction the meaning and scope of these practices undergo a dramatic change.

Theories of civil society have only acknowledged the contested nature of practices but do not account for the overwhelming possibility that this contestation 'always already' creates a tilt, an imbalance favouring the dominant power equations; instead they have only bestowed a hope—a promise—that this contestation will keep the civil society neutral and open, to be reconfigured and mobilized for the purposes of oppositional politics. This is why the theory and normative ideals of civil society also create the mirage through which its practices can work and gain their legitimacy and cannot be separated or exonerated from the concrete failures of civil society. Therefore, merely 'by demanding that civil society deliver what it promises in theory' only creates an inextricable circularity that entraps oppositional politics on the one hand, and legitimizes and reifies civil society in spite of its repeated failures, on the other. We cannot sufficiently interrogate civil society from its own vantage point but through the concrete trajectories of political movements that have dithered but not hesitated in experimenting with the possibilities of crossing the threshold, instead of opting to dovetail and fold themselves back into the very practices and ideals in civil society that have been the source and design for the way power disperses itself.

To begin with, in the second chapter on the human rights movements (HRM), we highlight the constitutive ambiguity in the relation between civil society and the state. Civil society in modern democracies is 'simultaneously' conceptualized as a space independent and separate from the domain of the state, and also as a space inextricably linked and possible only in relation with the (constitutional-democratic) state. Therefore, it is simultaneously claimed that there 'can be no freedom without the form of the state', and the essential civil society is that which is 'outside' the state. For Locke, civil society had no distinct existence apart from the state; it comes into being in providing for stable set of standing laws, impartial judges and coercive powers given to the state for effective enforcement. In the words of John Locke, 'wherever therefore any number of men are so united into one society, as to quit every one of his Executive Power of the Law of Nature, and to resign it to the public, there and there only is Political or Civil Society' (Locke 2002: 1690, 325). For Locke, then, there was no effective distinction—in terms of their origin and historical purpose—between the state and civil society.

The Enlightenment concept of civil society, by the end of the eighteenth century, demarcated a sphere of economy, commerce and science, independent of the state.[5] The idea of civil society as an independent domain, in modern democracies, has however taken various forms other than for the purposes of carrying out commercial transactions. In the post-colonial contexts, for instance, it has assumed a distinction between secular-liberal and religious-communal conceptions of civil society. 'The first presses the case for legal recognition of voluntary civil associations (political parties, unions, pressure groups, etc.). The second delimits as "civil society" a space of practices and activities unregulated by the "legal-constitutional state"...' (Kaviraj and Khilnani 2002: 30). Another version of civil society that has emerged as an independent site—independent of conflicting power relations that are projected to exist only in the state and the market—is the one furthered by contemporary neo-liberal reforms. Chandhoke observes that 'as part of the neo-liberal agenda, civil society has been relentlessly and deliberately stripped of its ambiguities, its dark areas, and its oppressions, and presented to us as an area of solidarity, self-help and goodwill' (Chandhoke 2003: 9–10). As stated above, what is of significance is that these versions of civil society—that dependent and framed by the state and those independent of it—in modern democracies, work themselves simultaneously with close interconnection and mutual influence.

In working simultaneously they re-emerge—condense—in ways that are in contrast to the original imagination. Civil society is imagined to enable expansion of freedom—in being independent and outside the state—and the state is expected to regulate and legislate against power relations within civil society—in working through its constitutional-democratic vision. However, in the emergent inter-connection between these two imaginations or versions of civil society, the imagination of civil society as an independent site blunts the capacities of a constitutional-democratic state in regulating the 'dark areas and oppressions' in civil society on the one hand, and the ideal of a constitutionally-constrained civil society blocks the process of inventing independent and effective space and instruments for oppositional politics, on the other. Thus, the failure of civil society to emerge either as a site for realization of justice as a 'rights-based civil society' or as an effective site for oppositional politics is linked to the process where the constitutional-democratic version of civil society constrains oppositional politics, while the independent version of civil society, as an independent site, fails to interrogate its own dark sides.[6] In the process what seems to emerge is not a democratic space that achieves mutual balance between the two versions, which is what is generally argued by the contemporary scholars of civil society, but a political condition dependent on the overreach of the state—to control 'anarchic' tendencies—at one end, and in celebration of civil society marked by oppositional politics, as a pure 'realm of freedom' at the other end. The tension or play between the two versions of the civil society does not result in the *mutual* expansion or institutionalization of freedom and rights but they get reconfigured in their moment of being pursued as mutually exclusive versions of civil society. This disconnect, bifurcation and binary opposition, however, is also a *moment of intersection* where both the versions of civil society entrench each other, in the operative dimension of politics, and that effectively consolidates and reproduces existing power relations in society at large.[7] In other words, the constitutional-democratic state increasingly regulates and controls the oppositional forces in civil society (without reflecting or expanding the limits of constitutional-vision), while civil society and those representing it as a site of independent operations define themselves exclusively in opposition to the state (without interrogating the various sources of power and hierarchies that inhabit civil society).

Foley and Edwards, in an important intervention, have conceptualized and invoked the 'Paradox of Civil Society' (Foley and Edwards 1996). They seem to put forth the argument that there are two versions of civil society—civil society is dependent in democratic states and asserts independence under authoritarian states—and therefore they operate in two neatly distinct contexts. However, as we observe in the context of political movements in India, in the actuality of modern democracies both versions of the civil society work together. What this account of Foley and Edwards, in any case, misses is that the democratic and authoritarian aspects of the state itself are not separate but in modern societies come together, mostly dependent on each other. It is only with the backing of certain kind of authoritarian coercive powers of the state that allow for representative democracy to function, while the aspect of representative democracy legitimizes the authoritarian use of power where the coercive apparatus itself does not depend or draw upon popular consent. Gramsci had observed that it is imperative that 'the apparatus of state coercive power "legally" enforce discipline on those who do not consent either actively or passively' (Gramsci 1971: 12). Both are necessary conditions for the state to exercise its sovereign power. One cannot work without the visible or invisible support of the other.[8]

As the democratic and coercive aspects of the state are inter-dependent, the two 'versions' of civil society in modern democracies cannot be neatly—spatially or temporally—segregated. It is in fact the failure *in* and *of* that civil society, which is dependent and framed by a constitutional-democratic state in realizing its democratic-egalitarian ideals that leads to the assertion *for* and *of* a civil society that is represented as a pure 'realm of freedom', uncoupled from and in opposition to the state, but also stripped of, in denial of, its own 'dark sides and oppressions'. Civil societies in opposition and with a self-representation of being 'outside' the state have emerged and existed, not merely in authoritarian regimes, but also in societies governed by constitutional-democratic-developmental states. The autonomous versions of civil society are born of the necessity to frame a space in opposition to the simultaneous overreach and failures of the constitutional-democratic-developmental state, and thereby construct an equally centralized and cohesive civil society that is flattened out. Political movements in India too in their zealous opposition to the state and also the corollary or residual civil society framed through the discourse of constitutional provisions, have slipped into and contributed in constructing civil society as a space that is not only independent but also is sought as a pure 'realm of freedom'. This can be grasped only when we observe how in modern democracies both the versions of civil society—in and out of state—work together in tandem, and one coming to the rescue—'aid-and-abetting'—of the other in creating an inextricable circularity for those political movements attempting to question structured power relations. In other words, as constitutional-democratic states fail to regulate structured power relations, newer and autonomous versions of civil society with a focus on opposing the state emerge but in the process only obscure the power relations within those 'autonomous' realms. These 'autonomous' realms are imagined and constructed as mirror images of the state—equally cohesive and centralized—in order to equip and strengthen themselves to face and withstand the transgressions of the state—executed in the name of constitution and democracy.

As we shall elaborate in the next chapter on the history and politics of HRM in India, the civil rights movement began with imagining itself as a harbinger of a nascent 'rights-based civil society' framed through the available legal provisions of the Constitution and autonomy of intermediary institutions. It sought to achieve both civil and political rights as well as social and economic rights based on this vision. However, with the near complete failure of the 'developmental state', its centralizing propensities expressed through 'deploying' the welfare policies for the purpose of consolidating authoritarian regimes (for instance in India the imposition of the Emergency and implementation of the '20 point programme' happened together—one in the name of the other), and the enactment of a series of draconian laws in the name of preserving 'law and order' and decoupling order and peace from issues of justice, that the human rights movement began to nudge towards an idea of civil society not only in opposition to the state but also in order to challenge the centralized political structure of the state it attempted to build and claim a 'cohesive civil society' as a pure 'realm of freedom', bereft of an interrogation of power and domination within this realm. In consolidating against the state, they felt the pressure of obscuring hierarchies within the civil society that might not have necessarily flown directly out of the state. They failed to notice that in 'merely' opposing the state these hierarchies do not naturally or automatically die and get transformed but in fact remain unattended to, and thereby expand and reproduce themselves. Political movements from representing and contesting aspects of civil society came to be the civil society. This is what I refer to as the *logic of circularity* of civil society, wherein apparent movement towards more democratic practices and ideals, the power relations, instead of being displaced, in fact get reproduced and consolidated. In the case of the HRM, it seems to have constructed what it believed to be more radical notions or versions of civil society—that which is outside the state as against that which is framed by or dependent on the state—while the two versions of the civil society remain inter-connected through the logic of reproducing power relations. Political movements in shifting from one to the other and between these versions are engulfed in a circular logic of power relations.

In actuality, when political movements in India turned a blind eye to power relations within the realm of the civil society in constructing it as a pure 'realm of freedom', the state gained a renewed role and legitimacy in regulating these movements and eroding their space and the legitimacy of their opposition. In fact, as we shall discuss, the failure to negotiate with oppressions of civil society resulted in the growing tension between various kinds of political movements, for instance, between human rights and Dalit, or Dalit and Naxalite; the singular focus of these movements on the state and in opposing its formidable hold, in itself undermined their efforts to negotiate with the power of the state as well as the power relations in the civil society. The ambiguous versions of the relation between state and civil society far from contributing, as it was argued by proponents and later scholars of civil society, in checking the excesses of the state by the mobilizations in the independent civil society at one end and providing legal protection of the state to those vulnerable in the civil society on the other, intersect to cut the critical edge, and discipline political movements within the contours of the 'civil' practices that are privileged in civil society. In other words, the regulatory powers of the state and mobilizing capacities of the civil society have often been thought to check the mutual excesses of these two domains; however, approaching this relation through the prism and experience of political movements tells us that working within the parameters of this relation only pushes the movements towards a 'false antithesis'—state versus civil society; in reality, state and civil society work in tandem (not in checking mutual excesses, but in obscuring them) to preserve power relations in both the domains. In other words, civil society in consonance with the state and civil society as autonomous of the state are two modalities of preserving structured power relations, and working through these constructions or imagined 'alternatives' only entraps political movements within the logic of points of *intersection* and *convergence* that consolidates and reproduces power relations. In order to circumvent this convoluted logic of power, political movements needed to experiment with complex combinatory postures that re-signified the available practices *beyond* their limited and structured scope within civil society. As we shall discuss in the following chapter, it was only towards the end of the 1990s that the human rights movement could effectively grapple with this circularity, created by the simultaneity of different versions of civil society due to its projected ambiguous relation with the state, and attempt in its place a set of 'alternative' combinatory practices.

As integral to civil society, another set of ambiguous practices that the HRM had to face, was the expectation of individuals to maximize their self-interest as 'bourgeois individuals' working around the ethics of competition, individualism, ego as self-actualization, pursuing private interests as making profits and accumulating wealth that is well protected through the founding principle of right to private property, yet, simultaneously, strive for as citizens to build common interests of the society as such through the embodiment of 'civic virtues' and 'moral sentiments'. Civil society was to stand for competition in the economy as well as for the solidarity in society necessary for all collective and co-operative activities. Therefore, civil society is representative of the ethics of the free market at one end and the civic virtues that underpin the 'moral character' of the citizen through his or her involvement and commitment to the collective life, at the other end. In fact, the unique quality of civil society was sought precisely in succeeding in building 'civic virtues' to coexist with the virtues of market and free enterprise in the political economy, since both are foundational to the way civil society has evolved and expected to work.

> Hegel openly and Adam Smith not so openly, were perfectly aware of the many incivilities that civil society was capable of. In effect, they realized at the very moment that they conceptualized civil society as the *differentia specifica* of the modern age, that the acquisitive instincts and predatory passions of the inhabitants need to be tamed and moderated through various means...Neither for Adam Smith, nor for Hegel, was the sphere capable of reproducing itself, without deliberate intervention. (Chandhoke 2003: 28)

While Hegel reposed faith in the state to instantiate universality, Adam Smith argued for the nurturing of 'moral sentiments'. Civil society therefore, in its modern version, as developed by scholars such as Robert

Putnam and Francis Fukuyama, represents the nature of civic virtues on the one hand, and the virtues of free market economy on the other. For Putnam, the three crucial aspects of civic virtues in modern democracies are the active participation in public life, trustworthiness and reciprocity on the basis of which social bonds are created and nurtured (Putnam 1995; Fukuyama 1995).

Again revisiting this constitutive dilemma—expecting the self-interest of the 'bourgeois-individual' and the 'civic virtues' of the 'citizen-individual' to counter-balance each other—through the experience and experiments of contemporary political movements, we find that far from state or abstract moral sentiments succeeding in 'the taming of civil society' and in the democratization of the market, what we have witnessed is the increasing 'marketization of society' and emergence of 'market societies'. This again is not merely the hiatus between the theory or ideal of civil society and its concrete manifestation, but civil society and its relation with democracy itself works through such latent norms, where 'virtues' of competition, efficiency and accumulation are not merely foundational to the market but also are the defining features—as 'meritocracy'—for the practices of civil society.[9] The HRM noted that, civil society as a projected neutral site for a play between powerful, structured and entrenched interests and ostensibly counter-balanced with values, as moral sentiments, with an appendage-like status, 'always already' tilts towards preserving the status-quo, and also is potent enough to engulf political movements themselves into this vortex of mutual competition and imagining a zero-sum game. The HRM confronted this intersection latent in the practices of the citizen in civil society and the 'bourgeois-man' in pursuit of private interests, in the increasing conversion of particularities—*differentia specifica*—of different political movements themselves into *particularisms* with irreducible differences, negotiated through the prism of 'interest-group' dynamics. Again, as feminists have noted, for instance, the discourse of rights—foundational to civil society—inherently has a competitive ethic; they can 'restrict connectedness rather than enhance it'.[10] It is in this context, of moving beyond neutralized spheres, that the HRM revisited the distinction between interests and values, and foregrounded the need to go *beyond* the meta-construct of self-interest in its search for a more durable basis for a *politics of post-civil society*.

In the third chapter, based on the study of the history and politics of the Dalit movement in India, it is argued that yet another contriving dilemma that Dalit politics had to negotiate within the portals of civil society was the simultaneous privileging of (secular) voluntary-associational activity on the one hand, and celebration of 'politics of difference', including various cultural and ascriptive-based identities, as representative of plurality indispensable for a vibrant democracy, on the other. For Hegel, civil society was also a realm of mutual recognition between individuals, and in that sense, a site for what Charles Taylor refers to as 'Politics of Recognition'. Even the notions of civility that are foundational to civil society are realized through mutual recognition between individuals of different cultural and social groups as possessing equal 'moral worth'. These modalities of recognition assume various forms in modern democracies, including that of assertion of various cultural identities, and in the context of India assertion of ascriptive identities related to birth as 'identity politics', since civil society also privileges the principles of pluralism and acknowledgement of plural values. However, civil society on the other hand is also the site for associational activity (based on professional and other such secular practices), since civil society is also governed by the imperatives of (abstract) citizenship and autonomy of intermediary institutions (such as universities, banks, among others) grounded in principles of merit and efficiency as pillars of the 'nation building' efforts. What this tension is expected to yield, as again scholars of civil society claim, is 'an agonistic vision of citizenship in which universal elements are not imposed from above, but are the outcome of projects in which social forces change themselves in constituting alliances with other political identities' (Purvis and Hunt 1999: 457).

However, what we observe based on the different shifts in Dalit politics, is that in this conflict between finding *dignity* or recognition in expressing particularistic identities, and *mobility* by carrying out more secular-associational activity for partaking in the more universal (national) domain of law, rights and democratic institutions, the groups asserting identity in civil society, in fact, experience *mobility without dignity*. In other words, while they might achieve certain assurances from the state and in law as citizens, for instance policies of protective discrimination for Dalits in India, socially they remain slighted, and stigmatized for raising and pursuing what are generally perceived as sectarian interests. In allowing a certain kind of entry into the discourses of citizenship in civil society, there is a subtle stamp of robbing these very social and cultural groups of 'a sense of self' without shame. The very processes of civility hold within them modalities of incivility and indignity.[11] In other words, the processes that hold a 'promise' of extending the civility through inclusive policies and practices, in fact produce their own set of indignities as stigma and humiliation.

The simultaneity of the experience of indignity for pursuing 'sectarian' goals and ostensibly enjoying equal 'moral worth' through legal subjectivity, then have spiralling effects on the response of these social groups that get 'internally' split across conflicting imaginations, as Dalits versus the scheduled castes, and thereby pushed to adopt essentialized strategies to claim a sense of cohesiveness and agency. Through the study of Dalit politics in India, we could observe that as a response to this duality in the operations of civil society, Dalit politics expressed as *mobility without dignity*, reasserts through exclusivist and essentialized identity politics. This assertion of Dalit politics as identity politics, again, meets two distinct responses from civil society, one of further stigmatizing them for being closed, inward-looking and morally self-enclosed and arrogating essentialized discourses, and the other of opening a route of gaining entry into civil society through the prevalent discourses of plurality and celebration of cultural identities. This entry into civil society of Dalit politics as cultural identities then disconnects such politics from social and economic agendas for equality; such stand-alone cultural identities are further institutionalized through (liberal) discourses of secularism, tolerance and multiculturalism that 'naturalise' differences, maintain 'harmony' and construct 'solidarity' or 'fraternity' by instantiating *difference as distance*. By creating a self-image of differences being natural and not historical, the discourses of civil society tend to 'resolve' the immanent conflicts between hierarchized social groups by maintaining distance between communities and social groups. This distance could be social when discourses plead for mutual tolerance, cultural when groups claim exclusivist and authentic identity and even spatial when they are ghettoized into 'distinct' and separate localities.

Nancy Fraser, in the context of second-wave feminist politics in the West, remarks:

> With the shift 'from redistribution to recognition' came a powerful pressure to transform second-wave feminism into a variant of identity politics...In practice, the tendency was to subordinate social-economic struggles to struggles for recognition, while in the academy, feminist cultural theory began to eclipse feminist social theory. What had began as a needed corrective to economism devolved in time into equally one-sided culturalism. Thus, instead of arriving at a broader, richer paradigm that could encompass both redistribution and recognition, second-wave feminists effectively traded one truncated paradigm for another. (Fraser 2009: 108)

This 'trading off' is the only way political movements such as those forged by the Dalits gain re-entry into the well guarded portals of civil society. Thus, they are caught in a veritable *logic of circularity*—where entry into civil society for Dalits is made possible as 'naturalised' cultural entities, but this moment of assertion of identity and ostensibly gaining dignity and 'empowerment' is blocked through the disconnect with social and economic agendas, constituted by and as the 'ambiguities' of civil society, and thus fail to move forward in 'arriving at a broader, richer paradigm that could encompass both redistribution and recognition'. The *logic of circularity* of civil society, expressed as 'trading off', is what Dalit politics in India precisely experienced in getting 'regionally enclosed'—as E. P. Thompson had referred to in the context of artificial divisions between economy and culture or base and superstructure—marked by a process of increasing 'culturalization of politics'. In the case of Dalit politics in India, it was more specifically expressed in 'retreating' from the dialectic between the universal and the particular, and instead claiming an exclusivist cultural identity that was purportedly authentic and self-enclosed, based on an organic 'lived experience' that 'only Dalits' had access to. While essentialization was deemed necessary to force-open the closures imposed by the civil society—imposed as indignity for pursuing 'sectarian' goals as against more secular ones, it was also a moment for the Dalit discourse itself to naturalize Dalithood—by birth— that ostensibly cannot be shared by non-Dalits. The distance imposed by the civil society translated/overlapped with the 'retreat' and exclusivist frames of Dalit politics.[12] However, towards the end of the 1990s, from this logic of circularity, Dalit politics moved on to find ways of combining demands for redistribution with recognition, of de-essentializing Dalit cultural identity so that 'internal' fractures and hierarchies within could be addressed and new political identities and subjectivities through inter-subjective dialogue and political engagement could be forged. These combinatory postures were articulated through a sustained interaction with the class politics as espoused by the Naxalite movement.

The Naxalite movement, in taking recourse to armed-militant modes of waging struggle, was in any case considered to be outside the boundaries of civility as prescribed and privileged by civil society. It is in course of its dialogue with the Dalit politics that the Naxalite movement realized the importance of open organizations, and also of moving beyond their exclusive focus on class, to a combination of a caste–class approach. While the Naxalite movement realized the significance of caste—in its social, economic, political and cultural dimensions—in reproducing power relations, the Dalit movement moved out of its essentialized politics to reframe its politics by addressing the question of 'classes within caste groups'. In combining the cultural, political and economic dimensions, and not in an additive fashion or carrying a 'trade-off' necessary to find a 'legitimate' entry into the realm of civil society, the political movements challenged the structured power relations and the discourses that privileged them. It is important to point out here that moving beyond civil society essentially involved and was possible only by forging new subjectivities that emerged through inter-subjective communication, which was again not purely or exclusively deliberative in nature but grounded in concrete political struggles. Political movements emerge as the agents of politics of post-civil society in entering into mutual relation with each other. It is more through an ongoing *relational process* that they emerge as agents and gain the capacity to identify and negotiate the *points of intersection* in civil society and the necessary agency to instantiate alternative set of terms, than as individual political movements. Special emphasis has therefore been laid, in this book, on the study of political movements in their continuous dialogue and mutual engagement with each other.

In Chapter 4, thinking with feminist politics will allow us to realize the *logic of circularity* created by yet another constitutive ambiguity of civil society, that between the exalted emphasis on law and legislation by the state and the processes of institutionalization—in contemporary times specially as *governance reforms*—on the one hand, and the expansion of agency of the excluded social groups through protest politics, but more as an emphasis on voluntary action—in contemporary times expressed through *market reforms*—on the other. Some scholars championing the cause of civil society such as Cohen and Arato, argue voluntary action of civil society is best and exclusively represented by 'social movements' themselves (Cohen and Arato 1992). Civil society then, is posited as a site that ostensibly expands space for associational and protest politics, and those demands that emerge from such voluntary activity are in course of time converted into legal postulates, in order to institutionalize, and make them a more permanent feature of the democratic polity. In other words, 'efforts in civil society will come to naught unless the state codifies these efforts in the form of law or regulation' (Chandhoke 2003: 55). In doing this, it is argued, civil society brings a semblance of equivalence between law and politics, i.e., politics only made good in law. The fragmentary pressures created by politics are made good by the unity created through law and institutionalization, and in this social groups that were earlier marginalized get empowered in the backing they get from the state. As Khilnani affirmatively notes:

> Civil society presupposes a concept of 'politics': a conception which both specifies the territorial and constitutional scope of politics, and recognizes an arena or set of practices which is subject to regular and punctual publicity, which provides a terrain upon which competing claims may be advanced and justified...In this respect, even in situations of great social heterogeneity, politics can function not simply to entrench social division, but it can act as a cohesive practice. (Kaviraj and Khilnani 2001: 26)

Legality as the baseline of civil society and legislations as the ultimate focus set for protest politics reflect the *point of intersection*—'cohesive practice'—of practices that otherwise look independent. The mediation by law for both defining the limits of the means and also the purpose or ends of political actions, as the women's movement realized, does not result in legality/institutionalization and political action mutually enriching and strengthening each other. On the contrary, emphasis on legislation as the end, *progressively and cumulatively* erodes the space for political action by converting political issues into technical issues engulfed in winding procedural demands. Increasing translation of political issues into procedural aspects of law also reflects the way state *but* encroaches on the 'free spaces' in civil society; while legality as defining the limits of the means that are imposed by the civil society also impacts the ends that are achievable within those prescribed limits.

Again, Chandhoke observes (however, does not interrogate this any further, in her quest to reinstate civil society as a legitimate domain of politics) how civil society can impose 'unconditional' limits, in its emphasis on legality, when she argues:

> What, however, civil society actors cannot do is to challenge the state in ways that it does not allow—through say militancy, howsoever justified this militancy may be in the face of the brutal exercise of state power and the equally brutal exercise of power by privileged groups in civil society itself. (Chandhoke 2003: 54)

Thus, scholars of civil society recognize the brutality of 'privileged groups in civil society', and also its absolute prohibition of (justified) militant methods by those opposing that brutality, yet they prefer to argue that civil society is the only terrain where political movements need to achieve their cherished goals. In other words, civil society through its 'neutralized' legality, forces a reconciliation with 'brutal exercise of state power and equally brutal exercise of power by privileged groups in civil society'. This replication and reproduction of power relations, expressed as reconciliation, excludes those forms or modes of political action, such as militant action, that can potentially moderate, regulate and displace the 'brutal exercise of power by privileged groups in civil society itself'. This point could be further explained through the observation K. G. Kannabiran makes, regarding the law of violence and violence of law, when he says 'if violence in society is perceived as a breach of the law, the law itself is equally violent and in fact has an even more debilitating effect because of its systematic and thorough ruthlessness backed by official sanction' (Kannabiran 2004: 1).

Similarly, reflecting on aiming for legislation either as the singular or as an overwhelming focus of the political movements, feminist politics arrived at the conclusion that this only contributes to creating circularity and thinning of agency, but not expansion of freedom and certainly not emancipation. Feminists in India have been circumspect about the demand for more legislation in order to arrest growing discrimination, domination and violence against women. They argue that more legislation and a legal discourse as such leads to increasing state control, individualization of the problem of structured power relations, de-politicization through erosion of space for collective mobilization and simplification of the problems that have cultural, economic and social roots, in converting them into 'technical' problems to be solved within the institutional framework. Institutionalization additionally creates the problem of translating the complex experiences of women into a language legible for legal discourse. However, in going 'beyond the law' there is again the risk of movements walking into the very politics of civil society, by willy-nilly privileging the methods of the NGOs that seem to further the discourse of 'getting-state-out-of-the-way', and thereby replacing the responsibilities of the state with that of individuals being responsible for their own actions, again in the name of expanding agency through voluntary participation. In questioning as well as in focusing on the law there seems to be a pre-set consequence of individualizing structured power relations or de-politicizing power relations in negotiating them outside their structural context. Thus, civil society creates a *logic of circularity* by reimposing its preconditions and pushing the movements to predetermined consequences—individualization and de-politicization; whether they reinforce legality or attempt to undermine it. Feminist politics attempted to circumvent precisely this circularity in interrogating the *points of intersection* in civil society, between law, public morality, civility, voluntary action, governance and governmentality, in the context of a political economy marred by a growing market economy. In comprehending the equivalence—in preserving power relations—between these practices that otherwise look disparate and capable of moderating each other, feminist politics throw light on the need for a set of new practices that are beyond the confinements of civil society and its accompanying ambiguities and convergence.

In Chapter 5, we deal with the claims of civil society that it remains the most *potential site* for the articulation of democratic politics because it allows for the proliferation of a multiplicity of practices as representative of different kinds of conflicting interests that exist. It also ensures an 'open-society' since it draws a wedge and separates the modality of operation of different spheres, primarily that of state, civil society and market. From the point of view of politics in civil society, those societies which obliterate this distinction either become totalitarian—excessively ordered and controlled by the state, or disintegrate into anarchy—excessively encroached by the logic of market or free associational activities of civil society. In other words, the 'separation' between the spheres allows for 'checks and balances' without any one of them transgressing the boundaries they need to be confined to, so that democracy is functional and vibrant.

As we have argued, civil society seems to achieve its *points of intersection* between the disparate practices and *convergence* with other spheres precisely through the multiplicity of its practices and claiming autonomy for different spheres. *Multiplicity and intersection* and *separation and convergence* then do not occur at different levels but fructify as modalities of the way power flows. In other words, the disparate practices that ought to represent a multiplicity of modalities of operation within civil society in practice actually coalesce and congeal, so does the logic of separate spheres that also is only a modality or a 'form' of convergence between them to reproduce and reinforce structured power relations.[13] 'Separation' is only a modality for convergence to work; 'this is to say that civil society, as we currently know it, is not only superfluous, but dangerous, as it presumes and reinforces both the state and corporate forms through the theory of autonomous spheres of activity' (Day 2005: 213).

However, the *points of intersection* within civil society and the *moment of convergence* with other spheres are made possible through a series of exclusions. Civil society excludes all those practices that can potentially disturb this arrangement and they are framed as the 'other' of the practices privileged in the state, civil society and market. Thus, civil society draws a series of binary oppositions between the practices it privileges and those that it excludes. For instance, legality excludes the illegal, modern the traditional, civil the uncivil, and so on. These are not 'given' or natural, though civil society constructs or projects them as such, but selectively built to suit the transactions within civil society and the imperatives of its interactions with other spheres. What is then legal or civil in civil society is not arbitrarily constructed but in accordance with the logic of maintaining existent equations between the three 'separate' spheres and power relations within each of them. For instance, challenging property relations or not honouring contracts is considered illegal, but advertisements that routinely flourish on giving either exaggerated images of their products or by making false claims, are not considered to be either illegal or uncivil, but as 'information' necessary to allow exchange relations and trade to grow in the market.[14] It can therefore be argued that multiplicity as intersection and separation as convergence is realized in and through the binary oppositions and the modality of bifurcating or dichotimizing practices within these spheres.

If power equations replicate through binary oppositions, how do we then disturb these binary oppositions? One possible way is to 'alternatively' privilege those practices that are excluded by the civil society, i.e., argue for illegality, incivility and tradition. This, it can be argued, potentially disturbs the balance and the scope of the practices that are privileged in civil society, state and market. However, this inversion, as we will discuss in the fifth chapter, does not amount to subversion, since the modality of maintaining power relations is not instantiated merely in the practices that are privileged and legitimized but at the very moment of drawing the binary opposition itself. In other words, privileging those practices that are excluded from civil society without questioning the methodology of constructing binary oppositions itself entails being engulfed in the *logic of circularity*, as it is constructed in civil society. For instance, as we discussed in relation to the feminist politics, in order to undermine the centrality of law, the women's movement did not have the easy option of going beyond the law or not taking recourse to legislations, which would have entailed letting the state off the hook and getting into the logic of neo-liberal reforms—the logic that individuals need to take responsibility for themselves, in the name of voluntary action and freedom.

The binary oppositions 'within' civil society and their grip on politics cannot be overcome in merely glorifying and emphasizing that which has been 'othered'. In other words, the tyranny of legality cannot be overcome by foregrounding illegality, civility by instantiating incivility, modernity by legitimizing tradition, institutions by celebrating simple minded voluntarism, and so on. This only further reifies and reinforces the dominant practices of civil society. Thus, in formulating the notion of 'political society' as a 'constitutive outside', as Partha Chatterjee does, one attempts to frame politics through those categories that have been excluded and undermined by the politics and discourse of civil society, without questioning the modality of constructing the binary opposition itself (Chatterjee 2004). Instead, Chatterjee further reinforces the binary approach by emphasizing and privileging those practices that have been considered illegal, uncivil and traditional as belonging to a 'separate' realm that he refers to as the 'political society', in an attempt to of course dislodge the hegemony of civil society. In the process, he builds another supra-binary between civil society and political society. This approach, however, cannot destabilize the hegemony of civil society but actually reifies civil society, projecting it 'as if' it were a pure realm of legality and civility.

In the same chapter on 'political society', we attempt to deal with this dilemma and ensuing circularity that civil society sets up. The notion of political society, in taking the binaries as 'given', attempts to draw an 'alternative' site that is constituted by all those practices that civil society shuns and delegitimizes, and thereby overlooks the fact that the *moment of the binary* is also the *moment of blocked dialectics*. Through the study of the new collectives against pollution in the industrial towns, it is critically argued that Chatterjee, in resorting to construct an 'alternative' domain of 'political society', valorizes the subaltern dependence on paralegal means which as 'survival strategies' and 'contextual negotiations' pushes them into a logic of demanding merely subsistence benefits from the state—'moral claims' in the language of political society—dependence on the good-will of the influential with cultural capital; and all this effectively culminates, I argue, in the thinning of the agency of the subaltern. In claiming an 'autonomous domain', the subaltern in fact gets more regulated by the dominant structures and power relations-*à la* Foucault. Autonomy represents itself as regulation.

In thinking with political movements in India, we learn that they never had the easy option of working in a neatly arranged alternative site, but had to draw various combinatory postures that of being 'in and out' or 'in-against-and-beyond'. Political movements in India, in contrast to the approach and methodology of the notion of political society, came to realize that binary constructions entail circularity that offer no easy way-out for circumventing and displacing power relations. By merely opting for the obverse practices by those excluded by the civil society only results, willy-nilly, in further entrenching and reifying the domain of civil society 'as-if' it were a realm of pure legality and civility. While in the operative part, the very constructions of the legality and civility are 'always already' contaminated by the illegal and the uncivil, which mark their 'foundational violence'. Legality itself is becoming illegal: '*When the Rule of Law is illegal*' to borrow from the title of Mattei and Nader's book, notions of peace and non-violence themselves hide structured or institutionalized violence, voluntary action itself produces discourses of withdrawal of state and pushing the responsibility to the individuals, 'politics of events' itself short-circuits politics as a process, language of rights itself in fracturing cooperative relations undermines the possibility of their realization and discourses of tolerance themselves institutionalize intolerance—in institutionalizing difference as distance, or in furthering identity politics as 'politics of presence' itself stigmatizes in undermining and de-coupling them from 'politics of ideas'. Political movements, therefore, had the challenging task of re-signifying the available practices in civil society without reifying them and exposing the power dynamics hidden in their interstices without the privilege of not engaging with them. In critiquing and highlighting the difference in the approach of 'political society' with that of the political movements, we shall attempt to elaborate on some of these dilemmas and/as circularity that practices of civil society entail.

In the final chapter, written in lieu of a conclusion, we shall take up the task of consolidating and putting together the insights and signposts that political movements are bringing into relief in course of negotiating power relations in civil society. The trajectory of these movements is by no means linear, and clear but chequered and marked by moments of slipping back, dithering and withdrawal. But praxis and conceptualizing in the context of praxis never was any different. It is in the conceptualization of *politics of post-civil society* that we shall attempt, in a tentative and preliminary sense, taking cues from the discourse and politics of contemporary political movements, in the last chapter of this book. The study of civil society has to be carried out with this emphasis on convergence with state and market, and consider this as constitutive and integral to the way it works rather than as contingent or contextual. The contemporary processes of neo-liberal reforms only make these characteristic features less hidden, and more obvious. However, scholars of civil society have often considered this as specific of only the civil society as it is emerging today, and therefore have made renewed pleas to invigorate the ideal-type notions of civil society, and—as part of the logic of circularity—ended up looking for means to fold these processes back into civil society in asking for its expansion and demanding of it to 'to deliver what it promises in theory'—only further reifying it.

Autonomy and Convergence

Any conceptualization of the *politics of post-civil society* can only be attempted in mapping the constitutive nature of the convergence between the state, civil society and the market. The trivalent nature of the process of convergence is in fact the defining feature of the 'context' in which political movements are mobilizing and operationalizing oppositional politics. The current context, as always in the past (only more visible and obvious now) is marked by all the three simultaneous processes of convergence:

1. Increasing support of the state to the unequal and formal exchange relations in the market;
2. Growing marketization of relations and processes in civil society;
3. Replication of the hierarchies in civil society in and through law.

Commenting on such an inter-link between the state, civil society and the market, Michael Walzer observes that:

> It is a false view of civil society, a bad sociology to claim that all that goes on in the marketplace is free exchange and that coercion is never an issue here. Market success overrides the limits of the (free) market in three closely related ways. First of all, radical inequalities of wealth generate their own coerciveness,

so that many exchanges are only formally free. Second, certain sorts of market power organised, say in corporate structure generate patterns of command and obedience in which the formalities of exchange give way to something that looks very much like government. And third, vast wealth and ownership or control of productive forces converts readily into government in the structural sense. Capital regularly and successfully calls upon the coercive power of the state. (Walzer 1984: 321–22)

State-Market Convergence

Without the backing and guided power of the state, markets cannot be 'free'. In fact the idea of being 'free' in markets 'always already' assumes the support of the state. Markets do not grow 'naturally'; as Frederic Jameson remarks, 'it must be brought about by decisive legislations and other interventionist means', and this as he says is as much true about the nineteenth century, that Polyani referred to as *The Great Transformation*, as it is for the period of Thatcher who proclaimed the irreversibility and singularity of marketization through her belief in the 'TINA factor' (Jameson 2000: 58); and this continues unabated till today's politics around the Eurozone. Legislations are made to change the legal regimes of the nations where 'free markets' are to be opened up in the name of 'structural adjustment' and strengthening of rule of law that again, Mattei and Nader refer to as the modern day '*Plunder*' assisted by the process '*When the Rule of Law is illegal*' (Mattei and Nader 2008). These changes are always brought through arm-twisting methods within the international financial bodies such as the World Trade Organization, the International Monetary Fund and the World Bank, through various methods, including imposing conditions on borrowing nations and suggesting legal changes through reforms in governance—in the name of 'good governance'. However, this is only one aspect or side of the story; this conformity in the legal regime is always backed by more brutal means that presuppose the coercive state power.

Observing this use of state power in its most brutal form to open up and privatize economies across the globe, Naomi Klein refers to it as '*The Shock Doctrine*' leading to the '*Rise of Disaster Capitalism*' (2007). Referring to the experiments of the 'Chicago school' she argues that it was part of a deliberate strategy to open up markets and sell off public property to private players, through a strategy of waiting for and coinciding the changes with the timing of natural disasters to occur, and before they slip back to what they refer to as the 'tyranny of the status quo'—'*intersection* between super-profits and megadisasters'.[15] She argues that 'now the same ideological program was being imposed via the most badly coercive means possible: under foreign military occupation after an invasion or immediately following a cataclysmic natural disaster. September 11 appeared to have provided Washington with the green light to stop asking countries if they wanted the US version of "free market and democracy" and to start imposing it with shock and awe military force' (Klein 2007: 11). This strategy of the state–market partnership, nationally and globally, in fact, was not invented post 9/11 but only perfected. Klein argues that it was part of the strategy of the spread of advanced capitalism that is visible in its most blatant form when rapid transformation of economy—tax cuts, free trade, privatized services, cuts to social spending and deregulation—was implemented soon after the coup by Pinochet in Chile, in Argentina in the seventies with the aid of 'terror' spread by the military junta, right up to the post 9/11 invasion and occupation of Iraq, and more recently, Libya.[16] Within nations both capitalist and also those claiming to be socialist, Klein argues, 'reforms' were introduced in a similar manner. In China in 1989, economic reforms followed the Tiananmen Square massacre, and in the USA, soon after the hurricane Katrina in New Orleans. These are the same forces clamping down in the Middle East in the name of spreading democracy, in 2012.[17] It is within the context of this kind of convergence that the sectoral analysis of civil society, state and market are strongly proclaimed, giving us an insight into their ideological role.[18]

Market–Civil Society Convergence

The state–market convergence, then, is not possible without either civil society–market or state–civil society convergence. Civil society and market converge with increasing marketization of social relations, both 'ideologically' and structurally. As we have already discussed, civil society is a site for individualism and pursuit of private interests, but this is sought to be moderated through nurturing 'moral sentiments', or regulated through legislations by the state, institutionalizing formal or contractual relations between citizens. In assuming the neutrality of the civil society is the implicit assumption that the state is unbiased (for instance, in class terms) and the market is marked only by exchange relations, whereby the rise of commercial societies made it possible for market relations to be set apart from personal relations based on solidarity and mutual empathy. 'For Adam Smith, for example, in pre-commercial societies all human social relations were pervaded by exchange relationships: it was only commercial societies that had successfully instituted a distinction between the realms of market exchange and personal relations' (Kaviraj and Khilnani 2002: 20). However, as we have argued, this institution of a distinction or separation itself is a modality for convergence.

This convergence is realized through a web of interconnected 'changes' introduced in political language and social ideology. It is therefore not a coincidence that the resurgence of civil society coincided with the emergence of 'Washington Consensus', where it becomes the watchword for the World Bank, the IMF, the U.S. treasury department, the MNCs and a site represented by the proliferation of the NGOs (Goonewarden 2004).[19] This process of freeing state executive from social responsibilities is aptly summed up in the World Bank's definition of civil society:

> Civil society consists of groups and organizations both formal and informal, which act independent of the state and market to promote diverse interests in society. Social capital, informal relations and trust which people bring together to take action is crucial to the participation and gives voice to those who may be locked out of more formal venues to affect change. (quoted from Harriss 2007)

The notion of groups acting 'independent of state and market', at one level exonerates state of its social responsibilities and at another level reinforces the rules of the market that individuals and groups need to fend for themselves and 'invest' the 'capital' they possess. Therefore, by the extension of this logic, groups who do not possess fiscal or financial capital, need to then 'invest' their 'social capital'—community ties and social bonds—to gain financial benefits and ameliorate their economic position. It is, however, pertinent to observe that three decades of 'experimenting' with Self-Help Groups (SHGs), and microcredit have neither resulted in formation of new classes (as in class mobility) nor accumulation of capital for marginalized social groups; on the contrary there has been a spurt of intra-subaltern conflicts, proliferation of social fragmentation and even in some cases reported suicides related to microcredit operations.

Civil society here, in political terms, therefore stands for 'democracy without the inconvenience of democratic politics and radical political action' (Ibid.). In fact, the percolation of this model is so deep that even the alternative movements for resistance against the processes of 'globalization and neo-liberal reforms' themselves adopt the NGO-type functioning to gain both a foothold in what is projected as the emerging global civil society—transnational, and in order to project 'alternatives' that *look* realistic to what has been projected as an 'irreversible process'. For instance, the role of the World Social Forum constituted by various NGOs, is itself 'a sign of the movement's defensive character, still unable to formulate an alternative hegemonic strategy' (Sader 2002: 93). This shift to NGO-ization of oppositional mobilization is made possible when the notions of the private subsume the public. The public gets redefined through a series of private acts, NGOs being one of them.[20] The ideals of substantive justice seem to assume within civil society more formal, symbolic or heuristic value wherein, willy-nilly, they assume the shape and purpose of creating a social or political mirage, if not an outright justification for growing inequalities due to increasing marketization-privatization, of social relations and 'public morality'. For instance, the ideals of justice, such as universal health care or education, themselves overlap or operate through the increasing 'privatization of the public'. We are witness to a more explicit change where the public—as in the State, for instance—is getting increasingly privatized in its role and purpose, while the private—as in the corporate—is beginning to perform more public activities through their expanding philanthropic activities that include support to health care and education, among many other such activities. The private, in assuming the duties of the public and the public in assuming the shape and scope of the private, is what finally aids the process of 'marketization of society' and assigning a symbolic value to the ideals of substantive justice.[21]

Further, civil society begins to represent a site where the distinctions between citizen and consumer collapse.[22] The identity of being a citizen is itself being reworked through the exchange relations and processes of consumption central to the domain of the market, making it possible to note that 'societies may have reached a historical threshold in which it is no longer possible to think such ideals as citizenship and democracy in the absence of consumption' (Canclini 2001: 20). It is a classic case where public morality, participation and rights are signified through the overlap or equivalence they enjoy with exchange relations in the market. Thus, dominant morality is signified through and as consumerism, participation as taking responsibility and not being dependent on the state and rights instantiated through the element of competitive ethic integral to them. The projected neutrality and universalism of citizenship—grounded in legality—are now reproduced through the identity of the consumer, grounded in exchange relations. This change, however, has been integral to the way civil society and market have evolved—as Frederic Jameson noted about the relation between state and market—rather than emerging in the present as a 'historical threshold'.[23] It is, perhaps, more appropriate to refer to the newly emerging *global reach* of this process—'time-space compression'—that David Harvey referred to, more than *global shift*, wherein now 'culture-ideology of consumerism serve to naturalize global capital everywhere' (Yudice 1995: 17).[24]

State–Civil Society Convergence

Finally, the convergence between state and civil society happens through the mediation and the reach of law. As we have already discussed, the reach of law transmutes—as expanding legal subjectivity—into increasing state control and instantiation of processes of individuation. At another level, it also reproduces—does not challenge—the social hierarchies in the silence of law in the name of maintaining the autonomy of civil society. As Anne Phillips observes, 'we do not find women in Masonic leagues, as we do not find men in the mother's union' (Phillips 2002: 75). Power relations—be they as increasing state control, or be they as reproduction of social hierarchies—as structured social processes, reinvent themselves.

It is these processes of reinvention that political movements attempt to negotiate with, in their myriad forms, by drawing forward–backward linkages in a distinct moment of 'dialectics of struggle'. Political movements collectively and in a relational sense emerge as agents of such a transformation by critiquing the critique offered by discourses of rights, plurality, tolerance, and so on, as it exists in the civil society with its capacity to create the *logic of circularity*. This coupled with a self-critique by the political movements, made possible through the emerging new subjectivities in the interstices of inter-subjective engagement, is what takes their politics and discourse beyond the neutrality of the language of ambiguities and paradoxes, which is what then is distinctly post-civil society about them.

Notes

1. Peter Drucker, in his book *Post-Capitalist Society,* makes one such claim when he argues that the USA now is representative of what is best in capitalism and also socialism. He cites instances such as workers' pension funds being invested in stocks and shares, and argues that it can therefore be claimed that workers have a share in the ownership of many corporate companies, and that welfare/egalitarian measures are being combined with the free market economies.

2. The recent manifestation of this dilemma in democracy and the role of civil society—as a zone of predictable unpredictability— could be observed with the anti-graft movement in India headed by Anna Hazare. While all he was demanding was a new legislation and a new institution to deal with corruption, the media argued that it would herald unprecedented changes in Indian democracy; even as it was being questioned by many as to how it could have any radical or even significant impact in controlling corruption without addressing its deeper roots in the nature of political economy. However, notwithstanding this, the debate was 'bounded and regulated' within the boundaries of what is a healthy equation between representative dynamics of democracy as against the associational aspects of civil society, without the debate ever spilling over to the link between corruption and on-going economic reforms and what has in effect happened to patron-client relations in a privatized economy. For an analysis of various political positions that emerged as commentaries on the anti-graft movement, see Gudavarthy 2011a.

3. The role and nature of political movements have often been framed through the discourse of civil society. Here I attempt the obverse: to 'frame' civil society and its

operations through the discourse and politics of political movements in the course of mobilizing their respective constituencies.

4. Conventionally, political movements have been differentiated from social movements on the basis of the former making a claim to political power as against the latter being disinterested in political power and operating within the social domain. However, following Foucault, after the 1970s, while industrial society was being disintegrated, there emerged the 'new domain and field' which Foucault calls 'the social' that neutralized the problematic relation between politics and economy. Civil society represents this neutralized/depoliticized relation between politics and economy. The term, political movements, expresses the idea that these political formations are attempting to understand power at its points of intersection and convergence between the social, political, cultural and social domains, better than the expression, social movements. I therefore prefer to refer to some of the movements that I study closely as political, rather than social movements, but not on the basis of their claims to state power. However, in the study of movements in India by various scholars, these terms have often been used interchangeably (see Shah 1985).

5. Refer to Keith Michael Baker, 'Enlightenment and the Institution of Society: Notes for a Conceptual History' in Sudipta Kaviraj and Sunil Khilnani (ed.) *Civil Society*, Cambridge University Press, Cambridge, 2002.

6. One such anxiety that was raised by many scholars in India was whether or not the popular mobilization by the far-right Hindutva forces belonged to the civil society, given its features of popular mobilization, participation which were also the ideals of civil society, but intended reimposing dominant hierarchical relations and majoritarianism that belied what civil society stood for (see Amritha Basu 2001).

7. For arguments that different versions and practices of civil society eventually and effectively, balance and mutually check each other to maintain democratic space as open and functional, especially in the context of India see Chadhoke 1995; Bhargava 2005; T. Jayaraman 2005.

8. There is an increasing 'interlocking of the ordinary and extraordinary' (Singh 2004). In India, the State has governed all through not merely through electoral politics and high politics of institutions but through repression and coercion manifested in the extra-judicial killings, cases of disappearance and enactment of a host of draconian laws (more on this in the chapter on the HRM). The democratic and repressive aspects coexist and are also mutually dependent. For instance, even as the State in India is seriously considering abolition of capital punishment, it is indifferent to the critique against resorting to extra-judicial killings (Lokaneeta 2011). Often those issues that are perceived to be beyond the frame of a constitutional-democratic state, such as challenges to state sovereignty (demands for secession) or property relations (demands for radical redistribution), are settled through the coercive apparatus of the state and thereby filter the issues that can be debated and put in the open—in the public sphere—in order to obtain popular consent.

9. Richard Dagger in his book *Civic Virtues* precisely raises this question of how rights lead to the emergence of excessive individualism, and thereby implies the decline of community-orientation. However, he argues that rights can be balanced with responsibilities; but, as we argue in the chapters to follow, this privileging of responsibility or (political) obligation takes the shape of formal-contractual relations and does not realize themselves as solidarity and fraternity (Dagger 1997).

10. The influence of this on democracy is visible in Habermas' arguments that advanced capitalist nations are today, like never before, prone to 'motivational crisis' bringing into crisis all forms of cooperative and collective activity, including taking part in representative-electoral politics visible in the declining voter turnout in the USA and

to some extent in Europe. This, however, has been converted in modern theories of liberal democracy, as in itself a new feature of the 'freedom' and leisure that these societies grant to their citizens, since modern forms of representation and the role of experts relieve citizens from the duties of vigilance and political participation. David Held explicitly argues for looking into the possibility of thinking of the 'right not to participate', as part of the repertoire of modern liberal democracies. He also further argues that the order of legitimacy of the state itself has undergone profound change and what we must be looking for today is not absolute legitimacy but 'strategic legitimacy', where citizens have a *quid pro quo* relation with the state, and know very well that state is biased towards certain classes of citizens; they nevertheless engage in bargaining for welfare and benefits of governmentality (Held 1993).

11. It is here that scholars of civil society and citizenship have been optimistic about the scope of the project of citizenship and democratic-institutional practices of civil society, as Purvis and Hunt argue that the project of citizenship 'is never complete but remains open to contestation and supplementation, and the theoretical elaboration of which is crucial to the development of democratic responses to the problem of the constitution of political community' (Purvis and Hunt 1999). The emphasis on the project of citizenship remaining 'open to contestation and supplementation' however misses the point of how these practices 'compel' movements to adopt more essentialized postures to get heard, which in turn stigmatizes these groups.

12. We could draw parallels here with the HRM. While the HRM constructed civil society as a 'pure' realm of freedom, as against a centralized state, Dalit politics as against a homogenized-secular civil society constructed essentialized—'pure'—identities that were disconnected from social and economic agendas and bereft of interrogation of 'internal' hierarchies and exclusions within Dalits, instead alluded to authenticity based on exclusive 'lived experience'. This, perhaps, allows us to explain the different 'forms' in which the 'logic of circularity' constrains oppositional political expressions, all of them nevertheless converging in reinforcing and reproducing existing power relations.

13. For instance, so long as the spheres operate on logics internal to them—production through wage-labour in the economy—then political and cultural domains can enjoy autonomy and proliferate with civil liberties and stand-alone cultural identities. However, the moment either the discourse of human rights or cultural politics bring within their fold issues related to political economy, for instance, ownership and questioning of private property, then the structures and practices of these 'autonomous' spheres begin to converge. This can also be read the other way round, the moment certain kind of cultural assertions are made—for instance those by the LGBT, then the state jumps in with legal sanctions of criminalizing it, so does economy/markets make jobs and social security unavailable to them.

14. For instance, invariably all brands selling toothpaste either claim shining white teeth or social popularity and quick visibility. Factually both are incorrect, but it is never thought that these companies should be penalized, instead often, the more the exaggeration, the better the reward. Crime and illegality are therefore often constructed in accordance with the prevalent imperatives within civil society, state and market.

15. This book only focuses on the intersection constructed by drawing equivalence between various social, economic, cultural and political practices. However, Klein here is drawing our attention to the possibility of even including 'natural disasters' to preserve dominant power relations, of course as environmentalists have argued many of the so-called natural disasters are actually 'man-made'. I partly allude to some of these concerns in my debate on pollution in the fifth chapter.

16. It is however interesting to observe that when state–market partnership is structural in nature and backed by brutal coercive power, within the academic circles and discourses this is rarely acknowledged and often termed as being 'reductionist' to argue this way. It was my experience while teaching the postgraduates at Jawaharlal Nehru University that any suggestion of this was always greeted by questions and doubts whether it was not too 'reductionist' to argue that way. It is true that the state therefore has both ideological dimension that works in this case through ideas regarding complexity—irreducibility—of modern systems or societies, which itself assumes the role of an 'ideological state apparatus' (ISA) in civil society represented by the universities and also the coercive dimension through its police, army and prisons, which is what accounts for it as the 'repressive state apparatus' (RSA). Those political forces that foreground this possibility of the coercive role of the state—including use of Intelligence agencies, deceit, stealth and manipulation—are critiqued for indulging in unwarranted 'conspiracy theories'. Thus, on the one hand, the critiques of reductionism and 'conspiracy theories', and the brutal use of coercive/manipulative powers by the state on the other, seem to work in tandem. The recent arrival of Wikileaks has only further confirmed what has been argued and widely believed about the state and its behind-the-scene machinations.

17. Klein suggests many more incidents including the Falklands War in 1982, the NATO attack on Belgrade in 1999, in Russia in 1993 when Boris Yeltsin set fire to the Parliament, all the way to the Bush administration in 2000. Along with these we could, perhaps, also point to the role of 'economic hit men' (EHM) who work on behalf of both the corporate and the governments, where loans are offered to developing countries and then followed up with access to natural resources, military cooperation and political support. Refer to John Perkins, *Confessions of an Economic Hit Man* (Plume New York, 2006). Commenting on the book, one of the commentators says that this book reveals 'how private multi-national companies *legally rob* the poor of the third world, country after country.'

18. Schumpeter brings to our attention the growing phenomenon of what he refers to as 'Khaki Capitalism' referring to the increasing 'military-industrial complex' (Schumpeter 2011). He argues that we need to take into account the extent to which the private industrial sector is dependent and in fact controlled or even owned by the military. He points to the interesting data regarding the army in Egypt controlling 10 per cent of the economy, in Pakistan it controls a US$15 billion empire, in China individuals in PLA were running 20,000 firms, the Revolutionary Guard in Iran runs more than 300 companies, and finally some 10 per cent of the bosses of the 500 biggest US companies are former military officers. To expect that the market be independent, or autonomous of the state power, and later remain neutral towards the classes and private interests in the market hasn't been actualized, neither in democracies, nor in military dictatorships. In this sense, capital—as long as its interests are served through this kind of convergence—is 'neutral' towards the nature and character of the state. It can continue its cohabitation with both forms of governance. It is again important to mark the emergent circularity here—the growing 'military-industrial complex' brings in demands for (liberal) democracy, like in the Middle East through 'Arab-Spring', but this does not necessarily entail a shift in the relation between state and capital. The shift to democracy, often, is actualized in a change of the 'form' of this relation. However, we cannot, by any stretch of imagination, based on this structural relation reach the conclusion that there is no, in political terms, difference between the two forms of governance. But where exactly do we locate the change—formal/substantive—and how do we take on board the benefits of, even if they were, 'formal' changes in the practice of democracy remain crucially

significant issues. In fact this was the focus of the now classical debate often famously referred to as the 'Miliband-Poulantzas debate'. Political movements in India have made some significant experiments in recombining the benefits of formal democracy and pushing for more substantive/structural changes—the binary in the civil society is transmuted into a dialectical relation.

19. As Goonewarden and Rankin ask,

> Is it not the valorization of civil society today part and parcel of the neo-liberal attack on the state as such and the attendant call for people to "get the government out of their lines" and finally start looking after themselves with the help of NGOs and "free enterprise". (Goonewarden 2004: 118)

20. It is also pertinent here to note that the nature of the dilemma in the way it was originally conceived 'always already' entailed an 'Impossibility of Society' as Laclau had framed it, and a complete closure of the possibility of moving towards structural change or substantive justice (Laclau 1990). It is a different matter that Laclau attributes the 'impossibility of society', as in the impossibility of realization of substantive solidarity due to the discursively constructed nature of social relations, which invariably have an 'excess' or 'surplus' meaning, leading to irreducibility of conflict of interests. While irreducibility is true in the sense of the impossibility and undesirability of reducing social relations to a homogeneous whole—a utopia that is eschatological in form and content; it can nevertheless still be possible to argue for a qualitative change in the nature of the 'conflict' itself—including a change in the modality of resolving them. This qualitative change is what Marx referred to as the 'end of pre-history' of 'mankind', though this is often interpreted either as end of politics (by the critiques)—in the sense of an end to conflicting interests, or end of ideology (by votaries of Communism)—in the sense of doing away with 'representation' and arrival of complete transparency or concurrence or absolute harmony in the subject-object relations. This was the focus, sum and substance of Althussers' critique of the French Communist party and its utopian belief about the post-revolutionary societies. He argued that even post-revolutionary societies cannot be self-evident—the complexity of social relations is irreducible and 'representation' works like a glue in keeping society together.

21. For instance, The Gates Foundation aims to 'enhance healthcare and reduce extreme poverty and expand educational opportunities'. It had an endowment of US$ 33.5 billion as of 31 December, 2009. In India, the Azim Premji Foundation was established in 2001, it works primarily in the area of primary education. In December 2010, Premji pledged to donate US$2 billion, which is considered to be the largest by any Indian billionaire. There can be any number of such examples that can be cited in terms of the growing philanthropic activity by the corporate. Including the collapse of consumerism and philanthropy, for instance McDonalds advertizes that the burger or sandwich that we eat benefits the farmer—it now carries the snapshots of the farmers on the coasters, so that we feel to have fulfilled 'social responsibility', while we are consuming.

22. This collapse comes ostensibly in supplanting the notions of citizens as 'moral agents' as Bhikhu Parekh put it, or as signifying the 'ethic of participation' or as agents who negotiate through the language of rights. However, a closer reading will allow us to understand that the very notions of public morality, participation as voluntary action and rights in instantiating a competitive ethic facilitate this process of collapse between the identity of a citizen and a consumer.

23. This global reach of consumerism—overreach—is instantiated and institutionalized—(naturalised) through various concomitant processes including that of the role of

media and communication revolution, often noted to be central to the purported 'expansion of civil society'. There is the transformation in the way culture—cultural identities—get constructed through the *mediation and mediatization* of culture and economy. For instance, Frederic Jameson notes that 'Commodity production is now a cultural phenomenon, in which you buy the product fully as much for its image as for its immediate use' (Jameson 2000: 53) while David Harvey notes the 'mediatized politics' shaped by images alone. In the case of Roland Reagan, he observes that media manufactured image of a 'Teflon president'—on whom no criticism sticks and no mistakes called to account—however it actually 'concealed a coherent politics'—such as cuts in the social welfare programmes (Harvey 1990/2008: 330).

24. As the discourses of tolerance naturalize social hierarchies and the differences that have been historically produced, the culture of consumerism naturalizes global capital and its accompanying impact on politics and democracy.

2

Human Rights Movements in India: State, Civil Society and Beyond

Civil society is constructed and made possible as a concrete and a tangible site, through an interface between a set of institutions and practices, at the heart of which are constitutionalism, citizenship, rule of law and democracy. These practices and their accompanying institutions lay down the character of the state as much as the nature of the civil society. One presupposes the other, as Michael Walzer (1995: 302) puts it, 'only a democratic state can create a democratic civil society (and) only a democratic civil society can sustain a democratic state'. It needs to be emphasized here that 'from Locke to Hegel civil society meant the establishment of institutions by a constitutional democratic state' (Gupta 1997: 305) for both the protection as well as the enlargement of the basic civil liberties of the citizens. It is then around the idea of citizens as 'autonomous agents'[1] that this foundational relation between a democratic state and a democratic civil society is made operative and becomes historically and socially sustainable. Therefore, while civil society does not include the state, it nevertheless strongly presupposes a state with 'limited powers'[2] and expects that through the project of citizenship it would not only push social groups to overcome their particularistic disadvantages based on ascriptive identities but also achieve a semblance of liberty and equality for one and all. In this frame of analysis civil society cannot, and ideally should not, overlook its linkages with the democratic state if only to put pressure on it, otherwise there is very little guarantee as to why or how a state should or will remain responsive to the expectations of its citizens.

The human rights movement (HRM) in India went through three distinct phases where it began within the limits set by the practices of civil society and then gradually marked new sets of political principles which questioned many of the assumptions on which civil society works in contemporary times. The first phase of the human rights movement in India in the 1970s began with a political discourse that exactly matches the above discussed reading of the 'idea of civil society'. The HRM imagined itself, for well over two decades, as the harbinger in forging a complementary relation between a newly adopted constitutional-democratic state and a nascent civil society. It put emphasis on the constitutional vision, autonomy and accountability of institutions, guaranteeing of basic rights for the citizens and a state limited by the principle of rule of law. However, by the mid-1980s, it could be argued, that there were attempts to break free from working within the confines of this understanding of civil society as inherently linked and dependent on the state, both due to the violation and the limitation with the constitutional vision. HRM began to question most of the assumptions surrounding the democratic state, marred by the frailties of citizenship and autonomous institutions, as being more constraining rather than liberating. The HRM, in its second phase, began to reimagine itself and thereby the realm of civil society as both independent and against the state, and as Cohen and Arato argue, exclusively represented by the various social and political movements[3] that exist outside the 'high politics' and institutional dynamics of the state to initiate and consolidate the processes of democratization. 'What the radical social struggles wished to create was a civil society that was beyond a "neutralized civil society" that works strictly only within the legal and constitutional limits set by the state' (Chandhoke 1998b: 39). In the process of overcoming a 'neutralized civil society', however, the HRM built and replaced it with an imaginary of civil society as a liberated space that is bereft of dominance, and allergic and suspicious of critical dialogue lest they fall victims to the machinations of the state. What abstract and formal citizenship did in clouding power equations in a 'neutralized civil society', the euphoric discourses of and about the political movements did in imagining a romanticized idea of civil society as a pure 'realm of freedom'. Civil society 'emerges in such formulations as something uncontaminated by those impulses that characterize other domains of human interaction…for civil society is neither conflictual nor marked with power relations as the other spheres are' (Chandhoke 2003: 242).

However, HRM's idealized understanding of social and political movements in the construction of civil society as a pure 'realm of freedom' were 'burst asunder' when it encountered power dynamics and conflicts between these various movements, vying to mobilize various social constituencies. There was no overarching dichotomy with an oppressive state on one side and liberating political struggles constituting the civil society on the other. The HRM, in fact, realized that such constructions of civil society as pure 'realms of freedom' were itself an inextricable part of the way power is constructed in modern societies. It is in negotiating with power dynamics constitutive of the civil society discourse that the

HRM began, in course of its third phase, to probe a range of issues that nudged them to arrive at political principles and practices that took them beyond the practices marking the contours of civil society, into the experimental portals of what we could refer to as a 'political society'—a site that politicizes, by identifying micropower dynamics, a large array of social conflicts. The conflict between civil society and the search for a political society was a site marked by new and searching combinatory political practices that went beyond the limits of abstract citizenship on the one hand and equally idealized imaginations of 'free spaces' and free zones on the other. The search for a new political society included, above all, looking for the possibilities of combining the arduous and 'critical task of building institutional support for democracy' with radically reinterpreted ideas of 'democratic space' that allows for recovering the agency of various marginalized and subordinated collectives, *within, between,* but also *outside of* organized political struggles.

The dynamic of the interface between institutionalized practices and radical political movements has to be comprehended, not through essentialized frames that uncritically bank on one or the other, but in opening up and grappling with the micro-foundations of power dynamics that are omnipresent. In other words, power in institutionalized practices needs to be overcome by toning them through radical political practices, while the later need to be tamed by compelling them to respect the principles within institutionalized practices. However, this process of overcoming and taming was not envisaged in the dichotomized and binary mould in which civil society imagines such a negotiation. For instance, the HRM, in course of constructing a new political society beyond civil society emphasized the importance of institutionalized practices such as rule of law and dialogue in preserving democracy not to dichotomize or de-legitimize militant political articulations by the subordinated groups, but only in order to politically contextualize them. In other words, while notions of civil and civility unilaterally exclude acts outside of law, the HRM, on the contrary, stresses on the possibility of 'democratic space' opening up due to the pressure that radical-militant politics are able to mount on the state, and compelling it into a dialogue on a range of issues beginning with land reforms to economic reforms on the one hand, and the institutionalized principles of rule of law keeping a check on the militant struggles and the excesses they might commit in either dealing with various social constituencies or other political movements, on the other. In pursuing such a path, the HRM was transforming the age-old founding principles of civil society, such as rule of law and deliberation into renewed political practices that operate in, and not obliterate, the context of militant (including armed) political movements. It is this re-signification of practices of civil society that marks the inauguration of a post-civil society discourse.

In the same breath, the HRM critiqued the idea that the civil society constructed through social and political movements can unproblematically mobilize and represent a romanticized collective will of 'the people', even if it is against the state, without themselves being accountable to the lateral power dynamics between the various political movements (Diamond 1994: 4). In other words, power is exercised not only by the state but also by political movements in course of mobilizing constituencies to achieve their stated goals. Here, the agency of the subaltern could well not be lying in but interrogated through (if not against) organized political movements, and here institutionalized practices could well play a more radical-democratic role in mediating the conflicts between political movements, or between specific political movements and their respective constituencies than what has been hitherto imagined. In the course of negotiating with this complex mosaic that the HRM is forging the new post-civil society discourse, where the terms of reference and practices envisioned are at odds and in excess with the discourse of civil society.

Finally, this chapter ends by critically looking at the dilemmas that emerge in course of inaugurating a post-civil society discourse. The terms of reference for the emerging political society can initiate hyper-politicization in the course of negotiating micropower dynamics, which can in turn lead to 'proliferation of particularisms' that can potentially threaten all forms of collectives and construe all modes of solidarity between political movements as being essentially hegemonic. The contemporary moment of the HRM seems to stress the need for a distinct 'moral language' as an antidote to the radical politicization being necessitated in post-civil society discourse. The contemporary HRM is attempting to explore whether 'morality has an intrinsic force of its own' (Churchich 1994: 11). The obvious question that needs to be asked in comprehending this shift—from the political to the moral as the basis of the post-civil society discourse—in the HRM is how different is taking recourse to a moral language from that of a discourse of civil/civility in civil society? After all, Gramsci equated civil society with dominant culture and values, and argued that it is by converting them into moral injunctions that they could endlessly replicate and reinforce themselves as the 'common sense' of the times; Or could it possibly be argued that invoking morality is a necessary mode of instantiating the new political practices that, as yet, lack the necessary (counter-) hegemonic status or capacity? As Slavoj Zizek (1997: 30) pointed out, 'the structure for ideological and political hegemony is thus always the struggle for the appropriation of the terms which are "spontaneously" experienced as "apolitical", as transcending political boundaries'. It is some of these shifts and dilemmas, based on a detailed historical account of the HRM, that need to be grasped in order to make sense of the emerging post-civil society discourse and politics in India.

The HRM has had a long history and made significant contribution in maintaining and transforming the democratic content of politics in India. The first organized initiative, perhaps, to form a civil liberties organization, was taken by Jawaharlal Nehru on 7 November 1936, with the founding of the Indian Civil Liberties Union (ICLU) with Rabindranath Tagore as its president. Rights were articulated not only as guarantees against arbitrary state action that was so much part of the British colonial rule, but also as necessary means to achieve a more just and egalitarian socio-economic order. It was this two-pronged strategy that was the basis of the anti-colonial struggle and the various instruments it set up, including the Motilal Nehru Committee of 1928 and the Karachi session of the Congress in 1931, which adopted the resolution on fundamental rights. The strategy was a derivative of the conceptual distinction between natural rights and the positivist tradition of articulating rights. In the natural rights tradition, rights are envisaged as inalienable, having their own origins in nature, while in the positivist tradition 'rights not only originate in the action of the state, but are also entirely dependent on it for their existence' (Singh 2005: 32). The state is the source and arbiter of rights and therefore can legitimately even take them away in certain rare and well-specified situations. The politics of the post-independence HRM was, in a sense, an attempt to negotiate the implications of these two distinct traditions of the rights discourse that were part of the anti-colonial struggle.[4]

The history of the post-independence HRM in India could be traced back to the early 1970s. The movement of the seventies was located in a liminal zone between Mrs Gandhi's coming to power and the emerging shift from the Nehruvian era gradually becoming evident in terms of the possibilities of the emergence of an authoritarian state on the one hand, and the continued expectations from a welfare state that was responsive to the popular demands of the polity and its marginalized, on the other. More than opposition to the state and the constitutional framework, it was the everyday misuse of the institutions and violation of procedures that formed the context for the beginning of the post-independence HRM in India.

State–Civil Society Complementarity

In a meeting of the Sarvodaya workers held in Bangalore in July 1972, Jayaprakash Narayan advocated that a broad-based organization should be formed for the preservation and strengthening of democracy in India and that the organization should consist of all those who cherished democratic values, but were not interested in power politics (Tarkunde 1991: 303). In an all-India conference convened in Delhi on April 13–14, 1974, a non-party organization called Citizens For Democracy (henceforth CFD) was formed with the objective of ensuring the *independence* and *autonomy*, for the purposes of democratic and constitutional functioning, of various institutions such as the judiciary, the press, radio, bureaucracy, the office of the President, the Election Commission and the Planning Commission, among others. This experiment of building a pressure group for the more effective and responsive functioning of state institutions was abruptly cut short with the imposition of Emergency in the country on 25 June 1975 under Article 352 of the Constitution on the grounds that the 'security and integrity of India was in grave peril due to internal disturbance'.[5] Jayaprakash Narayan and many of his followers were placed under preventive detention. After his release, there appeared to be a need to expand the scope of the CFD in order to protect the civil liberties or fundamental rights of the *citizens*. In a well-attended conference held in New Delhi in October 1976, J. B. Kriplani, in the absence of Jayaprakash Narayan, inaugurated the People's Union for Civil Liberties (henceforth PUCL) (Tarkunde 1991: 305).

The focus of the PUCL, given the immediate context of the Emergency and the recent memory of the larger legacy of the Nehruvian era, was limited to (*a*) the restoration of the rights curtailed or eliminated during the Emergency (undoing preventive detention law, curtailment of the jurisdiction of the courts, censorship on the press, and so on); (*b*) punishment to those responsible for excesses, through available legal recourse; (*c*) safeguards against taking arbitrary recourse to the Emergency provisions out of mere subjective considerations (Ram 1986: 91).

The PUCL was constituted by political figures and sections close to the Janata party apart from the Radical Humanist Association and the professional bodies of lawyers, academics and a few independent Gandhians. More than activism and mass mobilization, the thrust really was to draw eminent personalities who could exert pressure, moral or otherwise, on individuals and institutions. The issue of civil rights, which though had political connotations, was considered as essentially legal and therefore legal action was often considered to be the most effective method to make institutions responsive and to protect the rights of the common people, who were above all citizens of the country. State institutions, such as the judiciary, were considered to be effective representatives of civil societal concerns, as much as they were of state public policy.

On 23 March 1977, the Janata party came to power after the Emergency was lifted. The HRM temporarily lost its direction after this, as most of the office bearers of the PUCL, who had played an important role, were also the members of the Janata party. Ostensibly, there existed no clear and effective distinction between the state and civil society. And since institutional reforms and restoration of fundamental rights alone was the focus, the need for an independent human rights organization run by some of the prominent members of the PUCL, was no longer felt. In fact, 'at a national convention held in August 1977, top Janata leaders, like Krishna Kant, declared that there was hardly any need for a civil liberties movement as democrats had come to power' (CPDR 1991: 284). After a gap of a few years and with the return of Mrs Gandhi to power, the PUCL was revived in November 1980. A national convention of civil rights workers converted the PUCL into a membership organization. V. M. Tarkunde took over as the president, while Arun Shourie became its general secretary and Prof. Rajini Kothari was elected as the president of the Delhi unit. Their immediate concern was, following the earlier focus on institutions, to draft a new Prison Act and Jail Manual.

This in many ways was the first phase of the HRM—'The Civil Liberties Phase'—working within the framework of *state-civil society complementarity*. Organizations such as the PUCL perceived themselves as the harbingers of the emerging link between the state and the civil society in a newly formed nascent democracy. They were of the firm belief that:

> The link works both ways: on the one hand, these groups [such as the PUCL—my addition] breed ideas and give impulse to the system; on the other hand, the political system sets and modifies the frame of action for civil society. There is a constant flow and exchange between the two spheres. (Frevert 2005: 68)

Civil society was being mobilized not to stand outside the state, but to make the state more responsive, and recognize its constitutional obligations towards its citizens. It was understood that while a vibrant civil society is necessary to make the state accountable, it was equally important to recognize that the state and its policies legitimately determine how far the self-organizing powers of the citizens would reach. In other words, the state's constitutional framework guaranteed certain basic freedoms and they need to be effectively and progressively realized. It is due to this implicit understanding that PUCL never emphasized on mass mobilization as much as on taking recourse to available legal means.[6]

The *state–civil society complementarity* was to be pursued and further achieved around two conjoined programmes of (re)establishing the autonomy and independence of institutions of both the state and the civil society, and entrenching and strengthening the project of citizenship, by affectively realizing their civil, political and social rights. The various initiatives of the PUCL to restore the autonomy of the institutions such as the judiciary by protesting against the curtailment of the jurisdiction of the courts, was thought to be the precondition for the presence of the rule of law, necessary to curtail the arbitrary use of power and democratic transgressions. No meaningful equality before law could be presumed without the necessary neutrality, accountability and openness of the intermediary institutions. In turn, it however needs to be recognized that the PUCL believed that 'institutional autonomy of the judiciary draws sustenance from the axiomatic assumption that the state alone can guarantee essential freedoms to the individual' (Gupta 2004: 232). Similarly, it emphasized the autonomy of civil societal institutions such as the media and educational institutions by protesting against the censorship of the press, in order to have informed political participation to put in place an accountable and responsive state. It was also precisely for this reason that the PUCL, fairly early, had begun stressing the importance of electoral reforms, as the right to vote was an extremely potent tool to fight against discrimination, especially for the most vulnerable and marginalized social groups. However, in a highly segmented society like India, civil society based on 'meritocracy' (Elliot 2004: 23) and mere institutional autonomy was thought to be insufficient either to guarantee social equality or even to augment public welfare. Institutions could be greatly efficient, autonomous, and based on 'modern organizational and rational principles' and 'open to all categories of citizens' (Beteille 2004), yet, or precisely for this reason, deny entry to the disadvantaged groups.[7] Thus, along with emphasizing the autonomy of institutions, the PUCL also struggled to recover a 'rights-based civil society' where all citizens could have access to all fundamental rights.

The PUCL mobilized itself not only against the draconian provisions such as the preventive detention law and for safeguards against taking arbitrary recourse to emergency provisions and pressing for a new Prison Act, but also for positive social rights (such as the right to education) to achieve equality of status for all individuals and social groups, as citizens. Recognition of all individuals, cutting across their caste, class, gender and regional identities, as citizens would initially give them legal equality and eventually pull them out of their specific disadvantages, and duly accommodate them as part of the developmental goals of the state. Thus, for organizations such as the PUCL, in the first phase of the HRM, 'civil society as an ethic of freedom manifests itself in the modern democratic constitutional state by creating citizens and by upholding institutional autonomy' (Ibid.).[8]

State versus Civil Society

The nature of the state, however, underwent dramatic transformation. The flip side of the statist model of nation-building by Nehru became pronounced under Mrs Gandhi. Notwithstanding the welfare orientation of the state under Nehru, it was also developed as a highly centralized instrument to negotiate the different conflicts in the civil society. Commenting on this process, Bhikhu Parekh observes that:

> The state was the only conduit through which various parts of the society related to one another and was a party to all disputes and conflicts. It therefore became the sole centre of all political ambitions and energies and an arena of powerful ideological passions. (Parekh 1995: 44)

It was this inherent trend of centralization that Mrs Gandhi intended to strengthen when she initiated a process of 'deinstitutionalization' by undermining intra-party elections, offering dubious concepts such as 'committed bureaucracy' and 'committed judiciary', encouraging top-down approach to have hand-picked chief ministers in various states, misuse of Articles 356 and 352 (Brass 1992: 40–41). More importantly, Mrs Gandhi was using the idea of welfarism, which was foundational to the *state–civil society complementarity,* to further the authoritarian and centralizing tendencies. Centralized planning, the use of modern technology and the role of the 'experts' and technocrats became integral parts of governance. These methods, in the name of maintaining efficiency, achieving 'developmental' goals and preserving the 'unity and integrity' of the nation, in fact increasingly drew a wedge between politics or popular participation and the government.[9] This process, in a sense, was evident in the way a welfarist '20-point programme' was announced during the emergency. Welfarism and development were the new modes of enhancing state control and disengaging the masses from popular participation in the decision-making process. Further, this was the period when there was a fall in industrial growth. There were incidences of severe drought and as high as a 40 per cent rise in food prices. The social base of the state shifted to a newly emerging neo-rich or *lumpen* class, born largely out of the leakages of the first phase of development.[10] This class included the contractors, real estate dealers, liquor traders, renters, gamblers, speculators, cinema producers and actors (Haragopal and Balagopal 1998; Sethi 1975). The rise of the new classes was accompanied by a state that became increasingly coercive, evident in its use of force and rampant manipulation of legal procedures. For instance, those set free from preventive detention were brought back to prison—often arrested outside the court premises or at the doorstep of the prisons, on specific charges. A favourite device of some of the state governments was the implication of individuals in a number of inter-locking cases. There was horizontal as well as vertical inter-locking (Ram 1986: 93).

In this period, the Armed Forces (Special Powers) Act was used in Assam, the National Security Act was put on the statute and then amended twice to make it even more draconian, a Terrorist and Disruptive Activities (Prevention) Act were enacted and employed widely all the way from Punjab to Andhra Pradesh.[11]

This was broadly the social and the political context for the shift in the HRM from its earlier *state–civil society complementarity* framework to the second phase—'The Democratic Rights Phase'—during the 1980s, marked by a new *state versus civil society* framework. Civil society was now being renewed, unlike in the previous phase, for 'explaining the crisis of developmental state and providing an intellectual rationale for attacks on state power' (White 1994: 376). In such a context civil society made sense only in its confrontation with the state, and this perhaps was true of most of the post-colonial and developing societies that adopted an over-extended state, which presented a 'mystified and dehumanizing developmentalism' (Bayart 1986; also Chandhoke 1998b; Escobar 1992).The split in the PUCL and the formation of the Peoples Union for Democratic Rights (PUDR) in Delhi marked the beginning of this *confrontational* phase, exemplified in the new found proximity of the HRM with radical-militant struggles including the Marxist-Leninist organization's armed struggles and the nationality struggles in Kashmir and the north-eastern parts of India. Democratic rights perspective emerged when,

> a section of activists felt that the usage of the terms 'civil liberties' by the PUCL leaders restricted itself to (these) codified safeguards. The more radical activists used the category 'democratic rights' as a critique to the term 'civil liberties'. It implied the freedom to claim even non-codified rights, or, in other words, rights which citizens were not endowed with under the existent legal system. (Dutta 1998: 283)

The 'democratic rights' framework was critical of the way formal and procedural principles of liberalism and mere legal entitlements as citizens have come to be identified with democracy. Access to civil and political rights, in a society where economic exploitation is not 'directly dependent on juridical and political standing', initiates formal as against substantive democratization (Gudavarthy and Vijay 2000; Wood 1990: 72). Neither can democratization be equated with just periodic and free and fair elections. Such an equation only amounts to 'fallacy of electoralism' that grossly overlooks inequalities of wealth, power and social status 'making it difficult for even formal participation to be effective' (Jayal 2007: 3–4). This new framework marked the revival of the Association for Protection of Democratic Rights (APDR) in West Bengal, which later split with the formation of the Association for the Establishment of Democratic Rights (AEDR), on the issue that there are no democratic rights to 'protect' in India. This radical perspective also marked the revival of OPDR & AFDR in Punjab, CPDR in Bombay and formation of the *Manab Adhikar Sangharsh Samiti* (MASS) in Assam. In Andhra Pradesh, the Andhra Pradesh Civil and Democratic Rights Association (APCDR) was the first organization that came into existence and later split into the Andhra Pradesh Civil Liberties Committee (APCLC) and the OPDR, broadly representing two different factions of the CPI (ML), but both working within the new 'democratic rights' framework. Most of these organizations began working in close proximity with different radical-militant struggles in their states, such as the armed Naxalite movement and the militant nationality struggles that they believed best represented the new civil society that was confrontational and exclusively filled in the civil space.

The APCLC initially focused, in its struggle for democratic rights, on organizing fact-finding committees on 'encounter deaths' and lock-up deaths, providing legal assistance to the arrested activists of the various Marxist-Leninist parties, and protesting for the right to organize public meetings, processions and *dharnas* by the various mass organizations of the Naxalite groups. In its second state level convention, held in Warangal in May 1980, it adopted its manifesto and declared its central concerns to be the protection of people's right to struggle and protest, opposing the atrocities of the feudal landlords, capitalists and the state machinery, condemning police excesses and also fighting for the abolition of capital punishment (APCLC undated: 23). This was the activist phase of the HRM, which went beyond looking for mere legal remedies. Its members included leading lawyers, academics, artists, poets, journalists and students, apart from several full-time activists. Paradoxically, in spite of the shift to an activist phase, human rights organizations, contrary to building a vibrant, independent and separate movement, were more concerned with projecting themselves as a 'platform' or a 'forum' to 'shield' the radical political movements, and struggle on their behalf to protect their 'right to protest' and extend the legal and constitutional safeguards to the activists and leaders of these movements. The HRM was more than willing to play second fiddle to the militant democratic, or the Marxist-Leninist movements, and was convinced that there was an urgent need to use 'militant transformative methods' against the state in order to bring about a grand structural transformation. Such militant (at times violent) methods were justified since they were a response to 'more institutionalized versions of violence' that were 'performed non-violently' and can be appreciated only when we begin to notice 'the structured, routine and invisible violence going on right at the heart of our societies' and not merely look at 'acts and ignore situations of violence' (Parekh 1990: 131). It was convinced that in building a *confrontational civil society* it had a very limited, although significant, role to play by maintaining proximity with the radical militant organizations and their struggles. The proceedings of the APDR, after self-introspection, reached the conclusion that the, 'civil liberties organization (was) mainly characterized by acting as a *shield* of the democratic struggles carried on by the common people. In a sense, this role though *limited* (was) very important' (APDR 1991: 6). It also felt 'secondary' in terms of the capacity to mobilize people numerically, as 'the movement (was) limited to few individuals and limited sections of people' (Ibid.).

However, as the 1980s were also a phase of the emergence of various other organized political movements—women's, Dalit, regional, minority and environmental movements—apart from the Naxalite and nationality struggles, human rights organizations began to gradually extend their scope to protect the rights of the activists of these movements and their political concerns, which came to determine the character and contours of the civil society. Political movements came to represent the 'concerted action' and 'social self-organization' that is deemed indispensable for a vibrant civil society. Various types of issues of discriminations that the political movements were pursuing came to articulate themselves in the democratic rights language. The PUDR in 1984 investigated and published a booklet with the title *Who are the Guilty*, on the anti-Sikh riots in Delhi. It directly named some of the culprits belonging to the ruling Congress party. Some felt that with its publication, 'groups fighting for civil liberties and democratic rights acquired a national legitimacy' (Desai 1991). It was a fact that no other organization dared to so openly reveal the names of some of the most notorious history-sheeters. In Andhra Pradesh, the turning point came about with the gruesome *Karamchedu* massacre against the Dalits in July 1985. The APCLC investigated and again revealed the names of some of the upper caste landlords involved, and kept the issue politically alive, working in tandem with the Dalit organizations, till some of the culprits were physically eliminated by the armed squads of the then Peoples War Group.[12] Thereafter, the APCLC began to enlarge its work and investigate atrocities against women, such as dowry deaths and domestic violence, famine and hunger deaths in various districts, and issues related to environmental pollution. However, what is pertinent to note in this expansion of the HRM into various other social and political issues was the fact that it approached all these issues strictly through the *state versus civil society* prism, born out of the HRM's proximity with the Marxist-Leninist groups. For instance, it was the role of the ruling Congress party in organizing the pogrom against Sikhs that was stressed by the PUDR in its report *Who are the Guilty*, completely undermining any dialogue on the growing communalism in civil society. Once again, it was the caste (in this case *Kamma*) nexus that actively operated in the various state institutions (assembly, judiciary and the police) that was the focus of the APCLC's investigation. Not that these issues or for that matter the perspective was unimportant but the HRM was not, in any immediate sense, concerned with highlighting the existence and replication of power-relations and forms of discrimination at the civil societal level, such as the growing communalism and rigid caste hierarchies. It did not consider the possibility that all forms of violations of human rights need not have necessarily flown down directly from the state, although they might definitely have been actively patronized by it.

This issue of the violation of human rights at the civil societal level became starkly and rather poignantly evident with the killing of innocents or common people, accidentally, in the course of the military operations by the Naxalites against the police.[13] Human rights organizations took recourse to the argument, in reply to such incidents, that 'a civil rights organization was concerned only with the state violence and the concern for "private violence" does not fall under its purview'—a stand initially taken in the open letter written by the leaders of the APCLC to the Chief Minister in July 1985, and repeated thereafter *ad nauseam* whenever questioned about their concern and responsibility towards the victims of the 'private violence'. Some of the leading activist-intellectual representatives of the democratic rights phase, defending the actively 'biased' position, argued that:

> The reason is very simple. Whereas, in a law-based state like India, there exists an elaborate code, an entire ensemble of laws, procedures, institutions and enforcement agencies to deal with private violence or lawlessness, there is nothing comparable, no genuine checks or controls, to take care of peaceful or violent lawlessness of the state, which is potentially, and often in actual practice, the most powerful violator of democratic rights in society. (Singh 1993: 82)

However, this position stood in contrast to the interventions made by the APCLC, on more than one occasion, to mitigate the 'private violence' that erupted in the inter-group rivalry and killings between the various factions of the revolutionary parties. These interventions were undertaken more out of the proximity with the revolutionary parties rather than any sustained self-reflection on the issue as such. In spite of growing criticism from various quarters of the society and also the deliberate manipulative use of this apparent hiatus in the position of the HRM by the state,[14] the democratic rights organizations refused to critically reflect on their *state versus civil society* framework.

This initial reluctance could be understood in the immediate context of a repressive state, which, to counter the growth and expansion of the HRM was by then arresting and physically attacking and kidnapping the leading civil rights activists all over the country. To cite a few instances, in Assam, Parag Das—who had political and organizational proximity with the politics of the ULFA, was with the MASS and was a popular editor of a leading Assamese daily—was shot dead by SULFA (Surrendered ULFA) with the active connivance of the state police. In Andhra Pradesh, Gopi Rajanna, Narra Prabhakar Reddy and more recently Purshottam (all office bearers of the APCLC) were brutally killed by the police; K. Balagopal was attacked, assaulted with knuckle-dusters and kidnapped by an outfit referring to itself as *Prajabandhu* (in August 1989), and V. M. Tarkunde (the then President of the PUCL) and K. G. Kannabiran (long term president of the APCLC) were assaulted at a public meeting in Madurai. The later president of the APCLC, Laxman, was also kidnapped in November 2003 by surrendered Naxalites operating as private mercenaries, with the active involvement of the state police. Such growing number of physical attacks increasingly reduced those involved with the HRM to what Agamben refers to as '*homo sacer*', men reduced to bare life no longer covered by legal or civil rights (Agamben 2003), reinforcing the human rights organizations' understanding of the state being the primary, and perhaps the sole violator of human rights and thereby it vindicated their *state versus civil society* framework. These attacks coupled with the sacrifice and preparedness of the activists gave them a ready 'moral' reasoning of the correctness of their politics.

Civil society now signified a 'strong public' whose discourse encompasses both opinion formation, decision-making and political action, rather than a mere site for forming public opinion—or the 'weak public' (Fraser 2004: 102–3).[15] It further offered them the ready reasoning that these illegal methods adopted by the state only made the use of counter-violent strategies indispensable, and perhaps also civil, in building a *confrontational civil society*. Thus, the HRM was not prepared to reflect on the 'conceits of the civil society', and letting go the singular focus on the state, which only meant weakening of the civil society and the movements it constituted, and strengthening the state. The lurking fear was the larger possibility of equating and conflating the various types of violations and thereby 'letting the state off the hook'. They consciously worked, as much as possible, outside the formal institutions such as the courts, in an attempt to de-legitimize and minimize the arena of state control. Interestingly, while in the first phase of the HRM, it did not want to let the state off the hook by abdicating its constitutional responsibilities to the citizens, in the second phase it did not want it to be off the hook by missing any opportunity to dismantle and de-legitimize it. In an obverse way it reinforced the understanding that the nature of the civil society was guided by the nature of the state, exposing the delicate but formidable link between the two versions of the civil—complementary and confrontational.

Thus, the 1980s marked a rupture-like shift in the HRM with efforts to construct civil society as a pure 'realm of freedom' that squarely stood 'outside' the state, and constituted various militant and radical political movements. Organizations such as the PUDR and the APCLC strongly believed that what brought the various political movements in the civil society together was 'their shared perception that the state is the repository of coercive force which is frequently directed against the citizens. The fact that the state is a potential and actual transgressor of individual liberty and that its might must be collectively challenged gives coherence to the otherwise diverse units of civil society' (Mahajan 2004: 181). In other words, in order to seek autonomy and relentlessly expose the state the HRM laid emphasis on coherence rather than diversity in its version of the civil society (Shils 1991: 9).[16]

Ironically, with this emphasis on coherence the political movement discourse on civil society came a full circle. What the project of citizenship—through a 'rights-based civil society'—did with its provision for formal and legal equality in shrouding the social hierarchies in the first phase of the HRM, the idea of civil society as pure 'realm of freedom' bereft of power relations did in the 'democratic rights' phase. Here the oppressions in civil society were 'treated as dysfunctions in civil society. In principle, coercion belongs to the state while civil society is where freedom is rooted and human emancipation according to these arguments consists in the autonomy of civil society, its expansion and enrichment, (and) its liberation from the state…' (Wood 1990: 74). From *representing* the struggles against hierarchies in civil society, political movements slipped into assuming themselves as the *embodiment* of the civil society.[17] In other words, power relations in both versions of civil society—that which is framed by the state and that which deems to stand outside—remained, through different means, shrouded and thereby left to actively reproduce themselves. The two versions that in their moment of their relation with the state looked different, bifurcated, separate and opposed to each other were inextricably linked in their moment of replicating power relations.

Both the versions therefore supported and entailed each other mutually. The moment of separation was therefore also the *moment of intersection*. In engaging and withstanding the transgressions of the state and finding a way out of a legally 'neutralized civil society' the HRM actively constructed a 'cohesive civil society'. The HRM in moving from the 'rights-based' version of civil society to the notion of civil society as a pure 'realm of freedom' was replicating or instantiating the *logic of circularity*, where power relations by remaining shrouded consolidate themselves.

The rigid *state versus civil society* framework, however, became increasingly untenable with the beginning of the decade of 1990s. The context this time around was provided by the simultaneous unfolding of multiple contradictions manifested in the growing conflicts *within* and *between* various political movements, constituting the civil society. The HRM was, in a sense, caught unaware, and the radical articulations by the Dalit, women's and regional movements, not only against the state but also vis-à-vis each other escaped its rigid binaries and neat totalities. An important starting point for this could be traced to the *Koyyur* kidnap on 30 January 1993 in Andhra Pradesh when a tribal MLA was kidnapped from Vishakapatnam district by the PWG. Various Dalit organizations, the most prominent among them the Dalit Maha Sabha, raised serious objections to Dalit leaders who were (in any case far and few) weak and vulnerable, being picked up as 'soft targets' for fulfilling demands with which they had nothing to do. They raised pertinent ideological and political questions on what they referred to as the 'caste-blind politics' of the far-left groups.[18] The state too took its own time to react, allowing the new growing conflicts to brew. What came to the fore was not the fact that mere anti-state activity exhausted or addressed the concerns of the various political struggles, nor did it provide for unproblematically unifying them in a 'coherent civil society' that was believed to be marked by ideas of freedom and liberation.

The APCLC intervened to resolve the 'crisis', demanding the release of the kidnapped. Refuting their earlier position on 'private violence', perhaps for the first time, the then president of APCLC wrote:

> The practice of taking as hostages persons unconnected with the specific issue between the government and the PWG is a practice we in APCLC never approved of. We have been as human rights activists against this type of political practice. Whether the police hold people in illegal custody or the Naxalites kidnap and take as hostages persons unconnected with the specific issues involved our stand has been the same. (Kannabiran 1993: 495)[19]

The break from the rigid *state versus civil society* framework got further strengthened with the new questions:

> For human rights activists, Koyyuru (and earlier Gurthedu) (raised) issues regarding the concepts of human rights itself, the advisability of expanding the concept and thereby enlarging the filed of operation of human rights work. What should be its relations with radical and democratic movements? Has it any transforming role while operating the institutions available within a democratic set up? Should it merely confirm itself to maintaining a crime audit of the state? All such and related questions need to be debated. (Kannabiran 1993: 498)

This trend of problematizing power dynamics and human rights violations at the civil societal level got expressed and came to centre stage through the series of questions that the young activists of the APCLC raised, in their state and district level meetings. During the Kurnool convention in 1993, they began by raising a sensitive issue, by pointing out that a large number of those killed by the Naxalites as 'informers' were from the SC, ST and OBC communities, who, due to the absence of any type of social networking failed to get back into the so-called 'mainstream' life and often succumbed to the pressure by the police and passed on (sometimes very crucial) information about armed squads and their whereabouts, once they surrendered. Similarly, it was argued that there was 'silent' discrimination and violence against women by male members active in the various political movements, which could not be ignored as either 'personal' or a 'private' matter. Discussion papers with the old perspective reinforcing the *state versus civil society* framework arguing that there cannot be an independent 'human rights perspective' different and autonomous from and more importantly critical of the 'revolutionary perspective', and the new perspective bringing into relief a more critical approach to the civil societal violations, were printed and circulated among the members and the debate continued in all district level meetings for well over two years. A national convention on 'Democratic Movements and Human Rights Perspectives' was organized in Hyderabad in June 1996, to both go public with the debate as well as to gather the views of the other national level democratic rights organizations. Later, during the Guntur convention of the APCLC towards the end of 1997, they went for voting over the two contending perspectives and the APCLC was split, leading to the formation of a new organization called the Human Rights Forum (HRF).

Civil Society versus Political Society

This new split marked the beginning of the third phase of the HRM—'The Human Rights Phase'—now working with a new *civil society versus political society*[20] framework, where there was no easy recourse to the idea of civil society either as a site working on well grounded principles of autonomous institutions and citizenship or as a pure 'realm of freedom' represented by various political movements. The new site was neither in tandem or complementary, nor merely against the state. The immediate focus of the new framework, in identifying and constructing the new political society, was to both stress the importance of locating and condemning the human rights violations at the civil societal level, including those committed by the radical political movements, and thereby politicize a larger array of social issues; and to enumerate the inadequacy of maintaining or striving for the unity of various political struggles around the anti-state activity, without recognizing the independent sites and methods of dispersion of marginalization, and the possible areas of mutual conflicts between them and thereby the need to stress the autonomy of each movement. The HRM now wished to avoid the trap—the logic of circularity—of civil society that either identifies the practices of militant struggles as uncivil (from the point of view of the state—and its dependent idea of civil society) because they were illegal, or as essentially confrontational and therefore civil and moral (from the point of view of political movements—and its dependent idea of civil society) because they were mustering the cause of freedom and liberation. It was therefore, in identifying and questioning this *logic of circularity,* that the HRM was making attempts to move beyond civil society, in search of what was new in the quotidian.

The HRF, in its inaugural pamphlet, explained its differences with the 'democratic rights perspective' as against the new 'human rights perspective' that had foregrounded the adverse impact of human rights violations at the civil societal level. The pamphlet stated that 'we believe that unjust and unfair use of violence even by a popular movement must be openly condemned, not because it is violence but because it is unjust' (Human Rights Forum 2000: 4).

It further made a plea for treating all discriminations independently and at par and argued that:

> The political structure of the state and the social-economic structures of caste, class and gender have received some recognition as oppressive structures, but are yet to assume *equal importance*, in the eyes of the rights movement. The state–class framework continues to dominate for no cogent reason. But both caste and gender are major sources of not only violent suppression but also routine and insidious denial of rights. There is no scale on which their effect can be adjudged less severe than that of state and/or class. (Human Rights Forum 2000: 1)

Finally, emphasizing the inadequacy (and perhaps the impossibility) of a solidarity based on a 'coherent civil society' around just anti-state activity, it further argued that:

> The state–class framework that unconsciously guides our thinking of rights has come from militant- leftist movements and the problems of suppression they have faced from the state and the exploiting classes. But if we are ready to learn equally from the dalit movement and the women's movement and the politics of various minorities, religious, ethnic or linguistic groups then these movements have mostly sought to empower themselves by making use of and enlarging the democratic political space and the political and civil rights available in the present state and the political system. (Human Rights Forum 2000: 2)

Almost at the same time an independent organization by the name Committee of Concerned Citizens (CCC) came into existence. Its vision constituted a search for a new 'democratic space', initially between the state and the radical political movements, but also between the various conflicting interests within the civil society, and thereby foregrounding the difficulty of reconciling them within that constrained civic space. Interestingly it drew its members mostly from the various civil rights organizations in Andhra Pradesh, who had felt handicapped at the kind of stalemate the situation had reached between a repressive state and the civil rights organizations working within a rigid *state versus civil society* framework. In the foreword to the first report the committee published, it made it a point to proclaim that:

> The group which came to be known as the Committee of Concerned Citizens (*Puara Spandana Vedika*) was not formed at the instance of any authority or organization. It emerged on its own, open to reflect the voice of large democratic sections of the society which is tired at being reduced to a mute spectator in the game with peoples lives played by the state and the revolutionary parties. (Committee of Concerned Citizens 1998: 1)

The HRM began by looking for a new 'democratic space' between the state and revolution, and thinking through the cracks within the civil society. It is from this post-civil society vantage point that it wished to raise a series of questions at the behest of these new organizations mapped as the emergent political society. The framework that was guiding the HRM, based on the experience of past two phases, was an attempt to unravel and critique power relations in all its myriad forms (to reiterate—including those *within* and *between* the political movements themselves). However, the HRM realized that it was important to move beyond mere critique (either against the state or even against the political movements) since 'an exclusively critical attitude is useless as a guide for any transformative—as distinct from critical—activity excepting the seizure of power by force…' (Balagopal 1997: 84). It was, therefore, also necessary to build the required institutional support for the emerging dynamics beyond civil society. Political movements embodying the civil society exclusively privileged criticism as the 'pristine radical attitude' mostly against the state and avoided the 'question about the abilities of social movements to secure both stable and durable institutional forms and to embody self-limiting properties: if they are to govern, what governs them?' (Khilnani 2001: 32). These dual tasks—of critiquing and building institutions and norms or to put it differently attempting certain kind of 'radicalism with rules'[21]—were to be possible only in reimagining and re-signifying the existing principles and practices beyond the limits imposed on them by the civic sphere, to meet the changing political dynamics, and not in projecting 'as if' everything was waiting to be created 'for the first time in history'.[22]

'Radicalism with rules' was to emerge as the new sustainable basis for a post-civil society discourse, in order to simultaneously take up the task of critiquing and building institutions and norms, where one aspect of the process was not to confine and restrict or displace and supplant the other, but opening new modes of mutually reconfiguring each other for radically novel political practice. The founding principles of civil society, such as rule of law and constitutionalism, individual rights, civility and open-ended deliberation among others, needed to be reconfigured, rather than either continuing to practice them within the safe, civil and dichotomous mode in which they were available in the civil society or wholesomely critiquing or rejecting them as bourgeois principles or a mere 'juridical illusion' (Meszaros 1985). The activist-intellectuals of the HRF seem to have posed the issue in such terms as to reconfigure or re-signify the civil society principles, such as rule of law, when they argue that:

> The notion of Rule of Law was born, let us grant, in order to make the protection of private property from thieves a public duty rather than a private affair, in the interest of the accumulation of capital, but in due course the thieves too have found for themselves a few rights in the Rule of Law. This is particularly instructive, for thieves are not a 'class' in any sense, nor have they been able to exert pressure upon society in their interest, unlike say the working class, which has picked up the notion of Rule of Law and reinterpreted it in its interest to get some rights for itself...The idea that all significant social ideas are (in the ultimate analysis) the expression of the interests of some class is therefore basically a partial truth. (Balagopal 1997: 97)

Further, the HRM argued, the generalized practice of rule of law need not necessarily, as it is done in civil society, dichotomize or invalidate those modes of protest that the subordinate groups and political movements struggling on their behalf chose to adopt, including armed-militant methods.[23] To recount what HRF stated in its inaugural pamphlet, they condemned violence by popular movements 'not because it is violence but because it is unjust'. Even the CCC in course of its negotiations with the

Naxalites never made a unilateral demand to 'lay down arms' that is often mandatory in initiating dialogue through 'peace talks' and in spite of it being the precondition set by the government of the day.[24] On the contrary, the HRM perceived the possibility of a reconfigured 'democratic rule of law' creating the necessary 'democratic space' for militant movements, which can also be made, in turn, more answerable, and in the process smudging the baseline between legality and illegality. Only militant politics willing to abide by the imperatives of a 'democratic rule of law' could mount legitimate pressure on a state that is otherwise non-responsive to enter into a dialogue on a range of issues including livelihood and basic survival of scores of vulnerable classes of people.

In foregrounding a re-signified idea of rule of law, HRM was also going beyond the confinements of dichtomized notions of dialogue— dialogue versus militant politics—as they are framed within the limits of a civil society. Such binary constructions of practices of deliberation and dialogue become a hegemonic project in the name of civility and in setting the absolute precondition of preeminence of the maintenance of 'law and order', which in turn justifies the use of coercion, in the name of sovereignty. The HRM, in exposing the hegemonic equivalence between these practices within civil society, attempted to politically contextualize them, in arguing that civility—that inflects itself as maintenance of 'law and order' and reiterating the sovereign power of the state—as an absolute precondition, in fact, inhibits a free and fair dialogue and the possibility of an 'ideal speech situation', since it is often super imposed as a mode of conduct so that it can 'protect liberal democratic societies from the danger of extremes of the partisanship which it itself generates' (Shils 1991: 14).

At the same time, however, the HRM denied the political movements the opportunity of taking recourse to the safe postures available within the civil society that belied accountability. For instance, the civil society discourse made it possible to pose the simple equation of 'people against governments'. In fact, the very resurgence of the idea of civil society, during the east European crisis, is based on the 'magnificent phrase'—'we the people'. 'In the roundtable talks of 1989, one side went under the name "party-governmental" while the other side was called—and called itself—societal' (Geremek 1992: 6). The Solidarity movement sought to unite all the social forces of the society in a single all-encompassing civil society. There was, therefore, the need to move beyond the politics of civil society that equates political struggles with 'the people' around 'an awesome emotional unity' (Ibid.: 12), and instead pose a series of questions that found their true meaning beyond the contours of a civil society. Such questions included whether the revolutionary groups can claim that all their actions were actions *by* 'the people'? Can all actions (read excesses) of the revolutionary party be condoned because they were carried in the larger interests of 'the people'? In what ways were the politics of militant movements responsible, and what ought to be their response, to the growing suffering of the varied and segregated collectives and individuals in a condition of 'circular violence' between the state and militant movements? Similarly, they also stressed the need to engage with the available democratic opportunities, for instance, provided by the new institutions after the 73rd Amendment, for the disadvantaged groups such as the Dalits and women and therefore the need for periodic elections without violence; it is in this context that the HRM impressed upon the Naxalite parties to rethink their call for boycott of elections. Critiquing the 'democratic rights' framework, the HRM now argued that availing the (constitutional-democratic) institutions and procedures and achieving substantive democracy does not have to be necessarily a mutually exclusive exercise (notwithstanding the difference between them being real and significant in analyzing democratic processes). In fact they can aid each other, provided we transmute them in comprehending that civil society practices and institutions of formal democracy 'represent a contradictory unity of advance and retreat both an enhancement and a devaluation of democracy' (Wood 1990: 72). Finally, the CCC unequivocally condemned the brutality of the Naxalite parties in dealing with 'the people' 'as no less abominable than the third degree methods used in police camps' (Committee of Concerned Citizens 1998). Such excesses not only further brutalized the society but also reduced the 'democratic space' for individuals and collectives to fearlessly express their opinion, dissent and choice of political action alike, and it thereby robs 'the people' of the necessary rich experience, to take control of their lives, indispensable for an enriched existence even in the post-revolutionary societies.[25]

Hidden beneath these formulations was the recasting of the relations between individual and collective rights. Civil society discourse is again prone to the ambiguity—either the weakness of eulogizing and romanticizing the oneness of the masses as 'the people' or zealously guarding and privileging the notion of individual rights as hyper-separated from the social or the collective. The HRM in raising some of the above issues was suggesting that 'while the difference between individual-centered rights and collectivity centered rights is real enough, the two are not mutually exclusive or always enemies of each other' (Balagopal 1997: 91). They need to be recast as essentially complementary to each other. While most individual rights, such as the right to free speech presupposes communication and thereby some idea of collective, similarly most collective rights need to be supplemented by individual rights, to mitigate disadvantages and inequalities within the collectives. Individuals also require rights not just within but also against the collective, for instance, right of the individual worker not to join a strike or in above case not to support the Maoist's call to boycott elections; the right of a member of a nationality to dissent and speak up against excesses committed by the nationality struggles and other armed movements and so on. The emerging post-civil society discourse through its various such combinatory postures—between formal and substantive democracy; rule of law and militant modes of protest; dialogue-civility and revolutionary politics; legality and illegality or law and politics;[26] and individual and collective rights—subverts neatly designed arenas, either by the state/citizenship or radical political movements, and transforms all that is social or 'civil' into political.

In this context of changes inaugurated by the HRM, the political movements in general, and the revolutionary parties in particular, also made their bid to the post-civil society discourse in laying a claim to be engaging with both the conflicts in the civil society as well as being accountable and responsible to allow free political participation by the vulnerable classes amongst 'the people' themselves. They argued that the revolutionary parties did recognize the conflicts in the civil society and therefore:

> It is exactly here that the masses should be guided by the revolutionary leadership to understand the contradictions among the people and the united front that they have to forge in order to make the revolution successful. When they understand these two things then the excesses in people's courts, the occupation of land of even some middle class peasantry on some occasions and other wrong ways of dealing with contradictions among the people will get automatically solved. (Ravi 1993: 1471)

Similarly, the revolutionary process, they claimed, was engaged with the issue of encouraging 'mass participation'. However, the human rights groups need to realize that it is in course of such a process that there were bound to be mistakes and excesses and it is un-dialectical to imagine the process to be otherwise. It was therefore important to realize that:

> When the leadership itself deals with the village-level contradictions it is likely to reduce the excesses, but when the initiative is left to the masses then such anarchy is bound to be there in an anti-feudal struggle, but their experience will leave in them a higher level of consciousness. The first option is absolutely impractical and even if it is practical, which is preferable...which is the correct mass line? Which is centralizing the power? Which will guarantee the future egalitarian society? The initiative of the masses or the superimposed directions from the leadership? (Ibid.)

It is amidst this emerging post-civil society framework that the CCC initiated a process for a new kind of dialogue through the peace talks between the state and the revolutionary parties. Talks during 15–18 October 2004 commenced on the basic premise that both the state and the revolutionary movements should strive to be accountable to reduce the perpetual condition of fear and uncertainty for the vulnerable sections of the society and it is their choice and voice that needs to be prioritized over everything else, which can be made possible only by adhering to the renewed principles in their combinatory mode.[27]

However, in course of negotiating with the renewed attempts at instantiating the transmuted principles and operationalizing the post-civil society framework as a durable basis for politics, the HRM realized that it will have to further confront and negotiate with the larger prism or the meta-organizing principle of civil society—the foundational idea of self-interest. In nudging political movements towards a self-reflective process, where they were required to not merely question power relations as they were evident in their structured and institutionalized patterns in society at large but also to introspect within as to how much were their own struggles prone to reproducing and replicating them, the HRM confronted the dilemma as to how much were movements equipped to instantiate self-reflection when they are working within and through the language of interests as it is institutionalized in civil society. 'In fact, all the classical exponents of civil society were perfectly alive to the fact that civil society is not only fragile, but also self-destructive... We cannot assume that people will relate to each other on grounds other than rank individualism and self-interested actions' (Chandhoke 2003: 28). Hobbes, Adam Smith, Hegel, Tocqueville and Marx were of the singular opinion that civil society was organized around self-interest that manifested itself, depending on the nature and scope of the activity, as self-seeking individualism, egoism, greed, self-indulgence and aggressive competition manifested not just in the market but also in the civic sphere itself through the language of rights. For instance, as feminists have pointed out, rights promote atomistic individualism and self-seeking behaviour that enhance hyper-separation from the collective, and therefore were essentially (and epistemically) male-centric.[28] Each of the philosophers suggested their own chosen alternatives to either curb or arrest the unabated growth of rank self-interest. While Hegel bestowed his faith in the professional associations emerging from the structure of production relations by providing a sense of collective purpose, Tocqueville privileged all associational activity—from churches and literary and scientific societies to recreational bodies, though he strongly felt that 'political institutions were the mother of all institutions' since they taught the general idea of association itself—which nurtured civic virtues; Adam Smith trusted a more abstract social psychology that throws up 'moral sentiments' capable of (with the help of the state) designing a moral order.

The HRM for one felt that in such formulations the counter-values got reduced to stand-alone principles or practices and get no preferred status over that of self-interest, and are left to themselves to jostle for space within the civil society. Moreover, in a civil society that privileges self-interest all 'moral sentiments' as constraints become formal, and in the process social collectives are reduced to being only juridical and contractual in nature without any semblance of possibility for solidarity and 'deep understandings'. These restrictions would therefore be inadequate in preventing a political society from 'splitting into warring factions or degenerating into a congeries of inward-looking particularistic interests'?[29] The HRM could, in a sense, quickly grasp the difficulty in unproblematically looking up to the same political movements for instantiating the post-civil society norms and principles, even if they recognized and lay a bid for the new combinatory principles, as long as they were themselves organized and mobilized around the struggles for various kinds of interests.[30]

It is in this context that the HRM seems to be suggesting a more explicit shift from an interest-centric to a *value-centric* frame, as a durable basis of the post-civil society discourse and politics. A value-centric framework would no doubt recognize that interests and the struggles around them are the most important source for new values and that interests are always conceptualized and experienced as values and not as only 'bare interests'. However, 'activity around interests, to the extent that it is successful, generates and spreads new values in society. But that is again derivative or secondary. In this derivative or secondary sense, political activity is value-activity, and again importantly so, but only in the derivative or secondary sense. Primarily it is centered on interests, not always necessarily narrow or selfish, sometimes very broad indeed, but interests nevertheless' (Balagopal Forthcoming). In other words, while interests are concrete manifestations of values, the latter cannot be reduced to the former. Protection and even struggle for values can be '*a task by itself*', necessitating a different order of political practice, which is often not, or perhaps cannot be, carried out by political movements struggling for specific and concrete interests. In this sense, there seems to be a subtle but a very significant shift in the HRM, in articulating the need to realize the more universal and certainly a distinct appeal and reach of values, which are difficult both to imagine and practice within and through the discourse and politics of civil society structured around and limited by self-interest. This distinctness can be both realized and at the same time made the durable basis of politics only in a post-civil society framework.

The Contemporary Moment: Beyond the Political?

The HRM, in its search for a constitutive basis for politics of post-civil society, seems to be reformulating its *civil society versus political society* framework by underpinning a new ethical dimension.[31] In doing this, it is going further in arguing that not only is it inadequate to frame values in terms of interests but also to only look for a material—as social or even political—basis (however indispensable it might be) for values. On the contrary, the interface between interests and values needs to be recast on the premise 'that not only does our moral sense have a social basis (as historical materialists tell us) but our social devices also have a moral basis' (Balagopal 1997: 96). The fact that particular interests are always framed and fought for, by the various political struggles, on the basis of universal principles, such as equity or justice, is characteristic of a deep and an inherent 'human moral sense'. Therefore, in transmuting the civil society based practices, such as the language of rights, it needs to be recognized that 'primarily rights are ethical norms and any attempt to treat them as primarily or explicitly political can only lead to sectarian divisions and stagnation in the human rights movement'.[32] In such a framework the HRM itself cannot remain *exclusively* a political movement but needs to explicitly foreground the ethical dimension; and therefore the 'political movement and human rights movement as such exist in two planes the planes of interests and values' (Balagopal Forthcoming). This relocation of the HRM in the ethical domain is being sought as a way of rethinking the way social transformation has occurred in history in course of the struggles of the oppressed where 'what they have fought is not oppression *as such* but the oppression of the Other that has hurt their interests'.[33] The struggle against oppression *as such* happens or is possible only at the realm of ethics or morals. The struggle against oppression *as such* 'has wrongly been seen as a direct continuation of the struggle against injustice. This notion that the force that is necessary to destroy unjust social structures will by itself lead to the reconstruction of society on a just basis... has been sufficiently proved an illusion by the happenings of this century' (Balagopal 1995: 60).

The struggles in the 'material' or the political realm, in spite of being particularistic instances of different ethical norms, do not necessarily entrench or consolidate a generic moral foundation for the society as such.[34] The HRM has to become the embodiment of the human struggle to restore (universal) ethics/values, while political movements continue to protect (particularistic) interests of various social groups. The HRM, therefore, needs to work at the intersection of a new 'democratic space' beyond civil society, and has the difficult task of standing at a distance, yet working in tandem with the political movements. It needs to maintain its autonomy in order to generate a discourse of an ethical praxis, and maintain proximity so that it can effectively cut across all the political struggles. The HRM, thus, has the distinct task of *bringing out* values hidden within and produced by the various political struggles and also life situations; apply these values to new areas of social life not imagined by the specific political movements, which have brought them into being and also in turn apply such norms even to the movements themselves; and finally, institutionalize them in a more generic way so that humanity does not have to struggle all over again for these values. Thus, the HRM has the simultaneous task of working in tandem with political movements to bring to the fore values that accompany the political struggles for specific interests, and critique the political struggles by cautioning the limits of interest-based struggles and finally institutionalize—by generalizing and taking values beyond the context of specific political struggles and in applying the same values as standards in evaluating the practice of the political movements themselves—thus combining the critique with the necessity of institutionalization as generalization.

Notwithstanding the close relation that the HRM is drawing between interests and the struggles for them and values, doesn't the privileging of a distinct practice for and around values *as such* and founding the new basis of politics in an inherent trait of the species—its deep 'moral sense', in itself point towards a decisive retreat from the political into the realm of the abstract moral? How is this *retreat* different from that of the civil society privileging the social or civil/civility? How is this *abstract* of the HRM different from the abstract citizenship or equally idealized imagination of civil society as a pure 'realm of freedom', which is what the HRM intended to dislocate in its attempts for radical politicization? The idea that universality or universal concerns are themselves not born out of a historically conditioned political practice but a 'human moral sense' that is abstract, ahistorical and in the ultimate sense hegemonic in being abstract and ahistorical—was what was singularly critiqued in radical political thought across time and specific theoretical posturing.

Marx and Engels rejected it as a 'moral dogma' that 'has its permanent principles which stand above history'; Sartre critiqued it as 'bourgeois morality', which is 'like bourgeois law abstract'; Trotsky rejected it as 'transcendental moral norms' inadequate to respond to the 'question of expediency'; Althusser as 'Abstract Humanism'; Norman Geras as 'empty moralizing' where 'mere moral exhortation is incapable of accomplishing human liberation' and Judith Butler as 'tropes of normative universality' which is 'itself a powerful and forceful conceptual practice that sublimates, disguises and extends its own power play'.[35] To sum it all up, moral 'idealism' encapsulated different but interrelated claims:

First, that moral principles, values, attitudes and ideals are independent of, not dependent on, historically changing material circumstances i.e. social practices especially economic practices; second, that being independent they are external and unchanging; third, that they are universal i.e. valid for everybody; fourth that it is they that shape material social reality. (Edgley and Brisset 1990: 27)

Paradoxically, this attempt of locating the HRM *exclusively* within an abstract ethical domain in fact, comes as a response to the concrete historical experience of persistently facing the divide between the moral and political dimensions that already exist at a subterranean level in the discourses of the various political movements, which does not mean that there is no moral dimension within these movements, but that they have a specific kind of abstract and insular moralism disconnected from the on-going political struggles.[36] Ironically, in responding to the already existing moral essentialism of the political movements, the HRM seems to slip into obverse moralism of its own kind by condemning the political movements to a delimited struggle for interests and arrogating to itself the 'larger' task of entrenching abstract ethics.[37] The contemporary response of the HRM could be traced to some of the variants of moral essentialism it had to face in course of its interaction with the various political movements.

Firstly, the more existentialist of reasons for such a shift in the HRM—from the political to the moral—could be traced to the fact that socially (caste, class and gender wise) most of the activists who seem to be gravitating towards such arguments for a *bifurcation*, between the political and the ethical, belong to the more 'privileged' upper echelons. They often face a serious sense of isolation, as political movements around them are demanding exclusive organic linkages with those who wish to lead them or even be part of their struggles.[38] This self-valorization (or in fact moralization) of identities is perceived by the HRM as a shift of the political movements into an insular mode of pursuing exclusivist interests, fraught with pragmatic responses *to* and *within* the emerging political dynamic, and most importantly, bereft of a moral dimension. The HRM therefore wishes to now superimpose and externally inject its own variant of an abstract ethical dimension that will open the way for a democratic dialogue and a space for all those who are not organically linked to these movements.

Secondly, the nature of the social base, the middle class, of the HRM was always a suspect. The militant left movement always characterized it as 'petty bourgeoisie' in a derogatory sense and often mockingly referred to it as the 'middle class wing of revolution'. Many activists in the HRM themselves shared this perception, as this anecdote sharply puts forth the ambiguity:

> At a discussion in Delhi (under the auspices of the PUCL) the problem of 'legitimacy' of human rights activism, astonishingly surfaced and there was even some talk of the need for human rights communities to 'woo the middle classes' back to the value/mission ... (n)ot long ago many leading human rights communities critiqued, rightly (*prescinding the question of moral opportunism in practice of politics*) the middle class support to the anti-mandal agitation. (Baxi 1998: 349)

In another context a long-term vice-president of the APCLC and now member of the CCC argues, 'in fact, the middle class become spineless and loses the nerve against a repressive state. Some liberal activists shift their stand very fast. They not only compromise but also gradually degenerate into a self seeking and self aggrandizing class of individuals' (Haragopal 1998: 367). This perceived inherent moral weakness of the middle class never allowed the HRM to articulate itself as an independent and credible political movement, apart from the other related reasons stated earlier.[39] The HRM therefore now feels the need to pose issues in explicit moral/ethical terms, both as a response and the means to overcome this perceived handicap. This compulsive tension within the HRM would persist as long as they are not prepared to do an independent (as it continues to share this perception of middle class with the militant left groups) and a more differentiated, including a positive reading of the middle class and its contribution to the various organized movements.

While some scholars of civil society equate the processes of democratizing politics in civil society with the growth of middle class and professional groups since they are associated with modernization (White 1994), others believe that in places such as Singapore where democracy is under duress 'the regime has co-opted middle class...by appeals to social harmony and Asian values' (Elliot 2004: 31). In contrast, Marxism, Stalinism and Maoism have generally linked social progress to the elimination of the middle class (Brenkman 1999). Both these versions of analysis perceive a monolithic character of the middle class; either equates democracy or perpetuation of hegemonic relations with the rise and role of the middle class. While in the operative part of politics the middle class seems to perform a more variegated role of, on the one hand, arresting radical change, and on the other, enabling social force in foregrounding certain issues that are not easily amenable to 'immediate experience' and popular mobilization. Raymond Williams, critiquing the conventional position of the radical left groups on the role of the middle class, argues that:

> The significance of predominant middle class leadership or membership of the new movements and campaigns is not to be found in some reductive analysis of

the determined agencies of change. It is, first in the fact that of some available social distance, an area for affordable dissent. It is, second, in the fact that many of the most important elements of the new movements and campaigns are radically dependent on access to independent information, typically though not exclusively through higher education and that some of the most decisive facts cannot be generated from immediate experience but only from conscious analyses. (Williams 1983: 252)

And definitely the HRM is one such movement dependent on 'available social distance' and involved in constructing a refracted 'political culture', which at times (though not always) is difficult to 'generate from immediate experience'.[40] Thus, while civil society discourse equates democracy with middle class, radical political movements (specially the militant left organizations) equate it with their 'elimination', both of the positions eventually result in shunning concrete analysis and replacing the political by moralization of one or the other kind.[41] It would, perhaps, augment well for a post-civil society discourse to comprehend the necessity to make a more nuanced reading of the contribution of the middle class to such an emergent discourse and politics. It can be argued that while undue privileging of the middle classes can lead to elite assertions over public space, it is this class that also allows for raising issues at a distance from 'immediate experience', including those such as environmental and ecological issues in the recent past. It is only through such an approach that political movements can circumvent the bifurcated either/or and thereby a moralizing approach of the scholars of civil society towards the historical and political role of the middle class.

Finally, moral/ethical resolution to avoid 'stagnation' in the HRM is sought due to the moral *ad hoc*-ism within the Marxist theory, reflected in the radical left movements with their refusal to develop consistent political principles around the means–ends issue. Moral language could, therefore, be read as the residual effect of the proximity of the HRM with militant Marxist-Leninist struggles, in the 'democratic rights' phase. Steven Lukes, in his interesting study on 'Marxism and Morality', argues that, on the one hand, Marxism has 'claimed that morality is a form of ideology, and thus social in origin, illusory in content, and serving class interests… and that the Marxist critique of both capitalism and political economy is not moral but scientific… on the other hand Marx's and Marxist writings abound in moral judgments, implicit and explicit' (Lukes 1985: 3). This unexplored continuum between ethics and politics re-emerges as moral *ad hoc*-ism mostly on the basis of 'consequentialist reasoning' about revolutionary ethics. For instance, while Marleau Ponty proposed some kind of ultra-consequentialism 'in which the very meaning of an action is determined by its long-term results' (Lukes 1985: 137), others such as Herbert Marcuse argued for limitations on revolutionary violence by establishing 'general norms' and E. P. Thompson recommended humanist attitudes 'whenever and to the degree that contingencies allow', so that they do not negate the very end for which the revolution is a means (quoted from Geras 1990: 29 and 34).[42] Beyond such contingent moral advocacy Marxist theoreticians were hesitant of suggesting the means of converting moral principles into political norms and vice versa. Radical left movements failed to conceptualize what constituted 'revolutionary violence'. Some attempts on the part of the HRM to engage on issues of what are the permissible or impermissible 'strategies' and 'tactics' mostly remained aborted. For instance, they did discuss norms such as strictly avoiding civilians being killed;[43] innocents being taken hostage;[44] using third degree methods such as maiming, disfiguring and torture,[45] and slow death by burning[46] which however did not evolve into either a consistent dialogue or fructified into a set of concrete norms or praxis. It came to be generally believed that, as Trotsky contended, 'revolution comes down to a form of war and as such cannot be constrained by general or transcendental moral norms' (Geras 1990: 33).[47] It is this loss of such historical moments in concretizing values that re-emerges as the eternal wait for the moment of pure morality (very much like the elusive 'last instance' in Althusser). Strangely, radical left movement (against which the HRM complains of absence of explicit recognition of morality) was accused precisely of pure/abstract moralism by the feminists (which we shall focus upon in the fourth chapter) during the Telangana armed struggle. As absence of morality is a problem now, presence of morality was a problem then.

To conclude, the HRM in its attempts to instantiate the post-civil society discourse formulated in the various combinatory postures and their grounding in the proposed shift to a value-centric framework, needs to further strengthen and build on the foundational linkage it drew between interests and values. This, perhaps, is only possible with contextualizing the necessity as to why political movements resort to moralization and closures and what linkages does it have with the way power is structured in the civil society. Such a critical political dialogue is possible only when the political movements, in turn, are assured that the proposed combinatory postures and the value-centric framework of the post-civil society kind, recognizes struggles, conflicts and antagonisms as 'inherent to every human society and that determines our very ontological condition' (Mouffe 1993: 3). In this contemporary 'explosion of particularisms', there is an inextricable collapse between conflict, coexistence and empowerment. Neither can they be separated nor can one set of practices be privileged over the other. As Zigmut Bauman rightly suggests, 'without conflict, no engagement, without engagement no hope for coexistence...Conflict, I suggest, is in the liquid stage of modernity the prevalent form of coexistence. No longer can it be treated as a temporary irritant- a hiccup' (Bauman 2001: 138). It is in recognizing this 'collapse' and that there is no separate mode or level to practice values that we can avoid open conflicts being 'replaced by a confrontation between non-negotiable moral values and essentialist identities' (Mouffe 1993: 6). In other words, there needs to be a more sustained deliberation, as to how and when do political movements transgress the limits posed by interest-based politics into deeper engagement that entails coexistence and solidarity beyond formal, juridical, and contractual relations that mar the civic space called civil society.

It is in this context that we need to be realize that, as the HRM is pushing for, politics cannot simply be represented by the already instituted categories such as self interest or practices, such as rights, that are conditioned and constrained by the language of self-interest and competitive ethic; even if they are used in and by oppositional movements, they only end up reifying and reproducing existing instrumentalities and ends that they in fact purport to oppose. Such reification symbolizes a minimalist approach and agenda that fails to transgress the dominant sites such as civil society. 'It is as if we are afraid to "come out" from the categories that, uncomfortable and contradictory as the lives they afford us may be, at least supply us with a place in the polis and with the mask of representation and authority' (Finn 1996: 174–75). It is from such encircling barbed wires, operating as the *logic of circularity* in civil society, that we need to step out, not just by critiquing but also, as the HRM argued, by transmuting the existing principles into new practices and institutional designs that lay the foundations—not just 'neutralized rules'—for oppositional politics beyond the limits of a civil society. This is best possible when the proposed combinatory postures and their grounding in values are worked through the political movements themselves, and in further enhancing their political character and interrogating their changing dynamic, rather than assuming them to be static or necessarily self-enclosed.

It is again in this context that one needs to be sensitive to the changes that political movements are undergoing in course of negotiating power relations in their myriad forms. In contemporary polity, political movements across the spectrum are increasingly finding it difficult to be exclusivist in terms of pursuing their interests, either externally or internally. They are subjected to the processes of implosion, where no identity or social group can ever be closed off, and instead are radically opened up externally, and more so internally to new demands and constantly imbricated in dialogic processes of democratization, which then gain expression in new subjectivities around inter-subjective communication necessarily entailing combination of interests and values beyond the immediacy, along with other combinatory practices. We shall attempt to analyze, as a continuation of the dialogue opened in this chapter, how these new subjectivities and processes are exemplified, among others in the contemporary Dalit and Naxalite movements and more so in the emerging interface and ensuing interstices between these struggles. It is to understand the emerging inter-subjectivity and its implications for the post-civil society political identities and practices that we now turn to in the next chapter.

Notes

1. Hawthorn (Hawthorn 2001) believes that one is a citizen in a civil society only if they are protected from the intrusions of the state into 'ones reserved domain' (p. 276).
2. See Edward Shils 'The Virtue of Civil Society', *Government and Opposition*, 26(1) (Winter 1991): 3–20.
3. See Cohen and Arato 1992.
4. See Aswini Ray (2003) for a more detailed historical narrative, and also the collection of papers submitted to the Indian civil liberties conference held in Madras on 16–17 July 1949, titled 'Civil Liberties In India'. I am thankful to Ujjwal Kumar Singh for suggesting this important collection.
5. Bipin Chandra in his book (2003) completely ignores the role of JP in building the civil liberties movement and therefore reaches a one-sided conclusion that 'Total Revolution' had 'fascist tendencies'.
6. Refer to K. Balagopal (1987). He argues that even during this period:

   > extensive use was made of the Preventive Detention Act, the Armed Forces (Special Powers) Act and the Defence of India Rules; over wide areas the army was employed and the promulgation of "Disturbed Areas" was affected. But all these were mainly against the tribal nationalities of the north-east and the communist-led peasants and workers in the rest of the country. This did not spoil the state's reputation for constitutionality very much.

7. Refer for a more detailed account of the growing contradiction between meritocracy and professionalism, and issues of social justice in educational institutions in India, (Ajay Gudavarthy 2004).
8. It is another matter that scholars such as Krishna Kumar would doubt the very need to invoke the idea of civil society when we are interested in democratic constitutional state and citizenship. He argues:

   > The deeper question, however, must be whether we need the concept of civil society at all... if we are concerned about the abuses of state power, with recognition and promoting pluralism and diversity, with defending rights... what is wrong with the language and terms of such concepts as Constitutionalism, citizenship and democracy? None of these, it appears, needs to invoke the concept of civil society. (Kumar 1993: 390–91)

9. For a detailed account of this process, see Partha Chatterjee (1994); also see Rajini Kothari (1988).

10. See Breman 2002, for an explanation of the term *lumpen* class or *lumpen* capital.

11. (Balagopal 1987: 42). He in fact informs that there were a host of lesser enactments like the Postal bill, the amendment to the Commissions of Enquiry Act, etc. Refer to other articles in the same special issue of the Lokayan Bulletin on Civil Liberties, for similar details, especially Sumanta Banerjee.

12. People's War Group (PWG), after their merger with the Maoist Communist Centre of Bihar was renamed the Communist Party of India (Maoist), prior to the peace talks with the Government of Andhra Pradesh, in October 2004.

13. Common people also lost their lives sometimes, or rather most of the time when they were instrumentally used as 'shields' deliberately by the police. For instance, police opts to travel in public transport that common people use rather than their official vehicles when they have to visit remote areas as part of their 'combing operations'.

14. Often state officials, bureaucrats and the police argued that this entailed both 'double standards' as well as exposed the proximity the HRM had with the 'outlawed' organizations.

15. Within the liberal tradition, civil society was envisaged as a 'space where citizens could meet in order to socialize with their fellow-citizens, to exchange ideas and discuss issues of common concern, to form political opinion. *It was not a sphere where those opinions translated into political action* and decision-making' (Frevert 2005: 63). Such a distinction between thought and action emanates from the classical liberal formulation of J. S. Mill granting 'absolute freedom of opinion and sentiment on all subjects, practical or speculative, scientific, moral, or theological' (Mill 1963: 138), coupled with elaborate restrictions on 'freedom to act'. The earlier phase of the HRM was close to this kind of liberal articulation and therefore left the action to the state, which combines legislative and administrative powers.

16. In the resurgence of civil society, post East European crisis, the emphasis on coherence was a constitutive core. As Slavoz Zizek observes, the Solidarity movement necessarily represented coherence of all conflicting social forces against Communism.

> Conservative nationalists accused the Communists of betraying Polish interests to the Soviet masters; business oriented individuals saw in them an obstacle to unbridled capitalist activity; for the Catholic church, Communists were amoral atheists; for the farmers they represented the force of violent modernization which put the rural life off the rails; for artists and intellectuals, Communism was synonymous with oppression and stupid consensus; workers saw themselves not only exploited by the party bureaucracy, but even further humiliated this was done on their behalf; old disillusioned leftists saw betrayal of true socialism. (Zizek 1997: 31)

17. As an homology it wouldn't perhaps be inappropriate to recount the observation of Satish Deshpande that the middle class in India moved from representing the nation to themselves becoming *the* nation (Deshpande 2004).

18. For a detailed debate between the Dalit and Marxist-Leninist groups in Andhra Pradesh and their changing perception of each other, refer, Ajay Gudavarthy (2005), the revised version of which forms the third chapter of this book.

19. Also see Haragopal 1993.

20. The concept of political society used here does not strictly refer to the way it has been recently conceptualized by Partha Chatterjee, and instead intends to refer to a broader process of politicizing a larger array of social issues and practices. However, it cannot be denied that there are overlaps in terms of common concern to critique the hegemonic

practices in civil society and to map it as a site of power relations and in putting in perspective the need to politically, rather than force of any kind, negotiate with the choices, radical or otherwise, made by the subalterns. For Partha Chatterjee's idea of political society refer to his book (2004). The discussion around this concept will be the focus of the fifth chapter of this book.

21. I have borrowed this phrase 'radicalism with rules' from the title of a sub-section in the book by China Mieville (2006).

22. As we had argued earlier, the 'as if' modality is one of the ways civil society creates the mirage between multiplicity and intersection. For a more detailed argument on how civil society is dependent on the 'as if' modality to create binary constructions refer 'Omar Kutty' 'Civic Anxieties and Dalit Democratic Culture' (Gudavarthy 2012a).

23. As Neera Chandhoke points out regarding the choice of modes of protest that actors in civil society have:

> they can use sanctioned means of protest—moving the courts, strikes, public action, protests, and marches—as long as these remain within the rule of law…
> What, however, civil society actors cannot do is to challenge the state in ways that it does not allow-through say militancy… (Chandhoke 2003: 54)

24. In fact, Arundhati Roy, exasperated with the indifference of the State in dealing with the demands made by the Narmada Bachao Andolan (NBA) and the endless suffering of Medha Patkar and others, observed that the NBA is not taken seriously in spite of or just because it's a peaceful and a non-violent struggle, while the militant groups from the north-east and the Naxalite parties have succeeded in pressurizing the state to enter into a reasoned dialogue with them.

25. The growing significance of the shift in the HRM could also be felt in the response of the PWG to these observations of the CCC. The PWG later in their reply observed, 'though there are some short comings in the report of the concerned citizens, we feel that the Committee of Concerned Citizens has exhibited an essentially *democratic approach*' (Committee of Concerned Citizens 1998: 18).

26. We shall explore in greater detail the relation between law, rights and politics in the fourth chapter of this book.

27. Refer for a detailed account of the recent peace talks between the Government of Andhra Pradesh and the Communist Party of India (Maoist), (Committee of Concerned Citizens 2006).

28. Chapter 4 of this book looks into the response of women's struggles to the issue of law and rights in some detail.

29. See, for a series of similar questions being discussed, Foley and Edwards 1996.

30. It is around this issue of inadequacy in exploring the limitation of the interest based politics that we focused in our critique of Partha Chatterjee's notion of 'political society'. It is also for this reason that I emphasize on differentiating my use of political society in this chapter and elaborate this criticism in the fifth chapter.

31. The following position is being primarily articulated by Dr K. Balagopal (leading human rights activist and theoretician and office bearer of the HRF) with a few members and activists of HRF and other political movements gravitating towards such a position reflecting the possibility of a new *political society versus ethical society* framework. However, it is yet to take a definitive institutional form though again there are hints of HRF being implicitly driven by this new shift, and therefore I prefer to refer to this new framework as a moment rather than a definitive phase of the HRM.

32. (Balagopal. Forthcoming). For a brief summary of the contents of this forthcoming book refer, Ajay Gudavarthy and G. Vijay (2004). Upendra Baxi also seems to agree with the essential moral underpinnings of the HRM, and argues that:

> the social theory of human rights, of necessity, has to find bases for ethical judgment concerning "good" and "bad" social movements…It does seek to provide a "predetermined directionality" in human social development by articulating an ethic of power, whether in state, civil society, or the market. (2002: 120–21)

It is, however, not clear as to how does he place this 'ethical judgment' vis-à-vis the political in 'social movements' in general and the HRM in particular. Though he seems to agree with the idea that there is some essential distinction between the way the HRM relates to the idea of (political) 'power' and the way other 'social movements' do, and it is therefore 'then understandable that most contemporary social theory and history of new social movements does not focus on human rights movements as a social movement' (Ibid.).

33. (Balagopal 1995: 59). Similar ideas of emancipation going beyond the achievement of immediate interests can be located in a large array of writers with different ideological frameworks. For instance, Paulo Friere, the famous Latin American philosopher and educationist argues that in order for radical social struggles:

> to have meaning, the oppressed must not in seeking to regain their humanity become in turn oppressors of the oppressors, but rather restorers of the humanity of both…this then is the great historical and humanist task of the oppressed: to liberate themselves and their oppressors as well. (1972: 31)

Gandhi again argued that oppressed need to hate oppression, such as the practice of untouchability, and not the oppressor and therefore there is no place for violence and the need to incorporate into our struggles the necessary efforts for the 'change of heart' of the oppressor. See Raghavan Iyer (1978).

34. This idea of separation between the 'material' and the 'moral' that has emerged in the context of the present day HRM locating itself vis-à-vis the various radical struggles, strangely seems to have parallels with the way the anti-colonial national movement perceived itself vis-à-vis the colonial rulers. Partha Chatterjee observes: 'Anti-colonial nationalism creates its own domain of sovereignty within colonial society *well before it begins its political battle* with the imperial power. It does this by dividing the world of social institutions and practices into two domains- the material and the spiritual' [emphasis my addition] (1993: 6). It was this separation that was later super-imposed on the 'political' struggle against colonialism. For a critique of such a separation and its dualistic implications (which is perhaps relevant in the context of present day HRM too, and the new direction marked by the ethical dimension it seems to be taking) in a graded society like India, see G. Aloysius (1998).

35. One must add here that most of these theories operate, as the HRM has pointed out, within the confines of interests, which have been socialized beyond the self. For instance, Marxism would argue that class interests and not moral conviction drive the masses to change their society.

36. In fact, the construction of *political society* by the HRM, as opposed to civil society, was an attempt at critiquing moralization; this for instance is evident in the self-valorization of each movement or for that matter moralizing the arena of civil society as against the state, or the choice and preparedness of the subalterns, and instead initiate a process of politicization. But here having initiated the process there seems to be an apparent retreat only to reintroduce the moral–political divide.

37. This divide therefore lets the political movements 'off the hook' by reconciling to their struggles within the realm of interests. Some scholars have suggested in course of their response to this formulation, that what is called for, instead of the divide between the moral and the political dimensions, is 'transforming the moral self into the political self and the moral questions into political ones. This certainly does not call for super-imposing an arrogant moral discourse on the politically disunited people's movements...' (Arun K. Patnaik 1995: 1202). Also refer (Gudavarthy 1996).

38. For instance, the Dalit Maha Sabha makes it a point to emphasize that 'only Dalits' shall occupy the dais in all their meetings and no upper caste activist, however sympathetic and radical she/he might be, shall be allowed to do so. This process of 'othering' makes all others permanent 'outsiders' to the movement. This indeed is a variant of moral essentialism of the Dalit movement. However, the question as to why political movements take this route of essentialism to find a space for themselves in the dominant civil society needs to be historicized and understood in the way power is structured in the civil society, and also as a moment in the trajectory of political movement's struggle to move beyond. A more detailed account of this is presented in the next chapter.

39. Further, whenever individuals within the HRM raised questions that were uncomfortable for the radical left struggles they juxtaposed the sacrifice of the militant underground activists as against the comfortable 'middle class lives' of the human rights activists. The level of sacrifice thereby settled the authenticity and correctness of the political positions. Often, in private the human rights activists expressed discontent over, what they referred to as a silent '*moral* black mail'; while those activists in the HRM close to the radical left groups valorized such arguments. There is a different kind of moralization operating here, as compared to the previous point. There is a (de)moralisation of the middle class in terms of its permanent lack of morality.

40. Other scholars who have been following the HRM in India closely, based on field work, express a similar kind of opinion.

> Thus, at its core the CRM (the Civil Rights Movement) is a movement for a specific kind of "political culture"—a culture that socializes a society with democratic temperament. A belief in the possibility of institutionalization and protection of norms and practices that govern the state–society relationship is central to the efforts of the CRM...This is both the strength and weakness of the movement...It is (also) a weakness in the sense that it imposes severe constraints on the mobilization potential of the CRM. Vast masses, who have to struggle for their basic daily-bread, cannot be mobilized into the fold of the CRM. Even if the CRM could mobilize the masses against a background of severe repression, it would be more an ad hoc type of mobilization...Thus owing to its objective—generating democratic culture—the CRM, at least the core of it, is, bound to be, oriented towards the middle classes. (Kakarala 1993: 415–16)

41. Analysis of the middle class and its political role has become even more complex in countries like India where the post-liberalization middle class has become vastly differentiated, making even the use of a common reference as 'middle' class very difficult. See Satish Deshpande (2000) and Leela Fernandes (2007), both of whom map the emergence of 'new middle classes'.

42. Here, while 'general norms' can become abstract moralism, contingent attitudes can slip into pragmatism. The challenge really is, how do we generate political principles that emerge into moral norms, which are in turn open to political practice? How do we combine the self-belief and certainty required for political praxis with open-endedness

necessary to avoid abstract moralism? In one of the powerful memoirs of a communist revolutionary from South Africa, the author writes,

> In 1975 I was a young, very idealistic revolutionary, and I was prepared to die for my beliefs. I felt a strong connection with all those who had gone before me, and with all those who had faced similar tortures; and I felt a responsibility to the traditions of our liberation movement. That is what gave me strength. That is what made my resistance possible. And that is why I did not simply succumb to torture or lapse into despair. Writing this now, 24 years after my arrest, I don't seem as single-minded as I was back then. I now tend to see myself as having been rather naïve. All the same, it remains true that single-mindedness was the weapon that got me through. (Suttner 2001: 3)

In other words, how do we generate activists who fight for socialism with certainty and yet are open-ended about its success? For an initial discussion (by no means exhaustive or sufficient) on this issue, refer, Norman Geras (1995). Also refer Kate Soper (1987). Further discussion on this point would be carried out in the last chapter of this book.

43. This issue came up after an incident where a train was set on fire by left-wing militants in Warangal, resulting in the death of a number of passengers. However, the PWG later claimed responsibility and apologized to the families of the victims.

44. Most important of the spate of kidnappings was that of the tribal leader in Koyyur, referred to earlier in this chapter, before which was the incident involving the kidnap of seven IAS officers, which included S. R. Sankaran, often referred to as the '*Guthedu* kidnap' who was not only an upright officer working for the poor but also later spearheaded the CCC that was active in initiating the peace talks between the revolutionaries and the state.

45. This issue was raised generally in relation to the killing of 'informers' but more specifically it came into focus when a young girl was wrongly detained by the squad members of the PWG and tortured to extract information.

46. This specific issue came into focus more recently when the Maoists set fire to the huts of those they perceived to be belonging to the Salwa Judum (a state-sponsored anti-Maoist outfit in Chattisgarh). In the process many women and few children lost their lives.

47. Refer for some incisive observations on the sociology of armed movements and the difficulty and their reluctance to evolve norms (Balagopal 2006).

3

Dalit and Naxalite Struggles: Political Identities Beyond Identity Politics

The corollary idea to the core practices of civil society in the civic or the social sphere, which we discussed in the previous chapter, is its emphasis on associational life through voluntary action. Michael Walzer refers to civil society as 'the space of un-coerced human association and also the set of relational networks—formed for the sake of family, faith, interest and ideology—that fill this space' (Walzer 1995: 1). 'Un-coerced human association' takes different forms including forming voluntary organizations, clubs, NGOs and political movements, among other things. Voluntary associations are so central to the idea of civil society as they are expected to create an inter-related space that at one level curbs the power of centralizing institutions of the state and at another level nurtures constructive social norms, reinforces 'generalized trust and cooperation', and overcomes inward orientation created by ascriptive identities, instead encouraging and celebrating pluralism.

> Associations promote pluralism by enabling multiple interests to be represented, different functions to be performed and a range of capacities to be developed. No one set of organizations could hope to cover more than a small subsection of these roles, capacities and interests, so pluralism *within* civil society is essential. (Edwards 2010: 30)

It is this principle of pluralism that also allows for and emphasizes voluntary associations beyond ascriptive or 'primordial' ties and paves way, as Robert Putnam argues, for the creation of generalized trust that in turn makes political activity and democracy possible and vibrant.

Caste-based struggles in India, in terms of their interaction with the practices of civil society—with particular emphasis on voluntary action, links with the constitutional-democratic state and celebration of pluralism—can also be mapped into three distinct phases. These different phases can be analyzed in the context of the Dalit movement's ongoing dialogue with the Naxalite movement that was mobilizing the same social constituency, from of course a different ideological vantage point. Though the trajectory is somewhat different and chequered in comparison to that of the HRM, the essential efforts can be read as a struggle to negotiate the limits imposed on Dalit politics by the way power is structured in civil society. Though the caste system is based on ascriptive identities assigned on the basis of birth, caste-based organizations and struggles go beyond that, giving themselves a voluntary character. The political role of caste struggles in India has not only progressively initiated what has been referred to as the process of 'secularization of caste' but also has recast them into the mould of 'intentional associations', which 'challenges the ascribed-voluntary dichotomy, opening the space for a third, hybrid category. It also overrides the distinction between the realms of freedom and un-freedom sought to be superimposed on this dichotomy' (Rudolph 2008: 279).

The first phase of the Dalit movement, with specific reference to and a close study of the dynamics in the southern state of Andhra Pradesh, could be read as Dalit politics gradually claiming more space by contesting the exclusive emphasis on open-ended voluntary associational life in civil society and displacing it with politics that emerge from various kinds of combinations of ascriptive and voluntary characteristics.[1] Caste associations and struggles provide the necessary channels of communication and mobilization that connects the large sections of the various castes to the processes of 'high politics' and political democracy for demanding rights and benefits in the civil society; and in the process they also radically politicize the caste groups, to provide ideological avenues to critically interrogate their own particularistic identity and to convert caste from being merely imposed by the dominant and so-called upper castes— making it rigid, insular and structured—to that of 'self-given' by raising issues of claiming agency through struggle for dignity and self-respect. In the process of such mobilization, caste associations do accrue all the typical features of organizations in a civil society as Llyod Rudoplh points out, such as voluntary membership, leadership not by heredity but on the basis of those who can most effectively articulate their demands and organizations that have 'offices, membership, incipient bureaucratization, publications, and a quasi-legislative process expressed through conferences, delegates, and resolutions' (Rudolph 2008: 7).[2]

However, Dalit struggles in India in general and Andhra Pradesh in particular, have realized that particularistic and cultural articulations are in perpetual tension with certain central features of civil society such as citizenship, contractual relations based on right to exit, primacy to individual rights, merit based fairness, among others, and therefore their acceptability within the institutional contours and language of civil society was always partial and suspect. The imperatives of recognizing individuals as primarily legal, formal and equal citizens in a civil society is too strong to easily accommodate and recognize the dialectical mode of mobilizing particularistic Dalit collectives to achieve a more universal condition of eradicating caste. In the struggle between universal and equal citizenship and particularistic identity there is an inherent tension in accepting the strategy of, as Ramanohar Lohia once put it, 'use caste to fight caste'. For the majority of professionals, planners, bureaucrats and economic elites dominating the civil society such modes of mobilization do not signify democratization and expansion of freedom; instead they bring into relief practices that are in pursuit of sectarian and selfish demands and interests violating the basic norms of 'social duty and discipline' necessary for 'nation building'. Dalit struggles are therefore in endemic tension with and 'deeply trouble those committed to the progressive realization of a liberal democratic or socialist society and state. The individual must precede the group in time and importance for the contractual civil society or the ideological collective to have meaning and validity' (Rudolph 2008: 59).

Dalit political mobilization in India is caught between gaining acknowledgement for contributing to (universal) democracy by partaking in, for instance, elections set in motion by a constitutional-democratic state and thereby enriching the portals of civil society on the one hand, and being condemned for pursuing (particular) socially fragmented interests, on the other. Such simultaneity—of being acknowledged and condemned—draws an increasing wedge between achieving (particularistic) benefits and claiming (social) dignity, making the processes of discrimination ever more insidious. In other words, while engaging with the processes of civil society allows Dalit movement to be recognized as being civil and following 'civic virtue' and thereby empowers it, bringing and stamping it with its particularistic traits robs it of its legitimate claims to dignity and recognition, and thereby simultaneously disempowers it. For instance, the constitutional-democratic state recognizes the legitimacy of 'special' claims by Dalits and implements policies of protective discrimination or reservations (as they are known in their distinct version in India) in order to provide new opportunities for the legally constituted 'scheduled castes' in civil society; however, the same policies have also been the instruments that actively represented the Dalits as existing in 'perpetual passivity', objectified as subjects of 'charity rather than parity', as faceless 'statistical entities' and get suspended in a state of indignity. The Dalit movement manufactured a series of strategies to avail the benefits as available in and through the generic and core practices—laws, state policies and the project of citizenship—of civil society, and yet recognized the need to step outside in order to compensate the damage to particularistic identity experienced as loss of dignity that is accumulated due to this very availing—*marking a unique dialectic between the universal and the particular*. Thus, the first phase of the Dalit movement, unlike the HRM, began with a tension with politics and discourse of civil society—neither being able to accommodate, get accommodated nor reject it, maintaining one step outside it in order to negotiate with the 'empowerment-disempowerment dilemma' that was debilitating and represented the way power was structured in the civil sphere.

It was in the second phase of the Dalit movement in the early 1990s that, in negotiating with this inherent tension with the domain of civil society, the Dalit struggles withdrew from the unique universal–particular dialectic and moved increasingly towards celebration of particularism—where identities were inward-looking and self-enclosed—that found strong resonance with the privileging of the ideal of pluralism in the civil society. In the course of the close study of the second phase we realize the distinct character of pluralism in civil society, which while offering a critique of inward-looking identities, actually pushes and corners political struggles to precisely produce such identities. In other words, ironically, while on the one hand civil society despises ascriptive identifications, on the other, in the course of celebrating a 'politics of difference' and a 'politics of recognition' it in fact privileges identity politics in the name of plurality and diversity, revealing certain foundational aspects about civil society. As E. M. Wood has argued, 'Hegel's identification of "civil" with "bourgeois" society was more than just a fluke of the German language' (Wood 1995: 240). 'Bourgeois society' in fact presupposes a modern economy that does not depend on 'extra-economic' modes of accumulation but is dependent on purely economic modes—wage labour. It is this 'separation' of the economic from the political and cultural that allows for the emergence of an 'autonomous' social and civil sphere with activities that are expected not to have a direct impact on the economic processes. Civil society therefore unproblematically articulates, accepts, modifies, prefers and privileges those forms of struggles that are grounded in and maintain this ostensible 'separation'.[3] However, this *moment of separation* between the economy and politics is also a *moment of convergence*—in replicating power relations in its myriad forms—when political identities are disciplined into emerging as stand-alone cultural identities withdrawing from their unique dialectic between the particular and the universal.

The insidious modes of robbing the Dalit struggle of dignity and self-respect that it witnessed in its first phase frustrates and throttles the movement into an avalanche-like phenomenal growth of identity politics for recognition that is framed in a manner that singularly undermines the possibility of combining such demands with all other issues, including those of economic redistribution. It is this shift, or rather shrinkage, to the 'identitarian' mode that gained the Dalit movement a renewed acceptability within civil society through its discourse of plurality and in a sense allowed it to 'resolve' the tension it felt in the earlier phase. The Dalit movement during such a phase is represented by the processes of valorizing and essentializing its own culture and in the process producing a self-enclosed identity. This shift signifies a withdrawal, from the unique universal-particular dialectic, where particularism replaces particularity, ghettoizing itself by taking recourse to an exclusivist and self-enclosed language of 'lived experience'—Dalits alone can speak on behalf of Dalits and that it cannot be a shared identity or politics. The exclusive 'identitarian' turn accompanied or signified by withdrawal from a larger political agenda (for instance, of combining demands of recognition with that of redistribution) and ghettoization made the Dalit struggles susceptible to, what Slavoj Zizek in the context of the privileging of pluralism through the discourse of multiculturalism calls 'racism at a distance'—allowing racism to be practiced by the distance created between communities through spatial and social ghettoization and through naturalization of differences between communities. This is akin to what Foucault had observed with regard to modern power in civil society where autonomy—in this case felt and framed through a withdrawal—itself meant and implied increasing self-regulation. Civil society is in fact a 'new form of social power, in which many of the coercive functions that once belonged to the state were relocated in the "private" sphere…It is, in a sense, this "privatization" of public power that has created the historically novel realm of civil society' (Wood 1995: 254). The overlap between Dalit struggles celebrating their *withdrawal as autonomy* with that of civil society discourse privileging *distance as pluralism* not only made its politics essentialized and insular both internally and externally, but also bifurcated and dichtomized the demands for recognition against those for redistribution—in not disturbing the structural equilibrium in the civil society Dalit politics gained renewed acceptance.

The contemporary third phase of the Dalit struggles, with the growth of the new phenomenon of the sub-caste movement on the one hand and through a renewed and sustained dialogue with the Naxalite movement entailing a recovery of the common ground it had shared with the latter in earlier political articulations (such as the *Dalit Panthers*) on the other, signifies an attempt to move beyond the limitations imposed by the civil society. In its contemporary articulation in the context of conflicts between the Dalit sub-castes, for instance, Dalit scholars have argued that 'the category of Dalit negates the *dichotomously* perceived and posed categories like "privileged" and "underprivileged" or the "forwards" and the "backwards". This negation is particularly influenced by the consideration that these binary or vertical oppositions tend to neglect the horizontal tensions within them. Thus, these categories inadequately capture the specific realities and underplay the need for internal critique' (Guru 2001: 103). In articulating new combinatory practices—internal critique combined with inter-subjective communication with other democratic struggles such as in this case the Naxalite movement; overcoming the bifurcation between the demands for recognition and those for redistribution with a new caste-class approach, among other such formulations that we shall discuss in some detail—that essentially represents a post-civil society approach, the Dalit movement intended to circumvent insidious modes of power. These processes are analyzed in some detail through a narrative based on three major massacres against Dalits in Karamchedu in 1985, Chundur in 1991 and Vempentta in 1998 in the southern state of Andhra Pradesh.

Karamchedu: Foray Into or Out of Civil Society?

The contemporary independent Dalit movement in India originated with the growing sense of subordination, including various organized massacres of Dalits by the so-called upper castes across the country amongst which one of the most brazen and also brutal and therefore significant to the emerging Dalit protest politics was in Karamchedu, in coastal Andhra Pradesh, in 1985. The Karamchedu massacre had its roots in the complex economic, political and cultural changes this village witnessed over the past quarter century. In the 1970s the small Kamma peasants of Karamchedu who were well versed with tobacco cultivation began to migrate to far off districts like Karimnagar in the Telangana region of Andhra Pradesh and began to cultivate tobacco on larger portions of land, 'while the migrant Kamma farmers struck gold in tobacco and cotton cultivation elsewhere, the others in Karamchedu did experience the spill-over effects' (Andhra Pradesh Civil Liberties Committee 1985a: 5). The 'scheduled castes' filled this vacuum and graduated to share cropping and field tenancy. Most 'scheduled caste' families graduated to become small peasants. Some among the youth also got educated and acquired jobs.[4]

These changes in the economic position of the 'scheduled castes' came into conflict with their extremely demeaning social position in the village, including practices of untouchability, extreme subordination, sexual exploitation of women and bonded labour. All of these discriminatory practices began to be questioned and *experienced* in a changed context.

Politically, Karamchedu did have a history of Left politics, which made a decisive difference to their consciousness.

> 'Almost isolating the landlords, the Kamma small peasants, tenants and agricultural labourers along with the harijans and others aligned themselves with the communist party. In the 1950's, Karamchedu was a veritable bastion of the communist party and the major segment of Kamma settlement in the village is even now unbelievably called Moscow' (Andhra Pradesh Civil Liberties Committee 1985a: 2).

The contradictions between all these 'levels' that found expression in the increasing conflicts and tensions compounded to only result in the ghastly massacre of 17 July 1985. The incident was representative of the growing cultural assertion by the Dalits across the country, and the intolerance to the changing situation on the part of the so-called upper castes, which in this case was expressed by the Kammas. On 16 July a Kamma boy watered his buffalo at the steps of the water tank of the Dalits, letting out the soiled water into the tank meant for the purpose of supplying drinking water to the Dalits. A lame Dalit youth and a young Dalit woman protested against this. This immediate incident resulted in the organized massacre in the early hours of 17 July, killing six and injuring around 25 men and women who after that had permanently deformed bodies and minds (Ibid.: 9).

Immediately after the incident, villagers ran to the nearby Chirala town and set up a camp (*shibiram*). It is around this camp that Dalit struggle with demands and issues 'specific' to Dalits emerged in the context of Andhra Pradesh. Initially, Dalit leaders began to mobilize Dalits all over the state around the issue of cultural assertion against the dominance of upper castes. This assertion for an independent and a voluntary movement demanded autonomy from both the state institutions and the mainstream parties and also the radical Left movement led by the various Marxist-Leninist (henceforth ML) groups. Dalit leaders protested and rejected ML groups' depiction of the incident as 'landlord's attack against labourers' (title of the pamphlet distributed by People's War Group). Instead, they argued it was the 'Kamma landlords' attack on 'Madiga coolies'. Along with demanding autonomy from the ML groups, Dalit leaders rejected state institutions and even Dalit leaders working within them, both political representatives as well as bureaucrats. Dalit bureaucrats were characterized as 'Dalit dalaries' or Dalit compradors (Illiah 1995b: 27).

As a symbolic representation of an autonomous and also a voluntary struggle, Dalit leaders decided that 'only Dalits' would occupy the dais and address others on the issue of Karamchedu. It is pertinent to note that the Dalit movement was drawing its voluntary character not in severing its ascriptive base but in precisely activating that for the purposes of protest politics. It was decided that no so-called upper caste, however radical and sympathetic to the Dalit cause, would be allowed. This demand of 'only Dalits' was one of the earliest forms in which autonomy got articulated in Andhra Pradesh. All those Dalits who were part of the communist movement were now discursively re-articulated as 'Dalit communists' (Illiah 1995b: 6). Ambedkarism emerged as the guiding philosophy for an independent Dalit 'social revolution', which was later referred to as a 'New Dalit Democratic Revolution' *both as a continuation and to counter* the ML group's exclusively class-based struggle for 'New Democratic Revolution'. Such alternate discursive articulations on the one hand created conditions for movements to rethink their position vis-à-vis each other, and on the other the idea was to give Dalit activism a distinct intentional and political character beyond mere primordial and ascriptive features that limit their access to legitimately belong and work in a civil society. In course of two months struggle after the incident, Dalit leaders also argued that there was a need for 'Dalit organic intellectuals', who could alone conceptualize the aspirations of Dalits and provide the much needed 'social network'—to counter the social capital of those influential because of their 'higher' caste status—that is essential to consolidate the space within the civil society.

The struggle to both rehabilitate the Dalits who left Karamchedu and punish the culprits began soon after. Fifteenth August was observed as a black day, followed by *dharnas*, and indefinite hunger strikes. However none of this could pressurize the government to take proactive measures. On 1 September 1985, finally a public meeting was organized where Dalits from all over the state were mobilized rallying under the slogan 'Chalo Chirala'. The PWG's cultural wing *Jana Natya Mandali* took an active part and its lead singer Gaddar (who himself was a Dalit) inaugurated the meeting (Ratnam 1998: 111). This signified both the proximity an independent Dalit movement wished to have with ML groups such as the PWG, as well as its firm resolve to maintain autonomy by projecting Dalit leaders, writers, singers and conceptualizing a discourse specific to the problems of Dalits arising from their perceived lower caste status.

At the end of this historic meeting, the formation of a state level autonomous Dalit organization—Dalit Maha Sabha (DMS)—was formally announced. Two prominent Dalit leaders were elected unanimously as its office bearers. Again the choice of the leaders, apart from following the popular elected representative model, typically resembled the processes in a civil society and was based exclusively on the capacity of these individuals to voice and articulate the aspirations of the Dalits, rather than either their clout as political leaders, or wealth, muscle power or a principle of heredity. Later, in February 1986, the DMS held its first state level conference at Tenali and released its manifesto. It created interest among various sections of the society in general and ML groups in particular as it was the first attempt to articulate and conceptualize the idea of an autonomous Dalit movement.

The manifesto was, again, an attempt to negotiate, incorporate and expand the consciousness built around Marxist struggles in the state. In the manifesto Dalits were defined not as particular castes or social groups, subjected to particular forms of discrimination and oppression. Instead, all peoples belonging to various religions, castes and classes subjected to various forms of economic, social and cultural discriminations were all together referred to as Dalits (in a sense, drawing from the Marxist idea but laying emphasis on 'creating' a 'universal subject'). It in fact very specifically declared that those socially discriminated through the practice of untouchability was only a fraction of this larger identity called Dalit. Thus, it opened up a *unique dialectic between the particular and the universal* where 'particularity or difference is valued but not particularism, which absolutizes it. The universal is valued but not universalism, at least not of the kind that sets itself in opposition to and despises the particular' (Parekh 2008: 3).[5]

It was part of the DMS' agenda to struggle and to realize this 'hegemonic unity' among the poor peasants from all castes, including the so-called upper castes. This autonomous strategy of transformation was understood to be part of the principles and organizational work envisaged primarily by Buddha, Phule and Ambedkar. The DMS believed that historically, the Congress party offered only piecemeal benefits and never implemented more fundamental demands of transformation, including economic change possible through land reforms and implementation of minimum wages. Communist parties, on the other hand, suffered from 'economic determinism' and neglected various forms of social discriminations. An independent Dalit movement was therefore aiming at 'social revolution' as well as a 'cultural revolution', along with socialization of land and capital (APDM 1985: 6).

The DMS was, however, ambiguous about political power. It declared that in order to remain away from 'political temptations' it would not admit people who were earlier members of any political party (Ibid.: 13). In other words, it wished to remain as a conventional civil society organization at the grassroots without an agenda of capture of political power, with its important demands being land, education, water, library facilities and the right to information, which would contribute to obliterate social discriminations. The DMS not only made land the focus of its struggle but also kept distance from parliamentary politics, to keep open its option of carrying out joint activity with the ML parties. It recognized the need for support from militant-armed organizations in order to achieve its demands.

History, in a sense, was repeating itself with the DMS formulating a programme partially similar to the Dalit Panthers in the 1970s, which made the 'genuine radical Left' or the revolutionary organizations carrying out class struggle their immediate friends. However, their struggle was not just against the existing class system but what they ingeniously referred to as 'Hindu feudal order' (Dalitha Pantherla Manifesto 1996: 15). The Dalit Panthers very forthrightly conceptualized that all struggles based on caste, devoid of a generic and broader social and economic concerns were all 'casteist struggles'. They therefore believed that for the emancipation of Dalits, there was a need for 'total revolution', which included the fight for socialism and not 'pseudo-nationalization' and therefore legal petitioning, demands for subsidies and electoral methods were considered obsolete (Ibid.: 20), as much as any resort to a self-enclosed understanding of what the category or notion of the Dalit represented.

However, the DMS, unlike the Dalit Panthers along with militant struggles took up legal battles against the so-called upper caste culprits in most of the cases. For instance, in the Karamchedu massacre it filed cases against the main accused (Chenchu Ramaiah) behind the massacre. The government also constituted a judicial enquiry under the pressure of the DMS, which however declared that 'it could not find any clear cut reason behind the massacre, hence it is inconclusive' (Ratnam 1998: 117). While the court case dragged on inconclusively on 6 April 1989, a PWG guerrilla squad physically eliminated the main accused. The PWG also condemned the DMS for its legal struggle abandoning its initial revolutionary and agitational struggle. Dalit leaders however argued that, though the PWGs act gained a lot of admiration among Dalits, it is important to pursue legal and constitutional means as long as Dalits had trust in them and thereby empowered them. It was part of the dialectics of the struggle by the DMS to use as well as to expose the laws, judiciary, police and the entire state machinery of the caste bias they suffer from. The Dalit movement, without denying the need for militant struggles, pursued other forms of struggle as well. Dalit leaders believed that the specific form of oppression of Dalits made it necessary to carry out the struggle on various fronts. It is in this context of recognizing the dependence on state institutions that some of the Dalit leaders in the DMS began to differ and argue that 'political power for Dalits' and active state intervention was in fact not only the essence of an independent Dalit movement but also an integral part of the political vision of Ambedkar. As some Dalit scholars have argued, 'Ambedkar invested faith and confidence in the state for restoring citizenship to the Indian Dalits. He argued strongly for state intervention because he was not sure and he was deeply suspicious of the Hindu public sphere' (Guru 2005: 263).

The multi-pronged strategy that kept distance from electoral politics and the idea of 'capture of political power' while maintaining proximity with the militant Left parties on the one hand and negotiating with available legal and other avenues within the state institutions, along with keeping open, and sometimes emphasizing, the idea of the need for state intervention and use of political power on the other, besides a unique dialectic between the particular and the universal, demonstrated a complex mosaic of uneven relation that the Dalit struggles were forging *with* and *within* civil society. They were not making an easy choice between a civil society that worked only in consonance with a constitutional-democratic state and a civil society as represented by political movements that stood opposed to the idea of the political structure of the state. Unlike the HRM that moved from working with one version to the other between its initial phase of 'civil liberties' to its later phase of 'democratic rights', the Dalit movement was in fact reconfiguring civil society as a 'mediating space' (Jayaram 2005); while making claims and forays into civil society they also had one step outside to counter the limits posed by both the ideological (caste) bias of the institutions of civil society, and also to recognize the power relations that were integral to the 'Hindu public sphere' avoiding a romantic view of civil society as a pure 'realm of freedom'. Somewhat akin to the—human rights—perspective of the HRM in its third phase, the Dalit movement too sought to explore the possibility of democratization by spinning complex dynamics through the interface between democratic institutions and radical protest politics.

It is within this backdrop of an emerging critique and tension with practices and institutions in and related to civil society that DMS officially launched its journal called 'Nalupu' (Black), in April 1989. Its focus and purpose clearly reflected this need to evolve a broader strategy for the Dalit movement that was conscious of the need to *work within* as well as in *tension with* civil society. The president of DMS edited 'Nalupu'. However, it is interesting to note that the editorial board had leading civil rights activists, academics and journalists from the so-called upper castes along with Dalit writers. The structure and issues in focus in the journal were also symptomatic of the 'broader cause' Dalit movement stood for in Andhra Pradesh, beyond highlighting discriminations on the basis of caste. In a sense, it was interested in comprehending the possible linkages between these other modes of domination and exclusion, and the caste system. It carried detailed discussions on political movements such as the anti-arrack movement, and on issues such as problem of housing, health policies of the government leading to 'brain drain' in the medical field, privatization of education and its implications, struggles in Kashmir and other international issues. Most of these issues were analyzed with an ideological proximity to Left politics, and therefore intensely reflected on the need and the possibility of forging solidarity with ML parties like the PWG and yet fight for the benefits, such as the policies of affirmative action, the existing socio-legal system offered.

In this context, it repeatedly argued through its editorials that the ML movement was a political struggle for demands affecting the lives of scores of adivasis and Dalits. It also argued that the violence indulged in by the Naxalite groups was only a 'counter violence' to the violence perpetuated by the State, and therefore there was nothing 'uncivil' about it. Nalupu protested against the ban on the PWG and the series of 'fake encounters' against them and focused throughout on the issue of land and various militant land struggles taking place in remote villages of Andhra Pradesh and that revolution was a plausible means of transforming the society (Nalupu 1991). At the same time, it stressed the significance of using the available legal and constitutional means. The 'Nalupu' carried a series of articles on various state institutions. For instance, it constantly argued that Panchayat Raj institutions (PRIs) should be used for the empowerment of the weaker social groups, along with the various legal provisions in favour of carrying out land reforms (Nalupu 1991).[6]

'Nalupu', at the same time, also projected the caste bias among some of the ML groups, for instance it carried a detailed coverage of an incident on 7 March 1993, where activists of the CPI (ML) Praja Pantha attacked and killed a Dalit boy, due to organizational differences between them and Dr Ambedker Yuvajana Sangham. They criticized the 'sectarian tendencies' in the ML groups, and the social power it imposed and replicated, which made any meaningful dialogue and alliance politically problematic. Again, the reasoning for such a complex discourse—critiquing and making use of state institutions and legal mechanisms on the one hand, and critiquing and working in tandem with the ML organizations on the other—could be traced to the tension between the need to avail of benefits—legal redressal, policies of protective discrimination, among others, through state-constituted categories as 'scheduled castes'—and the need to align with struggles beyond caste both for exploring the implications they had for emancipation from caste-related oppression and also to counter the accompanying objectification and stigmatization that getting reduced to availing of 'special' benefits that state-constituted categories entailed. While they recognized that these benefits could be part of a necessary condition to forge new subjectivities, they also felt the need of politics beyond mere legality or state-constituted categories. In other words, the Dalit movement was looking to reconfigure the available practices, ideas and institutions in the civil society by not only combining different versions of the civil society that related to the democratic-constitutional state and that represented by the radical political movements, but also being acutely conscious of the power dynamics inherent to civil society. The Dalit movement was therefore in and out of civil society.

Writings in 'Nalupu' further reflected the acute awareness of dealing with the power dynamics in the civil society, in highlighting the caste-class complexities. For instance, it reported incidents of attacks by the OBCs on the Dalits, which posed new challenges in expanding the contours of the Dalit movement by forging new subjectivities by addressing the emerging 'internal' dynamics around the issue of larger unity of the *bahujans*. It agreed with Ambedkar's interpretation that caste is both base and superstructure (Nalupu 1991). Hierarchies and accompanying power in civil society was structured around political, cultural and economic dimensions. Civil society, while allowing for change through some of its practices, was also a site that structures and perpetuates inequalities. Caste can therefore be fought only in association with other forms of struggle (which can themselves again replicate hierarchies and its accompanying power) and carrying a sustained inter-subjective dialogue, and setting for itself an agenda that interconnects various dimensions of power on the one hand and make use of various modalities within, outside and against civil society on the other. The Dalit movement in this phase was deeply conscious of the limitations of circumscribing its politics within mere celebration of 'politics of identity' and instead argued for new modes of imagining the possibilities of raising demands for recognition without narrowing the scope to struggle for redistribution and other political agendas of representation. Its framework certainly went beyond mere ideals of plurality and difference that unite:

> diverse human beings all free and equal, without suppressing their differences or denying their special needs. But the "politics of identity" reveals its limitations, both theoretical and political, the moment we try to situate class differences within its democratic vision. Is it possible to imagine class differences without exploitation and domination? (Wood 1995: 258)

The integral link between caste and class was the defining frame of the Dalit struggle under the leadership of the DMS.

The Dalit movement under the leadership of the DMS and its ideological propaganda through 'Nalupu' provided conditions for a fuller articulation of its inherent tension with the politics of civil society in proposing: (*a*) the need to pursue both militant as well as legal methods; (*b*) articulating a broader identity of Dalit around caste–class dimensions; (*c*) emphasizing ideological unity between Ambedkarism and Marxism for innovative combinatory discursive articulations; (*d*) realizing the need for proximity with radical Left struggles around social, cultural and economic issues.

Though 'Nalupu' was published for a short span of four years (1989–93), when it was discontinued, 'every educated Dalit and the whole Dalit community felt that their potent leader had vanished' (Illiah 1995b: 38). In fact, in most of the issues of Nalupu it was repeatedly propagated that it was not just a journal, like those available to self-enclosed and mere opinion-making readers in a civil society, but was intended to create political action and therefore was a 'movement' by itself.[7] It was akin to what Melucci referred to as 'movements as messages' without necessarily, as Melucci intended, discounting the 'existence of systemic conflicts' (Melucci 1989: 39).

It is, however, pertinent to ask whether the Naxalite movement was in a position to grapple and coordinate with the dialectical mode of negotiating with power dimensions in civil society expressed through the changing material, discursive and strategic dimensions, initiated by the Dalit movement. To begin with, it was reluctant to accept ideological combination of Marxism with Ambedkarism, that found a reflection in the co-primacy of cultural issues with economic (land) struggles and combining armed-militant struggles with using legal-institutional means. This in many ways for the Naxalite movement meant diluting revolution and gravitating towards reformism. This was reflected, more immediately, in the refusal to recognize the Dalit movement as an independent political struggle, and its accompanying perspective of locating itself *in,against and beyond* civil society. They, on the contrary, strongly believed in the centrality of the armed wing and a hierarchized relation with various 'mass organizations'.[8] Therefore the Dalit movement could not fit into their scheme of political organization and modes of protest and mobilization. In fact, building 'mass organizations' was considered for a very long time as compromising with revolutionary politics. By the end of the 1970s and early 1980s, due to various historical reasons, most of the Marxist-Leninist (ML) groups did begin to experiment with alternative forms of mobilization.

Revising their earlier aversion, they began to organize 'open' 'mass organizations'. Thus the People's War's Central Committee wrote in the early eighties that, 'today almost no revolutionary group in our country clearly holds it as in the 70s that either building "mass organizations itself is revisionism" or "carrying out partial struggles itself in revisionism"' (Central Committee CPI (ML) People's War 1981: 6). However, they continued to enjoy very little autonomy and were considered 'secondary' in forging a revolution. 'Mass organizations' were characterized as mere 'Propaganda agencies' or 'recruitment centres' (Sudhakar 1998: 42). They were divided into three broad types on the basis of the nature of work they carried out. Firstly, there were the 'secret mass organizations' that propagated revolutionary (read armed) politics and recruited members for the party. Secondly, there were the 'open mass organizations', which used the available legal-democratic and constitutional means to build 'pressure, expose the state and contribute to further revolutionary politics'. Thirdly, there were the 'cover organizations', which aligned with non-party organizations and carried the agenda of anti-feudal and anti-imperialist struggles into these organizations. Such 'tactics', they considered, were necessary in conditions of extreme repression by the state (Kendra Rajakeeya Nirmana Sameeksha 2001: 110). Most of these categories of 'mass organizations' reflected the necessity of propagating the centralized agenda of 'new democratic revolution' into various sections of the society rather than trying to develop independent methods of integrating diversified sections and their particularistic demands into the overall goal of forging a socialist revolution, while maintaining their specificities. It is with this backdrop that the Naxalite movement dealt with the independent Dalit movement as one of 'its' 'mass organizations' and looked to 'co-opt' it both by entering the leadership positions and by characterizing it as a 'partial' struggle (the metaphor used was a 'stream that needs to flow back into the ocean').

Ironically, while the Dalit movement was struggling to find space for its dialectical mode of working and negotiating with the well-defined contours of civil society, radical and democratic struggles such as the Naxalite movement found the new frontiers being inaugurated unacceptable. Revolutionary struggles were preoccupied with charting out a 'coherent civil society', through their 'mass organizations', that was exclusively marked out from and essentially stood outside/against the repressive state. Their yardstick for judging other political movements was their antagonism and distance with the state. In terms of such an evaluation the Dalit movement and its multiple strategies looked at best as ideological confusion, and at worst as pragmatic manipulation. They were attempting, as we traced in the previous chapter, through the discourses of the human rights organizations—during the democratic rights phase when the HRM was close to the Marxist-Leninist parties—to construct (a coherent) civil society as a pure 'realm of freedom', and in pursuit of such a path the Dalit struggles looked like 'diluting revolution and gravitating towards reformism' due to their engagement with state institutions, law and legal subjectivity. Dalit struggles now had the burden of making sense of a formidable convergence between the two versions of civil society—the constitutional-democratic civil society and the civil society that stood outside the state represented by political movements—in this case the Naxalite movement and its 'mass organizations'. Both versions of civil society looked to *intersect* in marginalizing the assertions by the Dalit movement, and the dialectical mode in which it was attempting to operate. While the constitutional-democratic state was failing in implementing laws effectively and was suspicious of the Dalit movement's proximity to militant-left organizations, the revolutionary organizations were circumspect about Dalit movement's engagement with the state and were reluctant to politically accept the new ideological formations—combining Ambedkarism and Marxism—in their bid to construct a 'coherent civil society'. In both these processes Dalit movement sensed its own marginalization, and replication of caste hierarchies. It is in this context of this formidable *convergence* that had the potential to completely marginalize the Dalit politics that it had to reassert itself through a new language of authenticity and identity. It, perhaps, reached the conclusion that 'only Dalits' could understand the necessity of the specificity of Dalit politics, and without this organic link other political processes, however sympathetic they were, failed to grasp the logic behind their political articulations. The assertion of the emerging identitarian turn, ironically, found its fullest articulation possible within and through the discourse of pluralism and celebration of 'politics of difference' as they were privileged within the contours of civil society itself. Dalit politics now increasingly found pursuing its earlier dialectical mode less feasible, and more burdensome. Instead, a cultural assertion seemed to open up new spaces to reoccupy civil society on the one hand and force-open a dialogue on more equal terms with the Naxalite movement on the other.

Chundur: Identity Politics and a Disciplining Civil Society

It was to explore further the possibilities of critical dialogue on the exclusionary modalities of the Naxalite movement, and finding a way to reconcile autonomy in claiming specificity with achieving a common ground, that the Dalit writers started yet another journal called 'Edureeta' (Swimming against the Tide), in May 1990. Two important Dalit leaders who were previously part of the Naxalite movement (while the editor of the journal came out of the UCCRI (ML) group, another important member of the editorial board was previously a COC member of the PWG) started it. They together also started the Marxist-Leninist Centre. It is interesting to note that while the journal declared its perspective as 'Marxist-Leninist' and as a 'journal for revolutionary politics', none of the ML parties owned it but it was the Dalit organizations and writers who identified with it. A more explicit articulation of an ideological basis for solidarity in a synthesis of Ambedkarism and Marxism was acceptable to most of the Dalit groups, not so for many of the ML parties. Edureeta's editorial declared that the purpose of the journal is to: (*a*) Critique the anti-democratic, authoritarian tendencies within the various revolutionary groups vis-à-vis the newly emerging caste and gender perspectives; (*b*) Invite discussions on caste by both revolutionary groups and autonomous Dalit organizations. It was supposed to be a platform for all progressive groups to negotiate their theoretical and ideological differences so as to make unity between them a possibility (Rao 1991). Pushing the need for more self-reflection, 'Edureeta' declared itself as autonomous of both the Dalit movement led by the DMS and also the various revolutionary groups. From the lack of engagement with the state as a marker for claiming autonomy for a political movement, the new dynamics initiated by 'Edureeta' shifted the focus in emphasizing on negotiating with power dynamics internal and integral to the 'democratic space' that was being claimed 'autonomous' of and from the state. 'Edureeta' strongly believed that critical intervention into the politics of both the Dalit and the Naxalite movement alone would make a meaningful dialogue between them possible and purposeful. As for the Dalit movement, (*a*) It was critical of the DMS falling into the trap of excessive dependence in focusing on appealing to the same upper caste state, which was itself perpetuating caste discrimination; (*b*) It analyzed the shifts in the programme of the DMS and cautioned it against its politics of mobilizing just SCs and STs and not addressing issues concerning the Bahujans and other poorer communities, which was what was originally intended by the category 'Dalit'; (*c*) It also criticized the DMS for neglecting its original agenda to struggle for land and other economic issues and instead getting restricted to demanding compensation and reservations from the government. It argued that the Dalit movement in course of time had restricted itself to the 'socio-cultural' domain and fought as if Dalits could be emancipated without addressing the issue of growing economic inequalities that can be abated only through redistribution of land. 'Edureeta' was definitely in search of a new framework that could further radicalize the Dalit movement against any possibilities of getting ghettoized. In a sense it was furthering the agenda set by the DMS but interestingly found a method of critiquing it for wavering—critiquing the critique—to advance its cause.

On the other hand, it raised a series of critical issues on the practice of ML groups in the state. Among various other criticisms it highlighted that though ML groups expressed outward support for autonomous Dalit (and also the women's movement, which will be the focus of the next chapter) movement by being active within them, they always attempted to either merge these movements with the ML groups or tried to take over the leadership positions so that they could be subsumed under class struggle. Similarly, it was also pointed out that ML groups hegemonized the discourse over autonomy by branding all those seeking autonomy as 'revisionists,' 'careerists,' 'opportunists', 'stooges of ruling class' and 'agents of imperialism'. This was so primarily because they believed in recognizing autonomy or plurality of political expressions only as a 'tactic' to accommodate these independent struggles as they enjoy 'mass support'. It was also argued that constituting most of the separate anti-caste and women's wings by ML parties was again only a 'tactical' move and these organizations did not enjoy any organizational or ideological autonomy (Ibid.). In the political discourse on autonomy as privileging plurality of political ideologies and organizational forms, 'Edureeta' pointed towards a significant dichotomy between 'tactical' notions of autonomy as against 'substantive'. The debate on the political and ideological legitimacy of a 'tactical' approach as a strategy of transformation, opened up new dimensions in the ongoing dialogue on the need to reconcile the need for *plurality with commonality* or solidarity between different political articulations and their agendas, the need to maintain particularity while forging linkages between different social sections and their varied political demands in the economic, political, and cultural realms.

The dichotomization of tactical and substantive notion of autonomy by the militant-democratic movements was now sought to be understood in the face of entrenched and structural inequalities in the civil society. In other words, the question that was being raised was as to what kind of autonomy or plurality between the various political movements can maintain their specificities, yet substantively overcome the structured inequalities within the civil society? The Dalit movement now organized and deliberating on the basis of the experience gained in the course of the first phase of its mobilization was now aware that:

> There is (an) emerging (a) conflict between the civil society and Dalit society. The first is formed by the consolidation of both ideological and structural forces of caste Hindu denominations. The Dalit society, too, is reborn and reshaped by their exposure to new rights and violent resistance from the savarnas. (Nagaraj 1993: 8)

It felt there was an impending need to build Dalit resistance that can reconcile the need for plurality with the necessity to contest and overcome structured—economic, political and cultural—inequalities in the civil society.

With the intervention of 'Edureeta' in the ongoing dialogue between the Dalit groups and the ML organizations, it got concretized in terms of (*a*) distribution of land on the basis of caste; (*b*) making it mandatory to have 'only Dalits' as leaders in all ML groups and (*c*) to theoretically accept the combined philosophy of Ambedkarism—Marxism as the only alternative for the Indian situation. These alternatives got further legitimized at the beginning of the 1990s with the massacre against Dalits in Chundur. It was again retaliation by the so-called upper caste communities, in response to not just demands for higher wages or land, but about identity assertion by the Dalits for self-respect and dignity. This time in Chundur on 6 August 1991 more than 10 Dalits were brutally killed (APCLC 1991: 8, 13). Immediately after the incident, in spite of the fierce ideological differences, the ML and the Dalit groups formed the Joint Action Committee, with DMS, CPI (ML) Vimochana, UCCRI (ML), the Socialist Revolutionary Forum and the Ambedkar Youth Association. What was significant about the joint activity was, unlike before, ready acceptance to incorporate the issues 'internal' to the Dalit and ML movements. While the Dalits openly declared that 'counter violence' is essential for the Dalit movement (they now demanded that they would bury the dead right in the middle of the village and were ready to confront the so-called upper castes, unlike the Karamchedu victims who refused to go back to the village and confined the struggle to a nearby town), the ML groups accepted that cultural and issues of recognition such as dignity and self-respect would be the focus of the struggle and also that 'only Dalits' would lead the struggle. These exchanges clearly reflected the complexity that included on the one hand the experiment to carry forward the inter-subjective communication and the possibility of solidarity between the democratic movements and on the other hand to fiercely maintain the specificity of each movement and its own identity.

However, after the initial instantiation of this mutual exchange and incorporation of the agenda and strategies internal to each of the political movements, brought to the fore at the time of the 'crisis' marked by the massacre in Chundur, the public discourse began to take a different turn. The preparedness demonstrated to 'give and take' at the time of the crisis did not necessarily become the integral part of the political repertoire of the movements. On the contrary, the return to 'normalcy' pushed the movements to make a cost-benefit analysis of what they had 'gained and lost' in the course of the changes they made to their agenda and strategies in the immediacy of the 'crisis'. The qualitative distinction between *process* and *events* seems to enact its impact in ensuing openings/inclusion, and closures/exclusion. The 'changes' in the agenda and strategy of the Dalit and Naxalite movements, made at the time of 'crisis', suddenly began to be articulated as (undue) concessions that were made, and thereby the mutual expectations of the movements from each other went up, so did the anxiety to preserve their own specificity. However, the heightened expectations were played out in the context of 'normalcy' where there was no impending or pressing need to make changes or stick to those made at the times of the 'crisis'. The *play* between events and process, expressed in terms of a relation between 'crisis' and 'normalcy', seem to assume what E. P. Thompson refers to (in the context of the growing arms race) as 'gathering determinism' (Thompson 1985). The *play* between events/crisis and process/normalcy itself assumes an independent capacity to determine the consequences. Each of the movements that made amendments by incorporating the agenda and strategies of 'other' movements perceived as external to it, begins to feel the anxiety of losing its specificity due to the 'concessions' they made and interpret all changes made at the time of specific events that occur as 'crisis' as mere tactics and not substantive in nature and content. The propensity that exists at the time of specific events seems to fizzle out when they return to what they perceive as the normal or regular process of politics. Ironically, the trend to engage in a dialogue as a process gets highlighted and even consolidated by specific events but only to be short-circuited once the events die down. In this case of the ongoing dialogue between the Dalit and Naxalite movements, while specific events—like the massacre against Dalits—highlighted and momentarily consolidated their efforts to mutually influence each other, once the events passed by the movements failed to get back to the 'normalcy' of the process, and instead reinforced the existing and perceived hiatus between them.

Between the Dalit and the Naxalite movements, the ongoing dialogue got short-circuited and reinforced the bifurcated approach, expressed through a series of binaries between process and events, substantive and formal or tactical changes. These binaries then mapped themselves onto the larger grids of caste–class approach that the movements were attempting to rework through. In this mapping (or rather morphing), the movements re-presented themselves through and in claiming authentic versions of their ideological positions. While the Naxalite movement reclaimed the need for a more vigorous class mobilization, the Dalit movement moved towards claiming a more enclosed 'politics of recognition' as a way of reclaiming the specificity of each of the movements that they perceived to have diluted in the course of mutually accommodating each other. In reinforcing the bifurcated approach, the Dalit movement struck a commonality with the approach of civil society. The Dalit movement, in claiming its specificity through a renewed emphasis on enclosed 'politics of recognition', found its resonance and equivalence with the discourse of plurality and 'politics of difference' that already have a privileged and a celebratory position within civil society. Amongst the various practices and discourses central to civil society is the discourse of plurality as celebration of 'politics of difference', in that, as E. M. Wood observed, these cultural identities are celebrated in separation from the economic-class differences in which these cultural identities are located. The new identity assertion and articulation by the Dalit movement then worked like a wild card entry into the distinguished circles of civil society, gaining it a new sense of dignity and recognition that it had perceived to be losing. However, this new twist to an exclusive 'politics of recognition' in Dalit politics while allowing it a new sense of dignity and identity in its renewed entry into the portals of civil society, robs it of its earlier caste–class approach and its capacity to struggle against structured economic and social inequalities.

Nancy Fraser observed that the discourse of 'politics of difference' while allowing for celebration of cultural differences cannot be helpful in dealing with class differences, resulting in a 'recognition-redistribution dilemma'—strategies that are ideal for 'politics of recognition' wean away political movements in their struggle for politics of redistribution. Differences needed to assert cultural distinctions block the processes of forging solidarity that are necessary to struggle against common economic or class exploitation. The specificity of the discourse of plurality in civil society operates in the context of the logic of already existing and entrenched structured inequalities in this domain. As Walzer observes,

> Whether or not it includes market associations, civil society reflects and is likely to reinforce and augment the effects of inequality. This is so because every organized group is also a mobilization of resources; the more resources its members bring with them the stronger the group. The stronger the group, the more is it able to enhance the impact of the resources it collects. Hence, it is a general rule of civil society that its strongest members get stronger. (Walzer 2002: 39)

This 'general rule' then conditions and constrains the options that can be or are in effect exercised by the political movements.

The moment of empowerment for Dalit movement in gaining a new identity through the discourses of plurality and cultural politics in civil society is also a moment of distancing itself from aligning with class politics and struggling against institutionalized patterns of social inequalities. It is not that 'politics of recognition' cannot be reworked in order to overcome the 'recognition-redistribution dilemma' but its instantiation as identity politics is what makes this bridge very difficult. However, it is a sociological reality that identity and culture as stand-alone categories are constructed politically due to the kind of imperatives we have mapped but that does not remove or distance the impact of economic and social inequalities on these identities. Thus, Dalit politics faces a new challenge with its entry into civil society. While it can culturally assert, this new space comes as a 'trade-off' against its earlier sustained struggles again economic inequalities and its sustained dialogue with the Naxalite movement. However, it needs to be simultaneously realized that inter-relating various kinds (economic, political, and cultural) of agendas, in order to circumvent and displace power dynamics in civil society, has no simple or independent site to operate in. It has to be achieved by *claiming an identity* and in turn *negotiating* structured power: the simultaneity of the challenge can be blinding and excruciating. The political movements are therefore further pushed, within civil society, to internally consolidate themselves (read essentialize) in order to create and maintain the momentum and claim specificity to be recognized and heard.

In other words, while the cultural identities are essentialized in order to find space for specificity, the bifurcated scope (culture supplanting economy) of these struggles also erodes the exclusivity and dignity to their identities under the impact of existing and exasperating economic inequalities. While ideologically and politically movements need to negotiate power in all its forms—economic, political and cultural—simultaneously, sociologically and experientially they get serialized. While all along they need to struggle incessantly to move towards 'shifting networks of multiple intersecting differences', in order to circumvent structured power relations, the 'materiality of politics' condition them in constraining the simultaneity. Again, reflecting on the complexity of this process in the context of the anti-racist struggles in the United States, Nancy Fraser (Fraser 2008: 38–39) observes that:

> the long-term goal of deconstructive anti-racism is a culture in which hierarchical racial dichotomies are replaced by de-massified and shifting networks of multiple intersecting differences…Its principal drawback, again, is that both deconstructive-anti-racist cultural politics and socialist-anti-racist economic politics are far removed from the immediate interests and identities of most people of colour, as these are currently culturally constructed.

In other words, the processes augmenting inequalities, which are entrenched in civil society, as Walzer observed, themselves push movements to take recourse to exclusivist identity politics. Dalit politics, thus, faces yet another binary between its ideological imperatives—of forging a caste–class approach—and the compelling logic of its experiential dimensions.

The beginnings of this shift to a more identitarian emphasis could be traced to the new emphasis in 'Edureeta' on the demand that 'only Dalits'—meaning SCs and STs—take over the leadership positions within the revolutionary parties, disconnected from their earlier parallel emphasis on caste–class approach and search to combine Ambedkarism and Marxism. Various editorials in 'Edureeta' argued that most of the leaders of ML groups came from the upper castes and the petty bourgeois strata who joined the movement during the student days from elite institutions. Their 'petty bourgeois' and 'upper caste' tendencies, it argued, invariably got reflected later on in their functioning and decisions. They also suggested that Naxalite leaders such as T. Nagi Reddy, Com. Pulla Reddy were all essentially, in spite of their radical credentials, upper caste leaders belonging to the landed community. The movement therefore failed to get organically integrated at the grassroots where Dalits constitute the struggling majority. As a possible solution, they suggested that it should be made *mandatory* to have only members coming from SC, ST and OBC communities of the society to assume leadership positions. Most of the Dalit organizations fiercely agreed and propagated this idea in Andhra Pradesh. They felt that it was agreed that only by mutually adopting and incorporating the principles evolved in each movement that they could forge solidarity. While the Dalit movement was taking up the land issue and recognizing armed method as valid and a legitimate political method, ML groups should incorporate the principle of distributing land in accordance with caste, so as making it *mandatory* to have 'only Dalits' and bahujans as their leaders (Rao 1991). This shift to a new found emphasis on the 'politics of presence' presumed 'that changing the composition of decision-making bodies changes the character of the issues and policies discussed' (Phillips 1995: 167). This demand to make available leadership positions for Dalits became a nodal point in framing the terms of public discourse for struggles against caste based discrimination, and their dialogue with the radical Left organizations.

The various ML groups, in response, rejected making 'only Dalits' in leadership positions mandatory as a means to overcome the problem of 'tactical approach' and its separation from the more substantive change and the growing fragmentation between democratic movements. They countered the challenge of the new 'politics of presence' by reinforcing the framework of 'politics of ideas' by arguing that communists are those who have genuinely overcome caste, class and gender prejudices and therefore to fix them in these categories (acquired by birth) is a reductionism and an unacceptable turn to identity politics. They further argued that such propositions emanated from the underlying assumption of the experiment in 'Edureeta' to combine or equate Marxism with Ambedkarism, which would always remain an aborted attempt, as Ambedkar at worst was a 'petty bourgeois reformer' and at best a 'radical reformer'. They cited instances of atrocities on SCs and STs as part of the repression on the armed movements in Tebhaga and Telangana that Ambedkar did not condemn, reflecting a narrow and constitutionally constrained notion of transformation (Rao 1991). The response from the ML groups foregrounded an opposition between 'politics of ideas' and 'politics of presence' that had its impact for a very long time to come in the emerging public discourse on inter-subjectivity between the Dalit and the Naxalite movements in Andhra Pradesh. In this emergent opposition and the binary construction, the point that 'it is in relation between ideas and presence that we can best hope to find a fairer system of representation, not in a false opposition between one or the other' (Phillips 1995: 25), was lost.

It was at this critical juncture in the history of the autonomous Dalit movement in Andhra Pradesh that Bahujan Samaj Party (BSP) emerged to occupy the social and political space created by the former, further exemplifying and entrenching identity politics through its amenable link with electoral politics. Electoral politics have a distinct tone and tenor of their own. They privilege modalities that are amenable to raising social and political issues that reflect the more immediate experience, and by more identifiable social collectives, rather than more generic or dispersed agendas such as, for instance, environmental issues that concern everyone across the globe, and do not have a 'natural' constituency. Electoral representative politics, while on the one hand allowed caste-based collectives to undergo a process of 'secularization' and therefore a foray into the portals of civil society, on the other, over a period of time, converted them into exclusivist collectives engaged in the process of bargaining and foregrounding interests that are of immediate concern. Yet again, the unique circular mode in which social power in civil society worked exemplified itself in the tryst between electoral politics and identity politics, congratulating and complementing caste groups for assuming a more voluntary and secular nature in mobilizing for popular electoral politics, but condemning and delegitimizing it when, as a result of such mobilization, these social groups get internally condensed, in order to use the 'creative power of community', including their numerical strength. Thus, while BSP is dignified for its foray into electoral politics, it is critiqued and stigmatized for indulging in a 'narrow' politics of 'vote bank'.

At the second state level convention of the DMS, in 1988 at Vizag, strong differences emerged among the leadership of the DMS over the issue of alliance with BSP. A section of the DMS (led by its president) was for alliance and an active role in electoral politics. They issued a pamphlet titled 'BSP Evarikosam, Endukosam' ('BSP, For Whom and Why') to explain their position. Another section of the DMS boycotted and argued for the need to remain autonomous from all party politics and working more as a front for 'social revolution' through a dialectical articulation combining agitational-militant politics with popular mobilization rather than convert exclusively into a political party to take part in parliamentary politics

(Ratnam 1998: 119). However, DMS, the Dalit Kala Mandir, Dalit Writers, Artist, and Intellectual United Front (DWAIUF), the Ambedkar Youth Association and also a few Dalits in various revolutionary organizations, gravitated and finally joined the BSP.

One of the immediate reasons and gains that the Dalit movement perceived with its merger with the BSP was its success in drawing together the Dalits (SCs and STs) and the Bahujans (OBCs), which the autonomous Dalit movement, with its caste–class approach had failed to do. It was observed that with the combination of identitarian cultural politics with mobilization for political power there was an upsurge in the backward castes, whose youth especially in northern Telangana districts gravitated towards the BSP (Srinivasulu 1994: 2386). Kanshi Ram in the course of his campaign argued that it was due to the BSP's efforts that the OBCs gained new consciousness and to counter it the Congress party was trying to vie them through various means, a part of which was in constituting the 'OBC Commission'. The combination of being a political movement and a political party apparently created a larger space for Dalit politics than what an autonomous movement could.

Simultaneously, the BSP had to counter the consciousness—of forging unity and interconnecting economic, political and cultural agendas—that the ML groups in their sustained dialogue with the Dalit movement had already built among the Dalits of the state. Some of the Dalit writers characterized the rise of the BSP as itself the 'social revolution', which the ML groups had failed to carry out. They also argued that with the BSP gaining power at the centre there would be 'total revolution' and this is what is the 'Indianized version' of the 'New Democratic Revolution' and after this there was only 'Socialist Revolution' to achieve. As Ambedkar had envisaged, the BSP would establish the aspired 'State Socialism'. Not only was the revolutionary language appropriated by the BSP but also their agenda. Its leaders announced that land reforms would be implemented in the Telangana region. Further, it would lift the ban on the PWG, call back paramilitary forces and stop all the fake encounters (Rao 1994: 10). The leaders of the various Dalit groups attempted to pursue the idea of some kind of continued proximity with the ML parties even from within the BSP. However, 'parliamentary path versus armed revolt' emerged as the most significant dichotomy and important ML groups like the PWG, now distanced themselves from the Dalit politics, as pursued by the BSP. Thus, the legal constitutional means combined with foray into parliamentary politics now became the key or even an exclusive strategy of the Dalit movement for achieving both political power and social transformation. The careful balance it was attempting between agitational-militant means and legal-constitutional means could not be maintained anymore, and this, in the course of time, had its telling impact on the way Dalit movement framed its agenda through the language of an exclusive cultural identity and community.

Though the BSP could not gain any seats in the assembly elections, it propelled a process of conversion of Dalit socio-political movement into a movement with a singular focus on gaining political power. In the post-BSP phase in Andhra Pradesh, Dalit organizations, inspired by the success of the BSP in Uttar Pradesh and other states, made independent attempts to come together and form political fronts and continued to pursue electoral politics as the strategy for empowerment. One such significant experiment was the formation of the Mahajan Front, with around 22 prominent Dalit organizations. It constituted important sub-caste Dalit mass organizations such as the Madiga Dandora and Mala Samarabheri, among others. The Mahajan Front, however, attempted to appropriate, like the BSP, the revolutionary language and declared that they would be more radical than the BSP, as they understood the distinction between 'social justice' and 'socialist justice'. Their struggle was supposedly, as Ambedkar had articulated, against both 'Brahmanism and Capitalism' (Mahajan Front 1999: 2). However, in actuality:

> what this led to, though, was a kind of dual systems theory, (that was integral to even Ambedkar's own approach—my addition), which saw capitalism and Brahmanism (casteism) as separate systems of exploitation, one to be fought by class struggle and the other by caste struggle…The dual systems of "capitalism" and "Brahmanism" provided useful rhetoric and a rule-of-thumb for analysis, but it Left the question of the connection between the two systems completely unresolved. (Omvedt 2001: 146–47)

Some of the revolutionary parties, such as the CPI (ML) Janashakti, and their experiments were squarely based on a 'dual system' approach. It formed its 'mass front' DAFODAM—a United Front of Dalits and Minorities. DAFODAM however took a more exclusivist identitarian approach, without a corresponding linkage to a class perspective. The idea of autonomy got articulated through segregated or 'separated' parallel struggles. While the armed wing (guerilla squads) carried out class politics, the 'mass organization' attempted to carry parallel identity based caste politics. Autonomy as segregated politics led to many splits within the CPI (ML) Janashakti. Many of its cadre raised pertinent points, about Ambedkar not addressing the issue of land reforms and Communism, and Buddhism being part of the ruling class ideology. How could these ideological systems be the exclusive basis of a 'mass front' of a Communist party? (Pamphlet 1994).[9] These arguments, over a period of time, resulted in CPI (ML) Janashakti splitting into many groups—CPI (ML) Janashakti (Rajanna), CPI (ML) Janashakti (Veeranna) and the 17 May Group (CPI (ML) Janashakti undated). These splits were significant as they manifested the point that autonomy or plurality could not be interpreted as leading parallel—dichotomized—struggles with segregated ideological bases as a replacement to the earlier dialectical mode that was conscious of the difficulty and complexity of addressing various dimensions of domination and marginalization simultaneously, and in their interconnectedness.

Ironically, it was around the same period that CPI (ML) People's War encouraged the formation of anti-caste 'mass organizations', rebuking their earlier stand against building separate organizations for caste. It is interesting to observe the dynamics of the political arena, as the Dalit movement moved towards a more identitarian politics, the ML organizations changed their approach towards a more inclusive caste–class framework. In spite of or precisely due to the inter-related switch in the approaches the *differences and/as distance* between movements continued. It should be pointed out that those 'mass organizations' against caste atrocities were formed as a result of various issues raised by the Dalit cadre within the CPI (ML) People's War party, as well as under the influence of a strong and autonomous Dalit movement. Many of the important leaders of PWG Left the revolutionary party to join the Dalit movement. They questioned the reasons behind the absence of Dalits in the leadership, despite a relentless struggle for over three decades, and their reluctance in accepting promoting them to leadership ranks as *mandatory*.

As a response to some of these questions, in an International Seminar organized by CPI (ML) Janashakti on '*Marxism-Leninism, Mao-Tse Tung Thought and Revolutionary Movements*' during 9–12 March 1995, in Hyderabad, the CPI (ML) People's War presented a paper entitled 'Special Features of Indian Revolution and Marxist Approach Towards Resolution of those Problems'. In many ways, their presentation was considered as a reflection of the change in the approach of the party towards the caste question. Amidst various other specificities for revolutionary politics in India that they enumerated, such as the absence of a unified revolutionary party, existence of highly centralized State machinery, specificity of nationality struggles, problem of communalism, existence of Parliament and other legislative bodies, caste was identified as a significant problem peculiar to the Indian situation. It accepted that the:

> general tendency among the Communists has been to treat the question of caste mechanically as a super-structural category that could be eliminated once the existing social system is changed through a social revolution or to treat it as a question to be taken up only after the resolution of class struggle… it did not formulate a concrete programme and plan of action to tackle the caste question. (COC CPI (ML) People's War 1995: 14)

Though it stressed that complete resolution is possible only after the New Democratic Revolution, they nevertheless transformed Marx's famous dictum to discursively rearticulate it as 'all hitherto history of India is the history of class and caste struggles' (COC CPI (ML) People's War 1995). They acknowledged the contributions of 'reformers' such as Buddha, Basavanna, Narayan Guru, Jyoti Rao Phule and Ambedkar, whose writings and ideas were extensively propagated by the autonomous Dalit movement born after the Karamchedu massacre in 1985. Regarding autonomous Dalit organizations they however observed that: 'we must adopt the policy of forging a common front with the cadres of such organizations on specific issues related to caste discrimination while taking care to expose the bourgeois reformist nature and limitations of their leadership' (Ibid.: 16).

It is with this understanding that they encouraged the formation of new anti-caste 'mass organizations'. Kula Nirmulana Porata Samithi (KNPS) was formed in Vijayawada in 1998. It held its second state level conference on 18–19 February, 2001 in Ongole. Various other 'mass organizations' took part in these proceedings, which included the APCMS, the VIRASAM, the APCLC, the Rational Society and the BC Rights Protection Committee. These were mostly organizations which broadly agreed with the People's War Group. The resolutions adopted in these proceedings reflected the approach to integrate Dalit problems and movement with various other political and economic struggles, which also affected Dalits. The resolutions included struggles against privatization of the economy, declared handloom workers' suicides as 'government murders', were against cuts in the welfare budget and demanded the punishment of the culprits of atrocities against Dalits (Kula Nirmulana 2001: 24). It was argued that the Dalit movement had to struggle against all those issues that affected not Dalits alone but also other impoverished sections of the society as well, which ironically was the initial perspective of the Dalit movement under the leadership of the DMS.

In the manifesto of the KNPS it raised one of the pertinent points, as a critique against the identity based formulation privileging 'only Dalits', regarding 'classes within caste groups'. While the autonomous Dalit movement perceived the new classes as an empowerment of Dalits, KNPS argued that this nascent bourgeois class among the Dalits was interested in the slogan 'political power to Dalits' as it had already acquired economic power. This class also had a nexus with the traditional 'feudal ruling classes' (Kula Nirmulana Samithi Pranalika undated: 14). The KNPS once again sought to link Dalit movement with the Communist movement through struggles against feudalism and imperialism. Similarly, it raised the issue of eradication—annihilation— of caste identities by deconstructing them as against their consolidation by the autonomous Dalit movement and saw this as possible only through the interface of caste based politics with an agenda against growing class inequalities. KNPS wished to foreground the point that 'in this context, questions of recognition are serving less to supplement, complicate and enrich redistributive struggles than to marginalize, eclipse and displace them' (Fraser 2000: 108).

It claimed it is because of this integrated caste–class approach that the KNPS could address various issues related to emerging conflicts between BCs and Dalits, and various sub-castes within Dalits more effectively than the Dalit movement, which had no means of negotiating them through the prism of identity politics (Pamphlet 1999). The KNPS also approached the issue of privatization of the economy through its caste–class approach in a dialectical mode; while it demanded reservations in the private sector for Dalits it also mobilized them in struggles against privatization of economy as such. In spite of its broad agreement with the People's War Group, the KNPS took no open stand on making a choice between armed struggle and electoral politics. The KNPS with its broad dialectically linked caste–class approach, not only once again attempted to negotiate with the 'problem of displacement' of class/redistributive issues that was integral to the 'identity model' but also seemed to have been effective in mobilizing Dalits and aligning them to revolutionary politics.

The Dalit movement, as a *response* to such radical re-articulation by the Naxalite movement, however only further entrenched and solidified its turn to identitarian politics that it had set in motion for some time now. The newly emerged 'organic intellectuals' among the Dalit community made further appeals to forge a self-enclosed identity, based on the claims to authenticity that they now argued ensued from the exclusive 'lived experience' that 'only Dalits' had an access to as a result of their birth and suffering social stigma and ostracism. On the basis of this renewed cultural framing and as a consequence of increasing 'culturalization of politics' the Dalit scholars began to further argue that:

> the makers of history themselves should become the writers of history so that the interaction between history and the makers of history is a living interaction. In this sense, both Western and Indian upper caste scholars/historians were the 'other' and wrote the Dalit Bahujan history in their voice. Hence, the very difference between 'others' and 'us' distorted the living spirit of that history… The organicness, therefore, is more fundamental for perceiving the reality in its true spirit. (Illiah 2004: 227)[10]

'The organicness', it was argued, helps articulate ideological projects from radically alternative 'Dalit-Bahujan epistemology' where 'the Dalit-Bahujans have their own theory of knowledge which produces and reproduces itself in the day-to-day interaction with *prakruti* (nature)…' (Illiah 2001: 110). This mode of arguing was further entrenched with not just 'epistemological claims' for authentic representations but also in terms of ethical/moral claims that had no place for the 'outsider'. 'It is just that non-Dalits have no moral right to theorise about Dalits' since there is a deep-seated 'inability to either recover or throw up an alternative concept (happens) because these scholars choose to theorize Dalit experience standing outside Dalit experience' (Guru 2002: 5004). It is pertinent to observe that this switch to a moral language or moral authenticity and the mutual spiraling impact such a discourse had on other democratic movements, for instance on the HRM's invocation of 'abstract morality' that we discussed in some detail in the previous chapter.

Dalit scholars during this phase argued that the uniqueness of these claims rests on the exclusivity of this experience—an experience that cannot be replicated. In other words, 'the lived experience of Dalits is not about sharing their lifestyles, living with them and being like them, but being them in the sense you cannot be anything else.... lived experience is not about freedom of experience but about the lack of freedom in experience' (Sarukkai 2007: 4045). The claims to authenticity therefore emerge from a closure, where neither can the experience be shared nor can it be replicated. It also closes the avenues to understand the internal mechanisms of generating knowledge through what was sought in the earlier phase—an inter-subjectivity; since this is a knowledge now considered to be born out of an internally closed 'lived experience' of and by 'only Dalits'. There emerged, it seems, a shift in this unproblematic collapse between an 'experience of being a subject and experience about the subject', with a sense of completeness unto itself. It was not interrogated whether this 'social' completeness of the experience in the sense of opening a 'dialogue (only) between their own history and their ongoing struggles' (Illiah 2004: 227), could well generate insularity. As there is a dimension of external 'incommunicability' that restricts the possibility of 'inter-subjective communication' there could as well be a strong dimension of internal insularity that incapacitates dialogue between the various fragments of the 'lived experience', for instance, between Dalit women and their more dominant male counterparts, or between various sub-castes within the Dalits (which is what eventually happened, and what we will focus on in the next section of this chapter).

'Lived experience' as an originary point of explanation and not as an epiphenomena of larger processes raises very many questions about the veracity of the identity politics that flow out of them. As Joan Scott argues, 'grounding exclusively on experience renders invisible the *historicity* of experience and reproduces the very terms and conditions upon which that experience is in fact founded- and therefore cannot contribute to transformation' (Scott 1992: 24). In other words, for the given experience to be interrogated there is a simultaneous need to own up, self-reflect and distance—*in-against-and-beyond*—one's self from her lived experience. Otherwise the experience is prone to be susceptible to available dominant forms of practices and articulation, and would actively replicate them. The purport of these propositions is not to argue that experience is merely a construct of the structures, linguistic or otherwise[11], but to foreground the point of the possibility that it is never epistemically self-sufficient since 'experience is not a clear datum but a complex of elements in need of clarification and reflection' (Martin 1990: 48). This reflection, as against essentialism and the inability to relate to socio-historical dynamics, is located in the interstices of 'inter-subjective communication', which the Dalit movement itself emphasized, in order to arrive at more combinatory postures, before it took such an exclusivist identitarian turn.

As we argued and attempted to lay out so far, the switch to identity politics can itself be made sense of in its complex interface with the way social power is constituted in the civil society, however, the nature and texture of such an interface is determined by the specificity of history, memory, language, symbols and other social dimensions in every society. While the new turn to identity politics got locked with the discourses of plurality and celebration of distinct cultural identities in civil society, the nature of this inter-locking in turn is determined by the specific—historical, linguistic and symbolic—discourses that dominate the performative aspects of a civil society. In other words, how civil society comes to be constructed as a public sphere. In its role as the public sphere, civil society becomes, 'a non-legislative, extra-judicial, public space in which societal differences, social problems, public policy, government action and matters of community and cultural identity are developed and debated' (McClain and Fleming 2000: 312). It signifies the modalities through which common problems are framed, debated and thought to be resolved; where shared interests are sought to be forged, and above all 'a willingness to cede some territory to others, the ability to see something of oneself in those who are different and work together more effectively as a result…' (Edwards 2010: 64), the modality of generating a civic space for 'peaceful' resolution of conflicts.

The construction of such a public sphere in a segregated and hierarchized society like India not only remains in a state of permanent 'making' but also is difficult to trace as to who or what in history actually lead to such a public based on a semblance of 'consensus' and dialogue. There would always be claims and counter-claims, for instance the claim of 'nation in the making' by the nationalist leaders during the anti-colonial struggle are countered as 'Nationalism without a Nation' by the contemporary Dalit scholars. However, given the proximity between state, nation and civil society as public sphere, one cannot be presumed either without or disconnected from the other. In this context, perhaps the nature of the anti-colonial movement and its leadership continues to frame and determine the tone and texture of civil society as public sphere. In this the role of Gandhi and the language, and symbols he introduced into public life in order to create civil society as public sphere, remains singularly pertinent.[12] The impact of the language and symbols he introduced in the course of the anti-colonial mobilization continue to influence the domain of public policy, institutions and political processes, especially in offering terms to legitimately 'resolve' conflicts, and provide moral subjectivity as integral to cultural identities.

Gandhi, as has been well documented and researched, predominantly used the philosophy, language and symbols of Hinduism, in order to create a civic space with 'a willingness to cede some territory to others', especially in the context of the question of caste (Chatterjee 2006; Moore 1985). His symbols of fasts and ashrams, his language of 'Ram Rajya' or that in the bhajans he insisted on being sung before public meetings or his philosophy of sathyagraha were integral to his creation of a moral self that was in turn the source and foundational basis for non-violence and attempts to construct a civic space for 'peaceful resolution of conflicts'. Within this context, it is intriguing and significant, for our discussion here, the centrality of the category of 'experience' in operationalizing the philosophical/moral, linguistic/semantic and symbolic/performative propositions into real-time practices of a public sphere. The convergence between the privileging of experiential—as against cognitive— categories in Gandhi then, and Dalit politics now offer us insights into the labyrinthine terrain on which political movements operate, in order to reclaim legitimate civic space within the constructed domain of civil society as public sphere.

The Gandhian approach to constructing the dominant Hindu public sphere, against which, rather ironically, both Dalits and even feminists have in the recent past been unequivocally critical, was also marked and constrained by the same existential/experiential mode to which Dalit politics have turned to with the emergence of the identitarian politics. Gandhian ideas, 'about very specific political strategies in specific contexts flowed from ideas that were very remote from politics' (Bilgrami 2003: 4159). For instance, the idea of Brahmacharya had a crucial link to the Gandhian idea of politics. Gandhi argued, 'Brahmacharya does not mean merely physical self-control. It means much more. It means complete control over all the senses...I have not acquired that control over my thoughts...there is perhaps a flaw somewhere which accounts for the apparent failure of leadership...'[13] Therefore, Gandhian political praxis reveals very little compared to what it hides, a complex 'internal' process, which invariably includes 'things which are known only to oneself and one's Maker. These are clearly incommunicable' (Gandhi 2007: 8). Gandhi's 'voice of conscience', was the only 'tyrant' he was willing to 'surrender' himself—he could recognize no higher court of appeal than 'the court of conscience'—and it provided him with a moral experience—the experience of truth, which is an experiential and not a cognitive notion inextricably tied to a 'lived experience'. The dictates of this 'still small voice' were final, and provided him with unquestionable guidance to his 'political' praxis. As early as 1916, Gandhi wrote, 'there come to us moments in life when about some things we need no proof from without. A little voice within us tells us you are on the right track...'[14] It is this 'individual conscience' that Gandhi was concerned with socializing 'rather than internalizing the social conscience' (Ibid.: 123).[15]

The experience of the conscience (or truth or God) cannot assume moral proportions unless it is a part of one's 'lived experience'. If 'lived experience' is all about an absolute lack of choice or freedom, Gandhi precisely emphasized this lack in formulating his idea of a true Satyagrahi, who has the compelling obligation, 'to suffer for one's beliefs to the point of spiritual isolation and even public ridicule, involving if necessary political martyrdom and even physical death'.[16] Actualizing the dictates of the conscience are tied up, not with unbounded freedom to act, but in realizing the absolute lack of it, and therefore 'the civil resister of Gandhi's conception cannot protest at being put into prison for the violation of laws that he regards as immoral and unjust. He *meekly* and willingly *submits* to the penalty of disobedience and cheerfully accepts jail discipline and its attendant hardships....' [emphases my addition] (Ibid.: 155). These strictures or obligations of the conscience, in a sense, are stronger than the ascriptive constraints. The point is by emphasizing the centrality of obligation (directed inwards—towards one's conscience) Gandhi wished to equalize the moral burden on one and all, and thereby neutralize the various social hierarchies and inequalities. He felt by generalizing the language of obligations internally he wished to make external differences irrelevant. These obligations would generate similar (though arrived at individually) lived experience for everyone. What he sought to change was not the material condition so much as the moral condition. However, the possibility that such generalization in a hierarchized society, such as India, might lead to 'moral purification' of everyone yet leave the social hierarchies untouched was completely overlooked. In other words, oppression was an 'abstract moral condition' without being linked to the concrete social, economic, material and historical conditions.[17] This delinking or 'separation' in fact has been the consequence of, and critique against, Gandhian philosophy, and has a parallel with the approach that

Dalit movement adopted in course of and as a consequence of its shift to identity politics.

Further, the ideas, knowledge and praxis generated on the basis of such inwardly oriented lived experience in Gandhi is also (again very much like the identity claims of the Dalits) exclusive, rather than social. It can be neither replicated nor available as 'political principles'. 'For him (Gandhi) conscience and its deliverances, though relevant to others, are not the well-spring of principles. Morals is (sic) only about conscience, not at all about principles' (Bilgrami 2003: 4162). There is therefore insularity about the way Gandhi pursued his morals and the political praxis that flows out of a closed internally 'lived experience' between him and his 'maker'. These 'metaphysical presuppositions' and 'unprovable assumptions'[18] are themselves unquestionable as they are not open to cognition but constitute an inexplicable moral experience. However, Bilgrami affirmatively argues, 'the romance in this morality is radiant. Somehow goodness, good acts enter the world and affect everyone else. To ask how exactly they do that is to be vulgar, to spoil the romance. Goodness is a sort of mysterious contagion' (Bilgrami 2003.: 4163). Further, for Bilgrami, the inexplicability of the experience, 'far from encouraging self-enclosed moral subjects', in fact is an extremely humanizing exercise since Gandhi severed the link between moral belief and moral criticism. In other words, Satygrahis are 'moral exemplars', who are fully confident about the moral values they wish to exemplify. However they do not arrogate to themselves the moral superiority to criticize others, but only to persuade them by setting an example. Therefore, 'at most we may be disappointed in others that they will not follow our example, and at least part of the disappointment in ourselves that our example has not taken hold' (Ibid.). While this aspect of disappointment might seem to keep in place a continuous process of self-reflection and self-criticism, it however is only formal. The method of persuading others might be open and self-critical, but the moral values at stake are non-negotiable.[19] This can often reduce the others to mute spectators with little choice in the offering. The parties that disagree might be 'forced' into an unthought-out consensus on compassionate grounds. Gandhi was of the firm belief that 'the eyes of their understanding are opened *not by argument* but by the suffering of the satyagrahi'. To draw a parallel, we could argue that the Dalit movement in its identitarian avatar too replicates a similar process of narrowing the scope for inter-subjective communication that was integral to imagining strategies of deconstruction to destabilize caste hierarchies and make available the category of Dalit to new forms of radical interpretation and appropriation. There is a need to underline the replication in replacing deliberative processes—arguments—by self-enclosed experiential claims.

Thus, in switching to experiential categories the Dalit movement seems to produce a counter-narrative to that already dominating the public sphere through the language and centrality that Gandhi gave to 'moral experience', in as much as sharing the contours of the experiential discourse that was found to be more legitimate and foundational to public sphere in comparison to legal, institutional and cognitive practices.

However, the identity politics of Dalits in being too strongly bound within the experiential confines of demands for recognition willy-nilly seem to entrench the social practices they in fact had wished to transcend, in the previous phase. There was, perhaps, a pressing need to recognize that social groups and the processes that they were caught in were not 'regionally enclosed' but part of, as E. P. Thompson put it, an 'integrated material life'. It is therefore 'important to see that, while members of groups that have experienced historical exclusion, contempt, or obloquy may indeed need new social practices in order to flourish. What they are seeking is not always *recognition*' (Appiah 2006: 20). Given identity or experience, many a times, could merely be a vantage point to make sense of social life, engage with given political processes, rather than offer an unproblematic resource for oppositional politics. Whether it was the Gandhian construct of Hindu public sphere or contemporary Dalit identity politics operating within the limits of civil society in articulating its politics through the exclusive language of pluralism as assertion of cultural identities, both ended up setting a minimalist agenda of transformation that could be excruciatingly self-defeating. Thus,

> it's equally important not to pursue a politics of recognition too far. If recognition entails taking notice of one's identity in social life, then the development of strong norms of identification can become not liberating but oppressive...there is no clear line between recognition and a new kind of oppression. (Ibid.: 20–21)

This oppression could be felt strongly more than anywhere else internally in terms of closing off a critical dialogue between various constituents of a social group. Maintaining *internal silence* well became a precondition for laying a claim to authenticity. Such entrapments could eventually incapacitate Dalit politics from raising a series of questions that are central to the kind of transformative politics that were initially envisaged by the Dalit movement with its caste–class approach. These could include processes where

> with the spread of education...by virtue of their detachment from their setting and production relations [supervisory jobs on behalf of the owner or administrative/quasi-administrative jobs on behalf of the State] (they) do represent a transition in class. There has even emerged a section of Dalit

bourgeois, relatively small though, in the form of contractors, small-scale industrialists, petrol pump owners, transporters and of late certain service vendors.... They mark the emergence of a new age prototype of Dalit petty bourgeois that reflects a weird combination of belief in neoliberal ideology, faith in identity politics and communitarian convictions. (Teltumbde 2007: 293–94)[20]

Along with this insularity there emerged an ironical convergence with the very politics of the dominant Hindu public sphere, which operationalized the ideals of morality bereft of materiality, and plurality and identity 'separated' from the problems of social and economic inequalities. It is in course of negotiating, and negating such an entrapment within Dalit politics and out of adverse implication of 'politics of authenticity' for more vulnerable of the sub-castes that new modes of framing or reintegrating social, economic, political and cultural issues emerged in the new movement by the various sub-castes within Dalits, yet again attempting to displace the existent discourses (of power) entrenched within civil society.[21]

Vempentta: Civil Society versus 'Dalit Society'

It took another major massacre against the Dalits for the earlier aborted debates to revive. However, the context this time around was much more complex, very similar to the one the HRM faced, symptomatic of multiple levels of contradictions represented by growing conflicts *within* and *between* various political movements. The Dalit movement, by the mid-1990s had to negotiate not only with other political movements, including the ML parties and the growing women's movement in the state raising issues specific to Dalit women, but also the 'internal' demand for autonomy and justice from the sub-caste groups. The sub-caste movement foregrounded the historical fact that Dalits were never a homogenous group, either culturally or economically and were always:

> internally differentiated in terms of occupations, numerical strength, geographical spread and ritual status...There is a clearly recognized hierarchy among them, with each group exhibiting specific styles of life...In spite of the diversity that exists within them, they have been ascribed a common identity by the Constitution. (Ramaswamy 1986: 399)

The sub-caste movement in order to negotiate with this reality, raised issues similar to the demands made previously by the ML movement and its caste-based organizations such as the KNPS around a caste–class framework after the Chundur massacre—the question of 'classes within caste groups'. It was in 1995 that the contemporary version of the sub-caste movement represented and led by the Madiga Reservation Porata Samithi (MRPS) came into existence.[22] Both the important leaders of this movement, Krishna Madiga and Krupakar Madiga, had previous association with the organizations of the Naxalite parties. The MRPS revisited the caste–class framework, beyond the identity model, in raising the issue of 'classes within caste groups' that got consolidated due to the disproportionate appropriation of reservations by the Mala community and demanded that 15 per cent quota allotted to the SCs in the state be subdivided and fixed quotas allotted to properly identified sub-groups of the 59 Dalit communities (Balagopal 2000: 1076). The MRPS, very much like the PWG-backed KNPS, also opened up the debate on those 90 per cent of the Madigas who resided in villages and needed land and not just reservation as part of public policy guided by the principle of protective discrimination. The MRPS also debated on whether privatization of economy would benefit or rob the Dalit communities of whatever opportunities they had and the need to align with other movements struggling against processes that expand and entrench private capital. Similarly, various organizations pressed upon the MRPS to demand 50 per cent reservations for women to be implemented within the sub-division of SC reservations into A, B, C and D groups.

MRPS was responding to the unfair consolidation of benefits and opportunities that emerged as institutionalized trends and patterns in education, employment and land holdings, among other social, economic and political arenas. It could be observed that 'educational institutions have been availed of between Malas and Madigas broadly in the ratio of 64:36' (Sankaran 1998: 210).[23] By the 1980s the percentage of literates among Malas had gone up to 12.9 per cent in comparison with 6.2 per cent among the Madigas. Similarly, within the 39 reserved seats in the state Assembly out of the total 294 Assembly seats, Malas had a representation to the tune of 70.50 per cent, while in comparison the Madigas had a representation of only 29.50 per cent. As for the public sector undertakings again the Malas had availed employment opportunities to the tune of 75.90 per cent, while the Madigas had a meagre 24.10 per cent of the available jobs. These figures assume an even more serious proportion when we compare this uneven division of opportunities in relation to the proportion of their population where Madigas constituted 46.94 per cent and Malas 40.99 per cent of the SC population (Muthaiah 2004: 191). Part of this consolidation of benefits accrued from the fact that while majority of the Malas resided in the more prosperous region of coastal Andhra Pradesh, Madigas hailed predominantly from the more backward regions of Telangana and Rayalseema. However, this does not negate the unequal distribution of resources and opportunities between the two sub-castes as 'even within a given region, there is not only social inequality among the Dalit castes but also inequality in the relative proportion of members of each community availing themselves of reservations' (Balagopal 2000: 1078).

Responding to the demands of MRPS the state government of Andhra Pradesh appointed a one man commission of enquiry with Justice Ramchandra Raju (retired) and he submitted his report in May 1997 supporting the need for sub-categorization (Sankaran 1998: 208). On 6 June 1997, the government issued a GO sub-dividing the SCs into four categories, with Group A consisting of about 12 castes such as Relli and others, Group B consisting of Madigas and others, Group C consisting of Malas and related castes, and finally, Group D consisting of Adi-Andhras who had benefited the most from the policy of reservations since it was promulgated (Balagopal 2000: 1078). By then, to counter the mobilization by the Madigas, the Malas started their own organization and named it the Mala Mahanadu, which approached the High Court, which on certain technical grounds held the GO *ultra vires* on 18 September 1997. The Malas continued to counter-mobilize with acrimonious arguments bordering on those offered by the so-called upper castes against 'protective discriminatory' measures in favour of Dalits. The Malas offered various ostensible reasons for the backwardness of the Madigas including their differential regional location, the fact that Madigas had caste-based occupations while the Malas had none and therefore got themselves educated and availed themselves of government jobs, and finally they made superficial appeals for joint struggle to enhance the percentage of reservations in proportion with the increase in the population of the SCs in Andhra Pradesh. None of these arguments demonstrated any willingness among the Malas to either accommodate the interests of the Madigas or rethink more substantially about the possibility of pursuing Dalit politics around issues that affected both the sub-castes. It was this compounded complexity that got exemplified in the Vempentta incident involving violence between the sub-castes that pushed the Dalit movement to revisit some of its formulations in the earlier dialectical mode, as against its more recent turn to identity politics.

In Vempentta, a village in the Kurnool district of Rayalseema region in Andhra Pradesh, factionalism was the dominant culture. The entire economic, political, and social life of the village was under the control of the factions led by the landlords who had direct links (either as MLAs or through control over the representatives) with either the Telugu Desam

Party (TDP) or the Congress. Around 1980, the CPI (ML) Peoples War Group entered this village to build a struggle for land and increase in wages. Around 1996, under the party's leadership, the landless labourers occupied temple lands. This land was redistributed among 80 Madiga, 56 Mala and 129 backward caste and lower class (which included some so-called upper caste) families. Each family got half an acre land (Virasam 1998: 19–11). As there were more landless families among the Madiga community more land was distributed to them. These struggles and access to land definitely gave a sense of confidence and dignity to the Madiga families in the village. They were also now more openly part of the 'mass organization' of the Peoples War Group. This obviously earned the wrath of the so-called upper caste Reddy landlord family, which dominated the village, along with the ex-*sarpanch* who belonged to the BC community. As a counter strategy to the PWG, both the landlord and the ex-*sarpanch* mobilized the OBCs and the Malas of the village under the pretext that injustice was done to them in the distribution of the land. They went to the extent of organizing a social boycott of the Madiga families in the village, in a context where the state was already under the grip of a strong sub-caste (Madiga) movement lead by the MRPS.

Madiga families were forced to organize their own market to sell their harvest and their own panchayats. This further sharpened the conflict between the landlord, the Malas and the OBCs on the one hand and PWG and Madigas on the other. Along with this as part of organizational rivalry in the village, Pratighatana another ML organization ironically joined hands with the landlords to weaken the hold of PWG, which by then was popular among the landless labourers (predominantly Madigas) of the village. As part of this rising conflict, the PWG killed the ex-*sarpanch*, who as aforementioned was a BC. As a reaction to this, the already polarized village across caste–class lines flared up in a brutal massacre of men and women of the Madiga community, by the landlords with the active support of the Malas and OBCs on 16 July 1998. They lit a pyre and threw nine Madiga men into it after brutally killing them (after chopping off their hands and in some cases their heads).

This is the bare outline of the incident in Vempentta, which raised a number of questions, some new and some that were raised in the earlier phase of the Dalit movement: what was the nature of the contradiction in the village between caste and class? Could this be addressed within the limits of civil society signified by the identity politics that Dalit movement was currently pursuing? What then was the relation between conflicts between sub-castes and Dalit politics on the one hand and ML politics on the other? What is the role of the armed-militant strategy by the ML groups? These questions while divided the perspectives of Dalit, ML and human rights activists and organizations, also provided the new context for rearticulating the Dalit politics.

The new context articulated itself when all these organizations *spontaneously* formed a United Front to protest against the incident (i.e., primarily against the landlords and the connivance of the state). This United Front included to a name few, Dalit Bahujan Maha Sabaha, the BC Welfare Association, PUCL, APCLC, PDSU, POW-Stree Vimukti, AIPRF and VIRASAM, among others. On 2 August 1998, they organized a joint state level convention on the incident. This convention was meant, for the first time in the history of the political movements in Andhra Pradesh to discuss the differences and the possibility of *consensus* between these organizations. This step towards forming a united front was possible immediately after the incident in spite of the differences between these 'mass organizations', as all of them could perceive, in a dialectical mode that the emerging commonality of concerns and the evident overlap of issues coexisted with conflicts and power dynamics between them necessitating dialogic processes, replacing separatism and ghettoization. While issues of redistribution were now part of the sub-caste movement 'internal' to the Dalit movement, ML groups were becoming increasingly answerable and open to debate and discussion on caste-based violence that had aspirations for recognition and dignity encapsulated within their demands for mobility; yet again, demonstrating the point that political movements seem to react differently at the time of specific events that emerge as a crisis. The 'politics of events' that highlight the nature of debate that was part of the political process preceding those events, somehow also block the dialogue from fructifying into more sustained practices that become integral to the political repertoire of the different political movements. In this case, however, as we will discuss, the capacity of the 'politics of events' to short-circuit the process was minimized by the way MRPS carried on the dialogue much after such events.

Caste organizations such as the Dalit Bahujan Mahasabha have argued that one of the important dimensions of the incident was the 'caste blind politics' of the PWG. They could not foresee the possibility of mobilization on caste lines by the landlords. Not only could the landlords mobilize the Reddy families but also other OBC and Mala communities. Caste differences made collective mobilisation and hatred easy. Some Dalit writers have argued that Vempentta was always a 'Communist village' but there were never such incidents in the past. The reason being that the leadership of the Communist organizations was with the 'Reddy Communists' and therefore enjoyed the close patronage of the Reddy landlords. The Communist groups and the landlords entered into a conflicting situation because the leadership shifted into the hands of the

Dalits. It is interesting to observe that the leaders of the local squads of the PWG in Vempentta belonged to the Madiga community and which could very well be a reason why they had more following among the Madigas (DBMS 1998: 136).

Some of the Dalit writers also recognized that there was a caste contradiction between the SCs and the OBCs. It was because of this complex and graded situation that Ambedkar believed that violent and militant methods had a very limited role in socio-cultural transformation. They also argued neither squad action nor individual annihilation could be a solution for any of the problems as they reflect an apolitical-militarist approach, which by itself cannot handle caste contradictions. As a method of resolving sub-caste conflicts Dalit organizations suggested distribution of land and wealth in accordance with the 'population percentage of different castes' and the need for the Dalit-Bahujan groups to take control of the 'State power' (Ibid.: 70). However, as ML movements were struggling to negotiate with their earlier 'caste blind' politics, the Dalit movement, with its identitarian turn, had also failed to evolve a clear perspective and therefore remained largely a 'sub-caste' blind movement.

The PWG in its reply to the accusations of leading a 'caste blind struggle', argued that there were not only Madiga men and women among those killed but also four men belonging to the BC community, and it was also a fact that majority who took part in the massacre were men from the OBC community who were also the followers of the ex-*sarpanch*, other than a few Mala men who were traditionally with the landlord's faction. Similarly, they argued, land cannot be distributed on the basis of caste but on the basis of landlessness. For instance, there were powerful landed factional leaders from the BC community, how do we characterize these Bahujans? Replying to a phrase used by one of the Dalit writers, they wrote, it is 'Manu's justice' that was implemented in the Vempentta massacre, not by the so called upper castes, but by the ex-*sarpanch*, who was himself a BC. ML organizations argued, as the MRPS leading the sub-caste struggle later did, that only by recognizing the 'classes within these caste groups', was it possible to achieve unity among the Dalit-Bahujans (Guruvayya 1999: 40).

It was this renewed realization that 'politics of recognition' needed to be pursued not in the mould of mere identity politics that got ghettoized and insulated around the idea of authentic lived experience, but by forging new political identities and subjectivities that were prepared to negotiate with the 'recognition-redistribution dilemma' that would take Dalit movement beyond the contours of a dominant and a disciplining discourse of pluralism as 'mere' celebration of cultural identities in civil society. In other words, recognition does not have to be framed in a manner where it necessarily displaces issues of redistribution or it reifies group identities encouraging 'separatism, intolerance and chauvinism, patriarchalism and authoritarianism' (Fraser 2000: 108). The identity model treats misrecognition as 'a free-standing cultural harm' without its 'social-structural underpinnings' and thereby undermining its entwinement with and replication as 'institutionalized significations and norms' (Ibid.: 110). The problem of misrecognition, therefore, has to be approached, as Nancy Fraser suggests, as social subordination, signifying a shift from the identity model to a 'status model'. As Fraser puts it,

> from this perspective, misrecognition is neither a psychic deformation nor a free-standing cultural harm but an institutionalized relation of social subordination. To be misrecognised, accordingly, is not simply to be thought ill of, looked down upon or devalued in others' attitudes, beliefs or representations. It is rather to be denied the status of a full partner in social interaction, as a consequence of institutionalized patterns of cultural value that construes one as comparatively unworthy of respect or esteem. (Fraser 2000: 113–14)

The sub-caste movement signified this shift towards a 'status model' raising issues of 'institutionalized patterns' of discrimination in education, employment, land holdings and political representation, among others, and also connecting them with aspirations of recognition on the basis of claiming self-respect and dignity. The MRPS, therefore, did not make the struggle for recognition mutually exclusive with the struggles for distribution. Along with questioning the 'institutionalized patterns' of discrimination they also made independent claims to cultural recognition in a way that only further complemented the redistributive struggles. They took up a series of cultural issues to transform the social patterns of 'symbolic injustices' perpetrated through cultural domination, non-recognition and disrespect. To begin with, they put efforts to convert the signification attached to the term Madiga from being one of abuse and 'filth' to that of re-representing it by arguing that it is derived from the combination of *maha* (very) + *adi* (from the beginning) + *ga* (moving)—meaning the original inhabitants of India. The MRPS reclaimed self-respect by popularizing Madigas as the 'aborigine kings of India' (Muthaiah 2004: 186). The MRPS claimed a separate identity as well a separate status for themselves on the basis of historical legends and mythology.

The history of the Madigas could be ascertained from various social groups that are now known by different names, due to various historical reasons.

> Arundatiyar, for example, are Madigas who claim that Arundhati, the wife of sage Vasista, was of their caste. Jambavulu are also Madiga who trace their origin

to the ancient sage Jambhava. Again, Matangis whose ancestors have claimed to have ruled the Kannada country are also Madiga. (Uma 1986: 399)[24]

Similarly, reworking the symbols and 'tradition', which are an important component of any culture, the MRPS made their traditional musical instrument the drum the symbol of their movement, which was in fact called the 'dandora' referring to the practice of drumbeating. The MRPS argued that traditionally the drumbeating was carried out in service of the village *jajmani* system, but it would now symbolize the 'cry for justice'.[25] The sub-caste movement by the Madigas, similarly, resurrected their own caste deity, and publicly worshipped *Mathamma*, a form of *Adisakti*, as a symbol of energy and capacity to 'speak truth to the power' that the Dandora movement stood for. They claimed their historical legacy during the anti-colonial and anti-caste struggles by revoking the memory of Babu Jagjivan Ram, as against an exclusive emphasis on the role and ideas of Dr Ambedkar. However, the MRPS was careful not to denounce or decry the ideas and formulations by Ambedkar but in fact referred to them, and stress the parallels with the ideas of Dalit leaders from other sub-caste (i.e. other than the Mahar community). They specially referred to Ambedkar's notions of drawing a strong link between equality and fraternity or unity, to drive home the point that Madigas were demanding sub-categorisation to ultimately achieve the unity between the various Dalit sub-castes in order to realize the dream of Ambedkar to eventually annihilate caste.

The most impressive of all the symbolic acts that the MRPS invented was to:

> suffix the caste tag to their names...As "Madiga" has served as term of abuse, whether directed against a Madiga or otherwise, it was most discomfiting to be confronted by someone who wanted you to address him as "Krishna Madiga"... it must be said that this deliberately chosen tactic of the Madiga movement did as much as anything has ever done to puncture upper caste arrogance. (Balagopal 2000: 1077)

They have reworked each of the symbols diligently, whether it be suffixing name tags, upholding traditional musical instruments, revoking the memory of their own deity or past leadership without necessarily to simply valorize their culture or imagine a self-enclosed (moral) identity but in order to claim dignity and 'parity in participation'. For instance, while taking pride in their traditional skill of shoe-making or drum-beating the Madigas made demands to 'move out of the confines of inherited modes of low-paying toil based largely on traditional technology and commanding, within Hindu society, little social regard or opportunity of wider knowledge or social advancement' (Ibid.: 1078). The sub-caste movement was resisting the specific degradation and stagnation they were facing while culturally upholding and respecting all manual toil that they were involved with and also duly recognizing the knowledge-based skill it involves. In other words, they foregrounded the point that claiming an identity or *difference* need not be at odds with either culturally reworking new values for the society, like in this case upholding the dignity of manual labour in a society dominated by the Brahminical heirarchization between mental and manual labour, or in socially grounding these identities to make redistributive claims to be 'materially' uplifted.[26]

There are no essentialist assumptions that could be made of the role of the politics for recognition, and what the claims to *difference* entails need to be historically ascertained rather than predetermined once and for all. While on occasion, undoubtedly claims to recognition as identity politics can displace redistributive claims and reify group identity, as they did after the Chundur massacre and in the process they arrested dialogue and pushed forth exclusive claims to authenticity, on other instances they could be framed in a manner more complementary with other social, economic and political demands. Iris Marion Young, in her critique of Nancy Fraser's formulations, makes a similar emphasis on the possibility of complementarity between struggles claiming dignity and specificity of cultural identity, and those for economic equality. Nancy Fraser, in her earlier formulation, argued that all struggles for recognition as demanding 'group specificity' contradicted the transformative goal of redistribution, in the process producing what she termed as the 'recognition-redistribution dilemma'. Fraser, in the context of movements by the African Americans, argued that 'whereas the logic of redistribution is to put 'race' out of business as such, the logic of recognition is to valorize group specificity... How can anti-racists fight simultaneously to abolish 'race' and to valorize racialized group specificity? (Fraser 2008: 27). Disagreeing with such compulsive dichotomization, Young argued that:

> it may be true that some activities and writings of culturally affirming movements of people of color treat cultural empowerment and recognition as itself the substance of liberation. More often, however, those affirming cultural pride and identity for people of color understand such recognition as a means of economic justice and social equality. (Young 1997: 103)[27]

The distinction, in the context of caste struggles, can be best understood through the difference between Dalit politics as pursued after the Chundur massacre privileging an exclusive 'lived experience' that converts all 'others' as outsiders, and also puts on the back burner all demands related to land reforms, and minimum wages, among others. While the approach of the Dalit politics after the Karamchedu massacre, in its dialectical mode, was attempting to simultaneously create a cultural space by laying claim to specific cultural identity and connecting this to demands for economic redistribution and to attempts to forge unity with other political movements, such as the Naxalite struggle, that had a similar agenda of achieving economic equality. The sub-caste movement had, especially after the Vempentta massacre, even more strongly exemplified a variegated approach demanding cultural specificity, and connecting it to both deconstructive cultural politics as well as transformative economic redistribution, in order to achieve 'parity in participation'. This approach of the sub-caste movement resonates with the transformed position of Nancy Fraser who on realizing the need for different recognition strategies, later argued that:

> in some cases (misrecognised groups) may need to be unburdened of excessive ascribed or constructed distinctiveness. In other cases, they may need to have hitherto underacknowledged distinctiveness taken into account. In still other cases, they may need to shift the focus onto dominant or advantaged groups, outing the latter's distinctiveness, which has been falsely parading as universality. Alternatively, they may need to deconstruct the very terms in which the attributed differences are currently elaborated. Finally, they may need all of the above, or several of the above…and in combination with redistribution.[28] (Fraser 2000: 115–16)

Such an approach of combining differentiated claims of recognition with redistribution, not only opened renewed space to argue for all other sub-castes, including those that were 'below' the Madigas culturally and economically but also to wage 'battles' against the opposition to sub-categorization put up by the relatively more economically developed Malas, while keeping in view the historical fact that the Malas too have culturally suffered untouchability, and therefore they are potential partners in struggles against the socially subordinating caste system. In other words, the MRPS was conscious of both the need for unity with the Malas on cultural grounds and also to resist the new formation of 'classes within the caste groups'.[29] Both the attempt to recombine recognition with redistribution and resistance with unity took the sub-caste movement beyond both the limited celebration of exclusive identity politics as well as narrow self-interest based struggles and politicization, as institutionalized in civil society. While resisting the denial of what was rightfully due to the Madigas by the relatively more privileged and organized Malas, the sub-caste movement was also searching for avenues to forge joint struggles against the caste system as such. It was with this purpose that it reminded the Malas that the 'battle' for reservations was finally restricted to government educational institutions and government jobs which were in any case shrinking and fast turned into contractual jobs with low pay and little security. While the reality that the majority of scheduled castes lived in the rural areas and only 14 per cent lived in the 'urban agglomerations' is common to both the castes, and almost all Madigas and Malas living in the rural areas worked as landless agricultural labourers.

Intellectuals writing on behalf of the sub-caste movement also foregrounded the point that while each of the sub-caste community was distinct they were also inextricably united by the common characteristic of suffering untouchability. The rather tragic and poignant alliteration in history stands testimony to this:

> If in the Karamchedu incident, the Madigas were the victims, malas were the victims in Chundur incident. It makes no difference to the attackers and aggressors whether the untouchable community is mala or madiga. It is indeed to the lasting credit of the scheduled caste community that they stood united in all these cases of atrocities. (Sankaran 1998: 210)

And it is the weakening of this understanding of commonality that made the Vempentta massacre a possibility. The MRPS, with its emphasis on unity as much as resistance, took up common causes between both the dominant sub-castes; for instance they led the protests against the attempt by the government of Andhra Pradesh to assassinate popular ballad singer Gaddar (a Mala) in 1997. The MRPS believed that equality between the sub-castes was necessary for unity and fraternity that Dr Ambedkar insisted all through, and sub-categorization actually provides for the sub-castes to come together and inaugurate a 'golden period of unity' to address the larger common cause of struggle to dismantle and 'annihilate' the caste system (Muthaiah 2004: 207). The MRPS was thus simultaneously struggling to realize the ideals of Dalit poets and philosophers, such as Jashua, and also Bhoi Bheemanna who coined the term 'mamas' (Madigas + Malas) to integrate them on the basis of new subjectivity grounded in mutual respect (Chinnaiah 1998: 7).

The discourse of the MRPS while conscious of the need to combine resistance with unity with the more dominant Mala community was also equally aware of the need for justice and unity with castes that lay 'below' the Madigas. In this sense, the MRPS was willing to address and represent the issues of all other smaller sub-castes since the idea of justice through sub-categorization could be meaningfully raised only this way. Representing all other sub-castes invariably involved moving beyond the prism of narrow self-interest and progressively moving towards a realization that 'to condemn oppression is to condemn at least a little bit of oneself'. In other words, 'a caste oppressor is not an unbridgeable alien… for he is a part of everybody's identity' (Balagopal 2000: 1076).

The MRPS, thus, raised issues not just against the dominant Malas but was extremely conscious of the need for justice to be extended to those that Madigas themselves discriminated, including sub-castes such as Dakkalis and Madiga Sindhus, among others. Keeping this in mind the MRPS fought to protect the rights of some of the more discriminated sub-castes such as the Rellis and 12 such other castes, which were placed in Group A of the sub-categorization giving them the utmost priority even though the struggle for categorization was being led by the Madigas. The MRPS, in fact extended its support to not just other scheduled castes but even the backward castes such as the Lambada, Koya, Yadava, Gouda and others, who inspired by the Dandora movement were struggling for more equitable redistribution of resources and a more dignified recognition of their cultural practices.

There was thus a conscious attempt to reframe struggles against caste, in moving progressively towards claiming cultural specificity along with a politics of deconstruction that destabilizes all fixed caste identities on the ladder like caste structure and sustain a 'field of multiple, de-binarized, fluid and ever-shifting differences'. In other words, transformative remedies through deconstruction would 'redress disrespect by transforming the underlying cultural-valuational structure. By destabilizing existing group identities and differentiations, these remedies would not only raise the self-esteem of members of currently disrespected groups. They would change *everyone's* sense of belonging, affiliation, and self' (Fraser 2005: 83). Dandora was a self-proclaimed movement for justice 'for all'. The principle of justice 'for all' emerging from the sub-caste movement, signifies politics of deconstruction signifying an 'all-affected principle' demanding justice 'for all those affected by a given social structure or institution' (Ibid.: 82). The MRPS and intellectuals writing on their behalf in fact further argued that any form of *withdrawal*—like that witnessed after the Chundur massacre through the language of exclusivity—from such universal forms of justice would invariably result in the 'monopoly' of either the Brahmins or even the scheduled castes, or sections within them. Overlooking such universality, as distinguished from universalism, would entail a kind of 'Dalit fascism', very similar to what Kancha Illiah had referred to as 'spiritual fascism' of the savarnas (Muthaiah 2007: 30).

The MRPS, through renewed combinatory postures—of combining interests with universal concerns and politics of deconstruction—seem to have overcome the need, as the HRM, represented by the HRF, had argued in its contemporary moment, to dichotomize morality or ethics and politics or interests into two separate 'levels' or 'domains'. And also the need for these 'domains' to be represented by different movements, where while the HRM self-arrogated to itself the role of pushing ahead and sustaining new values or ethics and all other political movements were delimited to struggles for interests. The sub-caste movement radically combined the struggle for specific interests of various sub-castes with the universal and deconstructive 'all-affected principle'. In other words, it collapsed the distinction, made by the HRM, between fighting the oppression that 'hurt specific interests' and struggling against 'oppression as such', overcoming the problem of abstract moralism and replacing it by politicized ethics.

Similarly, the MRPS-led Dandora movement also seems to have addressed the problem of connecting radical politics to immediate experience. Dalit politics after the Chundur massacre had articulated identity politics based on the immediate 'lived experience' of Dalits themselves, without space or scope for groups and individuals from 'other' castes to either be part of or represent the Dalit struggles. Not just Dalit politics; in fact drawing continuity between radical and oppositional politics and the experience of specific constituencies has been a generic problem with critical politics (and theory) of all hues. Constructing new radical subjectivity, as Nancy Fraser (Fraser 1997a: 91) observes:

> has been the problem with socialism. Although cognitively compelling, it is experientially remote. The addition of deconstruction seems to exacerbate the problem. It could turn out to be too negative and reactive, i.e., too deconstructive, to inspire struggles on behalf of subordinated collectivities attached to their existing identities.

The MRPS not only has inspired a movement but it had succeeded in combining the demands of specific groups and identities with that of justice 'for all', simultaneously destabilizing the very given identities. Experience here works as a hinge connecting the immediate and specific interests with the ability to speak, represent and struggle on behalf of various other similarly placed 'specific' interests of other sub-castes, and backward castes.[30]

Finally, the MRPS had made an initial attempt in comprehending the issue of caste as not merely being 'bivalent', which is to combine cultural with economic discrimination, but being 'trivalent' to include the problems specific to political power or legal exclusion through state-constituted categories. Since legality is the baseline for civil society, and state-initiated legislation is the single most important mechanism to both govern as well as transform social relations, identifying marginalization specific to legal processes becomes an important mode of transgressing and going beyond the confinements of civil society. The problem of conceiving social issues such as caste only in terms of a 'bivalent' interaction between culture and economy is to neglect the specificity of state (political), where 'it becomes a kind of medium through which cultural and economic processes develop. The welfare state as a bureaucracy, the welfare state as a form of political power-classifying and indeed producing subjects, mixing therapeutic aid with punitive exercise of political power' (Feldman 2002: 417–18), and such other elements get neglected and sidelined. In other words, the MRPS perceived problems in conceptualizing state as 'neutral delivery service' and refocused its attention on how the state produces 'subjects, as bureaucratized, dependent and disciplined', through its processes of categorization and decision-making procedures. 'Ironically, the conceptually subordinate place of the state' in the 'bivalent' model, might itself 'be a reflection of the state's very centrality to the politics of redistribution and recognition'; Patchen Markell suggests that the 'grammar of recognition' might itself be depoliticizing—a handmaiden of classifying procedures of states, 'rendering their populations cognizable and manageable' (Ibid.: 418).[31]

The history of classification of the SCs in India goes back to the list of the 'depressed classes' or in some cases as 'exterior castes', as communities suffering from the stigma of untouchability were then referred to as, prepared by J. J. Hutton, as the Census Commissioner of India in 1931. This list was later adopted by the Government of India Act of 1935 for providing special protection to the 'depressed classes', which were listed in a schedule and therefore came to be referred to as the scheduled castes. 'The scheduled castes thus represent a constitutionally declared collection of castes, communities or groups, their defining characteristic being suffering from the traditional practice of untouchability' (Galanter 1984; Sankaran 1998: 209). After independence and the enactment of the Constitution in 1950, the President of India notified the list of scheduled castes in accordance with the provision of article 341, wherein the SCs 'have been specified separately in relation to each of the states and union territories' (Ibid.). Article 341 also categorically states that the list of scheduled castes can only be modified by the parliament. It was these two issues— the definition of scheduled castes and the provision for their modification only by the parliament—that became the contested grounds on which the full bench of the Andhra High Court pronounced the GO providing for sub-categorization as *ultra vires*. The High Court argued that sub-categorization by the Government of Andhra Pradesh implied an alteration of the list of scheduled castes, which can only be altered by the parliament and is not within the purview of the state governments. It further argued that since scheduled castes were identified as those castes which are 'absolutely' or 'most backward' among all castes identifying further backward castes would tantamount to keeping certain castes (i.e., those which are relatively developed) outside the list of scheduled castes. The court overlooked the historical origins of scheduled castes on the basis of the distinction between 'touchables' and untouchables or *savarnas* and *pachamas*, and had nothing as such to do with the degree of backwardness among the castes. It is a different matter that it is a reality that scheduled castes are the 'most backward' of all the castes. 'It is a rather strange procedure of interpretation that performs a semantic reversal and turns this descriptive or rhetorical expression into a definitive characteristic and argues that there is some scale of backwardness on which the castes can be placed...' (Balagopal 2000: 1079).

The Malas led their campaign against the sub-categorization using the judgment and the logic behind it and reiterating the point that 'all the specified and notified castes in the schedule are one single unit called Scheduled Castes'. They also argued that it was the obligation of Madigas as citizens to both respect the Courts and their legal pronouncements, and pushing for further mobilization for putting (what the Malas perceived as unjustified) pressure on the political and legal institutions amounted to encouraging chaos and anarchy in the state, which would in turn have adverse consequences for all other social groups and not just the Malas and Madigas. Such arguments that captured public imagination and the fact that the issue of sub-categorization was now *sub-judice* (and that too for a long time to come) made it difficult for the MRPS to organize further political mobilization, and the movement entered a long period of impasse.

This new situation confronted by the sub-caste movement raises a series of questions, including the issue of the relation between the dynamics of institutionalization and the dynamics of building political movements; how mutually exclusive are they or at least when do they actually become complementary? Similarly, this aspect of the emphasis on singularity within law as against heterogeneity and contradictoriness of social reality raises a number of conceptual issues with regard to political exclusion that follows taking recourse to legal methods. This then raises the point whether law, by definition, makes sense only in its singularity and by arresting the fluidity or complex heterogeneity of the social processes, or can it actually accommodate and assume a transient nature? Can law precede or work as an alternative or even a substitute to building a political or social consensus on a given issue? Does giving law a pre-ordinate position in the context of an ongoing political dialogue and mobilization aid the disadvantaged or does it in fact convert them from active participants who can more comprehensively transform given social order through alternative political means into passive subjects of law? Does law have an independent capacity of its own or is it actually only a concrete manifestation of state power? In this context then, does demanding more legislation empower or dis-empower the social groups involved in protest politics, and lead to the erosion or increase in state control?

All of these conceptual questions get more complicated when law is in the hands of a kind of political executive that wishes to consolidate power by 'managing' the 'populations' and insulating themselves from democratic accountability. As for the MRPS, it continued to, on the one hand, go back to political mobilization that it now found extremely difficult to build, and on the other, as Axel Honneth argued, to believe that they also need equal respect in legal relations, through the protective measures of the state, for self-respect, and therefore need to struggle for and around the demand for sub-categorization (Honneth 2001: 50).[32]

Dalit politics in India have substantially framed the emerging post-civil society discourse. They have reinstated their dialectical mode of functioning in order to circumvent the dispersed social power, and the disciplinary effects of the civil society made visible in its selective celebration of identity politics. Dalit politics has moved beyond framing recognition as identity politics or valorized culturalism with various discursive interventions and practices—including their recombining of a differentiated and multidimensional modes of pursuing recognition with redistribution; interlocking 'internal' resistance of sub-castes with an emphasis on the unity of Dalits on the basis of combining interests with universal concerns and politics of deconstruction, and also connecting radical and oppositional politics to immediate experience; finally, it has realized the need for a shift from a bivalent mode emphasizing culture and economy to a trivalent mode where the 'grammar of recognition' might in fact be a handmaiden of classifying procedures of states, which can convert active movements into mere passive state subjects.

Legality and the law-making processes remain foundational to the very construct of a civil society providing the 'social' arena as a 'manageable' site to the regulatory machinations of governmentality. Dalit politics, while increasingly growing aware of the inextricable inertia and intractability that such situations can push political movements into, continue to demand for legislations such as sub-categorization. Dalit politics could take a cue from feminist politics that has given much thought to this issue of moving 'beyond the law'. The women's movement in India has singularly contributed to the understanding of this issue of fragmentation of the social processes due to the interventions of the legal processes and the institutional design around it and the concomitant effect on limiting political mobilization and arresting the transformative process, rather than unproblematically complementing or supplementing its efforts. Feminists have therefore raised the issue as to whether it is worth focusing so much, as political movements have done in the past, to bring about legislative changes and even if they do where do such changes need to be placed within the dynamics of oppositional politics. It is thinking feminist politics, negotiating such transformative dilemmas, that is the focus of the discussion in the chapter to follow.

Notes

1. This is true of civil society not just in the southern continents but for the European and American civil societies as well, which are equally fraught with ethnic, religious and racial identities. 'Caste associations are very much like ethnic groups in America. The Polish, German, Irish and Latino clubs and associations in all major cities made up of members who have chosen to identify with them' (Rudoplh 2008: 278–79). Even the so called professional associations have the underlying pulls and pressures of ascriptive identities.

2. It is this quality of the movements to take on the features of a civil societal organization that begs for a more complex and contextualized analysis as to how exactly such struggles are negotiating with civil society as a space and what it means to move beyond it, rather than offer, as Partha Chatterjee does, another binary between civil society and political society as if they can be neatly mapped without being mutually imbricated. This will be the focus of our engagement in the fifth chapter of this book.

3. It is this ostensible 'separation' that also makes it a complex task to simultaneously accept and value 'formal democracy' and the accompanying liberal safeguards such as freedom of speech and rule of law and also internally rework them beyond the confinements imposed on them by liberalism, as we have argued in the second chapter of this book in connection with the emerging discourses of the HRM in its contemporary phase.

4. It is important to note here that the subjectivity produced through the legal category of being 'scheduled caste' is markedly different from that of Dalit. Dalit politics, as we will argue later, had to grapple with this split and re-signify and recombine the two, in order to overcome the possible passivity accompanying legal subjectivity, and the possible closure by forging self-enclosed subjects in claiming an exclusive culture and identity as Dalits.

5. The DMS, on one hand, was foregrounding the idea that Dalits alone should lead their struggles, and on the other, expanding the conventional meaning of Dalits—as scheduled castes—to include all those marginalized by the existent class and caste structures. This signified the nature of the unique dialectics between the universal and particular that was being articulated by the first phase of the Dalit movement.

6. This point of making use of the 'democratic space' in negotiating and working with the local Panchayat Raj institutions is very similar in its emphasis to the way CCC as part of the HRM argued and attempted to impress upon the Maoist movement.

7. One could perhaps argue that in form while the practice of maintaining and running journals was civil societal in nature the content and the mode of self-representation blurred the possibility of any such neat attribution.

8. It is interesting to note that within the parlance of the revolutionary parties, while the armed squads were equated with 'the party', which also had its own strategic, military and political wings, the organizations that were open, legal and registered were referred to as 'mass organisations'. Organizations with differing focus—Dalit, women, civil liberties—were all referred to as 'mass organizations'. It is important that both in terms of the undifferentiated etymological usage of the notion of 'mass', as well as the location of these organizations within the contours of 'civil' practices highlighted their overlap with the realm of civil society.

9. They raised similar points in their contribution to the official journal 'Red Star' under the title, 'Ambedkarism: Ideology for a New Ruling Class Alternative'.

10. Kancha Illiah's *Why I am Not a Hindu* (Illiah 1996) was one of the first attempts to explain the various everyday cultural practices of the Dalits that are distinct and at times completely at odds with the caste-Hindu practices. This semi-autobiographical existentialist mode of writing was attempted to confirm the point that the caste background and the accompanying experiential dimension of the scholar him/herself mattered in determining the nature of approach and content in analyzing issues related to caste.

11. As Joan Scott argues, 'experience is a linguistic event—the question then becomes how to analyze it', which presumes that experience is 'an epiphenomena originating entirely outside of the individual in the linguistic structures' (Joan Scott, op. cit.). It is another matter that Ernesto Laclau and Chantall Mouffe refuse to make any distinction between linguistic and extra-linguistic structures and are critical of Foucault for making such, what they believe to be untenable, distinctions (Laclau and Mouffe 1985; 1990). Also see 'Post-Marxism without Apologies' New Left Review 1990.

12. There are however, different approaches and standpoints on the relation between Gandhian politics and philosophy and civil society. While liberal scholars such as the Rudolphs argue that 'Gandhi was a talented and tireless creator of civil society' using ingenuous modes of mobilization, institutions such as Ashrams, which were the counterparts to the coffee-house in America, and symbols to create a dialogue with the illiterate masses and thereby give new forms to 'meanings associated with liberal and democratic spheres', post-colonial scholars such as Partha Chatterjee argue that Gandhi was a bitter critic of the liberal/western idea of civil society, and therefore presented new practices outside rationality, and new sites such as villages outside new urban centres. However, post-colonial scholars appropriate both Gandhian critique of civil society as well as the Dalit critique of civil society, without ever enquiring into why then, in spite of such commonality, are Dalits so critical of Gandhi (Rudolph and Rudolph 2006; Chatterjee 2006).

13. Rudolph and Rudolph (2006: 211).

14. Gandhi in *Young India* (Iyer 1972: 124). He also said, 'The satyagraha leader is useless when he acts against the prompting of his own conscience, surrounded as he must be by people holding all kind of views' (Ibid.: 299).

15. He therefore said, 'The human voice can never reach the distance that is conveyed by the still small voice of conscience. The only tyrant I accept in this world is the still small voice within' (Ibid.: 121).

16. Gandhi further argued,

> wherever a man's place is, whether the place which he has chosen or that in which he has been placed by a commander, then he ought to remain in the hour of danger, taking no account of death or anything else in comparison with disgrace. (Ibid.)

17. Phrase used by Madhu Kishwar (Kishwar 1985: 1699). I am thankful to Ramachandra Guha for suggesting and giving the reference to this article.

18. This is what Raghavan Iyer refers to as a possible way of understanding satyagraha (Iyer 1972: 287).

19. There are, however, accounts of Gandhian approach to building a public sphere being effectively dialogic in nature. See Bhattacharya (2005) and Rudolph (1967/2003).

20. Some other Dalit intellectuals have also observed that,

> those who masquerade as the champions of Dalit cause have been propagating with impunity their hideous perspective that serves nobody else but themselves.

It is merely cunning that they deploy to use Dalit cause for personal ends. In fact, there is a complete lack of social vigilance among the common Dalit masses whose practical reason is used by these self-appointed Dalit as well as non-Dalit 'messiahs'. (Guru 2005: 7–8)

21. The above arguments comparing the Gandhian philosophy and contemporary Dalit politics are borrowed from my previous publication (Gudavarthy 2008).
22. Though in the current phase the MRPS represented and restarted the struggle on behalf of the sub-castes, this issue was earlier raised and fought for by a number of organizations. As early as 1931, the Arundhatheeya Mahasabha was established as the first organization struggling for the upliftment of the Madigas, and later the Arundhatiya Bandhuseva Mandali was established in 1981 by the first generation Madiga employees (Muthaiah 2004: 188). Soon after that the Andhra Pradesh Madiga Sangham was started in 1982, followed by the Dakshina Bharatha Adijambhava/Arundathiya Samakhya in 1990 to be finally followed by the MRPS (Ibid.).
23. According to the 1991 census the total population of scheduled castes in Andhra Pradesh was 10,592,000, constituting 15.9 per cent of the population. While the population of SCs in India, again according to the 1991 census, was 138.2 million, representing approximately 16.48 per cent of the total population in India (Sankaran 1998: 209).
24. In fact, the claims to self-respect by the Madiga have not resulted in valorization but on the contrary the MRPS corrected and discouraged some of the popular legendary stories doing rounds, maligning the Mala. Earlier, for instance, the Madigas had began to believe that the 'Mala was born in the menstrual blood of Parvati, and so their name is derived from *maila* or polluting substance. But the Malas claim that they were born from Parvati's garland or "mala"' (Reddi 1951: 3). Further, in Andhra Pradesh, the Mala and Madiga are designated as the right-hand group and the left-hand group, based on an original myth that Sankyamuni and Yugamuni, the ancestors of the Holeya (Mala) and the Madiga, stood at the right and left side of the entrance, respectively (Ibid.: 4). The connotations of right and left took different meanings in later periods, one of them being that all the 'castes of the right hand section claim to be followers of Ramanuja, while the followers of the left-hand section claim to be Saivites' (Ibid.). The other meaning is that Madigas are referred to as the left-hand because of their traditional occupation, which was scavenging.
25. The president of the MRPS declared that their weapon was not a gun but a drum. He said they beat the drum so loudly that the ruling class will have to either heed their demands or the 'sound will tear their ear drums' (Muthaiah 2004: 187).
26. It is often seen in India that whenever the so-called upper castes have to protest against either declining job opportunities or even reservations to the disadvantaged groups, they protest either by offering free boot-polishing service or by sweeping the streets. What they intend to communicate is that performing some of these 'menial' services—because they are manual—are below the dignity of their caste status and lifestyles.
27. Though in her response Young seems to suggest that recognition being an end in itself actually displaces redistribution. It would, perhaps, be more apt to argue that the problem is not in fighting for recognition as an end but in framing it to explicitly displace redistribution, which can be done even when, for instance, using recognition as a means to not economic redistribution, but merely political power. In fact, not recognizing recognition as an end gives an impression that it is a second order demand of the political movements. Thus, recognition, as Amartya Sen argues with regard to democracy, is best conceptualized as both an end and also a means for democratizing social relations.

28. Fraser's transformed position emerged from both her debates with Young, cited above, as well as with Judith Butler (Butler 1997). These revisions appear in four of her writings (Fraser 1996; 1997a; 1997b and 2000).

29. In a sense, the MRPS was faced with a more complex reality than what Young recognizes when she argues that, 'so long as the cultural denigration of groups produces or reinforces structural economic oppressions, the two struggles are continuous' (Young 2008: 64). While in this case, the Malas were culturally as denigrated as the Madigas due to the practice of untouchability but were economically, relatively, more well off due to getting the overwhelming share of reservations. Further, the Malas themselves practised untouchability vis-à-vis the Madigas compounding the problem of conjoining economic struggles with those for recognition, and making the Malas partners in such a political movement.

30. Since the socialist agenda of class politics is experientially remote there have been various scholars who have suggested ways to overcome this hiatus. In that, the most significant of the arguments has been to understand class differences too as a form of misrecognition, wherein specific social groups, due to existing property relations, such as the workers, suffer from 'deficient recognition'. However, such an approach, as Fraser has pointed out, does not account for the political economy dimension including the workings of the market and technological innovations (Sayers 2005; Fraser and Honneth 2003).

31. Markell (2000).

32. Honneth, apart from achieving self-respect through equal legal relations, believes that self-confidence through love and care in intimate relations and self-esteem through trust in communities of shared values are indispensable to any idea of recognition.

4

Feminist Politics and Legal Subjectivity: Negotiating Transformative Dilemmas

T he politics of civil society along with, or in lieu of, associational life, also lays emphasis on legislation by the state. As Michael Edwards (2010: 60) argues:

> dealing explicitly with (these) inequalities is a precondition for societies that are civil, and this task must include government action to "level the playing field", legislate against discrimination, change the "rules of the game", protect labour and other standards, guarantee adequate social security and child care arrangements, and do all the other things that associational life, firms and families can't or won't do for themselves.

Civil society is founded on the premise that legislation by democratic governments, as Cicero once put it, makes citizens free to the degree that they are slaves to the law. Law emerges as a significant point of mediation when community bonds and traditional family ostensibly based on 'naturally' conditioned social relations such as gender, caste, ethnicity and kinship are replaced with (free and equal) legally constructed subjects. Marx in his celebrated essay 'On the Jewish Question' observes that the rise of democratic republics out of feudal social formations is inextricably tied up with the abolition of estate privileges engendering a civil society where pursuit of private interest is ordered by modern and secular law rather than birthright. It is this potential within modern law that feminists such as Mackinnon believe in exploring by compelling 'law to fulfil its universalist promise'. Thus, 'Mackinnon's legal theory and legislative proposals seek to emancipate women from these conditions by making the conditions themselves illegal, by politicizing them in the law' (Brown 1995: 130). Such formulations believe that feminists need to reform the masculinism in law and enable it to become an effective tool in overcoming the subordination of women. What women need to aspire for is a legal subjectivity to be gained through struggling for rights that grant individuals 'a sphere of bodily integrity and privacy and personhood' even if it were to assume in an abstract fashion the membership of an 'abstract community' (William 1991). In fact, equality by abstraction could well be what promises emancipation without objectification.

The women's movement as feminist politics in India, again studied in detail with reference to Andhra Pradesh but drawing examples from elsewhere, has had, since the public–private distinction was the overarching framework throughout, not distinct phases but three distinct *moments* in articulating its relation with law, for mediating their relation with not only civil society, but also state and market that were all considered the part of the same public. With the public–private distinction as the running thread, the women's movement has attempted to negotiate with structured power in civil society and other associated structures as part of the public. Within and due to this overarching distinction between the public and the private, the women's movement experienced distinct moments in negotiating with ensuing transformative dilemmas.

During the 1970s and 1980s, as the first moment in feminist articulation, the women's movement began negotiating with the dilemma regarding the place of law and state action in relation to gender issues—which it felt at best was ambivalent—and the visible gender-neutrality of the law and state a mode of dispensing indirect regulation on the freedom of women (Connell 1990; Mcintosh 1978). 'If the modern state is itself the "general patriarch"' (in Mies' evocative phrase), 'does it then make sense to expect such a state to legislate against gender discrimination?' (Connell 1990: 513). The period of the 1970s and 1980s witnessed women's movement taking multiple, contrasting and contested approaches pulling the movement in different directions; Upendra Baxi, who commented on similar ambiguities in the HRM, argued in this context that there were four sets of approaches within the women's movement.

> The 'nihilists'… suspect all law is a ruse to divert and deflect, and to depoliticize the nature and agenda of the struggle for women's emancipation. 'Evangelists' show, in deep contrast, an abiding commitment to the rule of law…The 'moderates' appreciate the potential role of law but believe that legal changes in themselves are not likely to usher significant social changes… The 'eclectics' will use it (law) without thinking much about the significance of the use of the law for social thought and action. (Gandhi 1992: 267–68)

He further added that 'legal order remains a big puzzle for those committed to struggle and action for the emancipation of women' (Ibid.). The 1980s were known as the 'golden era of legal reform'. Apart from expanding the scope of the women's movement to include issues such as right to employment, fair wages, price rise, education, health, nutrition and environment, among others, the period was also witness to a host of legal reforms including significant reforms such as that of the bill against rape and the Anti-Dowry Prohibition Act. In spite of the failure to effectively make them work for women or allow for free access to such legislations, feminists argued that 'the real value of the law reform campaigns were the campaigns themselves, because these helped to mobilize women and articulate political demands' (Mukhopadhyay 2007: 204). The 'puzzle' of law and state was for the women's movement characterized by being 'in and out of the state' (Ibid.: 206) or being simultaneously 'anti- and pro- state' (Phillips 2002: 82). It is their approach to law and state that determined and influenced their approach to civil society. Civil society was any way considered laden by power relations for women, since they were located or pushed to the private that was itself structured by residual power; it was the way they understood state and law that decided the nature of opportunities and purpose of action in civil society.

It was in the 1980s that the women's movement, in negotiating with 'multiple, contrasting and contested approaches' to law for mediating the relation between the public and the private, experienced its second distinct moment. Whenever movements have grappled with multiple strategies they seem to get caught in the *logic of circularity* that civil society operated through and reproduced structured power relations. However, as we have discussed in the previous chapters, it was only in working through multiple strategies that they could also make a new sense of their politics in order to overcome and circumvent power relations. The moments of dithering were also the moments of drawing new meaning and arriving at combinatory strategies necessary to confront entrenched power relations in civil society. In this case, the moments of dithering were marked by absence of street protest politics, in lieu of which emerged an emphasis on legal reform, unlike the palpable tension between political mobilization and struggling for legislation in the previous moment; alongside and inter-related with 'withdrawal' from street politics and emphasis on legal reform was the conversion to 'professionalization of feminism' and NGOization of women's movement, which included 'retreat' into (in the sense of getting restricted to) academic circles, new centres on women's studies in colleges and universities, professional and paid feminist activism, and local and foreign funded NGOs for women. In a sense, the women's movement assumed all the formal features of organizations that belonged to the civil society. However, what was, perhaps, distinct about the women's movement in this internalized moment was converting it into, in the context of Andhra Pradesh, an opportunity to raise issues of body, sexuality and such related issues that were not otherwise easy to raise in its more popular forms of protest in the public. In other words, the moment of formalization was also the moment of radical politicization. What was also distinct was that the processes of culturalization only lead to a more nuanced critique of the epistemic bias in moral language and moral foundations of the private. Unlike both the HRM and Dalit politics, feminist politics consistently foregrounded a critique of the language of morality, and could perceive the role of morality in persisting and perpetuating the public–private distinction, and therefore emphasized on a distinctly political discourse that got reflected in its slogan: 'personal is political'.

The third and the most contemporary moment in women's movement could be traced to the 1990s, marked by the neo-liberal reforms and the new hyper-role arrogated to and by the market. This moment, in the context of Andhra Pradesh, was marked by a return to street politics in the shape of the anti-liquor movement that was one of the largest and unprecedented collective struggles of the women's movement, drawing women from more than 800 villages. Along with state and civil society, women's movement had to reframe their strategies to include the new transformative dilemmas that emerged with the changing interface between state, civil society and market, though they were all located in the public. It had to now question itself as to whether some of its postulations to critique law and thereby the state and also civil society would strengthen, *ipso facto,* the social space and political legitimacy of the market, raising the question as to whether it is actually 'better to be dependent on the state rather than the market' (Dahlerup 1994: 118). However, instead of a possible bargain or 'trade-off' between the spheres, feminist politics arrived at the conclusion that there was hardly any choice left between state and market as modern forms of governance had blurred the two beyond their existence as 'separate spheres', while the domain of civil society constrained by legality was ineffective.

As the market requires a process of 'individualization of the subject', so do the developmental schemes of the state, such as the subsidies and loans, where the objects of the development are individuals as 'stake-holders'. 'The success of the schemes required the values of instrumentality and economic rationality, which compete with collective struggle' (Kamat 2002: 157). The increasing collapse between the modalities of law, state and the market through the reforms in governance entailed a new *convergence,* demanding new strategies that emphasize on countering the implications of the convergence on the part of the women's movement. In other words, new forms of governance made it possible to introduce legal reform in the context of economic reforms, where law instead of mitigating the ill-effects of neo-liberal reforms—growing social and structural inequalities—was in fact putting in place an ideology and modalities that augmented well for the market. Feminist politics, therefore, attempted a deeper epistemic understanding of the structure of law in and by itself, on the one hand, and the context in which state was entering a phase of hyper-legislation and the consequent ideological and social implications, on the other.

Feminist politics argued that it was not just about the character of the state that made its legislations suspect for the purposes of transformation but the law as such blocks multiplicity and 'flattens complexity'. It is in fact law because it has the propensity to fix and disallow backward–forward momentum of political processes; law was incapable as a political tool to look beyond conflicting relations legible to litigation and that necessarily required to be corrected through punitive action. With its intrinsic propensity towards fixity law reifies dominant positions and hegemonic understanding of those positions. Law 'recognizes' the multiplicity of religion, caste, sexual identity, marital status and class only in the moment of reification, and therefore 'difference' reinforces discrimination. It appropriates the strategies of political movements to reproduce them in their flattened institutionalized version that has 'aversion to diversity and multiplicity'. In fact, 'a law is not a law unless it holds for everyone' and it is 'natural' that law operates that way. Further, law 'stands above messy details' of everyday life and the invariable need for exceptions because it is this insularity of law that brings clarity to the particularities that look wayward.[1] Akeel Bilgrami notes that 'the idea of a law derives from something more basic than law itself, something like the idea of a principle, something of greater generality, greater abstraction…' (Bilgrami 2007: 324). The inward-looking structure of law necessarily undermines and is independent of 'what this or that group of citizens' response to the law will be (Ibid.: 320).

In other words, specific consequences of the law—specially those not intended by it—cannot be a part of the consideration in formulating the law itself often giving rise to a misplaced debate on the effectiveness-of-law as a policy against its ineffective implementation, as if there were no relation between the two. For instance, the various draconian laws in the past, such as TADA, POTA and AFSPA that have routinely suffered from misuse and gross violation of human rights have as much to do with the approach of police and armed forces, as they do with the nature of the provisions that make available gross degree of impunity to the forces that act 'under' these laws. Similar has been the experience with the Act against domestic violence that fails to take into account what women had been expecting in the context of violence in the family, and its manifold links with the changing nature of political economy. As feminists reflecting on the inadequacy of the Act wrote,

> it appears to us that when we set up the law/public institutions as the primary site of "action" for women, two processes get obscured. One, women's efforts to

regain "the effective ties of family/husband"; two, her actions outside the realm of law and institutions. (Suneetha 2006: 4358)

Thus, the history of feminist approach to legal subjectivity in civil society has been that of wading through the labyrinthine possibilities of using law to open spaces and guarding against these very openings turning on or into new closures.

Feminist politics has foregrounded the issue, not just of the limitation of this or that particular law and the rectifications that need to be carried out, but of the way legislation as such, both in its substantive as well as procedural aspects, proceeds and thereby constitutively limits what is possible to achieve within the contours of law. Since law is a foundational 'nodal point' of civil society, feminist politics highlight the need to articulate a politics that does not merely undermine law but necessitates the possibility of dialectically interlinking the critique of the singular focus that feminist politics at times was tempted into in bringing about legal reforms during the decades of the 1980s and also simultaneously argue that 'law and rights of citizenship...are (nevertheless) an option available to those who have been traditionally denied them under the conditions of long standing oppression' (Sunder Rajan 2003: 170). Post-civil society politics seek to overcome the *constitutive ambiguity* at the heart of civil society processes that allow for emancipatory discourses and practices such as 'progressive legislations' to reinforce, and yet hide, discriminatory effects, in the process, revealing the 'chameleon quality' of such instrumentalities. Thus, political movements needed to take necessary caution in adopting such instrumentalities by way of being constantly open to the new transformative dilemmas that took shape due to the kind of intersection and convergence they were prone to.

'Law as a Catalyst': Civilizing Law or Legitimizing Civil Society?

The centrality of law and legal subjectivity to the political processes in the evolution of civil society in India could be understood both in the context of the legacy of the colonial state and the overwhelming role of the developmental state in the post-independence period.[2] British colonial rule replaced the centrality of political legitimacy and popular consent with that of legality and rule of law. Western legal structures introduced by the British on the one hand consolidated the colonial rule and on the other legalized the social relations producing in the process legible and modern version of the categories of custom, religion and village.[3] Legality in effect became a mode of enlarging both (liberal) democracy and economy and their accompanying practices in the post-independence period. Institutionalization of practices by accommodating and also circumventing the processes of popular consent continues both in their external and internal versions in post-colonial countries such as India. Externally, 'exporting democracy' and its accompanying economic practices from the north to the south has heavily depended on transplanting legal structures, and therefore 'economic globalization is feeding the rule-of-law imperative by putting pressure on governments to offer the stability, transparency, and accountability that international investors demand' (Carothers 1998: 98). Similarly, internally with the growth of a global middle class that wields influence on the decision making processes of the state more on the basis of its 'cultural capital' rather than its capacity to impact the electoral results (Fernandes 2006), and with the transformation of the self-perception of the global middle class itself from representing the nation to becoming the nation (Deshpande 2000)[4], it has been possible to implement 'reforms by stealth' (Jenkins 1999) primarily and surreptitiously through bringing in changes in law, such as putting in place conformity laws, reinterpreting the rule of law as primarily honouring contractual relations, and maintaining 'law and order' in disconnect with democratic principles of equity and justice.

Such surreptitious change was possible not merely due to the colonial rule and its post-colonial legacy but the way law itself worked. 'In Weber's view, in order to understand political legitimacy under conditions of legal domination, it is not necessary to evaluate the content of the law. The existence of the law...provides its own ideological basis whatever its substantive content' (Hussain 2003: 71). Content of law, as such, was not relevant for legal domination, and for law itself to accrue a centrality in the political processes of a nation, but in fact, it works the other way round where the nation accrues its legitimate existence on the basis of enforcing a dominant and uniform legal structure. Law in terms of its structure is inward-looking and works in a self-referential manner generating its own code of technicality, as well as providing its own ideological justification without necessarily being open to negotiation or reflecting the substantive values of the society. In other words:

> Modern law provided the basis for the legitimacy of the modern state; without law, the state could only rule by force, making it no different than despotic regimes of the past. Thus, the idealized conception saw one uniform law, belonging to one nation, and administered uniformly by one state. (Verma 2006: 27) Legal domination and centralism was foundational to the way nations were imagined, where "law, nation and state came to justify each other." (Ibid.: 32)

During the colonial period, for both the social reformist as well as the nationalist movements, bringing about legal reforms was an important mode of instantiating the political idiom unto the popular imagination. It was both the imperatives of the colonial rule as well as the pressures from 'enlightened' individuals and groups that resulted in a series of legal enactments.[5] In fact, legal codification was accomplished in India much before the process was completed in England. 'India's major codes of law were completed in the 1860s. By 1882, the process of codification in India had essentially wound down, while codification only came to England between 1882 and 1893' (Hussain 2003: 40).

In Andhra Pradesh, the social reform movement was believed to be initiated by Kandukuri Veeresalingam in the late nineteenth century. He campaigned for the rehabilitation of widows, widow remarriage, women's education, against child marriage, superstition and the *devadasi* system.[6] Each of these issues in the course of time led to various changes in the legal system, resulting in a virtual collapse of the legal, political and the social domains. Alongside Veeresalingam there were various individuals and organizations campaigning for various issues concerning women. For instance, Raghupati Venkatratnam Naidu spearheaded campaigns against the practice of Sati, which played a pivotal role in bringing about the Act against Sati on 4 December 1829, making the burning and burying of all Hindu widows illegal and punishable.[7] Gurajada Apparao, a literary figure, through his writings highlighted the ill-effects of the practice of bride price or *kanyasulka,* which was also resulting in young girls getting married to men much older and in turn resulting in girls becoming widows at a young age.[8] A full bench consisting of Chief Justice Sir Arnold White and Justice Miller and Munroe ruled that a contract to make a payment to a father in consideration of giving his daughter in marriage was opposed to public policy with reference to Section 23 of the Indian Contract Act (Janaki 1999). Women's India Association was started with the efforts of Annie Beasant in 1917, with activities spawning many parts of south India with its headquarters in Madras. Many of its prominent members such as Margaret Cousins and Muthulakshmi Reddy were active in mobilizing campaigns of women's education and in abolition of child marriages. It again played a very important role in bringing about the Child Marriage Act and other laws relating to divorce and inheritance (Ibid.).

After the phase of social reforms, the next major period in which women's issues were addressed in Andhra Pradesh was during the Telangana armed struggle (1946–51), but this time without a specific focus on bringing in changes in law. The Telangana armed struggle paid attention to 'women's problems' such as wife beating, child care, hygiene and the right to breast-feed infants during work, and sexual violence; they also initiated action to get local authorities to construct lavatories for women, apart from the issues related to minimum wages. However, feminists in hindsight have been arguing that the frame in which these 'women's problems' were taken up was more in tune with reducing them to moral problems—what is the best or right to do, rather than attempting to understand them as structured power relations—to be dealt within the private realm through discussions, and contextual compromises arrived at as and when conflicts arose. 'Women's problems' were taken up without a focus either on bringing in legal changes or proposing a clear political programme to transform gender relations through public action. Feminists have also argued that the Communist party could not evolve a 'policy' on problems of childbirth, and unmarried women who joined the armed squads. The Communist party also considered single women and their sexuality a 'moral problem' that hampered the functioning and image of the party. Most issues, such as women comrades being forced to give away children after they were born, were settled as and when they arose and were 'diluted into a moral problem, with guilt at having violated family happiness. Once again there was no analysis on it as a political issue that had to be addressed if the movement was serious about women' (Stree Shakti Sanghatana 1989: 27). These moral terms according to which women were defined and judged were that of the private domain: 'the domain of the family, household, domestic labour and reproduction'.

The Telangana armed struggle was primarily against feudal order. Feudal oppression was structured around amassing of land and various discriminatory cultural practices relating to Dalits and women. Forty per cent of the area of the entire Hyderabad state came under the *jagirs* (i.e., hereditary property of those revenue officials who were loyal to the Asif Jahi Nizam), *samsthanams* (land under traditional Hindu rulers who paid annual tribute to the Nizam) and *sarf-e-khas* (land administered by Nizam and his family for their personal expenses). The remaining 60 per cent of the territory was directly under the administration of the state government and the *ryotwari* system operated here, wherein the middlemen played an important role in collecting huge land revenue. The middlemen amassed enormous stretches of land (for instance, the Pratap Reddy family possessed around 150,000 acres of land) and became landlords (Ibid.: 4). The complete centralization of ownership of land meant that the majority of the landless population was subjected to various de-humanizing practices; one of them being *vetti*, which meant free services, had to be rendered to the landlord by the people of various castes, such as the blacksmiths, carpenters and other castes rendering and dependent on manual labour. 'Most of the agricultural labourers on whom vetti obligations fell were from the lower and untouchable castes of Malas and Madigas' (Ibid.: 5); similarly, the tribals were exploited under the *bhagela* system. The bhagela serfs were customary retainers tied to their masters by debt. Unable to repay their debts, they continued to work as domestic or menial labourers, generation after generation. The conditions affecting women were 'doubly oppressive'. They were not only affected by the economic oppression of the landlord and the moneylender but also exploited physically and sexually. Rape was an everyday reality. Apart from all this the custom of *Adi bapa* or concubinage was prevalent. 'Adi bapa was a form of concubinage peculiar to Telangana where a young girl, usually from a bonded family, had to accompany the bride to her husband's house to tend to her mistress and to provide sexual services to the master' (Kannabiran and Lalitha 1989: 182). The nature of oppression of the so-called upper class/caste women was qualitatively different. Purdah, child marriage and early widowhood were some of the de-humanizing practices even among these upper-caste women but they did not feature prominently in the Telangana people's movement.

There was a shift in the political situation of the Hyderabad state with the assertion of cultural rights by the Telugu people with the establishment of Andhra Jana Sangham in 1921. 'Soon the Andhra Jana Sangham converted itself into the Andhra Maha Sabha (AMS) which was to be the focal point not only of the social and cultural but also of political activity' (Stree Shakti Sanghatana 1989: 8). The AMS was initially an assemblage of people with different views but gradually it came closer to Andhra Communist Party. Under the leadership of the Communists the AMS assumed the character of a 'mass organization'. By November 1946 the decision for armed resistance was taken and village defence squads were formed and struggle against the landlords of various districts intensified. This armed movement brought some radical changes in the otherwise rigid and oppressive feudal structure of the Telangana region. It is clear that the Communist party did take up women-oriented issues during the course of their struggle. However, the problem was the politics or lack of it behind these struggles. 'We do not find that there was an awareness of these gender-specific areas as valid sites of political struggle... mobilization around these issues drew their loyalty and support without leading to an increased awareness of the nature or source of that subordination' (Kannabiran and Lalitha 187). The party often found it very difficult to absorb women into its ranks risking its reputation and alienating public sympathy. There was often possibility of propaganda that if women enter in large numbers there would be no 'morality' left in the Communist party. Party leadership often took ambiguous stands on this, which led to the 'reinforcement of traditional ideologies'.

> So women had to fight against traditional beliefs and feudal outlook even to become a part of the political struggle. That supporting the women in these

personal struggles and politicizing the context of that struggle could have brought a new and progressive philosophy into existence was apparently a possibility which the party did not realize. (Stree Shakti Sanghatana 1989: 263)

Once women managed to enter the party and in some cases into the squads, they were often relegated to 'secondary' and 'supportive' roles. Though there was ideological recognition to transform traditional roles, 'everyday behaviour invariably relegated domestic chores to the women'. While few women carried guns they were generally helpful in cooking, taking messages and nursing wounded comrades.

In fact, P. Sunderayya's chapter on women in his *History of Telangana People's Struggle* refers to a letter from a young woman who joined the squad in 1950 and was an active cadre. She wrote, 'we women are still looked upon with the old outlook, that we are inferior. Any slip or mistake we commit our leaders come down very heavily on us… why have you not allowed any woman to participate in actual guerrilla raids on the enemy' (Ibid.: 24). Similarly, single women were considered a problem and those married with children were forced to leave them behind with families. The party considered these more as 'personal' problems of individual cadre rather than a political question that had important cultural dimensions. Single women were considered as a problem for the 'moral purity' of the party. There was an implicit but definite pressure to marry that operated on the women. Marriage was a way of defining in more clear terms the status of the women and also to avoid the problem of unwanted sexual relations. Further, single women and their sexuality were put through the disciplinary scanner of the party.

Women were warned under party discipline not to support other women under criticism. This delimited the focus of the party and often left it with no sophisticated analysis of the issues of culture and ideology. In other words, in turning away from issues of culture and consciousness and viewing organization purely as a matter of political organization—that struggling against 'larger' political structures—the old relationships of power and authority were not only reproduced but also reinforced. (Kannabiran and Lalitha 1989: 198)

There was definitely an attempt to settle these problems as and when they arouse but in an explicit moral, and not a political, idiom. Under severe state repression by the Indian army, the politburo of the party took the decision in 1951 to call off the movement after prolonged discussions.[9]

It was after almost 15 years that there was an opportunity to reassess the relation between women's issues and the left movement during the Srikakulam uprising of 1967–71. This movement was primarily based among the tribal people under the leadership of the Naxalites. It was a peasant revolt with people from both tribal areas and the plains. It was primarily against the landlord–state nexus and for access to forest produce and tribal lands. The movement in general did not generate women leadership in the guerrilla squads. Those women from the plains who did assume leadership positions were in fact often women who had relationship with the leadership of the party (either as their wives or as their daughters). However, the more significant aspect of this movement was that it formed separate women's organization, as part of the movement for the first time, in order to claim a more legitimate political status beyond the (moral) regulations within the private realm. Girijan Mahila Sangham was formed after the movement took a militant character. 'These Sanghams were instrumental in mobilizing women for meetings, processions, protest marches, public meetings and strikes' (Vindhya 1990: 37). However, it is important to comprehend that these Mahila Sangham's were 'loose associations which were structurally not always distinguishable from the main Girijan Sanghams' (Ibid.).

In the backdrop of the social reform movements pressing for legal changes followed by armed struggles of the Communists taking recourse to the moral language in resolving the 'women's question', it would be pertinent to understand what the specificity of the emergent relation between law and morality was. In a context where law, nation and state justified and reinforced each other in order to instantiate the 'concept of the political' and the public, those political expressions (such as the armed movements) pushed out of the public or the civil because of the violent means they adopted, and had no easy recourse to influence the law because of being located outside the dominant imagination of the nation, it seems expressed themselves through the language of (public) morality. Thus, the fault line was between law–nation–state–public–civil as against morality–violence–private–uncivil. The recourse to the language of morality by the armed movement, in such contexts, could be read as a modality of accessing the public, which would otherwise be approached and instantiated through that of law and 'high politics' within the limits of democratic institutions. As it is important to grasp the relation between law and morality, it could be equally significant, in the context of political movements perceived as uncivil and outside the public by the state and dominant civil society, due to their taking recourse to violent means of resistance, to comprehend the relation and mutual influence between externally imposed constructions of uncivility, and the recourse to the language of morality.[10]

Absolute closures by the dominant legal and political structures—state and civil society—and limits imposed on resistance against domination (agency) erupts in violence, taking recourse to violent means of protest in turn precludes the multiplicity of languages—legal, institutional, political—that the political struggles might have experimented with, in negotiating with the contesting political interests and structures. The congealing of space for political movements that come to be perceived as uncivil or outside the public often get expressed in taking recourse to both internal regulations[11]—reflected in increasing recourse to disciplinary methods and strict hierarchical organizational structures replacing political engagement—as well as opting for practices that look universal in nature—morality; political movements thereby attempt to intervene, influence and map their own set of ideas unto dominant structures and their practices that are already recognized as legitimate, through the moral idiom. Taking recourse to a moral–universal language, as opposed to political, serves this precise purpose of reserving a modality of intervening into the legitimate sphere of the public or the civil in forms that can speak to or influence the dominant structures. The interaction between law, morality and politics, in this context, has to be understood in the context of the interface between what come to be perceived as civil and uncivil political expressions.[12] The Communist party's mode of mobilization precisely reflected this conflict against the public or the civil sphere that congealed around state and its legal structures on the one hand, and a mosaic constituted by complex dynamics within and between the private/uncivil sphere, morality and violence, on the other.[13] However, the fact that the armed struggles, in their own self-perception and that of the civil sphere, were located outside the public or a civic space, where the women's movement and the 'women's question' was also relegated to, did not make the relation between the women's movement and the militant-Communist politics any easy, revealing the complexities and dilemmas involved in the divide between the public and the private. In other words, while the Communist movement and women's movement found themselves relegated to the uncivil/private sphere by the dominant processes of civil society, the equation between them was not one of consensus and bonhomie.

The decades between the 1970s and 1980s for feminist politics were marked by attempts to gain autonomy from the radical left movements and its regulatory moral language. While the armed movements were perceived (both by the dominant civil society and the state and to an extent by the movements themselves) outside the dominant public, but for feminist politics they were part of the 'same' public. In other words, the women's movement was of the opinion that gendered spaces were created as much by the political movements, as the State, civil society and market, against which the movements were waging justified battles. In this sense, they all belonged to the 'same' public. The line between the public and the private itself seems to constantly change unavailable to any neat categorization, 'sometimes we call everything which is not the state "private" including the market. Sometimes the term private is attached only to the family, everything else being public' (Dahlrerup 1994: 121). In other words, it was during this period that the feminist politics discovered that there was no social or even a political space available that was not contaminated by gendered power relations. It was the same approach that dictated their understanding of civil society,

> generally speaking, feminists have juxtaposed the private, domestic sphere to the public sphere of the state and/or the economy. In these instances, civil society is conflated with the state, the economy, or both, a move that generally leads to a neglect of various intermediary institutions. (Dean 1992: 380)

We need to here note the pertinent difference with other political movements, since at least momentarily and relatively the civil sphere was accessed by the civil rights movement during its 'civil liberties' phase and the Dalit movement in its repeated attempts to re-enter the portals of civil society.[14] However, the women's movement to the contrary, found itself at the receiving end of multiple exclusions.

It was with the public–private distinction as a beacon that feminist politics was straddling multiple and contradictory paths that could never be easily settled, or coalesced or contained into the contours of civil society and therefore feminists '...have also been acutely aware that strategies for change have to intervene in a number of levels. This is not necessarily (indeed rarely) discussed under the rubric of civil society' (Phillips 2002: 76). Therefore, as Anne Phillips observes, 'feminists have been less interested in where to draw the line between civil society and state', since in the final analysis 'a feminist looks around the world and sees much the same patterns repeating themselves in every sphere of existence whether this be family, market, civil society, or the institutions of the state' (Ibid.: 74). Thus, they were struggling within and with a liminality to 'civilize' the law without legalizing the civil society, and impact the civil society using 'law-as-a-catalyst', to avoid being pushed back to the private, without at the same time legitimizing the civil sphere itself.

> Feminist theorists have a distinct approach to locating and patrolling the civil society/government boundary. Freedom for association argues for independence from government intervention, but the need to enforce equal protection laws and the desirability of various forms of state support for groups argues for intervention. (Rosenblum 2002: 155)

The decade of the 1970s was marked by the formation of various separate women's groups seeking varying levels of autonomy from the overwhelming influence of the Marxist-Leninist groups and the armed struggle led by them. Not only were women's issues brought to the forefront but also the relation with the ML parties began, for the first time, to be more openly debated about and conceptualized in political and ideological terms. It is however interesting to note that in all these separate women's groups, it was either the sympathizers or former members of the ML groups who were in the leadership ranks. Along with the Telangana and Srikakulam armed movements, various CPI (ML) groups continued to inspire the youth in the urban areas, largely from the middle classes. This inspiration was coupled with the increasing conflict women of the urban middle classes entered into with their 'family values' at home. Women students began to take active part in the movements such as anti-price rise, along with CPI ML student groups such as the Progressive Democratic Students Union (PDSU). However, in course of their interaction with the leadership that was essentially constituted by men from radical-left organizations in such movements, they realized that it was necessary to have separate women's organizations not only to discuss and prioritize women's issues but also to mobilize and provide more opportunities for women themselves to take up leadership positions. This sparked off discussions with M-L student organizations whether it was necessary to have separate women's organizations. However, 'the principal response of male students was that it was anti-Marxist to have a separate women's organization, that women are not a class by themselves; that only an economic revolution would ultimately and automatically emancipate women...' (Lalitha 1998: 5).

It was difficult to break away from the radical Left parties because historically they were the only political formations, after the period of social reform, which provided women with the necessary space to mobilize, which was otherwise unavailable within the newly evolving public domain that was in consonance rather than in conflict with the vice like grip of the dominant value system against women. At the same time they felt the pressing need of a distinct perspective and politics that could foreground the issues specific to women, which could no longer be secondary or subordinate to the ML parties or constrained within the private-moral realm in which they were negotiated. This journey to autonomy was difficult since the alternative of working with or within the civil society was found to be extremely difficult as the civil or the public sphere itself harboured and reserved private values/realms for women to operate in since, as feminists argued, 'civil society so often conjured up a masculine realm' and more 'people exist in civil society already as women and men, and their positioning in sexual hierarchies will have a considerable effect on the kind of organizations they are most likely to join as well as their propensity to join any' (Phillips 2002: 76).

Women in political movements realized that they confronted categories and practices in the public domain, which suffered from an 'epistemic bias' against them and that they were offered a false choice of raising issues pertaining to them through these very categories. The public domain or the civil society was 'doubly oppressive', in excluding them due to an overwhelming patriarchal value system, and then offered them strategies that only further eclipsed their standpoint. For instance, civil society was founded on the centrality of law and its accompanying language of rights. However, feminists recognized that:

> the rights which structure juridical recognition are based on particular cognitive properties. These properties, which include rationality and autonomy, are masculine characteristics. When women have rights, then they are recognized only to the extent that they too are masculine, or conform to a masculine standard. (Dean 1992: 387)

Legality and its associated language of rights created a 'masculine realm' within the well recognized portals of civil society; this in turn relegated women's stand-point to the background—into the private—and proved insufficient in articulating their demands.

They had an ostensible choice to forge a selfhood or subjectivity with alternate categories such as good life, emotionality and obligation to which there was no recognition within the annals of public life in civil society, but that had the additional burden of the possibility of reinforcing a 'feminine' subjectivity against which they had began their struggle. For instance, feminists such as Nancy Hirschmann have argued that since women are bound to series of obligations, such as child care, to which consent is 'not only often unavailable but often of questionable relevance' it follows that 'a feminist ontology and epistemology would operate from the philosophical priority of obligation' (Hirscmann 1989: 1241). In other words, 'from a "feminist standpoint"', perhaps obligation needs to be taken as given and 'obligation is the standard against which other things, such as the freedom to act as one wishes, are measured...In this feminist conception, it is the assumption of obligation that demands an explanation of non-fulfillment' (Ibid.). However, Carole Pateman points out that rather than seeing this historical bondage and the experience of it as problematic, we begin to accept ideas such as obligation as a new feminist starting point for thinking about politics (Pateman 1992). She therefore argues, 'Feminists would be ill advised to give up the priority of freedom...[and replace it with obligation—my addition] and whether a political order in which all are cared for can be created if freedom for all is relinquished as a priority' (Ibid.: 182).[15]

There are interesting parallels here with the possibility of the women's movement articulating a politics exclusively around their own 'lived experience' as the Dalit movement did during the phase of identity politics after the Chundur massacre. Though sections of women's groups did articulate exclusive politics by and for women, based on their own 'lived experience', it never took the proportions that it did as in the case of the Dalit movement. This could, perhaps, be due to the insurmountable difficulty that women's movement faced with the public–private divide offering no easy choice. Since the Dalit movement had relative access in claiming the public sphere—based on ideas of community, numerical strength mustered for electoral politics that made it possible to capture political power—notwithstanding practices such as untouchability, they could articulate politics in the public sphere that exclusively belonged to and represented by the Dalits. In effect, the women's movement, in its relation with civil society, either had a choice of reifying their femininity or eclipsing into the masculine realms. It was this, rather difficult and chequered encounter with the public domain that was weighing heavy on them in deciding how to negotiate the terms of autonomy from the radical-left politics.

At a city convention held on 29 September 1974, an organization called the Progressive Organization of Women (POW) was formally established. The political and ideological relation with ML mass organizations was still very ambiguous; to the extent that it fought the power in the public it was an ally, but since it was also part of the same public—through its moral regulatory discourse—it was also responsible for replicating gendered languages and politics. It was felt at this stage, that separate women's organizations were necessary but the nature of autonomy was not clearly conceptualized. This transformative dilemma was clear from the manifesto of POW. To continue their tie with the ML groups on the one hand and yet proclaim some separateness on the other, they divided the manifesto into 'long term goals' and 'immediate demands'. While the long term goals referred to the fight against feudal economy, foreign exploitation, monopoly houses and fight for 'production-oriented education system' and propagating scientific socialism, the immediate demands included legislations against dowry, child marriage, obscene art degrading women and laws for implementation of equal pay for equal work, and inheritance rights. These demands were divided in a manner that made it possible to convert the private-moral logic within the radical Left strategies on the one hand, and to struggle for legislations within the civil society in order to attempt to confront and convert the centrality of legality on the other, into a political idiom. In other words, they maintained proximity with the radical Left protest politics to politicize their engagement with the public, and continued their negotiation with law independently in order to radicalize the private-moral logic that operated within the Left groups. They kept the debate open at both ends and therefore continued to raise pertinent questions, as one woman activist asked, 'due to the Marxist-Leninist orientation of POW, the struggle had to assume a "proletarian" base which was sought in the *bastees*. One is left wondering what middle class women can do "for" *bastee* women (or peasant women) unless they have first broken the sexist and patriarchal fetters which keep them down?' (Lalitha 1998: 60). Within a few years of functioning of the POW, Emergency was declared in the country. Most of the important members of the POW, including the president of the organization, were arrested and implicated in various cases. At the beginning of 1976 almost all the activities of POW were paralyzed and it was disbanded as an organization. It is interesting to observe that while in the beginning of its activities the POW claimed to have very few ML activists as its members, 'by the time state of Emergency had been declared eighty percent of the organizers of the POW had become members of the ML parties' (Ibid.). This gives us a clue as to how the strategy of the feminist politics kept multiple options to struggle against series of exclusions, as options closed in one they preferred to avail the others. They neither constructed absolute closures nor imagined unproblematic/un-gendered openings and spaces.

However, experiments such as that of the POW definitely brought onto the agenda the issue of autonomy of women's organizations from the radical Left groups. Immediately after the Emergency in 1977, the Stree Shakti Sanghatana (SSS), another autonomous women's organization, was formed with women who had leftist and liberal leanings. They attempted to work on issues they believed would be of priority to the women and also formulate a perspective closer to and specific to the experience of the 'third world' women. The new perspective was driven under the influence of global recognition given through the UN's Declaration of 1975 as the International Women's Year (8 March was celebrated for the first time as International Women's Day) and also the release of the historical report of the CSWC on the 'Status of Women in India'. Similarly, organizations such as the Mahila Samta Shramik Dal (MSSD) in Maharashtra began emphasizing the need to recognize the fact that 'sexual oppression' was common to women of all classes, castes and regions. Organizations such as the SSS and the MSSD were looking for a common subjectivity for the women of the developing world and therefore rallied women around issues such as, protest against rape, dowry and sexual violence within communal violence, among other demands such as the need for more women's hostels. This was a period which began witnessing 'enormous activism of the autonomous women's groups'. In Maharashtra, Sahada was a mass movement led by the Gram Swarajya Samiti (district organization for self-governance) with the active involvement of women's organizations to protest against firing on Bhil workers by rich farmers of that area; such campaigns were taken up partly to counter the 'annihilation line' of the Naxalites, which, the women's organizations felt, offered limited scope of participation for women. 'One of the main points of criticism against the Naxalites was their neglect of mass mobilization. In Sahada, therefore, the "mass line" was the guiding principle of action' (Mies 1976: 480). There were other protests against price-rise by women's organizations such as the United Women's Anti-Price Rise Front, and later the Nav Nirman in Gujarat.[16] Other organizations such as the Self-Employed Women's Association (SEWA) in Gujarat worked towards improving the conditions of work through training and offering technical aids. It is interesting to observe that while in Sahada the women were critical of the modes of protest adopted by Naxalites for providing limited political space for women, with an experiment such as SEWA the feminists were hesitant to identify with its 'reformist' methods and SEWA 'itself maintained a distance from the feminists, perhaps it felt they were "westernized", or too radical' (Kumar 1993: 103). The multiplicity and contradictoriness of the strategies reveals the difficulty in dealing with the public–private divide that manifests itself in many forms and changes the nature of its boundaries every time the women's groups attempted to either negotiate or rearrange them.

One Act Play: Privatization of the Public or Publicizing the Private?

However, these very attempts to experiment simultaneously with multiple strategies that the autonomous women's organizations began with seemed to have been short lived and congealed around them. While the previous experiment by the POW, in the context of Andhra Pradesh, ended with a merger back into the ML groups from whom they were demanding autonomy, the later experiment of starting an independent SSS 'merged' into the civil society. Initially the SSS began its work as a 'mass organization', by organizing street demonstrations and mobilizing women from across caste and class, then it gradually began to 'operate' as a pressure group, by moving the levers of governmental structures through the activism of few independent feminists, and later converted itself into a research group with the formation of the Feminist Study Circle in 1979.

The Feminist Study Circle concentrated on organizing discussions, public meetings and publications. Gradually, they could not however sustain their activity, and limited themselves to organizing discussions and bringing out a few publications, converting itself into a classical civil society organization. The 'civil-societization' of autonomous women's groups was partly the result of its failure to expand its own social base beyond the English-educated urban women working primarily in the metropolitan cities such as Hyderabad. Diabolically the traits of the cultural capital that enabled them, as women belonging to the urban middle class, to shrug off the private-moral logic as it worked within the closed doors of the family, and recover and reclaim agency, in turn also constrained them into taking a formal shape of a civil society organization—with a focus on floating discussion groups, voluntary organizations, and research centres—which distanced them from popular mobilization in general but of other classes in particular, in both rural and urban areas.

In other words, while they realized the significance of the agency provided by urban middle class conditions, without moralizing the nature of middle class itself like the HRM, they could not, however, forge links with social groups beyond their own class. In course of demanding autonomy, from the ML groups that were primarily mobilizing the rural poor in the hinterlands along class lines, autonomous women's groups *ipso facto* failed in organizing the rural women, and thereby failed to also take up issues that went beyond (urban) cultural agenda of life style (not that this was not important or not political but it was limited). While it was extremely important to articulate cultural issues and those of representation, but in course of responding to the 'economism' of the ML groups the autonomous women's groups gradually valorized their own version of self-limiting 'culturalism'. With the retreat from street politics, and the movement being focused excessively in and on urban areas, there was a gradual growth in the phenomenon of 'professionalization of feminism' and NGO-ization of the autonomous women's organizations.[17]

The shift to an exclusive *identity politics* due to culturalism in the Dalit movement is comparable with the *professionalization* of feminist politics in encountering a disciplining civil society that worked through a strict public–private divide. NGO-ization made politics localized, coupled with a certain degree of intractability created by the simultaneity of multiple strategies that the autonomous women's movement had adopted and the 'intractability of the oppression at the level of "the body" (which) lead(s) feminist practice to attempt to comprehend and contain it in the discourse of coherence and uniformity offered by the law' (Menon 2004: 13).[18] In a sense, this was also the period that witnessed the 'retreat' of feminist politics into 'operating' governmental structures for legal changes. Resorting to increasing legal battles further entrenched women's groups well within the boundaries of the civil society, and further undermined their capacity to build collective struggles that could challenge the limits posed by the discourses and categories of the civil society. Ironically, the recoiling of the movement and the visible 'withdrawal' from occupying of the (public) space through organized street politics, led to the opening up of new spaces for questioning the insidious modes in which the logic of the private-morality was incessantly working its way. The moment of formalization was also a moment of politicization; in an obverse way, it is akin to the way the moment of autonomy, in the Foucauldian frame, was also the mode of regulation.[19] Here, the moment of a closure (formalization) was also an opening up of the space for raising new issues of private-morality—in this case, sexuality and sexual freedom—that could not be perhaps easily raised when women's movement was involved with mobilizing larger collectives and involved with organizing street-protest politics.

The Formation of the Feminist Study Circle was the result of a controversy over a condolence resolution arranged for Chalam, a powerful literary writer known for his scathing critiques against societal moral regulation of women's sexuality and was known to have argued that nothing short of the demolition of family system will work to emancipate women from the tyranny of morality. As the leadership of one of the Communist parties, UCCRI (ML), was unhappy about this ideological drift of its women activists demanding an official endorsement of Chalam and his writings as integral to revolutionary politics, they had to resign to the party membership. There were also individuals who walked out of civil rights organizations such as the Organization for Protection of Democratic Rights (OPDR), where no autonomy for women's questions was being recognized, along with the former members of the SSS. It was during this period that the independent feminists revisited the private logic of morality by rallying behind the ideas foregrounded by Chalam (Volga: undated).

Chalam was an unconventional literary figure and a social critique; he drew his inspiration from the social reform programme of Kandukuri Veeresalingam, more for the way he foregrounded issues concerning women than the content of the reforms themselves.[20] Through his various literary writings he pioneered in highlighting the centrality of female sexuality in recovering the female subjectivity. He consciously attributed an 'aggressive sexuality' to his protagonists, and advocated 'free love' as a way to upturn the female subjectivity identified with sacrifice, self-denial and surrender of desire. 'It is only to the extent that the individual (or the woman in this case) lives out this adversarial relation, and fights against the norm that she is a human subject at all' (Vindhya 2000: 182). The control of the private-moral logic was so complete for Chalam that it was only in the moments of adversity that she reclaims subjectivity for herself. Chalam was forthright in articulating the idea that without an absolute right to sexual pleasure and desire, and reproductive freedom, we cannot even begin to frame the issues of women's subjectivity and it was therefore necessary to demolish all institutions that constrain such freedoms including those of family, marriage and the sanctity of monogamous relations. For Chalam, the various dimensions of power condensed around the private-moral logic, which reflected not just a mode of social control of women but the way power in general was ordered in the society. Social reordering of power relations was signified in a comprehensive way in achieving 'sexual relations without exploitation'.

Chalam, who was a member of the Brahmo Samaj, was expelled from the organization, ostracized by his relatives and refused housing in 'respectable' civil or public localities prompting him to move to live in peripheral locations of the then '*harijanwadas*' with dalits and Muslims.[21] In 1931, his novel *Maidanam* which was being serialized in a popular Telugu magazine was abruptly stopped since the 'readers protested against the brazenness of the story' (Vindhya 2000: 185), reflecting the fragility of belief in free speech and publication among the educated and 'informed' readership that was supposed to have been foundational to the expanding public sphere. It was precisely to counter the rationality of the civic sphere that Chalam often argued that what he wrote was drawn from the 'common man's rugged common sense' (Chalam 1976: 64).[22] While the emerging public sphere pushed out Chalam, ghettoizing him and his ideas, both figuratively and literally, the radical Left groups too seem to have exacerbated this process by missing the multiple ways in which politicization occurs; this demanded a strategy that comprehended the manifold interconnections that were only sometimes visible but mostly hidden or beyond the settled frames in which radical politics seemed to have got consolidated. The Left groups too declined to accept the significance of 'body' as a site for the centring of power relations, which for them reflected an 'individualistic' approach to a social problem, and the 'reification of the private emotional realm of subjectivity that Chalam established through the "romantic ambience" of his novels' (Vindhya 2000: 179).

While part of the anxiety of the radical Left groups, with the *logic of individuation* and the possibilities of reification were justified in the way autonomous women's groups transformed from 'mass organizations' to circumscribed and professionalized research groups, the potential of connecting the logic of 'bio-politics' to a wider collective struggle remained unattended to. While, at the same time, feminists continued to read the reluctance of the Left groups to adopt the issues they foregrounded as part of the private-moral logic that undermined the process of politicization and instead in its place valorized a process of moralization. They argued that, 'the challenge to the concept of revolutionary identity from feminism lies in that it allows into the political arena problems of sexuality and subjectivity which have so far tended to be suppressed in revolutionary discourse' (Vindhya 2000: 188).

The visible incommunicability between the two modes of instantiating the political signifies the growing interpenetration or rather the collapse between subjection and subjectivity. Forms of power are also the context for action; in this case foregrounding sexuality individuated—offering individual solutions—but also entered the public on its 'own terms', where 'the subject is an agent, even if not an autonomous agent'.

> Autonomous subjects would be able, at least in principle, to have experiences, to reason, to adopt beliefs, and to act, outside all social contexts...Agents, in contrast, exist only in specific social contexts, but these contexts never [completely—my addition] determine how they try to construct themselves. Although agents necessarily exist within regimes of power/knowledge...

they nevertheless retain certain capacity to 'modify this background' and thereby set new terms of discourse (Bevir 1999: 67). All political movements seem to arrogate to themselves this capacity to 'set new terms of discourse' without offering the same concession to the political acts of other struggles, leading to increasing incommunicability between them.[23]

Later in 1994, the birth centenary year of Chalam, feminists in Andhra Pradesh formed the Nurella Chalam Committee (Committee to celebrate Hundred Years of Chalam); they brought out a volume of essays reassessing the importance of Chalam in light of the ongoing debates and politics and organized public meetings in nearly twenty cities and towns in the state, intensely scrutinizing and revisiting, yet again, the debate on the links between politics, law, morality and civil society.[24] Elsewhere too in the country women were beginning to focus on similar issues, such as the increasing sexist modes of representation that was becoming part of the media, cinema and the burgeoning advertisement industry. Many of the women's organizations began to work for a separate law that could deal with this and help them bring into relief the problem of indecency. In August 1986, Parliament passed the Indecent Representation of Women (Protection) Bill in order to curb the growing sexist culture in the public domain. However, women's groups were intrigued by the language of the law that framed the provisions within a moral tone rather than bringing to the fore the dimension of social power that provides and creates space for such sexism. The Act explicitly defines indecency in Section 2(c) as 'depiction which is indecent and derogatory to women or is likely to deprave or injure public morality' (Shah 1992: 225). Women's groups argued that 'nowhere does the law specifically mention women, their degradation and discrimination or the power relations between the two sexes' (Ibid.: 226), instead harped on injury to 'public morality', which was constitutively ambiguous, and precisely due to its ambiguity, could enforce regulation on women in the name of maintaining public order, and in turn contributed to the definitional problems of obscenity, vulgarity and indecency.

These definitional problems never remained merely within either the discursive or just the cultural realm, but posed fresh challenges to feminist politics even in claiming economic rights for women. For instance, allegations of immorality and adultery have always been used to deny women the right to maintenance. Here again, law reflects the dominant patriarchal-sexual mores integral to the familial ideology. Clauses 4 and 5 of Section 125 of CRPC have made provisions where: (4) No woman shall be entitled to receive an allowance if she is living in adultery; (5) On proof that any wife (in) whose favour an order has been made under this section is living in adultery... the magistrate shall cancel the order. As Flavia Agnes puts it 'the layered and multiple contexts through which sexual morality surfaces, as per the norms of patriarchy, serve only one end: to challenge the legitimacy of women's claims' (Agnes 2009: 61). The moral regulation around sexual mores becomes even more starkly visible when legal enactments for monogamy (under the Hindu Marriages Act, 1955) are violated by men, by openly claiming a bigamous marriage, precisely to deny women their right to maintenance (Ibid.). Courts have not only made it difficult for women who are not legally wedded 'wives' to get their rights to maintenance but also overlooked the violation of law by men claiming bigamous marriages; it involved neither criminal nor civil proceedings against them.[25]

In Andhra Pradesh, as elsewhere, the *constitutive ambiguity in civil society*—of what constitutes public morality—had its effects on the response of the political movements to the issues of 'vulgarity' and 'obscenity' that they felt was part of the growing popular culture. One such major controversy around popular culture and public morality was the demand for legal intervention to ban a mainstream 'commercial' film titled 'Alluda Majaka' released in 1995, with Chiranjeevi in the lead role.[26] The incident involved popular mobilization by left wing and right wing organizations on one hand, and independent women's groups on the other, apart from the support from the 'fans clubs' of Chiranjeevi. It, in a sense, had representatives of all political formations as well as groups that belonged to a cross section of castes and classes. The controversy was around a few scenes where the hero 'Sitaram finds himself in a bedroom with Pappi (his fiancé) and her younger sister Bappi'. There was also a demand to ban the movie since it showed the hero (who belonged to a lower class background in the movie), to be making sexual advances towards his mother-in-law (from upper caste/class). However, the debate around the controversy was vertically divided between women's organizations of both the right as well as the left demanding a ban, and the fans clubs of Chiranjeevi with people overwhelmingly from the lower caste/class background, often referred to as 'masses' by film journalists and in popular cinema parlance, arguing that there was nothing vulgar or obscene about these incursions in the movie, and the ban would provoke them to commit mass suicides.

The point, however, was the 'disturbing similarity between the left, right and "apolitical" participants despite the difference in their location and stated concerns' (Srinivas 1999: 5), which was expressed in terms of framing the problem essentially as a moral issue in the language of obscenity and vulgarity, rather than in terms of power exercised on women's bodies and the politics of it.[27] Both the women's organizations of the Marxist-Leninist groups and the Bharatiya Janata Mahila Morcha (BJMM) of the Bhartiya Janata Party (BJP), lamented the breakdown of 'family values' on the one hand, and depicted the 'audiences as the victim of cinema', which was primarily constituted by the 'masses', on the other. Neither the women nor the 'masses' have an agency and both were primarily depicted as 'victim-subjects', with an additional possibility of attaching obscenity with the 'massification' of movies, and depiction of 'woman' quintessentially as one who belongs to the upper caste/class social location.[28] The more intriguing of formulations on the controversy was reflected in the observations of the film critics and journalists, who in a proper sense belong to the civil society. As some of them argued that 'the primary source of obscenity is the entry of the "sex-act"' into the public (as opposed to the private) domain via cinema. This is one of the reasons why the masses and obscenity go together. Unlike "us", the educated, middle-class section, 'they live under trees, in shacks and don't have privacy.... Their sex-act is reflected in films and they enjoy it.' (Ibid.: 10). Yet again, such arguments shifted the boundaries between the public and the private, where the public here belongs to the lower classes and castes, and it is their morality that operates in the enlarging public domain as popular culture, while the rest either belong to the private or to the 'civil' within the public. These distinctions, based on moral regulations, constrain women, both within the private, and also in determining their access to the public domain.[29] Ratna Kapur, reflecting on the issue of 'sex in public', observes:

> The result is that the sex laws work at times in highly contradictory ways for women and other sexual subgroups. Sometimes, the refusal to intervene is based on the construction of some sex as private, as part of a cultural and sacred space, and beyond legitimate intervention; and at other times legal intervention is justified if the sex is public, and transgresses cultural and sexual norms. The law is not used to protect public sex, and may even penalise it. There are also times when even private sexuality, such as homosexuality, is constructed as public and therefore subject to legitimate intervention by the law. Running through the shifting use of the public/private distinction lie assumptions about the private as space for the articulation and preservation of India cultural values, and women as the central repositories for these values. (Kapur 2005: 32)

It is in the context of negotiating with this shifting terrain between the public and the private in law and public discourses of morality on the one hand, and the inability of resolving such dilemmas in treating culture as a stand-alone variable on the other, that the feminist politics entered a third distinct moment. This moment, marked by the era of economic reforms bringing into relief market and its associated institutional practices as the third major dimension of power, projected the necessity of locating the issues related to women in relation to the changing political economy and of also in turn rethinking the place of state and civil society in their approach to this new context.

Feminizing the State: Economizing Culture and Politicizing the Civil

Paradoxically, the next moment of the women's movement began, in complete contrast to the previous moment, with one of the largest and most powerful collective movement by women in the post independence era, demanding complete prohibition of liquor.[30] The anti-arrack movement began in August 1992, in the remote village of Dubagunta of Nellore district. Women of the village stopped vending of arrack in their village after three men lost their way and got drowned in a water tank. Women stopped arrack carts and jeeps from entering the village. Eventually the village arrack shop was closed down and gave relief to women, from abject poverty and domestic violence. This important incident found its way into the reading material of the literacy primers for adult education. The

Dubagunta village incident was written as a story (*Advallu Ekamaithe—When Women Unite*), which was widely popularized by the Government-initiated Akshara Deepam Programme, actively aided by the volunteers of Jana Vignana Vedika (an organization of the CPI(M). Thereafter, the ostensibly innocuous literacy campaign created a wave among the women of, initially, Nellore district, and thereafter Chittoor and then in almost all the districts of the Telangana region (in roughly around 800 villages).

Most of the feminist organizations have argued that it was 'personal tragedies'—mostly domestic violence and distress—and other related socio-cultural issues (which in fact forced some to commit suicide) that led to the struggle against arrack. They observed that 'women kept bringing up the daily harassment they and their children suffered at the hands of men who came home drunk and in an abusive mood' (Anveshi 1993: 88). Women had become more confident and united against men even at 'public spaces' like the arrack shop. They overcame 'personal shame' in making both their husbands' abusive behaviour and the resistance they were offering public; thereby they challenged the constructions of public morality.

> We only need to remind ourselves of some of the methods women brought to bear in the course of the agitation such as attacking the contractors and excise department officials with "household weapons" like brooms and chilli powder, refusing to cook or eat and publicly shaming their men. (Ibid.: 90)

They, in other words, reframed the carefully constructed notions from Rousseau to Mill and of course Gandhi who insisted that women in the family were the seats of 'moral restraint' in an immoral world marked by 'trucking and bartering', and instead took to public action precisely to challenge the nexus around 'trucking and bartering' in the civil society beyond the limits of the boundaries set up by the institution of family. Challenging the relations within family was invariably linked to—and entailed going beyond—the way relations, institutions and categories were structured around man's acquisitive and accumulative self-interest in the civil society.

Household goods that were closely associated with their everyday life and identity were given a new political meaning and symbolically re-signified. Women in this movement in fact renegotiated the conventional divisions between the public and private, in order to comprehend the hidden linkages between family, domestic violence, and the state and the liquor lobby. In smudging the lines between the private and the public, women drew more stark links between culture (as in patriarchy) and the nature of the economic 'development model' that the state was pursuing, overcoming the false antithesis in both 'culturalism' and 'economism', which seem to have worked as frames for the interaction between the women's and left movement in the previous moment. In forging a collective struggle with private symbols, it managed to politicize the civil sphere with new issues of the family and domesticity that were not earlier part of the visible and the performative dimensions of the civic sphere. It helped overcome the earlier anxieties of the feminists as to how:

> the focus on State power obscures both the ways in which actors other than the State, such as the family, particularly men within the family, are invested with the power to violate the human rights of others within the family, and the ways in which the State is implicated in reinforcing the power of men within the traditional family. (Kapur 1996b: 5)

Women in the context of the anti-liquor movement understood and demonstrated that behind their abusive husbands was the whole support structure led by the arrack contractors, police, goondas, legislators, ministers, officials and bureaucrats (Kannabiran 1995: 166).

It is in linking the issues of culture to the changing nature of the political economy that 'the anti-liquor movement has not merely raised a women's question as being portrayed by the press and a section of the intelligentsia but also targeted its attack on the nexus between the so-called people's representatives, police and arrack contractors' (Reddy and Patnaik 1993: 1064). By realizing the nature and character of the edifice of the state and the profit-seeking machinations of the market, not only have the women in the anti-arrack struggle made personal issues political but also compelled other political movements of the left, and also the Dalit struggles to realize that family is as important a site of political mobilization as class and caste.

> While the women's success in reducing or even preventing arrack sales has directly affected the state and can be seen without much effort as a classical "political" action... The women are also articulating many domains of their life in political terms and as political issues. (Tharu 1994: 112)

Feminist groups further argued that the anti-arrack movement also brought forth novel and radical *forms of organization* and mobilization into the politics of collective struggles. Most of them argued that anti-arrack movement demonstrated a 'leaderless' collective, which was specific to the women's approach to street politics. According to them it was 'an extremely interesting outcome of the struggle (is) that there is no central leadership, (and) with women independently taking up local agitations and initiatives in their own villages, the movement is truly dispersed' (Anveshi 1993: 89).

This was the general pattern in almost all the villages, notwithstanding minor differences. They observed that:

> in some we were told to wait for a kind of spokesperson and listen to her. In some the literacy volunteers had played an initiating role, while in others all the women who had gathered to meet us wanted to speak collectively of their achievements. (Anveshi 1993)

The truly participative character was demonstrated by the fact that the state could not attack or curtail the movement by arresting key organizers. Anti-arrack movement had demonstrated the depth of democratic practice and that the struggle for empowerment of women cannot have a centralized leadership (Volga 1994: 180).[31]

The change in the nature of the social base of the movement seems to have brought to the fore a set of new forms of organization and a new set of issues, and in fact a new approach that was, in some ways distinct, to its previous moment that was restricted to the urban middle classes. As Dalit scholars reflecting on the movement argued, it was the caste/class background of the women activist in the anti-liquor movement that had made it possible to address some of the dilemmas of feminist politics—the problem of withdrawal from collective struggles, treating culture as a stand-alone variable that constrained their imagination in the previous moment—in negotiating with the civil society. Kancha Illiah argued:

> Whether one likes it or not the women cadre and leaders emerging from this movement will pose serious questions in future. The questions that the grassroots women pose to husbands, activists and parties-to entire civil society-will be radically different from the ones that the urban middle class women have posed so far. (Illiah 1992: 2408)[32]

The anti-liquor agitation politicized the civic by inaugurating open discussions by women on their experience within the closed doors of the family, and demanding necessary changes in the operations of the state and market. In doing this they also took the civil society practices of discussion and deliberation beyond the confines of cafes, research centres and the 'reading public' squarely to constitute the public and conjoin it with protest politics, conjoining and simultaneously generating public opinion and political action.

Further, in launching struggles without leaders and outside the confines of well-entrenched organizational structures, women confronted the totalization of the civil society in reducing them to an undifferentiated 'mass' or 'the people' to be lead and represented by leaders or political parties, yet or precisely because of this managed to forge active collective struggles that were sensitive to differentiations (within women) across caste and class.[33] The impact of the anti-liquor movement could be felt in the articulation of new and differentiated struggles. In 1994, Dalit women of the Madduru village in Kurnool district waged a significant land struggle, reflecting the enlarged consciousness after their participation in the anti arrack movement. Around 60 Dalit women formed the 'Ideal Women's Association' and decided to occupy the barren land at the outskirts of the village, belonging to the government but used as a field for grazing the cattle of the landlord. This, of course, led to a confrontation with the landlords and their goons, who finally attacked and forced Dalit men and women to flee to the nearby Kurnool town. Even in the post-land struggle phase at the camps put up, Dalit women were active, unlike the previous camps set up after the Karamchedu and Chundur massacres (Illiah 1995a: 1–2).

Elsewhere too, Dalit women began to raise a new set of questions. In Maharashtra, they questioned the 'populism' of peasant movements such as the Shetkari Sanghatana, for representing the interest of rich farmers, which directly contradicted the interest of Dalit agricultural labourers over the issue of minimum wages. Similarly, 'Dalit women (are) were also not well disposed to the eco-feminist call for development of environmental consciousness' (Guru 1995: 2549). Dalit men and women uprooted saplings planted by the social forestry department in the Aurangabad district as Dalits were denied both the land as well as access to common property resources of the village. Forging new struggles around land, common property resources, ecological issues and against liquor inaugurated a new set of issues at the core of which was the continued attempt to reconnect social, political, economic and cultural dimensions, as much as exploring the complex continuities and discontinuities across classes, castes and regional locations including the difference between urban and rural areas, and to understand their impact on forging collective struggles with internal differences and possible political contestations. In the process of expanding the scope of the political, as Rajeshwari Sunder Rajan argues, 'some kind of essentialism must be strategically involved to ground a feminist politics…but one that at the same time remains alert to differences among women' (Sunder Rajan 2003: 13).

The social crisis, in the context of the anti-liquor movement, as it got manifested in the rising levels of domestic violence, hunger, ill health, lack of education for children, constant debt, their belongings—the pots and pans pawned for buying *sara* (arrack)—and their mental anguish, had its roots, apart from the rigid and dominant patriarchal cultural values in the family, in the general economic crisis in the region. In the 1980s, unemployment was on the rise, there was no substantial increase in the wages, prices of essential commodities increased by 30–50 per cent, and the subsidized rice scheme (two rupees for a kilo of rice in Andhra Pradesh) was withdrawn (Ibid.). These policies were the direct outcome of the state's unwillingness to displease the affluent by taxing their growing wealth and the nexus with the liquor lobby, along with the civil contractors who came to have a strong hold on the state. Coupled with this withdrawal of welfare policies was a policy of the state to increase its revenues through excise duty. It was collecting not less than ₹12 billion in 1990–91, almost double of its previous year's income of ₹6.11 billion of excise duty in Andhra Pradesh. The consumption of arrack in the state increased from about 54 million litres in 1975–76 to 70 million litres in 1980–81 to 111 million litres by 1990–91. Nearly 70–80 per cent of the excise was accounted for by the revenue from arrack. The number of shops selling arrack increased from 7,159 in 1969–70 to about 22,803 by 1987–88. Though the number of shops declined to 16,436 in 1990–91, partly due to the campaign taken up by the CPI (ML) PWG in districts such as Warangal, Mahaboobnagar, Nizamabad and Karimnagar that were their strongholds, it was not commensurate with any corresponding decline in consumption of arrack. By 1990, in Nizamabad alone, out of 587 arrack shops 351 shops were closed. From this district out of the regular revenue of ₹60 million to the state government it could manage only ₹40 million. In October 1990, a new excise year began but due to the threat from the PWG there was no auction of arrack in the district.[34]

With pressure from the women's groups and a sustained struggle for well over two years on 16 January 1995 NTR, the then chief minister announced complete prohibition of liquor in the state. However, with the election of Chandrababu Naidu as the new chief minister, he revised the policy and reintroduced liquor from 1 April 1997, restricting the dry law to arrack. This reversal in the policy, it was argued was a necessary corollary for ushering a '*Swarna* Andhra Pradesh' through economic reforms and free market. Naidu argued that 'total prohibition is neither successful nor feasible because of the leakages within the state and from across the borders' (Rao 2004).[35] Liquor sales fetch an income touching ₹30 billion per annum, which could be spent for 'developmental activities'—including building schools, new health centres, providing loans and other subsidies, which were all part of the demands that women were making to ameliorate their condition—along with overcoming the huge deficit of over ₹80 billion that the state was facing, and to repay the loans from international financial institutions (mostly the World Bank) that were sought to develop new infrastructure, mostly roads, to attract new global investments, which amounted to nearly 225 billion.[36] With the lifting of prohibition it was argued that state finances would be put in order, and the 'same' demands women were making on the state could be fulfilled. In other words, the government pointed at the 'contradiction' in the arguments of the women's organizations where they wanted increasing 'developmental' activities by the state and at the same time blocked the most significant source of income from the 'ever-growing' excise duty. Such arguments in turn had links to the changing nature of the economy where the state increasingly became dependent on revenue from liquor, real estate and, more recently, mining—replacing manufacturing industry and agriculture.

The changing nature of the political economy with declining importance of productive classes, both agrarian as well as industrial, and the growth of middlemen/contractor classes—liquor and mining—and also civil—largely on the borrowings from the international financial organizations, that lead to an exponential growth of the construction industry—was instrumental in the new policy perspective of the state. The state policy was overwhelmingly influenced by the lobbying tactics of the distillers, liquor barons, hoteliers and contractors. A large number of ministers in the Cabinet, in both the Telugu Desam as well as the Congress governments, were themselves liquor contractors, who had joined active politics both due to the control they came to wield in their own local areas, and for being cash-rich that had become imperative to contest elections.[37] One could, perhaps, make a case that what was coming to replace the 'developmental state' was at the local level a 'contractor-type state' that has features of both a 'shrinking state' as well as an 'interventionist state' but was not adequately captured by these formulations. The specific features making the contractor-type state distinct are the aversion for long-term planning, institutional norms and procedures; quick money and dependence on speculative and financial capital; emphasis on distribution and consumption; and links with the leakages from the loans extended by the international financial institutions such as the World Bank.[38]

After lifting the prohibition the tax revenue from liquor sales in Andhra Pradesh has been the highest among the four south Indian states. According to the Women's Group for Empowerment, nearly 31,000 liquor vends were permitted across the state, with nearly two liquor shops in every village (Rao 2004). Apart from 14,000 unauthorized counters in their 'belts' using bunks and even the grocery shops to sell liquor. However, this growth in the revenues of the state, as argued by the government, did not get reflected in any noticeable increase in its 'developmental' activities, and on the contrary welfare policies such as subsidized electricity and cheap rice were withdrawn by the government under Naidu. This they argued was necessary for overcoming the fiscal deficit that had accumulated due to the decline in revenues of the state, as a result of the prohibition. In 2004 the Congress government came to power under Rajshekhar Reddy, it brought back the subsidy schemes such as free electricity for small farmers and the two-rupee rice scheme, and it came back to power by bringing the agrarian agenda back to the centre stage. However, the policy of earning revenues through the sale of liquor continued unabated, it in fact attempted, going a step further, to pass a GO allowing all villages with more than a population of 25,000 to open as many bars serving liquor as they can, again, it was argued, to generate further revenues for the 'developmental' activities. However, under popular pressure from women's groups and widespread criticism in the print media, it was stalled.

Thus, the women's movement against liquor was in response and to resist multiple processes that were closely inter-related. Amongst which it was responding to the refusal by the state to prohibit liquor and recognize the link between consumption of liquor and domestic violence, mental anguish, and the impact on health and instead it favoured generating revenues from the sale of liquor to take up 'developmental activities'; the growing nexus between the liquor lobby, legislators and police; increasing influence of the new contractor classes—civil, liquor and mining—in the context of economic reforms; increasing dependence on the financial assistance from international financial institutions to develop infrastructure, these institutions in turn pressed for reforms in governance, including fiscal accountability by cutting down subsidies and other welfare policies and putting in place a new institutional framework that was 'managed' more by 'experts' rather than being responsive to popular demands including those made by the political movements. It is in this context that the women's movement for prohibition of liquor was making attempts to mobilize and resist the approach of the government and foreground precisely the link between all these processes. It is against this background that we need to make sense of the state action through its legal interventions, in this context through the promulgation of the Domestic Violence Act, 2005, in order to curb the growing domestic violence across the country. How do we then understand the state on the one hand refusing to prohibit liquor in order to curb domestic violence but was proactive in making a legal intervention by introducing a new law against domestic violence? This can only be answered in relation to other pertinent questions that we need to raise including: Why does the state replace or juxtapose the economic, political and cultural demands of the women's movement with its own 'developmental' activities? Or why is that the state initiated 'developmental' activities had failed or refused to take cognizance of the interconnections between social, economic, political and cultural dimensions in the making of a demand, by the women's movement, to curb domestic violence by prohibiting liquor? What impact does such a legal intervention of the state have on a political movement that had managed to politicize the public or civic domain through forging a collective struggle, as an alternative to both (public) moral language and a process of intervening in the problem exclusively through a legal discourse? Finally, what impact does the new law actually have in arresting and reducing domestic violence?

To begin with, all these interventions and processes were inter-linked, however disparate they might look on the surface. One needs to understand the scope, nature and impact of the 'developmental' activities of the state—with a focus on building infrastructure or doling out subsidies and other welfare schemes—in the larger context of pursuing neo-liberal economic reforms and its associated political and institutional changes brought about through the reforms in governance ('governance reforms') and the later legal—technical interventions. In other words, the nature of 'developmental' activities of the state augment the process of economic reforms by building the necessary infrastructure and conceiving welfare policies as an abatement of the 'unavoidable' adverse impact—growing social and economic inequalities, and falling quality of life—of such reforms. These 'developmental' initiatives of the state were further pursued or backed by legal and institutional 'reforms' where new modalities of institutional practices were introduced to facilitate the imperatives of the private and global capital at one level—to put in place conformity laws, reduced role of the state, low transaction costs, pushing out social costs through reforms to labour laws, amongst other such changes, and make legal interventions to abate the social effects of inequalities and distress at another level—including such Acts as against domestic violence. However, it needs to be noted that the state made legal interventions, without addressing the structural—the inter-link between economic, political and cultural—causes of inequalities and distress. In other words, it introduced an Act against domestic violence, while obstructing social and economic conditions that the women's movement against liquor highlighted, and that were necessary to mitigate such violence. It is here, that legal interventions—introduced in lieu of or without social and economic initiatives—have specific kinds of adverse effects on the social groups for whom such legal, technical changes were intended to benefit. The practices of governance enhanced the role of legal and institutional changes without addressing the growing social distress and economic inequalities, and instead created practices that facilitated the very process of creating a larger disconnect—between politics/democracy and institutional response—by creating an institutional design that gains some immunity from popular democratic participation and aspirations, including those from protest politics.

Andhra Pradesh has been one of the states in India in the forefront in pursuing the economic reforms and heavily banking on the concept of 'good governance' to enable the state to play an effective role as a 'facilitator'. Based on the World Bank publication *Governance and Development* (1992), a whole range of new strategies was introduced.

> For instance, to improve efficiency in public administration, strategies such as introducing corporate management techniques into public administration; introducing profitability criteria; "contracting out" functions of government to NGOs or private agencies or sharing them (under public–private partnership— my addition); decentralization of levels of administration, marketization and the like have been adopted. . . . (Joseph 2001: 1012)

The new role of the state as a 'facilitator' demanded a new set of practices, where governance reforms offered these as flexible modes of coordination or 'heterarchy' between individuals, organizations and different sub-systems. The opening up of the markets through the processes of globalization and liberalization entailed 'a corresponding increase in the "unstructured complexity" of the economy on a world scale', which in turn necessitated 'attempts on various spatial scales (from local to global) to re-impose some structure and order through resort to heterarchic co-ordination' (Jessop 1998: 33). It is in the process of creating such coordination that new institutions and practices were created, including those such as setting up of the various regulatory commissions, and introducing the idea of 'embedded autonomy' and 'consumer management', e-governance and reliance on computers and the language of stakeholders (exemplified in state-run programmes such as *Janmabhoomi*), apart from changing the notion of chief minister (in the executive) into a CEO (resembling the nomenclature in the corporate).

Governance correspondingly also entailed and envisioned the conversion of the citizen who engaged with the state into essentially a consumer in the market, and thereby attempts to collapse the distinction between the two. To put it differently, citizenship itself comes to be defined, not in terms of negotiations with the state, but consumption of goods and 'services delivered by a plethora of agencies' (Chandhoke 2005: 1033; also see Canclini 2001). In other words, there was an attempt to link the rationality of consumption to the constitution of the altered forms of citizenship, where:

> for many men and women… the questions specific to citizenship, such as how we inform ourselves and who represents our interests, are answered more often than not through private consumption of commodities and media offerings than through the abstract rules of democracy or through participation in discredited political organizations. (Canclini 2001: 5)

This shift from the identity of being a citizen in civil society to that of an overwhelming identity of a consumer (where the distinction between market and the civil society gets blurred), is made possible with the shift in the state from being a political entity to converting itself into a technocratic facilitating edifice.

The state, as a corollary, to efficiently meet the demands of a consumer, begins to rely more on 'experts', where 'the appeal to a "committee of experts" will itself become an important instrument in resolving a political debate', and it also progressively reduces political problems into 'technical' problems. The state, under this scheme of things, takes recourse to more insular techniques and strategies that were less open to public argumentation and accountability. In course of carrying out 'governance reforms' more and more issues were projected as a subject matter outside the domain of politics and thereby it was argued that they need to be left to the discretion of the 'experts', who alone can handle these highly complex and technical matters. The state impresses upon its citizens/consumers that 'developmental' issues are more achievable outside the chaotic and uncertain political domain, thus not only diverging democratic processes from 'developmental' agenda but in fact projecting them, at times, as mutually exclusive.[39] As Habermas observed, the advanced capitalist countries witnessed the arresting of the spread of 'public sphere' with the arrival of corporate firms; similarly, the spread of global capital, in the form of new MNCs (and also loans from the fund-bank) to India was accompanied by an ideology that augments a process where 'the distance between expert cultures and the broader public grows greater. What accrues to a culture by virtue of specialized work and reflection does not come as a matter of course into the possession of everyday practice' (Habermas 1987: 326).

The role of experts is in turn accompanied by other technocratic processes such as, for instance, the centrality of technology in potentially solving not only economic issues of growth and productivity but also social/political issues involving questions of access to resources, and social hierarchies of caste and gender. In fact, before governance, as a set of institutional and ideological changes was introduced in India, it was preceded by a phase of rapid 'modernization' that attempted to make a 'tryst with the twenty first century', to put it in the language of the then Prime Minister Rajiv Gandhi. During the Rajiv Gandhi term (1984–89), he announced 'six technological missions', which included use of satellites for resolving the problem of drinking water, importing technology to rapidly increase production of edible oil to overcome foreign exchange deficit, telecom revolution to inter-connect the market by connecting every village, 'operation blackboard' to provide infrastructure to all primary schools in villages to resolve the problem of illiteracy, 'white revolution' with advanced dairy technology to double the production of milk for domestic as well as for the purposes of export and an immunization programme to eradicate polio. (Chandra 2000)[40] These technological missions under Sam Pitroda as the 'expert' scientific advisor to the central government, were sought not only to solve economic problems of growth, and deficit, among others but also as a means to resolve caste conflicts, gender discrimination, and regional disparities.[41] This process seems to have been revived with the constitution of Knowledge Commission recently, and it is worth noting that it has brought back Sam Pitroda into the public life as the Chairman of the Commission.[42] The technocratic state can then lay a claim to legitimately enter a whole range of social and institutional sites, since the problems generated by the growing technocracy—for instance, new working conditions that were introduced after global outsourcing was made possible due to new technological innovations in communication—can be resolved only by other and better technocratic measures. These could include, for instance, the new psycho-medical techniques, widely recommended for those working with the new BPOs, which could make them efficient without a need to change the working conditions that included long hours, night shifts, and less time for leisure; or it could be an offer to freely perform hysterectomies that can solve the problem of 'unwanted' pregnancy without a guarantee against growing sexual assaults on women.[43]

The 'developmental' activities/practices of the state, and their impact on civil society, were then well ensconced within this logic of governance. The practices of governance initiated, along with putting in place a 'technocratic state', a corresponding process of 'NGO-ization' as a mark of the spirit of voluntary action in civil society. The necessary correspondence between a technocratic state and NGOs in civil society comes into play both due to the underlying assumption that NGOs are apolitical, and can be more easily subsumed under the technocratic notions of efficiency, and also in celebration of the value and spirit of voluntary action. The process of NGO-ization was introduced, alongside or as part of the new governance practices, through new programmes such as the Self-Help Groups (SHGs) also known as the DWACRA groups under the aegis of the state government programme called the Development of Women and Children in Rural Area in Andhra Pradesh. SHGs were essentially envisaged to work as a 'safety net' for the distressed women in the villages. There were about 465,000 SHGs spread across various districts of Andhra Pradesh, covering nearly 6.17 million poor women. Andhra Pradesh alone had about nearly half of the SHGs organized in the country, with at least one SHG in most villages and with about 15–20 groups in about 75 per cent of the villages (Department of Rural Development 1999). Further, the most significant associated microcredit programme, implemented through the SHGs, was based on the premise of reduced transaction costs (read efficiency) and 'obviating the need to pledge physical collateral', due to the 'innovative' organizational structure based on the principles of joint liability, peer monitoring, and peer pressure (read social capital in civil society).[44] In other words, it was based on the assumption of bringing efficiency in bringing together the ethics of individual responsibility and community participation. Other 'developmental' activities executed through the newly formed village cooperatives and *mandal* federations (under the aegis of Co-operative Societies Act 1955) included insurance services, and encouraging income-generating schemes such as the dairy and poultry projects.

However, as a result of the philosophy—of efficiency and individual and voluntary responsibility—and the context—market reforms—in which such initiatives were introduced, what has been widely observed is that the experiment of bringing about 'development' through SHGs and the microcredit programme failed to adequately ameliorate the economic position of the social groups, and instead increased the social stress in entailing the growing individualization of the problems that were earlier perceived at the level of the collective and negotiated at the level of the political—through the lens of caste, class and gender. These new initiatives far from tapping on the collective or communitarian resources, and expansion of 'social capital', microcredit programmes have had 'exclusionary pressures' on those members who were defaulters, having a 'detrimental effect on peer sympathy' on those even making late payment in repaying the credit amount (Kalpana 2005).[45] Similarly, such projects as the poultry or the new cash crops, as Sangeeta Kamat notes, in her study of the 'developmental' activities of the state for the adivasis, demanded imparting technical knowledge and skills such as amount of feed, importance of vaccines and other injectibles to increase the production, or the use of new and expensive variant of fertilizers and pesticides, in the process these activities 'individualize' the economic and concomitant social problems. Further, such measures, be it the new step to encourage insurance services or the state initiated health services, taken up to abate the adverse consequences of the social and economic distress, also reinforced the process of individualization. For instance, the health projects, taking recourse to the discourse of 'target groups' entailed an exclusive focus on the body, 'rather than on the multiple relations of power that create ill-health', such as the work conditions, low wages, deforestation of land, absence of good medical facilities, including the problem of pollution in new industrial towns (Kamat 2002).[46]

Thus, the solutions were sought increasingly at the level of individuals, or individual families, and the responsibility was increasingly pushed unto the individuals themselves, in the name of celebrating the new voluntary spirit. Since such programmes were 'managed' and operated through the NGOs, that were purportedly apolitical, they were sought to be perceived as outside the strict scope of the state. In the process, this matrix of practices, drew the fault lines between what were political and apolitical activities on the one hand, and generating ideological consensus on how the new set of policies and institutions were in the interests of all the classes and social groups in the civil society, since they 'collectively' participated in the decision-making process and were also the beneficiaries, on the other.[47] Undermining the focus on power relations was made possible with the shift of the emphasis to individual self-improvement, and 'entrepreneurial citizenship' as the new 'political' expression that ostensibly contributed to the success of the various 'developmental' schemes, on the basis of 'values of instrumentality and economic rationality'. The new ethics of individualization in fact directly competed and undermined the political space necessary for the collective struggles—initiating a process of de-politicization (Kamat 2002: 157).[48] The enlarging 'anti-politics machine' and the conjoined processes of individualization were all along made possible within the contours of the civil society, where the precept of individual responsibility for voluntary activity and associations seamlessly merged with the imperatives of the 'developmental' activities of the state and the competitive ethic of the market. In such contexts, 'civil society then becomes a code name for people assuming responsibility for their own lives' (Phillips 2002: 81).

Thus, the processes of governance introduced a new 'technocratic' state, new set of institutions that were insular from popular democratic pressures, new type of 'developmental' schemes linked to the market, increasing role of 'experts' and reliance on modern technology, NGO-ization of civil society through the introduction of new programmes such as the SHGs and microcredit, and the conversion of the citizen into predominantly a consumer dependent on 'services delivered by a plethora of agencies'. All these processes individually and cumulatively reinforced—marking a *logic of circularity*—de-politicization—as in undermining structured power relations and collective expressions—and individualization—making individual primarily responsible in the name of voluntary spirit. De-politicization and individualization, as feminists have pointed out, were also then precisely the implications of legal enactments of the state, especially when introduced not in consonance with social and economic changes but made in lieu of them.

The point being made here is that the impact of legal changes needs to be grasped through the context they were being introduced in. Legal enactments by themselves—even if they are 'progressive'—are not necessarily empowering. Thus, in a context where the state was withdrawing and converting into a technocratic edifice, civil society was being emptied of the language of citizenship and replaced with or read in consonance with that of the identity of consumers, whose demands were met through 'free' market and the voluntary spirit championed by the NGOs, the scope of legal enactments gets constrained, and reinforces the context in which they were being introduced. While the state introduces new laws as a counter or in the name of abating the adverse social conditions, for instance growing distress due to increasing domestic violence—the other institutional, conceptual, economic and social changes being introduced convert the scope of the legislation to suit—*points of intersection*—the logic and spirit of the context. Thus, a law against domestic violence instead of empowering women, and giving them palpable relief against violence, reinforces the logic of individual responsibility, and conversion of a political issue into a technical one, in 'resolving' issues of violence in family. The law—and the twin processes of de-politicization and individualization that were part of a range of practices introduced through reforms in governance, as we traced—in a sense frames women, and not domestic violence.

The history of struggle against domestic violence in India was a long and a contrived one. To put it briefly, it started with the campaigns against 'dowry deaths' in 1980s, only to realize that foregrounding a 'singular' cause for violence at home was actually shrouding the various other reasons and forms in which it occurred. Women's movement realized that the singularity was as much due to the imperatives of mobilization, as it was about speaking a language that is legible to law in demanding effective legal provisions and their implementation. Section 304B recognized violence and death in relation to dowry, while Section 498A was the first law to recognize domestic violence. The focus then shifted from dowry to violence in family, in all its forms including physical, sexual and mental. It also expanded the scope of remedies necessary, including the inter-relation with economic independence, access to the public domain, and the severe limitations of criminal law. It was some of these new ideas that were incorporated in the new law against domestic violence, unanimously passed on 24 August 2005 by the parliament. The new law recognized the rights of the second wife, it broadened the notion of violence even to include psychological and economic, right of women to live in their marital homes, provision of ad interim protection orders, creation of official division known as protection officers, specially trained to deal with cases of domestic violence, and provision for positive entitlements—maintenance, protection from future violence, and a right to custody over children (Suneetha 2005: 4102). However, the question remains, in spite of these 'progressive' changes in the provisions, what was the concrete impact of a legal enactment in arresting domestic violence, especially introduced in the kind of context—through reforms in governance—that we traced?

Women, in the course of the movement, in opposing domestic violence were 'seeking responsible husbands, a role in decision-making, self-respect and a dignified family life, which in itself often contributes to the violence they experience' (Suneetha 2005). They articulated some of these concerns through their own self-chosen means in the course of the anti-liquor movement, going beyond the 'victim-subject' image as well as pressing for other means that can potentially transform the masculine public realm, such as public shaming, without necessarily converting it into an open confrontation that needs a termination of the relations or abandoning the institution of family. In other words, they were looking for the intervention of the public, by disbanding the private, but not abandoning it. It was in the interstices of these spaces that they found both the possibility of continuing the relations and achieving freedom and dignity within them. It was with this end in mind, that women have always expressed a desire to live in the marital home; negotiate outside of law through caste and community networks, attempted to instrumentalize state institutions in order to turn them over to allow themselves new spaces; continued her 'bonds of conjugal love', and demands of affection, recognition and attention even as she experienced authority, abuse and violence; they recognized that family crushes rights along with protecting them when the distant and opaque structures of state and law were either indifferent or discriminatory, natal families have played a significant role in both subjugating women as well as in supporting them if they decided to take to legal recourse. Women in political movements realized that 'there is no single thread, when snapped, unravels the whole of state or the masculine domain', creating a need to draw backward and forward linkages and 'non-reductively capture their relation' (Brown 1995: 177). The question really was: will law allow for such transgressions?

It was therefore found by the feminist activists who studied the impact of the Act against domestic violence in arresting domestic violence and providing relief that women who approached state institutions to get relief under the provisions of the Act were invariably inconsistent in their approach, reflected in the high rate of withdrawal of cases filed against domestic violence, often raising the bogey of 'misuse' of legal provisions and thereby further confirming the need, in accordance with public morality, to socially and culturally control her. The difficulties that law creates could be substantive, procedural and discursive in nature. The problems of translating women's complaints, and experience into an institutional framework, involve ironing out of the 'unruly', and dithering self and replace it with a neat legal subjectivity. The political process of recovering the agency of women was replaced with an experience that gets constructed through 'certain established procedures, techniques and conventions'. It requires a projection of an 'abject victim-woman' who is in need of either protection or regulation for law to acknowledge the situation she has found herself in and to take cognizance of the offence (Suneetha 2006: 4359). The language of rights is not merely about empowering, but, as feminists have argued, it converts women into 'subjects of the state', silencing them due to their inability to translate their experience into legal categories/language, and inability to work in accordance with the demands of the competitive ethic innate to the language of rights. This silencing is what leads to increasing state control, construed as further justification for more (hyper-) legislation, and eventually individualizes women's problems leading to the collapse of the collective will and thereby reinforces the process of de-politicization. Law, in its own way, further reinforces the twin processes of individualization and de-politicization, through converting domestic violence into a technical issue caught up in institutional procedures and to be taken resort to by individual 'victims', and by framing women in flattened legal subjectivity that disallows transgressions necessary to account for the complex nature of the demands they were making.

Further, law mostly offers only simplified and standardized solutions such as levying penalty, rather than incorporate the familial and social conditions that women find themselves in requiring redressal and civil remedies that go beyond handing out fixed punishments. This process of creating legibility, uniformity and concomitant simplification—one-size-fits-all[49]—in fact, is the way power operates both within law and state, and it has very little to do with this or that state, or with good or bad laws. As James Scott observes:

> Suddenly, processes as disparate as the creation of permanent last names, standardization of weights and measures, the establishment of cadastral surveys and population registers, the invention of freehold tenure, the standardization of language and legal discourse, the design of cities, and the organization of transportation seemed comprehensible as attempts at legibility and simplification. In each case, officials took exceptionally complex, illegible, and local social practices... and created a standard grid whereby it could be centrally recorded and monitored. (Scott 1998: 2)

It is these underlying processes of simplification and standardization that act in blocking the effectiveness of state initiated changes. Even when state created new institutions such as family courts, women's police stations, counselling centres to promote non-legal solutions and reorder health care systems to address domestic violence, they remain crippled in taking into account the multiplicity of the needs or in countering unexpected consequences; as again James Scott remarks in the context of the 'developmental' activities with regard to planning: 'no one could specify, let alone calculate, the second—or third-order consequences or their interaction effects... the magnitude of their initial intervention was so great that many of their mis-steps could not be righted' (Scott 1998: 344).

Thus, legal interventions (such as against domestic violence) invoking public morality, governance reforms and its accompanying institutional changes and the 'developmental' activities through the NGOs were all various practices through which politics—as contestation of power—got undermined and sought to be replaced with these practices that were essentially enclosed systems that ran on their own set of terms and pre-given logic internal to them.[50] In the process, all such practices individually, and in interaction with each other, reinforced the processes of *individualization, de-politicization, simplification and standardization* of political issues. The operations of a civil society then work as a site for these practices to interact—*points of interaction*—and provide a formidable basis for each other. While public morality forms the basis for law, law becomes the mode of dispensing with and dispersing 'developmental' activities. Civil society, becomes a product of and a site for, multiple ensconced logics to interact, and produce distinct 'interaction effects'. The spaces available within civil society carry with them the traits and marks of these 'interaction effects'—where such spaces as they open up the possibility of intervention by the agents, they also congeal and turn into 'frozen categories'.

Civil society therefore works as a site where law might look like an effective tool to counter discrimination but in translating issues into the institutional, procedural and conceptual categories, it de-politicizes and individualizes the problems. The legal language of rights in civil society, as they promise to empower they also 'converge insidiously with the discourse of disciplinarity to produce a spectacularly potent mode of juridical-disciplinary domination' (Brown 1995: 137); leading to on the one hand expansive state control on all arenas of social life, and on the other offering a 'false concreteness' to legislation/legality that allows the dominant to appropriate them while denying 'empowerment' to the vulnerable at the other end through the very language of voluntary spirit—even agency—that can 'turn back upon the individuals all responsibility for her failures'. Women's movement had to therefore have a double-edged task of working through the spaces but going beyond the scope they allow within the confined realms of civil society. Feminist politics has parallels with those moments in the Dalit and the HRM where they were attempting similar reworking. Feminist politics then moved from needs to rights to get 'legitimate' recognition to various forms of discrimination and moved from rights to needs to avoid reification of their identities, and to not enter the public on the masculine terms that it operated. They might fight for legal enactments against dowry or domestic violence but relied on political movements to take a more comprehensive view of violence, drawing continuity between law and politics.[51] They foregrounded experience to recover the agency of the victims but looked for new subjectivity to go beyond its entrapments or reification within the legal categories of civil society. In such a search it was no longer just about bringing into relief 'women's issues' but, as the Dalit movement during its sub-caste phase emphasized on an 'all affected' principle, similarly women's movement during the anti-liquor struggle in questioning the domination and suffering in the private was effectively and comprehensively recasting the very terms of the public that was grounded in 'trucking and bartering'; instead was experimenting with the possibilities of a post-civil society discourse around shared or collective circumstances, and interdependence.[52] As Mackinnon puts it,

> Not only to be allowed to play with the boys but to question why the point and ethic of sports is competition. Not just to be taken seriously, but to ask why the definition of merit is membership in an elite. Not only to survive, with dignity and sexuality intact but to be able to measure achievement in other than dollars and to inhabit our bodies and express our sexuality in ways that are not scripted out of scrape of stereotype. (Mackinnon 1987: 28)

Post-civil society discourse posits on raising questions of this nature that expand the scope of the political, beyond the limits imposed by the structures of the civil society.

Politics of post-civil society, as we have argued with reference to various protest movements such as the HRM, Dalit, Naxalite and here the feminist politics, involved interlocking of contradictory positions, and pursuing a 'strategy of doubleness' so that the '…local and the global, the contingent and the systemic, practice and institution… enter into the dialectic of struggle' (Sunder Rajan 2003: 146). Feminist politics in shifting and sifting through the various moments has attempted to foreground civil society as a site where the place of legality and legislation cannot be looked upon as a stand-alone tool to grasp its affectivity or as bifurcated from other practices being introduced in civil society. Instead law emerges in its myriad interconnections—'interaction effects'—with 'developmental' activities of the state, public morality and economic reforms in the market that produce effects that are often contrary to what is intended or promised. The choice therefore was not to give up on law but to take its effects beyond those that civil society as a site of *intersection* constrains. This was possible in arriving at various combinatory postures where resorting to law and its standardization had to be juxtaposed vis-à-vis the collective struggles—aiming for fluidity—that were internally sensitive to differentiations of caste, class and region—against massification—which was possible through new organizational experiments—leaderless movements—that recombined the cultural issues with that of economic and political dimensions by expanding the social base and combining demands; so as to avoid the language of agency as voluntary activity to turn against itself and manufacture a new consensus for de-politicization and individualization of social/political conflicts. This was a complex route that assumed the 'dialectic of struggle' between institutions, practices and processes where there were no given frames but involved an effort when available categories/practices reach a dead end, to find new alleys to walk past. These passages were intended to create concrete and real transformative effects, and not merely a mirage—'false concreteness'.

As we have hopefully demonstrated, what was at the core of the political practice of contemporary movements was their 'strategy of doubleness' or 'dialectic of struggle' as an antidote to the false multiplicity of practices that civil society harbours, which contrary to creating free spaces in working together or in working as 'checks and balances', in fact, intersect and converge to congeal 'democratic space'. The expansion of 'democratic space' has to be sought within the interstices of these very practices—in working 'in-against-and-beyond' them. Any attempt at identifying processes outside of such a dialectic in creating a 'constitutive outside' by drawing a binary between the practices of civil society as against practices considered outside of civil society—for instance between civil versus the political, or legal versus illegal/paralegal—finally only reinforces the logic of the civil society, arresting transformation and transgressions, and reifying it through its *logic of circularity*. One such formulation that is potentially radical, and intends to go beyond civil society, but circumscribes itself into the micro-spaces created by the civil society without being attentive to the possible ways in which they can congeal/converge is the notion of 'political society', as formulated by Partha Chatterjee. In drawing the contrast between the approach of the political movements in their *moment of dialectic* from that of an approach of the notion of political society that essentially articulates through *moment of binaries* between the practices that are in and those considered out of civil society, there is only or merely a promise—or a provocation—of moving beyond. An elaborate discussion of this notion, in the next chapter, will possibly allow us to appreciate the point that the precondition for a politics of post-civil society is the dialectic itself found in its combinatory postures, rather than dispensing with it.

Notes

1. This division between inward-looking structure and waywardness of the everyday details is akin to the division between classical art, such as classical music or art cinema and the popular 'Bollywood' music or cinema. Scholars have drawn attention to the way these two forms take a different place in the imagination of the nation. While the classical is patronized by the State, the popular is disciplined and taxed. (Prasad 2007). It is interesting to further observe that the idea of aesthetics in the Classical is self-referential and insulated from the outside, and therefore 'sacred' and against easy or 'cheap' commercialization and has closer proximity with the methods of the developmental state; while the popular depends on the changing tastes and demands of the majority, and therefore more accessible but for this very reason also closer to the vagaries of commercialization and comes under the scrutiny of the state. Post-colonial scholars have only made a case for the first part of the distinction between high and low culture but very rarely reflected on the uncomfortable convergence with the market, which has often been central to scholars of Critical Theory (Fraser 2009).

2. We partially dealt with the ramifications of an overdeveloped developmental state in the second chapter, wherein not only was society held together through the centrality of the state but also the idea of democracy was truncated into a statist project and the democratic principles, practices and institutions that could arguably flourish in the interface between the state and society remained mostly symbolic and discursive in nature without ever translating into effective political practices. The principles of intra-party elections, federalism, among others remained untested under Nehru since the distinction between party and Government always remained fuzzy (see Brass 2001). In fact it was this legacy that later on regional parties at various points of time attempted to replicate in their tryst with democracy (read electoral politics) including parties as different as the CPI (M) in West Bengal and the Telugu Desam Party in Andhra Pradesh.

3. Uday Mehta, in his work *Liberalism and Empire,* articulates the mode in which liberalism promises universality and yet excludes various sections of the society in practice, including the populations in the colonies (see Mehta 1999). As Kapur puts it, 'Mill depicted India as chaotic, unfathomable and inscrutable, which made the Indian different. India was distant and removed in civilizational terms, India was infantile and backward and Mill argued that a society so different from the ruling power should not be entitled to liberty' (Kapur 2005: 24). It is the insertion of law that makes this claim to universality and exclusion possible.

4. For instance, it was because of the IT revolution, spearheaded by the new professional class that *Wired* ranked Bangalore at a high eleventh among 46 global technology hubs based on various parameters. However, some scholars such as M. S. S. Pandian believe that IT talk is more than the real expansion of IT in terms of its contribution to the growth rate and generation of employment (personal communication).

5. It is interesting to observe how legal reforms came in lieu of popular mobilization, which was also the case with the HRM in early Civil-Liberties phase working with state–civil society complementarity.

6. Veeresalingam was also instrumental in starting a literary journal called *Vivekavardhini* in 1874. Later in 1883 he started a monthly magazine meant for popular reading called *Sat Hita Bodhi.*

7. In Lata Mani's description this was a foundational moment in the history of women's politics.

8. Gurajada Appa Rao's play *Kanyasulkam* was very popular and was staged in many parts of Coastal Andhra.

9. Once the movement was called off, women were asked to go back to their homes, unaware of the fact that a majority of the women had joined the movement to escape this very 'home'. 'It was this lack of awareness of what it meant for them to go back and complacency of the assumption that the home was their place after all, that really hurt the women' (Stree Shakti Sanghatana 1989: 272). They all went back to the private world to bear the burden of their family. Some of them begged to feed their children, some carried liquor and worked as wage labourers and some (as a husband put it) were simply 'eating and sleeping'. They earned no means through their participation in the struggle to redefine their lives or give a new meaning to it even after the struggle. This clearly reflected how marginal they were to the politics of the struggle and how distant the struggle was, in this sense, from them. The fact that, for instance, women did not get land rights in the land redistribution programmes reflected the unchanged status of women.

10. In fact the violence by the armed movements is continued to be referred to as 'private violence' as against state violence. It is only recently that political movements have began to refer to it as 'political violence', in the sense of violence that is used to bring about political transformation. It is perhaps important to comprehend, in this context, that violence is resorted to when the agency that is granted by power, as in law, is insufficient to accomplish the political goals, such as land reforms that aim at significant structural or systemic change. Violence and power are therefore opposed though they are allied through the state (Arendt 1970).

> Violence manifests itself in any relationship between individuals, groups, or societies in which one denies the agency of the others by seeking to define for them actions they must perform. Power, in contrast, appears in any relationship… in which an individual does not have his action determined for him. (Bevir 1999: 73)

11. Internal regulation involves following a strict hierarchy in the organizational structure, as well as taking resort to a strong disciplinarian language, in order to present the movement as a very cohesive political formation. Women, as we will discuss in the following pages, often complained of being either subject to disciplining or issues raised by them reduced to moral factors. There is undoubtedly a link between disciplining, and the role of law and morality in bringing about and influencing the nature of closure that this interlocking entails.

12. Though it has been a concern as to whether 'immorality of a kind of behaviour can ever, by itself, be sufficient justification for making that kind of behaviour illegal' (Wasserstrom 1971: 1), legal philosophers have often argued that there are 'some logical connections between the concept of law (and its cognate concepts) and the concept of morality (and its cognate concepts)' (Ibid.).

13. The resorting to and justification of using violent means was as much about politics as about gaining a moral ground for the politics on the basis of the immense sacrifice it demands, which in turn settles the political authenticity or correctness of the choices and decisions made. Some of these aspects were dealt with in the chapter on the HRM, where the HRM itself took to a moral language in order to demand autonomy from the subordinate status it was reduced to vis-à-vis the Maoist politics.

14. The difference here could have a parallel with the distinction between discrimination and untouchability. While women were like the untouchables in the public, other political movements only felt discriminated and therefore as part of their political repertoire

working through the dominant public sphere was relatively a more plausible alternative. This parallel in the modes of untouchability against Dalits and women was noticed and commented upon by Ambedkar in many of his writings.

15. Hirschmann, however, in her reply to Pateman, reiterates: 'Women's subjugation has endured precisely because of theorists' refusal to incorporate the aspects of life typified in women's experience'. The point however is not to not take women's experience into account but how much of it can be taken as given for the purposes of transformative politics and negotiating, what we are identifying here as, transformative dilemmas. There are parallels here with the way Gandhi mobilized women during the national movement around a similar strategy of taking the social position of women as given, which I have dealt with at some length in another article (see Gudavarthy 2008).

16. It, perhaps, wouldn't be inappropriate to point out that women's mobilization against rising prices of domestic items, such as kerosene, representing them as 'women's issues' as if rising prices exclusively or even primarily concerned only women. This only further reinforced women's status as 'home makers'. They used rolling pins, *thalis,* and empty tins of ghee (clarified butter) as symbols of the anti-price rise agitation.

17. Withdrawal from street politics entailed focus on both important feminist leaders, and taking up issues related to women at much smaller levels by the NGOs. Ironically, it was the same process of individuation that the women's movement grew anxious about in course of resorting to struggles for legal reforms and using law as a means of empowerment.

18. This resort to coherence again is comparable to the way political movements, such as the civil rights movement during its democratic rights phase, attempted to build a coherent civil society, ignoring and undermining diversity, to struggle against the state. While in that case it was an attempt to build a coherent space 'outside' the state, here it was an attempt to build coherence through state based legal structures.

19. We have discussed this with regard to the period of identity politics in the Dalit movement, in the previous chapter.

20. Chalam was born on 18 May 1894 into a chaste Brahmin family with all strings attached to such an upbringing. He wrote about nine novels, 18 short stories and 14 major plays. Four books, which were commentaries on various social issues concerning women, apart from a treatise on women called *Stree* (*Woman*), and his autobiography, which reflected on the centrality of fear and regulation in the way everyday lives in general were structured and exemplified themselves in their most brazen form with regard to the various insidious and invisible forms in which women were controlled.

21. It is instructive here to recollect the parallels that Ambedkar drew in his celebrated essay 'The Annihilation of Caste' between the status of women and Dalits. According to him these were the only groups that suffered from untouchability. The only difference being Dalits suffered it routinely and women during their menstrual cycles, since they were considered polluted during that period. I made this point earlier, in a different context, see note 14.

22. Many Dalit writers, much later in fact, offered the same logic of questioning the dominant ethos of the society from the standpoint of a common sense. Kancha Illiah, for instance, argued that his writings reflect the 'methodology' that he learnt from his 'illiterate' mother and the shepherds of his caste who grazed the sheep (refer Illiah 2009). We reflect on the complexities of problematizing 'common sense' in such terms in the following chapter in the context of the question of framing agency in the 'political society'.

23. 'Different people adopt different beliefs and perform different actions against the background of the same social structure, so there must be at least an undecided space in

front of these structures where individuals decide what beliefs to hold and what actions to perform' (Bevir 1999: 68). This takes us to the structure–agency debate, which had attracted so much of attention during the 1980s (see Callinicos 2004; Anderson 1980; Giddens 1984).

24. The volume was edited by Volga titled *Nurella Chalam* (Sweccha Prachurunalu, Hyderabad 1994). Feminists also staged a play titled *Vallu Aruguru* (*Those Six*), bringing together six women protagonists from the different novels of Chalam to reassess the issues that Chalam reflected upon in his times.

25. See Agnes 2009 for a detailed account of various cases and the rulings of Supreme Court that involves judgments that invariably favour men, as law ends up punishing women for 'adultery' and also for being a 'mistress', if she was not legally wedded. The courts argued 'it is inconsequential that the man was treating the woman as wife. It is the intention of the legislature which is relevant and not the attitude of the party' (Ibid.: 62).

26. Telugu film industry is the largest in the country after Hindi. From 1981 an average of over 160 films were produced annually of which anywhere between a third to half were dubbed into Telugu, mostly from other south Indian cinemas. Andhra Pradesh has the highest number of cinema halls in the country. The number of cinema halls increased from 1,904 in 1981 to 3,080 in 1995 but declined to 2,763 in 2000. In the 80s and 90s the industry expanded rapidly even overtaking Hindi in number of productions on occasion (Srinivas 1999: 1).

27. Similar controversies were to follow with the release of films such as *Fire* (1996), where the Shiv Sena made a similar demand of banning the movie since it was 'obscene' and 'alien' to Indian culture; later there was debate surrounding the depiction of sexual abuse in *Bandit Queen* (1996), which again raised the difficulty of treading a thin line between vulgarity and honest depiction of sexual exploitation.

> Obscenity was the rallying point for the opponents of *Alluda Majaka*. Their diverse concerns found a meeting point in an anti-obscenity campaign. I wish to argue that individuals with otherwise differing institutional and political affiliations came together to form a *public* and that obscenity functioned as a 'gatekeeping concept' in their intervention in the debate on popular cinema. (Srinivas 1999: 6)

'Gatekeeping concept' is an expression coined by Arjun Appadurai to explain how certain concepts reduce the complexity by extrapolating issues outside the context (see Appadurai 1986).

28. 'The establishment of mass circulated film magazines from the late 1970s and phenomenal growth in fans' associations of film stars are indications of an increased lower class audience of cinema in this period' (Srinivas 1999: 1). There was also the problem of complete absence of the idea of women in imagining the 'masses', and while family refers to the upper castes, 'masses' or community refers to the lower caste/ classes. This, however, is not to argue that there are no patriarchal practices within the lower castes or classes, as sometimes is the case made in recovering the agency to these sections by the post-colonial scholars. We would discus more about this issue of agency of the subaltern in the next chapter on 'political society'.

29. The issue of access to the public domain again has complex inflections. For instance, with regard to the debate on Beauty Pageants, this was read contrastingly as growing access and independence of women to make their own choice, as against they being subjected to the processes of comercialization and thereby getting objectified.

30. There was, however, a relatively long history behind the anti-liquor agitation by women. The Shramik Saghatana in Sahada, in 1972, organized groups of Bhil women to go to 'liquor dens and break liquor pots' and this agitation continued for over a year. Several years earlier in Uttarakhand women took up similar agitations (Kumar 1993).

31. This, however, is not to deny the support from the state-level mass fronts like the Jana Vignana Vedika and Andhra Pradesh Dalit MahaSabha. In Nellore district alone, where the mass movement had initially begun, the movement was initially organized by the Anti Arrack Coordination Committee comprising 36 voluntary organizations. In Chittoor district there were 250 voluntary organizations comprising mostly village committees (Reddy and Patnaik 1993).

32. Reacting to this statement by an important leader of the caste movement in Andhra Pradesh, a section of feminists had referred to it as an 'utter misrepresentation of women's movement'. They had argued that there are no differences between urban upper caste feminists and the women in rural areas (Kannabiran 1995: 163). On the contrary, in the 1970s feminists had already supported and encouraged the practice of publicly speaking about domestic violence. However, feminists were criticized as urban middle class women who practise and propagate ideas relevant only to their lives and not to the lives of the rural women. Anti arrack movement has cleared this misconception. It is now clear that rural women also think about family and domestic violence and their ideas are no different from that of the urban feminists (Ibid.: 173).

33. It was during this time that the ML parties too took mobilization of women around certain specific issues seriously, overcoming simplified moral positions. It was only in 1991 that an independent organization, Krantikari Adivasi Mahila Sanghatana (KAMS) was built with a separate manifesto and flag. Gradually the movement to mobilize women on issues concerning them began and village-level committees were constituted in over 500 villages (AILRC 1993: 21). Much later during 5–12 August 1994, the first special meeting of women comrades was organized and a perspective paper for party members was finalized by April 1995. The running theme was to combine class struggle with women's issues without counter posing them (COC (PWG) 1995: 13). KAMS addressed various problems, such as, malnutrition, infant mortality, delivery deaths, protracted illness, illiteracy, superstitions, human sacrifice, black magic, and hunting down of women as sorcerers, and right to property or inheritance for the *adivasi* women.

34. Apart from these actions, the PWG drew inspiration from the anti-liquor agitation and forged new 'mass organizations' for women, and it also reflected in the increased recruitment of women cadre into the armed wing. By 1995, in Praja Guerilla Army (PGA) women constituted not less than 25 per cent and in the entire party membership, they constituted about 12 per cent (Kendra Rajakeeya Nirmana Sameeksha 2001: 129). Further, on 25 and 26 January 1994, they organized a national conference on women, with various 'mass organizations'. Out of the interaction between various women's groups, excepting those accepting foreign funding; 10 'mass organizations' came together in September 1995 to form the Andhra Pradesh Chaitanya Mahila Samakhya (APCMS). This women's federation mobilized women mostly in the various towns and cities of Andhra Pradesh (Mahila Margam 2000: 2).

35. It was rather impishly also argued that not many foreign investors, especially from the infotech sector, would opt to invest in Hyderabad if prohibition was in place.

36. This was said, when he introduced tax cuts for the film industry, and withdrew subsidies. This has links with the rich farmers in coastal Andhra becoming film producers and later taking to active politics, and influencing the state policy, including the specific policy of drawing income from liquor as the nature of this class was very similar and closely

linked to the liquor lobby. It is often the social views of this class that were reflected in the kind of films made by them, including the film *Alluda Majaka* that we discussed in the previous section.

37. More recently, in April 2012, there was a bitter controversy over the involvement of the state Congress President Botsa Satyanarayana, in running a

> liquor syndicate' in the coastal Andhra districts of Andhra Pradesh, which charged the consumers more than the retail price. One of the news dailies reported that 'In case of Satyanarayana, the ACB [Anti-Corruption Bureau—my addition] claims to have found proof linking him to shops in Vizianagaram. The ACB found that in auctions conducted by the government, many successful bidders were either workers or cashiers in liquor shops. In many cases they held BPL ration cards. Questioning how they could raise ₹5 million to ₹10 million for the licenses, an official said the investigation linked most of these shops to members of Satyanarayana's family. (Janyala, *Indian Express*, 12 April 2012)

Along with this, there were reports that many of the ministers, MLAs and bureaucrats had stakes in running the syndicate.

38. This needs a more detailed analysis and collection of data, which is however beyond the scope of the present study. What could however be argued is the nexus between the civil and liquor contractors, film producers and hoteliers, and their new influence on the state. This is partially reflected in the new policy direction of the state with increasing tax-benefits to films, emphasis on tourism to aid the hotel industry, complete state support to sale of liquor, and expansion of construction works, by way of expansion of roads, building highways, and distribution of contracts for new irrigation projects. Along with these, we could add the new Mining mafia that has joined the list, as demonstrated in the influence of the 'Reddy brothers' wielded on the state government of Karnataka in 2009. It required the Supreme Court to intervene to halt some of the illegal mining the Reddy brothers were involved in (Rudoplhs 2008; Bhadhuri 2010; Bardhan 2009).

39. Partha Chatterjee, in fact, suggested that this process of drawing a wedge between planning based on experts and politics, began soon after the Independence, with the appointment of the Planning Commission and development based on targets to be achieved through the five-year plans. He argues that,

> on the one hand, planning had to be a way of avoiding the unnecessary rigours of an industrial transition in so far as it affected the masses resident in India's villages. On the other hand, planning was to become a positive instrument for resolving conflict in a large and heterogeneous subcontinent. (Chatterjee 1998b: 60–61)

40. Also see, generally, for the rise of a technocratic state in India, Kothari 2005.

41. It is very unlikely that such technological interventions and modernization can solve complex social issues such as caste. On the contrary they could further reinforce rigid social hierarchies, as P. Sainath's example of incidents, in coastal Andhra Pradesh, witnessing the 'glass struggle' where separate glasses were being used by the hotels and tea shops for caste-Hindus and the Dalits, prove. After a series of protests by Dalit organizations these shop-owners introduced plastic cups ostensibly replacing the 'two glass system'—representing 'modernization' and new technology—however caste prejudices remained only unquestioned and got hidden under an abstract modernity introduced by the spread of market and new technological advances. P. Sainath reported on this through a series of articles in *The Hindu* from 1999 onwards. See P. Sainath, 'The Borderlines of Caste' (7 April 1999, *The Hindu*).

42. Sam Pitroda is largely considered responsible for the telecommunication revolution in India and specifically, the ubiquitous, yellow-signed Public Call Offices (PCO) that quickly brought cheap and easy domestic and international public telephones all over the country. In 2004, soon after Manmohan Singh took over as the Prime Minister, he invited Pitroda to take over as the chairman of the Knowledge Commission. It was considered to be a high-level advisory body to the Prime Minister of India, set up to give policy recommendations for improving knowledge-related institutions and infrastructure in the country, primarily driven by a technocratic and a meritocratic logic. In July 2009, the Government of India invited Sam Pitroda to head an expert committee on ICT in Railways. In October 2009, Sam Pitroda was appointed as Advisor to the Prime Minister of India on Public Information Infrastructure and Innovations with the rank of Cabinet Minister (refer http://en.wikipedia.org/wiki/Sam_Pitroda, accessed on 11-05-2012). Later, in April 2012, he was also declared to be a front runner for the post of President of India—the first 'citizen'.

43. Governance increasingly becomes not just a set of measures that levitate but a lens to assess the social, political and economic dimensions, and a set of 'real' practices that generate their own dilemmas and offer solutions within the set parameters. The practices that belonged to the public domain are virtually transplanted into enclosed corridors, and an alternate reference point is created that can take simulated practices of engaging in 'democratic exercises'. In contrast to market's 'procedural rationality' and government's 'bounded (hierarchic) rationality', governance is primarily based on 'reflexive rationality'.

> The key to its success is continued commitment to dialogue to generate and exchange more information, reducing opportunism through locking governance partners into a range of interdependent decisions over a mixture of short, medium and long-term time horizons; and building on the interdependencies and risks associated with "asset specificity" by encouraging solidarity among those involved. It thereby supplements market exchange and government hierarchy with institutionalized negotiations to mobilize consensus and build mutual understanding... (In) this sense the rationality of governance is dialogic rather than monologic and this requires an investment of time to work effectively (Jessop 1998: 29–30).

44. Microcredit and microenterprise projects have been part of the Emergency Social Fund of the World Bank, designed as a relief package for those countries undergoing structural reform (Weber 2001).

45. There were reported microcredit related suicides that followed farmer's suicides in some of the villages in Andhra Pradesh (P. Sainath). (There were again insurance policies introduced to mitigate the effects of risk involved with cash crop production, as a solution for farmer's suicides). Sainath did not seem impressed with the increase in the credit growth for the farm sector. On the contrary, over 3,000 rural banks have downed their shutters in the last decade. Between 1991 and 2003, the coverage of banks in the rural areas has come down from 58 per cent to 48 per cent. Those responsible for creating a mammoth ₹1,100 billion non-performing assets for the government-owned banks are being given the benefit of macro credit policies. 'Poor farmers are trapped in the commercial cycle of micro credit,' he said (see http://www.southasianpost.com/portal2/ff808081145157fb0114515da8f20001_Farmers_becoming_domestic_help.do.html Accessed on 12-04-2012). Also see Sainath 2007, 2008.

46. We shall take up the problem of pollution and ensuing individualization that undermines struggles, by exploring the idea of 'political society' as formulated by Partha

Chatterjee, in the next chapter. Among other things, 'political society' also argues in favour of strengthening of community with 'family like' bonds on the basis of micronegotiations.

47. These tasks are achieved through a change in the terms of reference. As the Charitable Trusts Act of 1950 states:

> The achievement of a political purpose, in the sense of arousing in the people the desire and instilling into them an imperative need to demand changes in the structure of administration and the mechanism by which they are governed... is not a Charitable purpose as being one "for the advancement of any other objective of general public utility within Section 9(4) of the Act." (quoted from Kamat 2002: 56)

48. To put it in Kamat's own words, developmental activity undermines politics as the 'ongoing discourse and struggle over the organization of social relations is made invisible and illegitimate within developmental practices' (Kamat 2002: 155).

49. One-size-fits-all has been the critique of the approach of governance reforms and the uniform changes suggested by international financial institutions across the globe in the name of 'structural-adjustment' that referred primarily to privatization, opening of markets and reducing protectionism, irrespective of the nature of economy and level of development of these various economies in Africa, Asia and Latin America (Stiglitz 2002; also see Gudavarthy 2009).

50. Again to put in the words of Scott who is intrigued by the parallels, 'Here, I believe there is something to the classical anarchist claim- that the state, with its positive law and central institutions, undermines individuals' capacities for autonomous self-governance- that might apply to the planning grids of high modernism as well' (Scott 1998: 349).

51. Similarly, Rajeshwari Sunder Rajan notes that feminists working on issues related to sex workers demanded full access to their human rights through decriminalizing sex work, but at the same time opposed prostitution as a system as such.

52. As Mackinnon evocatively argues,

> ...I think it is because we have no idea what women as women would have to say. I am evoking for women a role that we have yet to make, in the name of a voice that unsilenced, might say something that has never been heard. (Mackinnon 1987: 77)

5

Collectives against Pollution and 'Political Society': Implications of Uncivil Development

Political Society, as developed by Partha Chatterjee, is a potentially radical concept that purportedly is the 'constitutive outside' of civil society. He argues that civil society is a sphere of modern civil institutions governed by rationality, legality and contractual relations of entry and exit, of individual rights and citizenship, sovereignty and property relations. These principles and institutions of modernity, in postcolonial societies such as India, not only represent very limited elite sections of the society but also enter into an irreconcilable conflict with democracy. He therefore argues, 'civil society will appear as the closed association of modern elite groups, sequestered from the wider popular life of the communities, walled up within enclaves of civic freedom and rational law' (Chatterjee 2004: 77). The rest, in fact the majority, of the subaltern sections of the society, are thereby recognized, since they cannot be accommodated in the elite dominated civil society, not as rights-bearing citizens but as 'populations':

> Unlike the concept of citizen which carries the ethical connotation of participation in the sovereignty of the state, the concept of population makes avail to government functionaries a set of rationally manipulable instruments for reaching a large section of the inhabitants of a country as targets of their "policies"—economic policy, administrative policy, law and even political mobilization. (Ibid.: 34)

After Foucault, he argues, the regime secures legitimacy not on the basis of popular or political participation in the decision-making process but by claiming to provide well-being through governmental programmes to 'target' groups. The 'normative climate' of our times is such that national governments and also global agencies recognize the 'moral claims' of such populations that continue to live outside the civil society. It is this outside that Partha Chatterjee refers to as the political society marked by the 'politics emerging out of the developmental policies of government'. Chatterjee offers, on the basis of a field study, the intriguing example of the squatters in Calcutta who have been living on land illegally occupied, drawing illegal water and power connections, perilously close to the railway tracks. Governments, through 'governmental technologies', take cognizance of the 'moral claims' of such populations, although strictly speaking these claims cannot be addressed as rights. This sphere, and the populations it constitutes, survive by necessarily violating the rules of the modern civil society and instead draw upon 'the imaginative power of a traditional structure of community'. For instance, civil societal emphasis on civility and trust in situations of marked inequality not only offers a false promise to the poor but robs them of their right to struggle and protest (Edwards 2009); in a society with unequal access to law, emphasizing legality as a baseline criterion of civil society only permits the government to forcibly clear the slums, pavements and tribals in the name of development (Elliot 2004; Menon 2004). Thus, 'the politics of democratization must therefore be carried out not in the classical transactions between state and civil society but in the much less well-defined, legally ambiguous, contextually and strategically demarcated terrain of political society' (Chatterjee 1998a).

The idea of 'political society' is potentially radical in identifying that 'populations' that constitute this alternative site are neither agents of the state nor the civil society. They are constitutively outside (read excluded) to the process of political participation. 'For the sake of survival and livelihood, they have to negotiate with both state and civil society or public sphere, domains often led and occupied by the middle-class bourgeois subjects and social elites' (Kuan-Hsing Chen 2003). Chatterjee argues that not only the state but also the civil society using the well-recognized 'civil' norms could potentially become part of the power block and dominate and regulate the subaltern classes, for preserving its own dominant interests. The associations in civil society then are not only not accessible but also strongly act against the interests of those who reside in the political society, and therefore the modes of protest of the political society are not consistent with the principles and institutional norms of (liberal) civil society.

It is, however, recognized that:

> the problem with "political society" understood in this way is that the activities here would not necessarily conform to our understanding of what is "progressive" or "emancipatory". They could be struggles of squatters on government land to claim residence rights, but they could as easily be the effort of a religious sect to preserve the corpse of their leader in the belief of its resurrection or the decision of a village Panchayat to kill a woman accused of adultery. (Menon 2004)

These struggles more often than not fail 'the tests of legality and constitutionality set by civil society' (Ibid.). In order to therefore understand the alternative mode of operations in the political society we need to think beyond the modernity–tradition dichotomy, and instead see 'the "non-modern" as not just a station on the route to western modernity but as a condition that may lead us to a very different one' (Nigam 2005: 259). Chatterjee, for instance, cites the example of the death of Balak Brahmachari, whose followers instead believed that he had merely gone into a *samadhi* and refused for the cremation of the body, until it caused a health hazard, and the government officials had to negotiate and finally use force. This is a classic conflict between the perceived 'lumpen cultures' of those buried in tradition as against the small section of 'culturally equipped' citizens with rational values, representing the high ground of modernity.

Political society, in terms of its political practice, refers to a series of such 'contextual negotiations' with the state, and the powerful elite in the civil society. Be it to get the benefits of the developmental programmes or to regain the space for their cultural practices. 'By political society I mean a domain of institutions and activities where several mediations are carried out' (Chatterjee 1997). The populations can take recourse to 'strategically' use the political parties and 'consciously' play into their vote-bank strategies to gain 'subsistence benefits'; or bank upon other non-party political formations including non-governmental organizations, political movements or simply engage in a series of everyday 'contextual negotiations' with the state, to put pressure to recognize their 'moral claims' for welfare. The underlying assumption here being that power relations, in postcolonial societies, have to be approached in terms of their micro-foundations—integral to the process of 'microphisization' of power relations—that get reflected in the construction and administration of subjects or populations. In negotiating with such power dynamics, the subaltern resort to the 'politics of the possible' or 'politics of everyday life', i.e., negotiate power in its everyday aspect. In the course of negotiating power in its everyday aspect—and not through grand utopias—political society points towards the ostensible possibility where 'the actual transactions over the everyday distribution of rights and entitlements lead over time to substantial redefinitions of property and law within the actually existing modern state' (Chatterjee 2004: 75). This approach of Chatterjee has parallels with James Scott's analysis of 'everyday forms of peasant resistance', wherein he argues that the basic 'premise is that "routine" resistance of this kind may cumulatively have an appreciable impact on class and authority relations in the countryside' (Scott 1986: 1). In other words, structured power relations are made sense of and transformed by the subaltern through 'routine' and everyday resistance, through forms that they choose and those that are necessarily 'outside' the recognized practices of civility and legality.

Political society in framing its political practices is, therefore, questioning the role of party programmes—by centralized political formations—and institutionalized strategies of transformation. The process of transformation has to recognize those forms that are not yet legitimately referred to as political, and do not fall within the normative purview of established 'political principles'. In a sense, political society as a realm of politics can be comprehended and appreciated only when subaltern action is not approached through a normative order that is external to their context or outside the way they understand and perceive—through their 'own' experience—any given context. Some of these arguments are drawn from contemporary forms of post-structural analysis of politics, where the 'post' in post-colonialism is the 'post' in post-structuralism.[1] For instance, Melucci argues that 'there is an increase in the number of groups capable of organizing themselves, representing their interests and extracting advantages from processes of political exchange' (Melucci 1989: 169). He cites the 'new social movements' as an example of how social and political transformation occurs, not through grand structural change or 'rupture', but through the proliferation of contingent 'contextual negotiations' entailing 'molecular change'. However, these negotiations result in 'actual expansion of freedoms', which, as Chatterjee argues, are not otherwise possible within the 'classical' realm of the civil society.

To sum up, political society is an 'autonomous domain' outside the modern institutional framework of civil society. It is constituted, not by citizens, but 'populations'; puts pressure on the state, not through rights, but 'moral claims'; works, not through bourgeois law and institutions, but paralegal means, and everyday 'contextual negotiations' with authorities; these negotiations are mediated through middlemen who could be individuals who belong to the urban middle class with the necessary cultural capital (knowledge of English and that of legal and institutional procedures), or political representatives from various political parties or through NGOS and even political movements. These negotiations help the subaltern to achieve subsistence benefits, and guarantee everyday survival outside formal procedures. However, such negotiations, over a period of time, can lead to effective and substantive change, including transforming the existent property relations. Political society, therefore, poses a challenge to both state and the elite-dominated civil society.

Are the discourse and the politics of political society then, in any meaningful and substantive way, part of the emerging politics of post-civil society, as enunciated by the contemporary political movements in

India? Or, ironically, in spite of locating political society as the 'constitutive outside', could there be a strong *convergence* with the practices of civil society and thereby its *logic of circularity*? This chapter is an attempt to delve into some of the substantive differences between the approach of contemporary political movements in India, as we have discussed in the previous chapters, and that of political society, on the basis of a field study in Kazipally, a pollution-affected village in Andhra Pradesh. This case study helps us to reframe some of the practices that are central to the notion of political society, including the role of middlemen, context for adopting 'survival strategies', the question of agency in the ostensible voluntarism of the subaltern and the modalities of negotiating power relations through binary oppositions that civil society constructs, among other issues.[2] The case of the collectives against pollution in Kazipally, helps us demonstrate how sustained demands for the closure of the polluting industries based on collective mobilization and action was met with uncivil state repression in nexus with mafia and the economic elites (industrialists) in the market. This in turn pushed the collectives to break up and they were displaced by fragmented interest-group demands and everyday negotiations (or in the language of political society, 'contextual negotiations'), carried out either at the level of smaller groups (formed around available social stratifications) or even the individual. Making it increasingly difficult over a period of time to sustain collective political action that could demand and gain structural changes (in this case closure of industries; revival of agriculture), that were necessary for 'expansion of freedoms'.

Political society, as part of its political repertoire, is projected as a domain constituted by a multiplicity of political strategies, including that of political movements. However, as we argue, on the basis of the case study, that the imperatives of collective action, by the political movements, cannot unproblematically coexist with contextually demarcated 'strategic politics'. Instead, the modalities of 'contextual negotiations' nudge out, over a period of time, organized political movements, since they gain the patronage and recognition of the state, market and elites in the civil society. It would therefore necessarily become '*ambiguous*', as Chatterjee himself observes, to demarcate the 'governing principles of the political society' and the alternative 'forms of institutionalization' it would attempt. While it needs to be undoubtedly acknowledged that uncivil development is making it increasingly difficult for the subalterns to wage organized protest—in the form of contemporary political movements that we discussed in the previous chapters—and in fact pushing them towards survival strategies, wouldn't it be for this very reason, imperative to search for the signposts of alternative modes of protest that could actually bring them out of this now what seems to be a never-ending struggle for survival? Political society in its bid to constitutively contrast it with civil society ends up as a seamless domain of qualitatively distinct political actions—of radical political movements, political parties and non-party political formations for strategic and contextual negotiations—that in practice cannot actually coexist and are bound to enter into a conflict to mutually dislocate each other. The state, the market and the civil society, selectively and carefully support this process of dislocation, in privileging negotiations that are essentially dependent on their patronage, over organized protest politics that seem to make more substantive demands beyond subsistence benefits.[3] It is, therefore, also imperative to question if the 'contextual negotiations' actually, as Chatterjee claims, lead to substantive 'expansion of freedoms'? Would the state, in nexus with the elite in civil society and market, allow for such an expansion?

While it is democratic to politically recognize the strategies for survival, substantive democratization, it seems, requires struggles that lie beyond both survival strategies in political society as well as mere formal benefits and rights available in the civil society. It is as a consequence of the antinomies of flattened notions of subaltern politics that there emerges a convergence between *formal rights* in civil society and *survival strategies* in political society, which essentially implies reproduction of structured power relations and thereby an entrapment within the constraints—*logic of circularity*—of civil society. The notion of survival strategy is instantiated within Chatterjee's idea of political society through the language of 'moral claims', and also in alluding to the 'capabilities approach'. Unlike Chatterjee who believes that the 'capabilities approach' results in 'expansion of freedoms', Anne Phillips argues that:

> Capabilities approach has at its heart a neo-liberal agenda, (and) focuses on minimum necessary requirements; it retreats from the profound challenges of the struggle for human equality, not just between men and women, but across social groups both within or across nations, ensuring humans minimum has taken over from worries about the overall income gap. (Phillips 2001: 16–17)[4]

This convergence—in terms of gaining only formal or subsistence benefits—of political society with civil society, on the one hand, and distance and difference with the approach of political movements that are attempting through "dialectic of struggle" as exemplified in their combinatory postures to move beyond and circumvent the *logic of circularity* as instantiated in civil society on the other, could be further conceptualized, based on the practices and ensuing *ambiguities* that can be identified with the notion of political society:[5]

First, political society, as a postcolonial approach, is constructed as a critique of modernity and practices that accompany it, and alternatively privileges what it identifies as the organic praxis of the subaltern, expressed in local processes and practices, signifying democracy/democratization within an 'autonomous domain'. It could be argued that the binary opposition between modernity and democracy fails to recognize that 'the spurious organicism of local places—not to mention notions of belonging and difference—has the effect of spiriting projects of social justice out of sight' (Kaiwar 2005: 3733). In necessarily privileging practices that are outside the realm of the modern, and undermining an explicit project of 'social justice' or democratization, the notion of political society, willy-nilly, 'always already' entails formal notions and conditions of 'empowerment', that *intersect* with those instantiated in the civil society. For instance, it is perfectly possible to celebrate difference—those identities and processes outside the modern—without necessarily questioning the difference in economic or class terms. This wedge between the cultural framing of politics and the dynamics 'internal' to political economy was what we had observed earlier in the context of the negotiations by various political movements (they had to contend with this 'separation' in civil society; for instance, the Dalit movement as identity politics made a renewed entry into civil society through the discourse of plurality and 'politics of difference' but in the process obscured social and economic issues) and was integral to the politics and discourse of civil society itself. It can therefore be argued that political society and civil society overlap in taking recourse to the language of 'separation' of economic, political and cultural dimensions or processes. The fact that this projected 'separation' is actually a moment of *convergence*—a modality for the operation of 'modern' power relations—mutually reinforcing and thereby replicating dominant power relations in the State, civil society and the market is undermined and glossed over, in the way the notion of political society is formulated.

Second, in his more recent extension of the idea of political society, Chatterjee argues that, it overlaps with the domain of the non-corporate capital that is not marked exclusively by the logic of profiteering that defines the purpose of corporate capital, which exists in the market and works through the civil society. The working of the non-corporate capital that is driven by 'providing livelihood needs', overlaps with the policies of State that provides 'welfare' and subsistence living to the populations, in order to reverse the effects of primitive accumulation. Drawing on concepts introduced by Kalyan Sanyal in his work on *Rethinking Capitalist Development*, such as 'de-capitalization' and 'reversal of the effects of primitive accumulation', Chatterjee argues that capitalism and its own mechanisms necessarily create an outside, finding expression in the 'informal sector' or the non-corporate capital that is not strictly governed by the principles of capital accumulation but more in terms of 'providing the livelihood needs'. Chatterjee argues that 'civil society is where corporate capital is hegemonic, whereas political society is the space of management of non-corporate capital' where 'given the logic of non-corporate capital…the function of these organizations (of the subaltern—my addition) is precisely to successfully operate within the rules of the market and of governmental regulations in order to ensure the livelihood needs of its members' (Chatterjee 2008: 58). Political society thus becomes a 'domain to manage non-corporate capital' emerging as 'another version of a negotiated social peace' (Nigam 2008: 62). Political society as a space, not for resistance, but for 'managing' social and political conflicts, and 'making it palatable for liberal tastes', replicates the strategy of civil society, which also curbs and manages protest and thereby social conflicts in underlining the notions of civility, legality, trust and social capital. In other words, while civil society emerges as a distinct 'social' domain and thereby plays an ideological—hegemony—role in managing political conflicts, political society too seems to 'manage' conflicts emerging in a residual realm of the non-corporate, and does not necessarily project ways and means of moving beyond the 'negotiated peace' but in fact as another version of such an equilibrium. Similarly, in believing that State only acts in the context of the non-corporate capital, and not in aiding and supporting the corporate capital, the concept of political society reifies the realms of market and civil society, 'as if' they were independent realms without being either linked to or dependent on the State. Therefore civil society and political society seem to overlap—converge—in terms of their ideological function.

Third, the idea of political society is purportedly opposed to the 'idea of civil society', in identifying and privileging the subaltern agency expressed through their organic—not spontaneous—political acts, as against 'abstract citizenship' in civil society that undermines the specificities of social groups and identities. However, the very model of retrieving agency to the subaltern is inextricably linked to 'the abstraction that generates an illusion of "authorship"…It removes the traces of belonging to a network-traces that always compromise the author's rights' (Certeau 1988: 44). The subaltern as 'an "author" in effect denies his real situation' or 'historical genesis' in order to create 'the fiction of a place of his own' (Ibid.).[6] The valorized ideas of autonomy and self-constituted subjectivity not only result in 'simple-minded voluntarism' but also effectively obscure the social hierarchies within 'communities' that represent and constitute an 'autonomous domain'. In the process, political society overlooks the intra-subaltern conflicts and the possibilities of fragmentation, and also hegemonization of the 'most vulnerable' among the subaltern, akin to the way citizenship in civil society obscures the specificity of social groups and conveniently assumes their 'tacit consent' to the social contract.[7]

Thus, while *abstract* notions of citizenship render participation as merely formal in civil society, equally *abstract* notions of community beyond the real limits of existing social hierarchies and hegemony render subaltern agency as valorized and self-enclosed in political society.

Finally, in articulating political society as the 'constitutive outside', Chatterjee reinforces a binary mode of analysis—such as legal/illegal—that is characteristic of a civil society; instead of transmuting, as political movements have attempted, the available civil society principles themselves into concrete conditions of protest and durable transformation.[8] For instance, the liberal principle of tolerance entails status quo, as Herbert Marcuse argued in his celebrated article 'Repressive Tolerance'. Marcuse argued that the principle of tolerance in equalizing diverse and contending claims, it also neutralizes counter-hegemonic narratives, which, in turn, reinforces existing dominant practices and classes that benefit from them (Marcuse 1965). However, tolerance also entails right to freedom of expression, which can be transmuted and re-signified beyond the constraints of 'repressive tolerance' that is implied within the limits of a civil society, so that we move towards 'a new order that is able to combine legality and dialogism and which may often take an extra-constitutional path, meaning dialogues beyond the prescribed conversations sanctioned by the constitution' (Samaddar 2007: 116).[9] Political society, however, reinforces the dichotomy and the prevalent *binary oppositions* in and of the civil society—legal/illegal, civil/uncivil, civil/political, modernity/democracy among others. In merely reinforcing and working through those practices kept out of the 'legitimate' domain of civility and legality, it takes the available dominant practices and their potential and implications as given on the one hand, and circumscribes the subaltern actions within the limits of the excluded practices, on the other. In taking the binary itself as given, political society necessarily remains de-historicized, contingent and restricts the agency and political action of the subaltern to the immediate and given conditions—living within the limits of the social relations 'they are born into'. It either valorizes everything that subaltern does as organic, and therefore authentic, or undermines the potential for resignification in dominant practices. For instance, in the binary opposition between civil/political, it would be ahistorical to ignore that practices and institutions recognized as civil today were themselves the result of political struggles in the past, and in privileging all acts of subaltern as political, it undermines the role of hegemony and the potential of the subaltern acts themselves to become hegemonic. Privileging (organic) experiential categories, as we had witnessed with Dalit politics as identity politics through their discourse of 'lived experience', does not necessarily entail dignifying or empowering the subaltern. In unproblematically privileging given experience, political society fails to understand that social justice itself is multilayered and that subaltern politics cannot be restricted, in the instance that Chatterjee suggests, to the limits imposed by governmentality (expressed in and as only interest-group politics) and cannot find its expression in its hyper-separation from collective action—the kind of 'separation' it, in fact, takes through the competitive language of rights in civil society. In other words, while it is necessary to *dignify the subaltern struggles* in all their forms, it is even more important to recognize their capacity to forge *struggles for dignity,* in order to move beyond the confinements of formal 'empowerment'—limited to the doles or claims for governmental care—imposed through the nexus between state, market and civil society.

It is these limitations that expose the substantive distance of the *politics of political society* from that of the *politics of political movements,* also marking its distance from the emerging *politics of post-civil society.* It is some of these overlaps with civil society, in terms of its implications and ensuing limitations that we shall focus and elaborate on the basis of a detailed field study.

Understanding New Industrialization: Capital-izing Un-civility

Kazipally is a village situated 35 kilometers towards the north-east of Hyderabad in the Ginnaram *mandal* of Medak district. Medak is one of the most backward districts of the state of Andhra Pradesh. The village has 506 households accounting for a total population of 3,000. The socio-economic background of the village is presented in Table 5.1:

Table 5.1: Occupational Statistics

S. No.	Category	No. of Households
1.	Small Cultivators	354
2.	Medium Cultivators	50
3.	Big Cultivators	10
4.	Rich Cultivators	6
5.	Landless Labourers	76
6.	Industrial Labourers	3
7.	Others	7
	Total	**506**

Source: Field study.

Table 5.2: Caste Statistics

S. No.	Caste	No. of Households
1.	Yadava	40
2.	Muthrasi	141
3.	Muslims	101
4.	Mangali	12
5.	Chakali	25
6.	Goud	10
7.	M. Kapu	5
8.	Madiga	172
	Total	**506**

Source: Field study by the author.

From the data in Table 5.2, it is evident that the amount of resources available to people who are victims of industrial pollution are very limited. Firstly, around 82 per cent of the total number of households is dependent on farming. Again, another 15 per cent of the households are engaged in agricultural labour for livelihoods. Taken together, around 97 per cent of the households are dependent on agriculture. The Green Peace report suggests that industrial pollution in this area has affected 2,000 acres of farmland besides contaminating well water to a depth level of 140 feet.[10] Pollution has displaced households from their traditional livelihoods and dispossessed people of their assets. These villagers do not have any alternative skills to be able to choose other employment avenues. As can be seen from the available evidence, local industries do not employ villagers. Thus, though the industries take subsidies from the government on the grounds that they would contribute towards the development of backward areas, in reality they do not provide the local population any employment opportunities or avenues of social mobility in terms of skill development. Some of the marginal and small farmers are also engaged in other activities for livelihood, and there is the possibility of generation of additional income for those engaged as washermen, or in occupations such as fisheries, vending of fruits grown on common lands, or rearing of livestock.

Industrialization in Kazipally had started during the post-Emergency period, when Indira Gandhi contested from the constituency of Medak in the 1980 general elections and won. This area was adopted as an Industrial Development Area (IDA). However, the rapid growth of industrialization in the town was witnessed only from 1989 onwards. Most of these industries, which started after 1989, operated on loan licensing and outsourcing by multinational and other large national corporations. Today there are about 50 industries in Kazipally and Gaddapothram. It has been recently found that of these 50 units, 35 have been operating without clearance certificates from the Central Pollution Control Board. The Commissionarate of Industries also does not have records about some of these industries.

The reason why multinational corporations, especially those from the USA, outsource their products is because it is estimated by Baumol and Oates that if the USA has to achieve zero discharge standards, it would cost the US economy US$2 billion. It was in 1989 that the Environmental Protection Agency (EPA) came into effect in the USA. The EPA had classified products, especially chemicals and metallic products, as Bio-Accumulant Toxins. Since these chemicals will not decompose, their discharge will lead to the accumulation of toxins in the environment. The term 'dirty goods', is also associated with this type of production. A 'dirty good' is defined as a good whose effluent treatment costs will exceed the value of the final product itself. Therefore, if the production of 'dirty goods' has to abide by the water, soil and air quality standards set by the law, it implicitly works out to be uneconomical. It is for this reason that the multinational corporations have chosen to produce these 'dirty goods' by loan licensing their products to 'Third World' producers. The national corporations on the other hand are outsourcing production of 'dirty goods' with the objective of securing ISO 2001 and other such quality certificates, acquiring which is a precondition for exporting their products to foreign markets. Such outsourced production is also undertaken by units in Kazipally and Gaddapotharam industrial areas. Among the multinational companies that have tie-ups with polluting industrial units, Shaw Wallace, the anti-AIDS vaccine being produced by the Bill Gates Foundation and Reddy Labs have been identified in our research. There could be many more such big players who could claim clean production for public consumption.

Interestingly, MODVAT, which was introduced in 1991, has provided a boost to small scale industries. Since MODVAT is a tax at the source, the small scale industries are benefitting as they are being given several subsidies on raw materials, excise tax and so on. Further, the small scale companies also recruit cheap labour. Therefore, MODVAT for them works out to be low. And this in turn implies that the big corporations get intermediaries or their outsourced products manufactured at lower prices than if these products were manufactured by these big corporations themselves. With Medak being a backward area, the incentive packages for industries here are very attractive. And though technically the region falls in Medak, it is at a distance of only 35 kilometers from the city, which assures access to infrastructure. This model of industrialization, referred to as the 'new industrialization', has been identified as generating high social costs both in terms of blatant violations of labour standards and environmental pollution (Vijay 1999; 2003). While the product market of the industries is non-local, the un-civility in the sense of violations of norms laid down by law is built into this model of industrialization. The intrinsic need for un-civil manufacturing practices propels a chain of un-civility seen in the lobbying with political circles, bribing of bureaucracy, nexus with the mafia and such other un-civil practices. Un-civility, in this sense, thus becomes indispensable and systemic.

Introducing 'Development': Pollution and Social Cost

The high pollution levels in the Kazipally tank are the outcome of dumping of industrial toxic effluents in it for the past 16 years. Several reports, including a technical report about the Kazi Cheruvu and the ground water by the environmental department of Jawaharlal Nehru Technological University (JNTU) in 1998, the monthly updates of quality of water in the tanks by the Andhra Pradesh Pollution Control Board (APPCB) and by the Committee constituted by the Andhra Pradesh High Court, chaired by Justice Gopal Rao, which submitted a Fact Finding Report in 2004, have all established irrefutable evidence about the alarming levels of damage done to these water bodies. As part of our research, we got water samples tested independently by Yagna Labs in 1997 and again by the Environmental Protection Training and Research Institute (EPTRI) in 2003 for comparing the quality of the water samples collected in similar locations. The results of these findings are given in Table 5.3:[11]

Table 5.3: Comparative Figures for 1997–2003 Water Sample Test Results

S. No.	Parameter	Normal Ranges	Sample 1		Sample 2		Sample 3		Sample 4	
			1997	2003	1997	2003	1997	2003	1997	2003
1.	pH	7–8.5	4.2	7.2	7.8	7.2	7.6	7.2	8.1	7.3
2.	Dissolved solid	500 mg/ltr	3900	2860	7600	2900	970	2865	7960	1860
3.	Chloride	200 mg/ltr	340	930	520	855	550	855	250	445
4.	Sulphates	200 mg/ltr	260	509	320	488	340	495	140	545
5.	Flouride	1.0 mg/ltr	1.8	.752	2.5	.759	2.3	.600	1.0	.666
6.	Magnesium	30 mg/ltr	300	347	300	346	300	272	180	347
7.	Calcium	75 mg/ltr	700	594	500	644	600	594	200	495

Source: Field study by the author 1997. Results based on tests conducted by Yagna Labs, Amberpet.

Field Work conducted by the author 2003. Results based on tests conducted by EPTRI Labs, Gachibowli.

The figures in Table 5.3 prove that not only are different chemicals present in way above the normal ranges in the water of Kazipally tank, but that for several indicators, the figures for 2003 show an increase in pollution levels over those observed in 1997. Although pollution levels have been controlled due to the long drawn battle by the people, this in no way absolves the regulating authorities, which continue to blatantly violate standards of pollution control by failing to control the presence of harmful chemicals beyond permissible limits in the water. In this way, the authorities are putting at risk the life, property and health of not only the local inhabitants but also of other life forms in the nature on which the community is dependent for its sustenance. The figures denoted in Table 5.3 therefore need to be assessed within this framework.

As a result of pollution, nearly 7,000 acres of land in 32 villages have been partially and completely destroyed (JNTU Report 1998). In addition, there have been several reports of loss of fish and of cattle, on which several rural communities depend for their livelihoods (field data, 1997–98, 2003–05). The health reports issued by Green Peace have made startling revelations about the health status of the inhabitants of the affected villages (please see Table 5.4).

Thus, we find that enormous damage has been done to the natural environment and huge social costs have been incurred by the local communities on account of industrial pollution.

This chapter focuses on collective action against pollution in an effort to explore how the idea of political society understood primarily

Table 5.4: Incidence of Disease in the Affected Villages

Disease/Organs Affected	Incidence of Occurence
Nervous System	3 times higher than the controlled group
Circulatory System	2 times higher than the controlled group
Respiratory System	3.81 times higher than the controlled group. 1 in 20 affected.
Digestive System	1.98 times higher than the controlled group
Blood and Blood-forming Organs	2.914 times higher than the controlled group. 1 in 35 persons are affected.
Endocrine, Nutritional and Metabolic Systems	1.84 times higher than the controlled group. 1 in 35 people are affected.
Neoplasms	11 times higher than the controlled groups
Skin and Subcutaneous Tissues	2.67 times higher than the controlled group
Congenital Malformations, Deformations and Chromosomal Abnormalities	3.93 times higher than the controlled group
Cancer	11 times higher than the controlled group

Source: GreenPeace, 2004.

as constituting various 'strategies' or 'contextual negotiations' with immediate interest-group politics for survival, becomes in practical terms unsustainable and also replicates the implications—reproducing entrenched power relations—that are civil-societal in nature. For this purpose, this study has analyzed three relevant social groups, that is, the farming community, youth and women, which are ideally suited for mobilization against the polluting industries, as all three of these groups have organized associations. This research study was also undertaken to examine what these associations were doing to tackle the problem of pollution, which affected the entire village community. The associations taken up for the study include the Kalushya Vyatireka Raitu Committee (KVRC) with a total membership of 40 farmers, the Shivaji Youth Association with a total membership of 50 members, and the DWCRA microcredit groups which together have about 100 women members. The study was conducted in two phases. An earlier study undertaken in 2003 had assessed and obtained responses from a sample of 40 farmers. A later survey done in 2005 was based on a sample of 30 respondents from all the three groups. Thus, this study is based on a total of 70 respondents. A structured questionnaire and informal interviews were used to collect primary data. As regards the collection of primary data, it was found that since the experience is a shared one among the respondents who belong to different homogeneous groups, there were repetitions in the narratives. This also leads to the conclusion that the responses of the sample can be taken to be the general view of the social groups represented by these associations.

Political Society: Interest-Group Politics or Collectives for Justice?

While studying the problem of pollution and its implications, we found that whenever people have raised structural questions through their collective political activity, they have faced uncivil means of repression from the coercive state apparatus like the police and also coercion from the organized mafia. This un-civility has weakened their political activity. The following is an account of the experience of Kazipally victims of industrial pollution when they raised such structural questions and tried to deal with the problem.

The conflict in the village centring around the issue of pollution of the village tank by industries assumed a collective form that raised structural demands. The demand made by the villagers for the shutting down of the polluting industries can be seen as a structural demand for several reasons. The villagers of Kazipally, as already pointed out, were predominantly dependent on agriculture and other traditional allied activities for their livelihood, before the pollution of their tank. The conflict was thus articulated as a conflict between farmers and the industry. Second, as has already been seen in the narrative on the nature of industrialization, these industrialists were outsiders in the regional sense of the term, as they predominantly belonged to the coastal Andhra and Rayalaseema regions of Andhra Pradesh. This regional dimension assumes special significance in the wake of rising aspirations for a separate Telangana statehood.[12]

Further, the regional dimension is of relevance in two other senses. Although the industrial policy outlines development of backward regions as one of the prime objectives of rural industrialization in the form of the policy for 'industrial development areas' and justifies the grant of subsidies and other such benefits, it has been found that the contribution of these industries towards development of these backward regions has been very limited. The local people were not given employment opportunities in these industries. Nor are the products manufactured by these industries meant for the local market.

It has also been found that the victims of pollution include several sections of the local population, including the landless, people rearing livestock, artisans and those employed in the traditional service sector, all of whom have suffered loss of income, livelihoods and assets, as also adverse impact on their health due to the setting up of these industries, which offer unfair competition to local crafts and small scale industry. They make huge profits, work through a nexus with individuals in power and exploit their capacity to manipulate the system for their vested interests. The resultant problem is thus not merely of pollution but has actually assumed the form of a conflict between specific social classes, and those marginalized, on one hand, pitched against the rich and the powerful, on the other. The demand by the local population for the permanent shutting down of polluting industries can thus be seen as an effort made by the farming community to deal with irresponsible industries; as also the spirited attempt of the local community as against the industrialists who are the outsiders; and it was also a demand of specific vulnerable social classes as against the rich and the powerful lobbies. In all these senses, the demand for a permanent shut down of the polluting industrial units becomes a structural demand.

The demand for permanently shutting down the polluted industries in Kazipally has, in fact, been raised on several occasions, starting way back in 1989. The villagers of Kazipally and several other affected villages, led by different organizations including the Forum Against Pollution, the

Jana Vigyana Vedika, among others, and the political representatives of these villages conducted rallies and *dharnas*.[13] However, the protestors were lathi-charged and their representatives arrested. Again in 1994, when the villagers initiated another campaign to oppose the industrialists, they were attacked by the mafia and despite putting up some resistance, they had to beat a retreat, with many of them even being forced to leave the villages, fearing threat to their lives. The villagers who fled the village after this episode were booked under cases including the attempt to murder. In another instance in 1995, the villagers, led by some of the political representatives, attacked the industries, and ransacked and assaulted the industrialists. Again, the agitating villagers were booked under the charge of attempt to murder and were framed for extortion. These acts of the subalterns bring into relief the role of 'contentious politics and collective actions' in constructing the political, and constituting their subjectivity. It cannot be a simple derivative, as political society seems to frame it, of their distance from the modern 'looking for the unconquered, the exotic, to find the autonomy and specificity of people's subjectivity' (Alam 1983: 47). It is the end-goals which the modes of mobilization intend to achieve that decide the nature of the protest rather than the 'traditional form'—social, religious or cultural—they assume. The response of the state and civil society also largely depends on this. In this case, the state came down heavily on the protestors since they were making demands that were structural in nature and also against the industrialists who were influential and well connected with the officials. It is therefore, very well possible that collective action can assume an 'unconquered and exotic' form, which might lie outside the modern institutional frames of civil society but still not make demands that are structural in nature, and instead make demands that are in fact in tune with the minimalism (formal) of civil society. In such cases of minimalism (subsistence), even if the collective action assumes 'traditional forms', civil society accommodates them within its own institutional logic. Political society in drawing a binary between the modern and traditional, or modernity and democracy fails to grasp the *points of intersection*—in reproducing, in this case, the privileges of dominant classes such as the industrialists—that the working of civil society actually facilitates.

Again in 2005, on the basis of an affidavit lodged by the Goa Foundation with the Supreme Court that several of these industries were functioning since 1994 without obtaining clearance certificates from the Central Pollution Control Board, the Supreme Court ordered for a public hearing. However, objections were raised by the villagers against the manner in which the public hearing was being conducted. While the Pollution Impact Assessment Reports had not reached several villages, the dates for the hearing were also not clearly disseminated among the villagers, some of whom even complained of receiving threatening calls trying to dissuade them from attending the public hearing. What comes across very clearly in all such instances was the fact that the state, and vested interests in the market, not only work in nexus but also often resort to coercive and manipulative mechanisms in order to reign in protest politics. However, political society now, and earlier 'the subaltern studies...more or less negate the possibility of manipulation, incitement and confusion' (Ibid.: 46), which have always been integral to the way power operates and replicates itself. Undermining these aspects in fact 'shuts off the whole field of external structural interaction and determination' and negates the 'historical constitution' or 'materiality of politics' (Hanlon 2000; Samaddar 2007).

Despite all these threats, however, the villagers mobilized themselves in huge numbers, attended court hearing and gave evidence against the industry. Seeing that it was going against them, the representatives of the industries sought to disturb the public hearing by beating up the Green Peace activists, which led to angry protests by the villagers. The Assistant Sub-Inspector (ASI) of Police suffered injuries in the ensuing fracas. Later, when the Green Peace activist and a researcher, who were involved in mobilizing the people, went to register an FIR at the police station, the Circle Inspector assaulted them again. When he realized that the victims were activists who had nothing to do with the protests of the villagers, the Additional Superintendent of Police tendered an apology to the activists, and assured that action would be initiated against the Circle Inspector. However, despite the registration of complaints against the industrial representatives and the Circle Inspector, no action was initiated in either case. Instead, 62 villagers, including both the Green Peace activist and the researcher, were booked under eight sections of the Indian Penal Code including Section 307, which provided for criminal proceedings for attempt to murder. The constables then went around the villages blackmailing the villagers with the threat that their names would be mentioned in the FIR for extortion of money. The sarpanch of Kazipally,[14] who had been supporting the industrialists, frightened the villagers by telling them that if a Green Peace activist and a researcher could be beaten up by the police for mobilizing against the industrialists, what would be the fate of ordinary villagers if they resorted to the same? This had the desired impact on the villagers, in whose perception the Green Peace activist and the researcher were amongst those who had connections with the urban elite in the civil society and access to the bureaucracy and even ministers in the state. If such people could be assaulted in the custody of the police, what protection would ordinary villagers have? This scared the villagers off sufficiently to keep them away from the public hearing on the second day, which was what the industrialists had intended to achieve.

On the second day of the public hearing, 12 DCM mini-buses were hired by the industrialists in which people were brought with the specific purpose of making statements in favour of the industrialists. Several villagers reported that the village heads (sarpanches) of some villages and some villagers had received bribes to give these statements. Thus, what was supposed to be a democratic process of allowing the villagers to vent their opinions freely was subverted by the representatives of the industrialists, who resorted to acts of un-civility, which were followed up by the police and which succeeded in intimidating the villagers to keep them away from the public hearing on the second and third days as well.

The narrative as above indicates that whenever structural demands around organized collective action are strengthened, the market, civil society and the state tend to exhibit un civility, aimed at suppressing the political activity of the people. The consequence of such un-civility of institutions is that the state loses its legitimacy and is seen to be unjustly siding with the dominant interests. The state apparatus, which in this case was represented by the Pollution Control Board (PCB) and the police, who were supposed to implement the law but actually took recourse to extra-judicial methods to subvert justice, thereby providing that the state can be manipulated into exhibiting arbitrary and inconsistent behaviour, which is severely damaging to its image of an objective arbiter in the event of disputes. Further, the failure of the state to initiate any action against the mafia-like elements because of their links with mainstream political parties, and its refusal to react to the acts of violence perpetrated by the industrialists against the villagers show that there was actually very little space for organized political protest, within the institutionalized 'legality' of the civil society. On the contrary, the more the political action reveals the limits of legality, the more devious forms the state and the elite adopt, and in the process the legal practices produce their own set of illegalities.

These *points of intersection*—between the legal and the illegal—demonstrate the fact that the binary opposition is a mode in which modern power operates. In order to displace or circumvent such power, merely stressing on those practices that have been excluded from being recognized as either legal or civil—in this case illegal or paralegal practices—as the domain of political society does, only reinforces the modalities of modern power in reifying the dominant practices and the domain of civil society, 'as if' it were a realm of pure legality, and thus becomes an integral part of the *logic of circularity* that civil society operates through.[15] It is such contexts that make it imperative to adopt, as many of the political movements did, complex combinatory postures to overcome the *logic of circularity*.

In this case, it could involve exposing law and its limits, yet availing the existing laws and simultaneously attempting re-signifying them beyond their Constitutional limits; it could also thereby involve contextualizing what are perceived as illegal or paralegal means, as uncivil or delegitimized practices but not in a *moment of binary opposition*, but through mutual engagement and in the *moment of dialectics of struggle*.

Political activity may display yet another trend in the wake of growing un-civility of the civil society in nexus with the state. It has been observed that as a result of the growing incidence of un-civility, what begins as a political activity for achieving structural demands (in this case closure of industries), gets juxtaposed—in a dichotomized mode—against immediate interest-based politics. The convergence between the state, civil society and market, as we elaborated, propels framing interest-group politics in such a way that they begin to gradually displace any notion of collective interests. It becomes increasingly difficult to raise questions of structured power relations and even questions of collective interest, and instead the subalterns are pushed into pursuing 'survival strategies' for 'subsistence benefits'. Interest-group politics, expressed through and as 'contextual negotiations' begin to look far more feasible and collective interests a distant utopia. The domain of civil society, in other words, manages to bifurcate the demands of immediacy from those against structured power relations, where otherwise interest-group politics should and could have themselves taken the form of collectives for justice. It is then again a modality of the way power operates in the elite-dominated civil society that draws an artificial wedge between interests and values or justice. While the HRM, as we had discussed in the second chapter, reinforced the binary by superimposing values over interests, with political society we observe that it displaces any need to pose questions of collective justice and assumes that they are necessarily subsumed under interest-group politics, just when civil society manages to 'separate' them. The point is not to either reinforce the separation or binary opposition or collapse them into a simple undifferentiated continuum, but in fact provide for political mediation as 'dialectic of struggle' that disallows any artificial separation between the two that civil society, in nexus with the state and through its uncivil practices, attempts to instantiate.[16] In other words, there is no essentialized relation between interests and values, but it is the manner in which these frames enable or disable dislodging entrenched power equations that eventually and effectively determines the nature of the relation.

In fact, this 'separation' of the issues of immediacy and experience from that of the collective and structural, and disallowing everyday processes and practices (negotiations) to have structural implications, unlike political society that assumes an unproblematic continuum, is itself a specific mode of operation and replication of the dominant structures of power. 'Domination works through actually constructing a seemingly dualistic world' that can take many forms and get imbricated in multitude of ways in everyday politics. For instance, in the Cartesian mould, there could be a separation of the physical from the mental mode of operation making it possible to read pursuit of dichotomized interest-group politics as a conscious *choice* of the subaltern and therefore it is possible to argue that 'it is in the immediate interests of most poor villagers to uphold the official realities in nearly all power laden contests' (Scott 1986: 321). Such constructions of the agency of the subaltern then assume that power is 'external to ordinary life' as in it is intangible and impersonal and therefore 'seems to stand outside actuality, outside events, outside time, outside community and outside personhood' (Mitchell 1990: 568). Thus, pursuit of exclusive and bifurcated interest-group politics, instead of being a moment of power, look like standing outside power and structures ostensibly enabling the subaltern in 'devising new ways in which they can choose how they should be governed' (Chatterjee 2004: 77).

In reality, we find that since society is stratified on the basis of several structures, the interests within this society too are stratified. In the case of any political activity initiated by such a stratified society without political mediation, the commonality of interests holds only symbolic significance, providing a ground for an artificial unity of the collective. While collective political activity and mediation mounts pressure on the system and creates conditions whereby the system is forced to accommodate the demands of the collective, the interest-group acts of individuals or small groups within a political society are always given the space to necessarily push through demands in their dichotomized mode. As a consequence of the 'subsistence benefits' accrued to the interest-based political society, such beneficiary groups increasingly find it difficult to suture their demands to a collective political activity that not only weakens but begins to look burdensome, where all forms of solidarity begin to be construed as hegemonic. In what follows we show the trends in interest-group politics in Kazipally, and thereby in 'the creation of what appears to us as the larger binary order of meaning versus reality that the effectiveness of modern forms of domination is to be understood' (Mitchell 1990: 559).

In other words, the 'modern forms of domination' that operate through the nexus between the state and the elite in the civil society allow for interest-groups to achieve only 'subsistence benefits' and increasingly depend on 'survival strategies' and 'contextual negotiations', necessarily in conflict with and in undermining the modalities of collective action that potentially hold the capacity to forge demands that are structural, and might question the *convergence* of interests between the state and the elites in the civil society. 'Modern forms of domination' present themselves through such binary oppositions that increasingly 'construct' the reality in such a way that only 'contextual negotiations' begin to look plausible (and sensible), and in fact projected as the preferred choice of the subaltern action. 'Political society', in exclusively privileging such negotiations, not only more or less misses the role of hegemonic machinations but also, as part of the *logic of circularity* in civil society, begins to read agency in 'simple voluntarism' and precisely at the moment when there is a process of thinning of agency by blocking the dialectic, the scope for political mediation. 'Thus, there is at least a potential contradiction', as political society is framed, 'between the claim that so-called hegemonic ideologies are not hegemonic in the sense that the poor see through them, and the argument that normative superstructures are essential to the functioning of authority' (Mitchell 1990: 549).

In 1989, soon after the people resorted to *dharnas* for raising structural demands against the industrialists, which was followed by their being subjected to lathi-charge and arrests, these collective/structural demands took the exclusive shape of interest-group politics.[17] Instead of asking for closure of the polluting units, the villagers demanded that they be given some livelihoods and (subsistence) income earning opportunities. The manufacturing process in the predominantly bulk drug and chemical industries produced dry ash as a residue. This ash was being used for brick-making in brick kilns located in the vicinity of the village. Apart from seeking employment in this subsidiary industry, the villagers were also offered to participate in other such works as managing water tankers, taking up construction contracts and other activities related to transportation. But they were, however, not offered employment in these industries. Some youth did get employment in the industries that were not directly responsible for polluting the *Kazi talab*. But these industries were located elsewhere at a much further distance from the village and even in these industries the youth could secure employment only as daily contract workers.

When the villagers ransacked the industries in 1995, although the industries did not close down their operations, a Memorandum of Understanding (MoU) was signed between the Model Industrial Association representing the industries and the village represented by its heads including the *Sarpanch* and the Zilla Parishad Chairman.[18] A sum of ₹400,000 was paid to the village. The construction of a community hall, village roads and such other activities considered to be village developmental activities were undertaken with these funds. In return, the villagers were asked to withdraw all the cases filed by them against the polluting industries. Some dissenting groups, however, persisted with the cases in the court. In 1998, all the polluting industries were closed on the basis of the directive by the Andhra Pradesh High Court. The industries, however, approached the Supreme Court and obtained a stay order against the closure order of the Supreme Court. In 1999, the Chief Minister of Andhra Pradesh, Chandrababu Naidu, made a statement on the issue of pollution, which had parallels to his approach on the question of earning revenues from the sale of liquor, in which he said that 'these industries were earning foreign currency for the country and that the pollution control authorities should go slow on the issue of pollution. If industries are harassed then it may impinge growth'.

In 2001, based on the case filed with it, the Supreme Court issued an order asking for closure of 18 industries listed as polluting units until they abided by the prescribed standards of water quality and hydraulic reduction of pollution. After a brief period of closure, the PCB, however, reopened the industries. During the same year, the Supreme Court gave a ruling stating that the industrialists had to pay compensation to the farmers whose lands have been damaged on account of pollution. The compensation amount paid was, however, a paltry sum of ₹1,700 per acre per annum. This amount was not even equivalent to the input costs incurred by the farmers on the seeds. Further, those who were landless did not receive any compensation. As part of the same judgment, potable drinking water from the river Manjira, which supplies water to Hyderabad city, was also to be supplied to the village.

In 2002, the village was able to get one of its demands approved on paper. The district collector ordered for repairs to be taken up on the Kazipally tank. The collector had ordered that a sum of ₹900,000 be collected from the industries for this purpose. The villagers were however disappointed after a brief period of excitement when Grasshoppers[19] had been sent to the village to begin the work. The day when the work was to begin saw a festive environment in the village with a *pooja* being performed at the site of the work. However, the Grasshoppers stopped work after removing only a few heaps of mud and never returned to resume the work. On being contacted about resuming the work, the collector of Medak told the village representatives that the industrialists were not willing to give the designated amount and that in fact the government was 'negotiating' with them for the same.

In 2003, the issue of pollution received considerable favourable media attention. The regional press and the regional electronic media extensively covered the issue. Several representations were made by K. G. Kannabiran (National President of the PUCL) on behalf of the people of Kazipally to the PCB. With the problem receiving renewed attention, a commission of enquiry was set up under the chairmanship of Justice Gopal Rao, a retired Chief Justice of the Andhra Pradesh High Court. The members of the Commission were quite taken aback by the condition of the tank when they paid a visit to the village. Following this visit, the villagers were asked to provide evidence of violations pertaining to pollution. The villagers began to act as vigilance teams and in the process, caught several industries letting out effluents into a stream carrying water to the tank and burning solid toxic wastes outside the premises of the industry. In view of these instances of violation of laws, a bond of ₹2.5 million was taken from the industries towards surety and they warned that in case of any further violations, they would have to forego the surety amount.

In 2004, Green Peace came out with its health report. The report compared the disease patterns in the pollution affected villages with those in the other villages that were not affected by pollution. The health report revealed several disturbing trends. It suggested that the occurrence of several types of diseases including congenital diseases and cancer was much higher in the pollution affected villages than in the non-polluted ones. Some diseases, in fact, showed an occurrence that was 200–300 times than in the non-polluted areas. After these findings, a need was felt for setting up at least a primary health centre with referral authority in the village, whereby the patients could avail of free treatment at government hospitals in the city. However, till date nothing has materialized and the village is still awaiting its primary health centre.

On the whole, therefore, we find that the victims of industrial pollution in Kazipally have not been able to achieve much in getting redressal or of getting rid of the polluting industries from their village. Although there have been several demands reflecting collective interests, they were not necessarily structural as we have defined it, including, employment opportunities in the industries, repairs to tanks, abiding by the quality standards, refraining industries from dumping untreated effluents into the village tank and setting up a health centre with referral authority, none of even these demands have so far been implemented.

Political Society: Of Middle Men and Processes of Fragmentation

In 1989 after villagers had secured the opportunities to sell the residual dry ash of the factories, or take up transport and construction contracts, a large number of villagers expressed their willingness to take up these works. The opportunities, in fact, seemed much fewer in number than the number of villagers willing to take up the promised work. This, in turn, led to feuds among the villagers as to get the work. The industrialists 'strategically' gave the local sarpanches the authority to decide on who could take up these works. The decision was 'strategic' in the sense that the Sarpanches could easily be lured on to the side of the industries as they received bribes from time to time. And given the frequent defections by the sarpanches on to the side of the industrialists, this system of allocating opportunities led to a situation wherein only the villagers who assured the industrialists that they would not raise an alarm about the worsening problem of pollution were to be given these opportunities. A section of the people fighting against pollution therefore withdrew from the struggle. This was also a result of their dependence on the industry for their livelihoods. So much so that the president of the Kalushya Vyatireka Raitu Committee (KVRC) (the Farmers Committee against Pollution), the main organization floated by the farmers to fight against pollution, actually started work on a construction contract in one of the most polluting industrial units. The farmers who were relatively better-off or had some assets like vehicles (tractors, etc, necessary to transport material for the construction) or who could mobilize labour were the beneficiaries.

Since the sarpanches were hand-in-glove with the industrialists, there were several other methods by which they could prevent the villagers from participating in the protest against pollution, while acting on behalf of the industries. It would be relevant to discuss some of these *means of control* here. In the backdrop of the displacement from their traditional occupations, especially agriculture, the farmers who were actively involved in the protest against pollution obviously could not secure opportunities within the industry. One of the active functionaries of the KVRC was earning his livelihood by engaging in unlicensed stone quarrying. This was possible for him because he owned a tractor which was used to transport the granite stones and concrete to construction companies. The farmer had taken a loan of ₹100,000 to engage labourers to do the work for him. After the work was completed the farmer paid the labourers their wages and when he was about to transport the material to the construction company, the sarpanch called the farmer and threatened him with arrest for having engaged in illegal stone quarrying. Frightened at the prospect of his arrest, and also of not being able to repay his loan, the farmer agreed to the sarpanch's diktat to withdraw from the protest against the industries. Thus, under duress, the farmer kept away from the KVRS.

Again in 1995, when the MoU was signed between the village heads and the Model Industrial Association, a substantial number of farmers did not approach the court with complaints about pollution. This was because they had received some of the amount out of the total of ₹400,000 paid by the industries as compensation for causing pollution in the village. This decision to pay compensation was also arbitrary as not all the farmers received the amount. Again, only those farmers who gave the assurance that they would keep away from the political activity against pollution were given the compensation. The ZPTC chairman, who was one of the signatories to the MoU, and himself owned about 40 acres of land in the village, was one such beneficiary of the compensation that was offered. He was a victim who had suffered the greatest loss in terms of the number of acres of land affected. This person was active in the mobilization of the farmers from 1989 onwards. After this episode, though he registered his presence in activities by villagers protesting against pollution now and then, he kept away from any further mobilization activity linked to the protest against pollution.

Yet another instance where one can observe the subversion of activity against industrial pollution was the way in which industries were dealing with the farmers whose cattle had been dying after drinking polluted water. Earlier, the farmers would take their cattle to the government veterinary hospital and after examination by doctors, obtain a certificate from them stating that the death of the cattle was perhaps on account of the consumption of toxic chemical water. This certificate was necessary for carrying out further forensic investigations on the dead cattle by the city-based government veterinary hospital, following which an FIR could be lodged with the police, on the basis of which a legal notice could be served, which would be used for demanding compensation for the dead cattle. All such complaints and cases would mean mounting evidence against the industries. Fearing this, the industrialists dissuaded villagers from going to government veterinary hospitals or registering complaints with the police. They said that those whose cattle die on account of consuming toxic water should instead approach the industries through their sarpanch. And over the years several villagers received compensation whenever they lost cattle. But the industrialists successfully ensured that there would be no evidence suggesting the loss of cattle was due to pollution caused by the industries.

In 2004, when panchayat elections were being held for the post of sarpanch, a new candidate stood with a single-point agenda: he would ensure that the problem of pollution would be solved in Kazipally village. This candidate was elected by the village. Soon after, this new sarpanch began serving notices to 50 industries accused of polluting. The industrialists were called to negotiate with the village. Thirty industrialists attended the negotiation meeting which was addressed by K. G. Kannabiran (PUCL) and G. Haragopal (APCLC), who were playing the role of mediators for the negotiations. In this negotiation, the sarpanch made a categorical statement that no compensation would be accepted by the village unless the industries completely stopped polluting the village tank and took up repair work for it. A second round of talks was scheduled to be held a few weeks later. Meanwhile, the sarpanch struck a private deal and accepted a package of compensation for the village and distributed some money amongst the villagers. Again, neither the tank repairs nor a reduction in pollution was achieved. And to top it all, at the public hearing held in 2005, this sarpanch made a statement that the development of the village was contingent upon industrialization, and strongly argued that the industries in the village should not be closed down.

These series of incidents bring to the fore the 'structural dependence' on political representatives—such as the sarpanch, in this case—and others such as the school teachers, local municipal officials, officers of the local police station and prominent middle class residents (among others that Chatterjee suggests) as middle men 'involved in the activities of the people', who according to Chatterjee offer new opportunities to work the system rather than entrench a 'patron-client relation'; Similarly, Chatterjee also argues, that the logic of 'competitive electoral mobilization', has afforded the subaltern 'a new strategic resource'. At one end of the spectrum, political society is valorized as an 'autonomous domain' and the subaltern attributed organic agency, at the other end the organic agency is replaced by a dependence on middle men with quite different persuasion and sensibilities. As Gayatri Spivak reviewing Chatterjee's work *Politics of the Governed* says, 'the book ends on a superb note of productive contradiction—when the author leaves popular politics and speaks in praise of "gathering of self-conscious people" to counter urbanization in the services of neo-liberalisation'. The contradiction manifests an unwillingness to wade through the expansive and variegated nature of conflicts that the materiality of politics involve, and instead delimits the struggles to 'claims for governmental care'. Political society also does a selective reading of the role of the middle men—*pyraveekars*—who have come into existence out of the poor social classes' dependence in negotiating with the colonial administration.[20]

> While the *pyraveekar* with one hand applies pressure, pushes the files, lubricates the process and extracts the benefits from the system, with the other hand he passes on incorrect information, misleads the target groups and makes a private fortune. It is the negative and exploitative dimension of the institution that speaks against it and calls for its elimination through appropriate measures. (Reddy and Haragopal 1985: 1161)

Similar to the plight of the villagers in Kazipally, Stuart Corbridge observes, based on his field work, that even in Vaishali district of Bihar the 'villagers are in dark about developmental schemes, duties of Panchayat officials and the rights of the poor. Panchayat members are then free to take up projects that are hard to audit' (Corbridge et al. 2005: 205).[21] Thus, when representatives of people, as in Kazipally, defect to the side of the polluters, those representing the people through political activism against pollution find themselves more vulnerable and political activists derived from among the common people of the village fail to sustain their resistance. In such circumstances, the political activism is given up for 'strategic politics', aspiring for either exclusive individual benefits represented by the growing culture of compensation or just the immediate needs of the community that do not address the problem of pollution as such.

On the whole, the different instances cited above indicate that what is described as 'strategic politics' or 'contextual negotiations' within the 'political society' may ensure social mobility in a very fragmented sense. In the above cases, for instance, the villagers received money from time to time because of their protest. Farmer activists of the KVRS who 'strategically' reduced the intensity of their struggle or kept away from any further activity either because they got employment opportunities in the industries or because they were dependent on the local administration for carrying on with their illegal income earning activities, could be seen as achieving some level of accommodation into the system. However, these small group 'strategies' and individual-centric negotiations for incentives effectively displaced the overall collective interest and collective action, both in terms of compelling the local people to give up collective demands like getting the tank repaired, preventing the dumping of toxic effluents into the village tank and getting a health centre for the village, among others, as also in terms of the cost that the community has had to bear by giving up the larger interest seen in the general health disorders suffered by the community on account of unabated pollution. Apart from these direct costs that the community has suffered, the 'strategic politics' has had long-term impact on the community life itself on the social fabric, social relations, and solidarity among the people. Far from, as Chatterjee professes, a situation where in the community would struggle 'collectively as a single family', all these factors have instead led to a certain kind of collapse of the sense of a collective, in a similar way as feminists had observed in relation to the implications of legal interventions against domestic violence, and introduction of 'community-oriented' microcredit programmes, without the accompanying social and economic changes, making sustained political activity itself very difficult. In the following few passages we enumerate these dimensions of the problem.

A local farmer Narasanna says:

> The Panchayat is corrupt and some leaders are even criminalized. There is no one to whom these leaders are accountable. Once the PCB closed down all the polluting industries, the Sarpanch went and gave no objection certificates and got these industries reopened. And we farmers are dependent on these industries for

our livelihoods; some supply water, some trade ash, some supply construction material and so on. If we participate in the protests we lose our livelihood…

The fact that the farmers in the village have associated themselves with different activities linked to the industries is an outcome of the severe pressures that they have been subjected to. In addition, their material needs and liabilities in terms of costs incurred on treating health disorders, the marriages of their daughters and the education of their children have also compelled the local people to give up their support for the agitation against pollution and quietly accept financial compensation by striking individual deals with functionaries of the polluting industries instead.

Similarly, Amina, the mother of one of the local farmers says, 'People unite if they see a possibility of a solution emerging from the protest. But if they see no such possibility, they prefer bargaining with the industrialists individually and get whatever they can.' Once the need to avail of opportunities are stamped by the processes of individualization—like the way women were 'reduced' to in dealing with the problem of domestic violence after the promulgation of the Act against Domestic Violence—as Padmaja, a DWCRA coordinator points out, 'Competitive culture increases, comparisons between families in terms of status grow. And individualistic behaviour leads to a weakening of the community.' As a consequence of individuation and induced competitive ethic—as with the language of rights—Venkataramani, another member active with the DWCRA, maintains: 'Of late there has been a lot of friction between families in the village. Families have stopped sharing problems, resources, or labour. The practice of extending mutual help amongst the members of the extended families has weakened.' During our field survey, we came across several cases of aged people complaining of not receiving care and being neglected by their families rather than acting as a 'single family', to use Chatterjee's expression. This can be seen as one of the most perceptible fall outs on the community life in the village.

What we could, perhaps, infer from this is that beyond a certain level of distress, social bonds within community cannot hold together and therefore the role and nature of the community cannot be taken either as given or necessarily constructed in 'creative ways' to mitigate the social and economic crisis, as the idea of political society formulates. Instead, community itself can come under stress and be replaced by growing intra-subaltern conflicts in the place of putting pressure on the state, or the elite within the civil society. Political society, in constructing the social relations through strong community bonds within and amongst the subaltern overlooks the impact of the changing nature of political economy on the community on the one hand, and the potential of social hierarchies within the community—as we observed with sub-caste related conflicts—to flare up as social conflicts on the other, instead it only looks at the possibility of community action in mitigating the adverse impact of the market. In other words, the processes in civil society—such as marginalization—cannot be 'regionally enclosed', and instead hold the potential to become more generic, spread and encompass all forms of social relations; wherein the processes of marginalization can be seen as a consequence reproduced within those social relations that are outside the formal contractual relations of the civil society, but under its impact exert power on the relatively weaker social groups, on the basis of the existing social hierarchies within the community, such as caste, or gender. In fact, it could be read that 'political society' instead of being a 'constitutive outside' or a zone of resistance, in fact is a residual domain that replicates the processes and practices of civil society. For instance, the justification for adopting paralegal means for survival emerges, not as a counter or as 'outside' of a civil domain that is marked by legality and civility but actually replicating the 'illegal' and 'uncivil' practices of the civil society itself. Thus, it makes it imperative to understand the 'social conditions which generate different organizational and ideological nuances' rather than essentializing the choices that the subaltern makes 'arising from the assertion of an irreducibility and autonomy of experience, and a simple minded voluntarism deriving from the insistence upon a capacity for self-determination' (Hanlon 2000: 82).

The 'agrarian culture' of the village, manifested earlier in the community spirit and the vibrant celebration of several local festivals, has also been one of the casualties of the uncivil development. The festivals are linked to the seasons and the agrarian economy in terms of their timing, and symbolism. The destruction of agriculture in the village due to unchecked pollution has also adversely affected the 'agrarian culture' of the village, reducing it to a mere collective minus the expression of this collectivity among the village population. Today, except for Moharram, during which both the Hindu and Muslim communities participate together in the festivities, none of the other festivals is celebrated with a strong sense of collectivity any longer. Narasimha, a local farmer, points out that 'earlier all the villagers were dependent on agriculture and there was lot of community life'. Bringing into relief the point that religious festivals might continue in form but might undergo substantive change in the content—reflecting the impact of the growing number of intra-subaltern conflicts—they accrue, in course of time, and therefore the mere 'use of religious symbols (then) is not what distinguishes one class from another but it is the use to which they are put' (Gupta 1985: 8).

Further, the fragmentation within the subaltern is visible in the mutual perceptions of social groups in the village; while farmers maintain that the youth have very little commitment towards the village, the youth allege that the farmers withdraw from the struggle as soon as they receive compensation. And the women are constrained by patriarchal structures of the village, which prevent them from taking independent decisions about acting against the problem of pollution. The interests of women are also perceived as those whose interests are limited to the family, and do not really have much social role to play. Since their main priority is perceived to be to promote livelihood of the male members within their families, the women can hardly be expected to play a constructive role in dealing with larger problems confronting the village such as the issue of industrial pollution. Thus, the village is today witness to the complete loss of solidarity—'moral passion', in Chatterjee's words—among different social groups. Consequently, youth associations, farmer's organization, and the DWACRA women are unable to work with one another. What will then sustain the sense of the collective seems to depend much on the nature of political mediation that bring to the fore the shared experiences of deprivation rather than 'investing their collective identity with a moral content'. However, Chatterjee believes that 'this is an equally crucial part of the politics of governed; to give to the empirical form of a population groups the moral attributes of a community' (Chatterjee 2004: 57).

This temptation to displace the *political with the moral*—a dilemma as we observed across political movements—is what is critiqued by the feminists, who best understand its implications in terms of forging and protecting the 'moral community' at the cost of reinforcing its internal hierarchies and discriminations. Based on her field work involving a series of interviews with the members of widows' organizations in Kerala, J. Devika believes that:

> Any effort to build a 'moral community' around widows and deserted women may be flawed not only because of the fragility noted earlier but also because it may upon the norm of chaste widowhood, which is not shared by other similar groups. For instance, insistence on building an identity around the chastity norm may make it impossible for the widows to build alliances with another group suffering remarkably similar disadvantages, the so-called tribal 'un-wed mothers' of Wayanad. Such alliances can be built only if the widows are able to forge political alliances that do not rely upon such moral unity, but highlight shared experiences of oppression and deprivation. Only this way may the widows escape reinstating intolerant identities and the threat of reinforcing social conservatism that Chatterjee acknowledges as existing in political society. (Devika 2007: 230)

This privileging of the political, then, does not emerge from an abstract anxiety to remain within the terrain of modernity but from the material conflicts and 'historical constitution' of the subjectivity of the subaltern that can be neither essentialized as completely self-constituted nor delimited to demands for mere governmental care. As Devika again notes in relation to the struggles of the widows' organizations:

Answering questions about demands, the activists rejected their confinement within a governmental category, to define themselves as an interest group with clear-cut claims upon the state. However, acutely aware that the sources of oppression suffered by the widow were multiple and located in all social domains, they articulated "group interest" in such a way as to reveal the complexity internal to the abstract category of "widow". This did indeed open up the possibility of counter-hegemonic politics that critique the founding conditions of widowhood itself.[22] (Devika 2007: 27–28)

Political society undoubtedly enables us to grasp the distinctiveness of the dynamics of the subalterns in opposition and contrast to the norms of the civil society. In this sense, it takes our understanding of the process of democratization beyond the classical, safe and settled domains of state and civil society. However, in mapping of the dynamics internal to this domain it comes out as flattened and dodges the *moment of the dialectic* and instead presents itself as a seamless 'alternative' site, reinforcing the *moment of binary* that is at the heart of the way power operates in civil society. First, the squatters of Calcutta could succeed in getting the State to recognize their 'claims' as a 'moral force' only as long as they do not enter into a conflict with major interests either in the State or the civil society, which would involve raising structural questions, as the villagers did in Kazipally; it is, therefore, (in)explicable as to why 'strategic politics' cannot prevent various slums from being demolished across the country and displaced people do not get rehabilitated by a state that acts 'contextually' and 'instrumentally'.[23] It is, therefore, part of a systemic logic to acknowledge 'strategic' interest-group negotiations, which would eventually displace organized collective action. It is untenable to consider that these varied protest forms could coexist within an undifferentiated 'political society'. Second, the sustenance of the 'political society' of the squatters around 'strategic politics' and its emergence as a 'community' or a 'single family' is an anomaly. On the contrary, 'strategic' or exclusive interest-group negotiations over a period of time only make the community more vulnerable, thereby pushing social groups and individuals to pursue individualized benefits. As the growing culture of compensation and declining solidarity between the youth, aged, farmers and women in Kazipally stands testimony, such 'negotiations' are squarely in conflict with the collective interests, and articulated around the available social stratifications. 'Community festivals' only come to remain as mere symbolic gestures of a collective life without the necessary resources that could sustain collective action for rehabilitation, employment and dignified living for the squatters in Calcutta or the closure of industries and revival of agriculture for the people of Kazipally. Finally, 'political society' as 'strategic politics' only reflects politics that generate perpetual insecurity for the vulnerable by nurturing unsustainable notions of mobility or which can be used only by social groups within the political society that are better equipped to gain the patronage of the middlemen such as the social elites, government functionaries and political leaders. Far from 'making a large array of connections with other groups in similar situations', as Chatterjee puts it, it merely increases the possibility of excluding the more vulnerable, such as the landless people without minimum resources or means of livelihood in Kazipally. For these sections of the society, the state, far from responding to their needs through 'welfare policies', as again Chatterjee believes, increasingly becomes uncivil while also aiding the uncivil developmental processes in the market. This was more than evident in situations wherein villagers have been implicated in false cases, and subjected to threats and physical assaults by the mafia during public hearings, apart from the brazenly biased police brutality seen in Kazipally.

Given these limitations with the politics of political society, they fail to take vulnerable social groups beyond the formalism that civil society offers, and instead presents another kind of formalism as 'subsistence benefits' that gets reflected in the perpetual dependence on 'survival strategies'. It is in this context that we need to emphasize the return to political movements and their chosen path of forging and constructing combinatory postures that offer a sustained 'dialectics of struggle'. This requires not merely 'culturalization of politics' but in fact 'politicization of culture', which includes finding ways of moving beyond the *binary alternatives* that civil society, and also political society, offer in myriad ways. As Chatterjee rightly observes that legality as the baseline of civil society undermines the various other forms that subalterns might resort to. However, this does not entail a neat alternative and self-enclosed site of political society working through paralegal means, but necessitates combinatory postures; politics that allows availing the various dominant practices in civil society by resignifying them through the spaces created in their interaction; as the HRM did with working through the principle of rule of law and also legitimizing and contextualizing militant protest politics, or in the way feminist politics was conscious of the *intersection* of the legislation against domestic violence with the 'developmental' activities of the state, where both implied the processes of de-politicization and individualization, and thereby necessitated resignifying law in combining it with protest politics, outside the limits imposed by the civil society.

Finally, political society in framing and privileging agency through 'strategic politics' or 'contextual negotiations' enters a self-defeating logic of fragmentation, and individualization of collective struggles, that feminist politics rued as a consequence of accessing legal provisions against domestic violence. However, this cannot be overcome either in forging 'moral communities'—'single family'—or by working their way through finding patrons—a 'gathering of self-conscious people'—who act like middlemen, as Chatterjee argues, but in expanding their social base and gaining awareness of internal differentiation, and in enlarging the interconnections between economic, political and cultural dimensions or agendas, as the Dalit movement pursued through the sub-caste movement in course of its sustained dialogue with the Naxalite movement. We need to therefore look more closely for such signposts in the articulations by the political movements and conceptualize and consolidate them into an 'alternative' radical post-civil society discourse and politics. We shall attempt, in a tentative and preliminary sense, such a theorization in the next and final chapter of this book, in lieu of a conclusion.

Notes

1. I am drawing from Anthony Appiah's evocative title of his article, 'Is the Post- in Postmodernism the Post- in Postcolonial?' (*Critical Inquiry*, Vol. 17, No. 2, Winter 1991).
2. I have elaborated on these issues, based on various case studies across India in the recent volume that I edited (Gudavarthy 2012a).
3. Arundhati Roy, in the course of personal communication, once observed that as long as farmers commit suicide there is tremendous response and sympathy from the elites and the middle-class; however, if they decide to take to protest, and in that an armed one, the same elite develops contempt. It could, therefore, be argued that the 'contextual negotiations' of political society become the more acceptable form of subaltern action, since it works within the limits of civility that civil society has set up.
4. This shift from questioning poverty to ensuring just the minimum gets manifested in many forms. Recently, the Planning Commission declared that ₹23 in rural areas and ₹32 in urban areas is the income necessary to be declared above the poverty line. It also manifests in the shift in politics that in 1970s were demanding land reforms are now busy protecting the existing land against 'land acquisition'.
5. It is more than a coincidence that both the domain of civil society as well as that of political society is constructed through a series of neutralized ambiguities and paradoxes. This signifies the convergence in the method and the politics of these two ostensibly 'separated' domains. It could therefore be argued that the moment of separation is the moment of convergence.
6. These terms, such as 'place of his own' and denial of his real situation seem to overlap with the way John Rawls formulates his theory of Justice around 'original point' and 'veil of ignorance'.

7. It must be acknowledged, though, that in his most recent exposition of the idea of political society, Chatterjee concedes the possibility of fragmentation of the subalterns, even if it is owing to, not the nature of the social structures, but governmentality. He argues:

> The intention is precisely to fragment the benefit-seekers and hence divide the potential opposition to the state. One of the most remarkable features of the recent agitations in India over the acquisition of land for industry is that despite the continued use of the old rhetoric of peasant solidarity, there are clearly significant sections of the people of these villages that do not join these agitations because they feel they stand to gain from the government policy. (Chatterjee 2008: 60)

8. Explaining the idea of a 'constitutive outside', Laclau, in the context of working class struggles, argues that:

> ...the conflict is not internal to capitalist relations of production (in which the worker counts merely as a seller of labour power) but between the relations of production and worker's identity outside of them. As we shall see, this constitutive outside is inherent to any antagonistic relationship. (Laclau 1990: 12)

And therefore history is stripped of any coherence or continuity with structures and practices that have existed earlier.

9. Refer Herbert Marcuse, 'Repressive Tolerance' for a detailed account of how certain rights or principles such as tolerance reinforce dominant hierarchies necessitating a shift to more subversive transmutation.

10. 'State of Community Health at Medak District', Green Peace India, Bangalore, 2004. Also see the Deccan Chronicle 'Dirty Nakkavagu Destroying Farmlands, Causing illness', 19 August 1996.

11. Though the Kazipally village is situated right below the *Kazi talab*, there is about 250 metres' distance from the actual location of the tank. This in a way dilutes the pollution by the time water reaches the village. We therefore collected different samples to show this variance as well. In Table 5.3, sample 1 has been collected directly from the tank. Sample 2 and 3 are from the canal. While sample 2 is from a location of the canal closer to the tank, Sample 3 is from a pointcloser to the village. Sample 4 is the bore water which was used for drinking purposes until recently. This primary data can be supplemented by other secondary data sources including data from Commissionarate of Industries, Green Peace, EPTRI and other reports.

12. See Ajay Gudavarthy (2011b) 'Tangles of Telangana' *Indian Express*, 11 July 2011, for an account of the movement for a separate Telangana statehood. Also Kodanda Ram Reddy (2007).

13. The most significant form being blockade of the national highway.

14. President of the village Panchayat.

15. Another instance that one can cite as a parallel is the growing resort to extra-judicial killings by the State. However, this happens in tandem with the State attempting to abolish capital punishment and become signatories to Conventions against Torture as a testimony of its 'liberal' credentials. Even as it 'legally' abolishes capital punishment, it increasingly resorts to extra-judicial killings (what are known as 'encounter killings') and cases of disappearances (that are, for instance, rampant in Kashmir, even as the State is willing to negotiate on Armed Forces Special Powers Act (AFSPA). Thus, it leads to an inter-locking—*logic of circularity*—between the ordinary and extra-ordinary laws on the one hand and extra-ordinary laws and extra-judicial practices on the other.

16. Interests and values or struggles for justice do not have an essentialized equation, where one either necessarily displaces the other as the HRM, to an extent argued, or necessarily exist only in a continuum, as political society foregrounds. For instance, as we had discussed in the third chapter on Dalit politics, during its third phase marked by the sub-caste struggles, that they forged continuity between struggles for interests with instantiation of more universal norms, such as the principle of 'all-affected'.

17. Here we could argue, that the subaltern, as Chatterjee does argue, see through the hegemonic machinations, but do not necessarily have the scope to articulate politics in accordance with that, and therefore retreat to means imposed by the state in nexus with the civil society. However, Chatterjee, in his model of simple voluntarism, fails to mark this as a retreat, since he valorises the choices of the subaltern outside all material contexts.

18. Chairman of the District Council.

19. Heavy engineering equipment used to dig mud out, popularly called a proclainer.

20. 'The *pyraveekar* is a middleman possessing professional skills in exerting pressure on the administrative system through what is known as *pyravee*—that is the art of approaching officials for favours and making the wheels of administration move in support of such favours' (Reddy and Haragopal 1985: 1149).

21. Chatterjee's positive reading of the middlemen also owes its source to the specific context of West Bengal where there is a certain kind of collapse between party and the government. In fact this collapse is very central to many of the assumptions and formulations around the idea of the political society. In fact Chandrababu Naidu, as the Chief Minister of Andhra Pradesh, also made attempts to replicate a similar experiment of collapsing the party and government through programmes such as DWACRA, and was wont to claiming that he too would 'like CPM' stay in power for the next 20 years. His party, however, lost the Assembly elections in 2004.

22. Devika notes, similar to the demands of structural nature in Kazipally, that the demands of the widows' organizations:

    were not limited to increasing and regularizing pensions but include measures to ensure upwards mobility from poverty, strongly reminiscent of the welfare demands in mid-twentieth century Kerala. Therefore, besides regular and better pensions, they demand free healthcare for senior widows, aid for the education and marriage of children of poor widows, projects for deserted women, land, housing, geriatric homes, legal aid and an enquiry commission to report on their issues. (Devika and Rajashree 2012: 223)

    They were also insistent that their claim to welfare pension was not as undignified recipients of the dole, but as a group of workers, comparable with "agricultural workers" or others who have worked hard for society. The widow was a "worker who has lost her employer". These demands reflect not merely "strategies" to gain governmental care but struggles to regain dignity through more integrated demands that belies any patronage that confines them to mere pragmatism.

23. Partha Chatterjee, however, cites the court order to evict the squatters and the increasing possibility of their being forcefully moved; 'thus it is quite possible for the equilibrium of strategic politics to shift enough for these squatters to be evicted tomorrow…Such is the tenuous logic of strategic politics in political society' (*Politics of the Governed*, Delhi: Permanent Black, 2003, p. 60). However, does not still acknowledge that such 'strategic politics' grow in lieu of organised political activity and cannot actually coexist with it in a 'political society'.

6

Towards a Politics of
Post-Civil Society

The contemporary times seem to be marked by a 'profound political disorientation' with the political movements losing the sense of achievement or direction with notions such as progress becoming complicated and counter-productive and the loss of innocence of the idea of truth, along with the realization of a misplaced hope that was placed, on sovereignty and ensuing rights, voluntary action and the possibility of democratization with institutionalization, law and accompanying morality, and abstract citizenship as well as identity politics, which are all foundational to the idea and promise of civil society. These categories seem to have become infinitely more complex when in interaction with each other and producing 'interaction effects' for the processes of democratization. Political movements face the intractability of power and its location, and they no longer seem to even have an access to claiming a neat separation between the oppressed and the oppressor, with an 'equation of truth and goodness on one side and power and oppression on the other side' (Brown 2001: 27). Neither violence enables movements to achieve goals, nor does non-violence and 'change of heart' proposition soften and appeal to the powerful. While there is a sense of despair and disappointment with democracy, there is reluctance and disbelieve about revolution. What, however, has not got suspended amidst all the 'paralyzing disorientation' is political action, reminding us of the Gramscian dictum—'pessimism of the intellect and optimism of the will'. Political movements in India appear to have forged struggles in the dark, often with neither the certainty of change nor the privilege to celebrate uncertainty; with neither the motivation of a utopia nor the strength to shrug off the burden of endlessness that seemed to have gripped the processes of transformation.

In such a context, the categories, ideas, practices, and institutions of the civil society have produced *constitutive ambiguities* and congealed 'democratic space'—through the projected hiatus between available practices and their intended effects—that promotes 'analytical impotence and political aimlessness', entailing social fatalism and an urge to withdraw from politics. The different sectors or modes of being in a society—state, civil society and market—are engaged in a process of 'shifting contradictions' that eventually imply a *convergence* of the practices of 'separate' domains in replicating power relations, rather than operating as 'checks and balances' against transgressions by these domains in a democracy. While state is expecting NGOs in civil society to take over its function of providing public goods, civil society is getting increasingly marketized—through principles of competition, efficiency and consumption, and (free) market in turn expects the backing and support of the state. They result in not merely lack of clarity for politics but lack of choice between the different modalities.[1] Thus, 'as an analytical concept, the contemporary notion of civil society and the sectoral models to which it is attached thus suffers from acute definitional fuzziness' (Edwards and Foley 2001: 4).

In a scenario of 'overlapping consensus' between the different sectors, civil society lays a claim to its legitimacy, in ostensibly providing a neutral ground for political action and in giving a false impression of a space that belongs to everyone. It came to be understood that civil society is best regarded as a neutral political force—neither belonged to the left nor to the right—and through this it is expected to enable democratic politics. Civil society today is being claimed by everyone beginning with new left radicals, right wing communitarians, World Bank, state initiated aid agencies, and the policy maker.[2] In fact, protecting and preserving the *neutrality* has itself become a radical agenda that civil society set up for political action. Contemporary critics of liberal democracy—who employ civil society as an integral idea—such as Chantal Mouffe, formulated an 'agonistic' perspective, that speaks of 'mobilizing power' rather than its elimination, and therefore, ostensibly critiques the idea of neutrality in liberal democracy, which, according to her, is a false way of 'eliminating power'. However, in her own model of 'agonistic democracy' as an ostensible 'alternative' to liberal democracy, the idea of neutrality is re-instantiated in her argument that all normative commitments are nothing but expressions of interests-power. She, therefore, believes, 'the very content of left and right will vary, but the dividing line should remain...' (Mouffe 2005: 120). Thus, leaves us with an unanswered question as to how do we demarcate and why should we prefer 'democratic' interests to anti-democratic interests? Along what lines do we make this distinction? And how exactly has this new 'agonistic model' of democracy overcome the problem of neutrality, when neutrality and constructing neutralised realms, become a modality through which modern power seems to operate?

Thus, in the face of working their way through the *intersection* of *multiplicity of practices* and *convergence* between the different *autonomous spheres* political movements seem to have no easy choice between being able to either step in or step outside the (ostensibly neutralized) norms of civil society. They are either disciplined and minimalized in accepting the available strategies in civil society or delegitimized and refused recognition in attempting to go beyond. In the event of taking up multiple strategies of confronting, accepting and circumventing the dominant structures, they appear to lose direction and the thread of their own thoughts and discourses. They then need to begin all over, but in a new context that they now find themselves in, and which in part is constructed out of their own volition—their voluntary action and 'agency'. The targets that need to be transformed to dislocate power also seem to be the sites on which the movements need to build on. Neither can they externalize or find the objective conditions that will guarantee them spontaneous mobilization, nor do they seem to internally possess unproblematic subjective capacity. What they however, cannot and did not abandon is political action, not as a choice but as the only means to achieve *mobility with dignity*. Though there cannot be a neat trajectory or a straight narrative that can be either traced or constructed, what can be sighted in the dithering *movements and moments* is the willingness to experiment, and inaugurate new discourses that are beyond the scope of the categories and practices they are given, born into and engaging with.

However, the act of going beyond—what I characterize as the moment of being 'post'—is 'not pre-figurative but is directly figurative'. It is 'not as pre-anything but as the immediate creation' (Holloway 2005: 272); as it gets reflected in the contemporary ecological discourses that have redefined justice not merely between social groups that exist in the present but to include 'inter-generational equity'—'future generations are not just to come but already present'. To put it differently, 'time can no longer be depicted as approaching a turning point where it veers back into the past or where the order of this world (or time itself) is apocalyptically transformed' (Luhmann 1982: 272). The future is presentified, it can either never begin or is already there; it is the 'absent present' that is evasively driving politics towards making it the 'presence present'.[3] It is a process of diligently working on the micro-foundations of power relations without losing the opportunity to create a 'meta-politics'. Political movements have internally worked their way through to create effects that carry the traces of being external to the dominant structures.[4] They have congealed at times to reinforce the logic they seem to be struggling against but only to make new sense of their arrest, and convert it into a context that allows them to raise new questions that often are signposts of the new possibilities to be realized.

We shall attempt to map, in this concluding chapter, as to what type of questions have political movements raised in what they potentially point

approach, replacing political mediation with moralization, breakdown of inter-subjectivity—internally it leads to the privileging of unitary voices, such as the English-educated, and urban middle classes—among the Dalits, and externally in blocking any possible dialogue with other political movements such as the women's and the Naxalite movement.

Civil society, in privileging identity politics through its discourses of plurality thus creates a Dalit subjectivity that is minimalist, symbolic, exclusively cultural, and naturalized, which is what Dalit politics actually and initially began its struggle against. The *logic of circularity* of civil society thus, brings back and instantiates all those features that Dalit politics were to struggle against, ironically now their practices themselves become the medium through which the logic of circularity of the civil society gets reproduced. In other words, plurality that creates space for articulating aspirations for recognition also fractures them from demands for redistribution and substantive economic mobility. Similarly, law that promises to empower also regulates and disciplines; civility and morality that offer opportunities to moderate marginalization also rob the vulnerable of the right to protest. This process constructs and constitutes our everyday 'reality', providing us with a lens that is 'always already' myopic. The myopia is not easily visible since domination occurs as autonomy, and distance as difference. As Callinicos reminds us that we are in times 'when empires constantly invoke the language of freedom and democracy to legitimize conquest and domination...' (Callinicos 2006: ix). The solutions that are offered 'through the looking glasses' and choices that are pushed through 'always already' presume and share the naturalization of the logic of power and the 'differences' it creates.[10]

Wendy Brown observes, with regard to the discourse of tolerance in civil society that presupposes essentialized identities and 'reduces conflict as rooted in ontologically natural hostility toward essentialized religion and cultural differences' (Brown 2006: 15). Thus, civil society, in celebrating the 'politics of difference', 'aims to separate and disperse us, and then naturalizes this social isolation as both a necessity (produced by difference) and a good (achieved by tolerance)' (Ibid.: 89). For instance, as we had observed with regard to some of the feminist subject-positions, there was the problem of unproblematically claiming feminine subject-hood on the basis of 'immediate experience' of women. Reinforcing care and motherhood as the core of femininity, as Nancy Hirshmann argued, could well replicate and feed into the dominant modes of discrimination. In other words, differences that are historically created through machinations of power when taken as given become naturalized; and then discourses of tolerance are offered, by the civil sphere, to mutate and moderate those power dynamics, which in fact only offer ways of reconciling with segregation and converting segregation into renewed patriarchy or 'mannered racialism'. Those working against power dynamics are then expected to work through discourses of tolerance as a critique of inequality, without ever raising the more substantive questions regarding the *context* in which those inequalities have got constituted, in the process the 'critique' itself works as a second-order discourse that constitutes and shields power—difference as discrimination. What takes over is a critique without a context or a morality without politics, or moralization as depoliticization, which 'involves removing a political phenomenon from comprehension of its historical emergence and from recognition of the powers that produce and contour it' (Brown 2006: 15).

Civil society as the site for the 'interaction effects', born out of the intercourse between the first- and second-order power discourses—between, in the example discussed above, authentic cultural identities (first-order power discourse) and tolerance (second-order power discourse)—creates an obscene choice between the immediate and the long-term; between events and process; between 'politics of presence' and ' politics of ideas', between the 'politics of the possible' or 'politics of the everyday life' or 'contextual negotiations' and the politics against structural inequalities. Each of these binaries reinforces the logic of circularity, while the former set of practices produces minimalist/symbolic solutions, the later seems too distanced for the purposes of mobilization and converting them into experiential categories necessary for mobilization. The political movements do not have the required gestation or the space to stand-on; to negotiate with this refracted aspect of power. The intractability of power dispersed through the 'interaction effects' strangely constitutes a logic where connecting the various loose ends and declaring a war on meta-structures opens the possibility of being construed as the hegemony of utopia and the 'incredulity of the meta-narrative'. It was these moments that were converted into movements for politics of post-civil society.

Post and Beyond: 'Dialectics of Struggle'

Political movements, as they seem inextricably caught in the logic of circularity and the vortex of 'interaction effects' also gain the capacity to comprehend the nature of the limits imposed, and convert them into a resource to raise new questions—the art of critiquing the critique. However, we can locate the beginnings of the art of critiquing the critique only if we are able to overcome the discomfort in pointing towards the moments that political movements are lost in the logic of circularity, since it is these moments that they convert into a resource.[11] As we witnessed with Dalit politics, the moment of identity politics got converted into a resource for the internally fragmented demands of the sub-caste movement, which in turn inaugurated a new set of practices and *political identities beyond identity politics* and its accompanying limits set *in* and *by* civil society. The sub-caste movement experimented, rather than moralizing, with combining unity between castes with resistance against the newly emerging 'classes within caste groups', and moving beyond claims to recognition as mere identity politics towards combining imperatives of recognition with demands for redistribution and justice 'for all'. They were not merely demanding their share 'against' those in dominant position but protesting along with, again not on behalf of, all other sub-castes who were less mobilized; it was not just a protest 'against' but 'in-against-and-beyond'. It was 'beyond' a mere critique, in the sense that critiquing the critique of domination invariably involved recognising that oppression is 'part of everybody's identity' and 'to condemn oppression is to condemn at least...a little bit of oneself'. They realized that this proposition of self-critique as the hinge connecting politics to justice alone can become the durable basis for the post-civil society practices, of allowing for solidarity to coexist with resistance and conflict. Solidarity and conflict are then not available in two—spatially or temporally—separate and enclosed domains, reflecting the challenge of simultaneity. While the discourses of civil society, such as those based on tolerance, segregated social groups to sustain 'co-existence', the practices of post-civil society radically altered this balance to allow resistance, conflict and self-critique to coexist as conditions of solidarity.

Similarly, the human rights movement struggled and dithered in order to search for alternative roots and routes to move beyond the meta-organizing principle of civil society—the grand old idea of self-interest. As discourses of tolerance naturalise social isolation as a necessity and a good, civil society essentializes self-interest as foundational to its own existence, and therefore Jeremy Bentham is forthright in arguing that 'for diet, nothing but self-regarding affection will serve; but for desert benevolence... is a very valuable addition' (Mansbridge 1990: 8). Whether its benevolence or altruism, as lived practices or political ideals, they can be recognized or practised in civil society only when they resemble or begin to function when circumscribed by the ambit of competition, efficiency and rational choice. In other words, they need to be disciplined into the mechanisms that civil society operates through and identifies with when converted or reduced into practices that guarantee the safe functioning of its foundational logic. The alternative values themselves need to internalize and map themselves unto practices, as a second-order discourse, that are privileged in civil society. As Amartya Sen, in preparing an index for household activities, argues: altruistic motivations 'should be seen in terms of an "as-if" market with implicit prices and not as non-market issues'; or, as Bina Agarwal puts it, 'short-term altruism might be in her long-term material self-interest' (quoted from Uberoi 2003: 215). The mode of creating parallels—the 'as-ifs'—is the *modus operandi* of civil society, making it imperative for political movements, such as the human rights and the feminist politics, to question whether 'the principle of altruism (is) to be only a paradoxical footnote to the narrative of material self-interest, a residual factor in the understanding of household dynamics?' (Ibid.: 217). How do we recover the essence of altruism without reifying the position of women in the 'private' sphere? When do care and mothering go beyond the constraints of obligation? When do trust and empathy overcome being vulnerable to patronage and reinforcing status quo, as they become susceptible in the Gandhian mode being dichotomized between spirituality for the masses and materiality for the classes? How do we retrieve altruism from becoming a 'general ideology of the subaltern in hierarchical societies', which 'turns people into willing doormats' (Bhargava 2000: 225). Is the way out to argue for 'reasonable self-interest', as against 'unrestrained egoism'? Or do we move beyond the understanding that self-interest is the 'anthropological foundation for democracy'? Human rights movement cleared the ground by way of foregrounding both the difficulty and the necessity of ensuring the practice of politicizing ethics, as the durable alternative basis for a post-civil society politics and discourse. In other words, how do ethics remain open-ended in so far as they do not assume absolutist and hegemonic proportions, but are sufficiently closed (bounded) to be put into practice, as a concrete medium and modality circumscribing the 'materiality of politics'?

The politics of politicizing ethics, moving beyond moralization, is representative of the attempt to grapple with the most insurmountable problem of our times, as to how to maintain open-endedness in thinking and in ideals—open to the 'not-yet' dimension of politics—and reconcile it with the imperative of the singularity of praxis. It is, in a sense, a political move to negotiate with the debilitating abdication of all normativity and projected neutrality of the civil society. The neutrality itself assumes a hegemonic dimension, when it gets replicated, as we noted with regard to the suggested alternative domain of 'political society', in reducing all politics to governmentality, in the name of avoiding imposing external normativity on the subaltern and taking their political choices—'contextual negotiations'—as given, without interrogating how this mode of framing voluntary action in itself, in actuality, leads to thinning of agency.[12] Politicizing ethics is to acknowledge the 'openness of uncertainty', which, however does not necessarily entail false neutrality or 'strategic void' in an 'epistemological wonderland' but a double-edged struggle to revolt against the denial of the 'not-yet' aspect of our identities, and aiming 'a becoming with no guarantees' (Holloway 2002: 207). It is not a politics without aims, but it is recognition of aims without assurances. Alain Badiou refers to it as 'dispersive flexibility' or 'political unbinding', where 'politics has no substantiality or community beyond the real transformation it manages to bring' (Badiou 2006: x). The 'real transformation' is inextricabily caught between what Carlos Nino refers to as 'historical constitution' and the denial of that constitution, between recognising the materiality and in attempting to surpass it. As Holloway puts it, 'only in so far as we are not the working class the question of emancipation can ever be posed' but only 'in so far as we are the working class we have the need to pose it' (Holloway 2002: 195).

It can therefore be suggested that politics of the post-civil society variant demands *informed detachment,* and not false neutrality. It demands a capacity to be in the midst of praxis and yet make a stark reading beyond the myopia that engulfs it, which is not always triumphant and could involve denouncing many aspects of the very praxis one is working through; it demands a rare capacity to combine an eye-for-detail or identifying the micro-foundations of power dynamics, with the seeming endlessness of the journey (sometimes even without milestones) to overcome or displace them. It demands the singularity of praxis that acknowledges the moment being transitory; where the past is acknowledged but not reified, future is presentified and the present is seen to hold alternative possibilities in being transitory; it demands a praxis that moulds the reality and yet instantiates the traces of its dispensability in its own acts of transformation. Following Badiou, one could argue that while 'ontological fabric of being is 'void', he still maintains that the 'ideo-logical' structure of any given situation is consistent, and quite capable of producing a reality effect' (Badiou 2006: x). It refers to a politics that 'constantly defies classification' yet does not reduce it to mere celebration of 'nihilism, or the ultra-sceptical attitude that nothing can be done' but recognizes the place of 'reality effect' along with the *problematic of institutionalization.*

The *problematic of institutionalization* refers to a political challenge of acknowledging and negotiating with meta-structures, such as the state, without replicating the logic inherent to them, the process of agents/agency getting converted into subjects/subjugation. Civil society, as we noted in the chapter on feminist politics, alternatively or together, privileges legislation and voluntary associational activity. However, in reality, they do not act in tandem or as complementary aspects as promised by the scholars of civil society, wherein voluntary action—as protest politics—walks in when legislation is not desirable or fails to achieve intended transformation in the demands. Instead, they can cancel out each other, where either it results in hyper-legislation and increasing state control and thereby erosion of space for political action; or it entails voluntary action—such as that by the NGOs—which involves abdication of responsibility by the state and shifting it over to those struggling for change—'victimizing the victims'. In other words, it's a choice between increasing state-control/ centralization and shifting of responsibilities to those making the demands; either it encroaches on your space or leaves you to your fate. How do you then arrest the process of centralization of power, without either getting sucked into and replicating the logic of the state, or turning a blind eye to it by letting-it-off-the-hook? How do you resist its expansionary designs and simultaneously make it responsive?

The response of political movements, to this *moment of doubleness*, involved experimenting across the spectrum from capture of the state power—in order to abolish it—to carnival as a form of disengaging with the state. Laying more emphasis on the monolithic character of the state, and its capacity to expand and centralize has lead to attempts to build equally cohesive and singular sites in opposition to it, such as those attempted by the human rights movement during its 'democratic rights' phase working within the 'state versus civil society' framework and in close proximity with the Naxalite groups. It attempted to build a unity between various democratic movements around a singular anti-state focus, undermining the conflicts and power plays within the civil society. Similarly, exploring the possibilities within the institutional framework of the state—attempting to make it more responsive—in such as demanding progressive legislations, was accompanied by the danger of converting political conflicts into technical and juridical matters, increasing state control and production of passive state-subjects. As we noted, in the case of the after-effects of the implementation of the legislation against domestic violence, the law simplified the issue by flattening out the contradictory demands of women, and depoliticized the process of negotiating with the power relations by individualizing the problem; or in the case of the demand of the sub-castes, it got locked up as an issue that was *sub judice*. State practices seem to congeal even as they respond and open spaces under popular pressure. Is the state then a centralized monolithic edifice or a mere ensemble of fragments, porous and thereby amenable to pressures and purposes of radical politics?

Alain Badiou argues that the state, 'instead of being all-embracing or totalitarian, is in fact something akin to a representative fiction, albeit a constitutive one' (Badiou 2006: vii). While Wendy Brown puts it as, a structure that is, 'highly concrete and an elaborate fiction, powerful and intangible, rigid and protean, potent and without boundaries, de-centred and centralizing, without agency, yet capable of tremendous economic, political and ecological effects' (Brown 1995: 174). It is this intractability of state power that has often resulted in bifurcated response and dichotomized binary strategies in negotiating with the state. Political movements have addressed themselves either exclusively to the 'concrete, powerful, rigid, and potent' dimensions of the state, and thereby believed that '...for any movement towards self-organization to succeed in breaking the power of capital, there has to be a moment of concentration and centralization' (Callinicos, eipcp.net); or sought to empower by manoeuvring the 'intangible, protean, and decentred' character of the state in exploring the possibilities of expanding the porous aspect of the state and gradually *dissolving* its power, in order to displace it. For such 'autonomous' methods, way out seems to be not to envisage a 'worker's state', which is a fundamental contradiction in terms because capital requires the centralizing functioning of the state, and not workers who are struggling against its very logic.[13] A state is a specific version of a 'social relation' that arises with the development of capitalism. It is not a neutral instrument that can be adopted, instead the thrust has to be, not on centralization and capture of state power but, on developing 'autonomous forms of action'; the idea is not to aim for power or counter-power, but to destroy it by working towards creating anti-power (Holloway 2002).

One way of doing this, as suggested by the autonomists, is to create an endless chain of differences. The leitmotif is therefore, continuous generation and maintenance of 'difference' between social actors, so that not only are new forms of domination 'discovered' but also existing identities can realize themselves to the fullest extent, without subsuming themselves under any other social group or being regulated by meta-structures or a cohesive civil sphere. Gilles Deleuze and Felix Guattari suggest that difference-creating desire could be guided by three principles. Firstly, 'Desiring-Production', i.e., desiring to desire or desire, is to be productive in the sense of creating differences or something new. Secondly, 'Desiring-machines', i.e. there is no given, natural or spontaneous desire, on contrary they are only a series of creative functions that make up an assemblage. Finally, 'Body without-organ' (BWO), it is where assemblages are creatively created because there is an unlimited and unblocked productivity of desire (Deleuze and Guattari 1988).[14] This process has to be continuous and is designated as the 'lines of flight'. By constructing these lines, segmentarity can be escaped and a pure flow of productivity created and ensured. In fact, creation or 'construction' of such 'autonomous forms' is, as some have argued, integral to the development of global capitalism, in its contemporary phase. According to Hardt and Negri, the rapid transformation in science, technology and the information revolution enables global capitalism to function as an autonomous 'Empire', outside the control and regulation of the state:

> We claim that Empire is better in the same way that Marx insists that capitalism is better than the forms of society and modes of production that came before it. In the same way today we can say that Empire does away with the cruel regimes of modern power and also increases the potential for liberation. (Negri and Hardt 2001: 43–44)

Civil society works through law and state legislation, project of citizenship, language of rights and pre-eminence of constitutionalism; in the process, as we have discussed, it only expands the control of the state. Can practices of post-civil society then, as a reversal of the emphasis on state, simply ignore, disengage or imagine emerging statelessness or construct 'lines of flight' as a desired alternative?[15] However, it needs to be acknowledged that there have been changes in the modalities of the state under the neo-liberal reforms; new practices in governance, as we noted in the chapter on feminist politics, have introduced more flexible modes of coordination or heterarchy, where a minimalist state is also interventionist.[16] However, these changes have only made the task of the political movements in negotiating with the state all the more complex. Political movements, in their contemporary moment have attempted, individually and collectively, to combine varied strategies in order to both engage, make it responsive and also avoid increasing its control and replicating its forms. They have worked both within and without; they have combined more militant protest politics against the repressive face of the state with resignifying the available institutional practices; these are neither merely reforms of a democracy, nor only cataclysmic events of a revolutionary kind—they are, in fact, a combination of reforms and a revolution, beyond the tyranny of the binary opposition. These combinatory or what we might refer to as *refolutionary* ('ref'-orm and rev-'olution') processes have emerged as the new modalities and basis for the politics of post-civil society.[17]

Refolutionary strategy, it could be argued, signifies the paradoxical mode of transforming meta-structures that *are not all powerful or all encompassing yet they are relatively more cohesive and centralised.* Refolutionary strategy has to be, accordingly, multidimensional, yet cohesive to transform the macro structures. It has to be multidimensional to the extent of including differentiated experience of various social groups and cohesive as to formidably transform these meta-institutions.[18] In other words, in opposition to revolution as the cataclysmic ushering in of a liberated society, it should be recognised that emancipatory collectives construct a towards as the 'alternative' *politics of post-civil society*; what are the adverse contexts that fructified into a 'resource', so that they could gain new insights for setting themselves radical agendas. The new conjunctures created do not stand out but are representative of the 'interstitial transformation' that stands, again as Holloway puts it, 'in-against-and-beyond'. To grasp the *movements and moments* that cross the threshold is to comprehend the simultaneity itself—of being 'in-against-and-beyond'. The over-determination opens up a profound complexity. As we had observed, for instance, during the identitarian turn of the Dalit politics that the simultaneity of the processes—dialogue with other political movements and claiming exclusivist identitarian articulation—could be read either as the insidious mode in which power was being dispersed and privatized, disciplining the dialectical articulations into more disaggregated and thus 'manageable' processes within the civil society, or as the simultaneity itself being a dialectical moment, given the fact that out of these dithering moments such movements emerged with new insights and strategies that are the signposts for moving beyond the *logic of circularity* that engulfed them.

Politics in the Waiting Lounge: Dithering Movements and Moments

Civil society creates the *logic of circularity* through its points of intersection between the various practices that look disparate, and through convergence with other spheres that look separate and autonomous of each other. It is this logic of circularity that represents itself and operationalizes itself through the very practices and strategies that political movements adopt. Thus, when political movements simultaneously, in order to overcome the logic of circularity, engage, circumvent, and undermine the practices of civil society, they seem to lose the thread of their own thoughts and get engulfed in the logic of circularity that they actually wished to overcome in adopting multiple strategies simultaneously. The political movements themselves, 'generating' and then negotiating this simultaneity, can inextricably get caught in the circularity—created by simultaneously transforming, engaging, withdrawing and circumventing the power relations—of it but then can also *transform* the circularity into a reflection that is an avenue for politics that is beyond civil society.

It is in the moments of getting caught in circularity that political movements had fell victim to the instinct to withdraw from politics and follow the vagaries of formality, legality, morality, authenticity, civility and plurality—supplanting *moments of dialectics* of struggle with drawing on *moments of binaries*—and settle into the ostensibly safe (dichotomized) havens of civil society. These moments—of arresting dialectics in becoming part of the logic of civil society—in the history of political movements, occurred when the practices of civil society subsumed and restricted the flow of political movements. For instance, it was the claims for authenticity as absence of inter-subjectivity that restricted movements from taking larger, interconnected—economic, political, and cultural—agendas, that in turn resulted in celebration of plurality, and exclusive emphasis on legality or/and morality as privileged in civil society. There is no 'origin' point to trace them but they occur in compounded complexity. We could map the same trajectory in different ways, but what they would perhaps converge into is the arrest of the 'dialectics of struggle'. Politics and political action were kept on hold or accompanied by moral injunctions where 'believes that bind a political order become fetishes' (Brown 2001: 28). In other words, it was through the practices of civil society (for instance, discourses of plurality) that the practices of political movements (for instance, claiming authenticity) operationalized the *logic of circularity*. However, it was the same moments that through self-critique and also critiquing the critique in civil society that political movements *converted* them into moments of dialectics. It is important to trace the moments of being caught in the *logic of circularity*, in order to understand both, how movements themselves became part of this circularity or rather how circularity operationalized itself through the practices of the political movements themselves, and also to observe how political movements converted the moments that arrested dialectics, *progressively and cumulatively*, into a 'resource' to make the necessary transition beyond the logic of circularity. The moments, that were internal to the *logic of circularity*, was what each of the political movements faced, in course of reworking their way but nevertheless blinded by the vicious cycle of the circularity generated by the multiplicity of their own strategies, as a response to the points of intersection and being sucked into the whirlpool or quicksand of congealed space in and of civil society.[5]

Let us discuss, as an instance of how the political movements were arrested within the *logic of circularity*, the example of Dalit politics as identity politics, in tracing how the various variables begin to interact and create the circularity through intersection and convergence. Identity politics, again not to miss created by the very processes of power—the very logic of circularity created by instantiating both secular/universal project of citizenship as well as celebration of ascriptive/cultural identities—in civil society that we traced earlier, lead to stigmatization of Dalit politics, which in course of countering humiliation and claiming dignity made exclusivist wide variety of actions to transform the oppression they face in myriad and insidious forms. Of course, such a construction might include cataclysmic events and militant action but they do not qualify as the only mode of protest for radical change, or signify all-encompassing fundamental transformation. This then is the paradox of a refolution. It is a partial act yet comprises the consent of all social groups; negotiates macro structures, yet they are not all powerful and all encompassing; it includes militant protest and changes that occur as a quantum leap, yet combines them with resignifying existing institutional practices; this entire combination completes not *just* a revolution but a refolution.

Political movements, as we analyzed in the course of this book, have precisely attempted such innovative combinatory postures in resignifying the available institutional practices and political principles. They have forged dialogues that allowed them to reflect on their own praxis, as much as critically engage with that of other political movements. In the process, each movement individually and all the movements collectively inaugurated new modes of transformation. Human rights movement, on its part, began working within the limits of constitutionality and law, only to break into a 'democratic rights' phase that was unwilling to engage with the state and its institutional framework and instead aligned itself with militant-radical protest politics and their 'revolutionary perspective'; eventually, and riding on the experience of the previous phases, it moved on to look for ways of combining militant politics with resignifying the available institutional practices such as the rule of law. They have attempted such a resignification when globally there is a shift in the role and implication of such a principle as rule of law, from that of an ideal enabling social justice, to that of an 'imperial ideology'—marked by a context when rule of law is 'receiving so much attention now because of its centrality to both democracy and the market economy in the era marked by a wave of transitions to both' (Carothers 1998: 97). The principle of rule of law is consolidating the ongoing process of enforcing market economies by breaking-open 'protectionism' that smaller and weaker economies followed, in the first phase of the history of post-colonial countries. Strengthening rule of law today by global forces implies the institutionalization of the 'basic elements of a modern market economy such as property rights and contracts' (Ibid.), making it possible therefore to 'export' rule of law (and democracy), and confirming its inextricable link with market that Hayek had proposed in his campaign for the libertarian-right. As Mattei and Nader argue that in contemporary international order rule of law is justifying 'looting to the paradoxical point of being itself illegal' (Mattei and Nader 2008: 3).[19] The growing illegality of law is a situation, as Judith Butler remarks, marking the 'violent hold that law lays upon life'.

However, it is in such a context that the human rights movement has attempted to resignify the meanings of rule of law, not only to check the 'all-intrusive powers' of the state but also to create the necessary 'democratic space' for the radical-militant armed movements to mobilize. It had initiated the process of 'peace talks' between the Maoists and the State not to compel the former to 'lay down arms' or 'abjure violence' or to invite them to join the 'mainstream' but in order to contextualise the use of 'political violence' by radical-revolutionary movements. It was also to contextualize the idea of peace itself, which, according to them, made sense only conjoint with justice and not bereft of it—peace as justice. It was compelling the state to limit itself to rule in accordance with the rule of law—as equality before law—while exposing the limits of the rule by law—as instantiating only formal equality—and also simultaneously expanding the meaning and scope of rule of law—in terms of not formal but substantive justice—(re)signifying the simultaneity of being 'in-against-and-beyond'. The traces of which can be observed, in the shift from mere citizenship to emphasis on 'active citizenship', from mere rule of law to emphasis on 'democratic rule of law'. In this resignification, the principle and practice of rule of law no longer meant dichotomization of dialogue and militant politics or law and violence, as it is supposed to be within the contours of civil society. It, instead, drew novel continuities and explored the 'interstitial space'. 'In other words, the law turns against itself and spawns versions of itself which oppose and proliferate its animating purposes' (Butler 2000: 346).

Institutional practices are, therefore, not necessarily mutually exclusive with militant protest and mobilizational politics but can be converted into sites for—refolutionary—'further making' and 'reoccupation' where 'in its resignifications, the law itself is transmuted into that which opposes and exceeds its original purposes' (Ibid.: 345).[20] In situations where civil society succeeds—through its binary approach—stalling such processes of combining different modalities of negotiating with the state, the politics of protest are disciplined into staying within the limits imposed from above. As we noted with politics in 'political society', where the subjects of protest remain as governmentalized categories—populations—carrying 'contextual negotiations' and thereby expanding the control and dependence on the state. 'Political society' becomes a domain for 'negotiated social peace' (without justice), acting as a buffer or a safety-valve that is similar to what the hegemonic realm of civil society—through its emphasis on civility and legality as the baseline—does. 'Political society' as a realm of subaltern politics in failing to move beyond governmentality, entails a thinning of the agency of the actors involved, as we witnessed with the collectives against pollution in Kazipally. How then are the actors of the post-civil society variant supposed to expand their agency?

Politics of post-civil society can be pursued only by the simultaneity of multiple actors in differential social locations. Post-civil society is, not merely continuous—in a temporal sense—but necessarily a relational process—in a spatial sense; it is not merely beyond heroic acts but also, simultaneously, beyond being delimited to 'politics of events' and also against getting reduced to 'contextual negotiations'. Its processes of transformation are not merely against instrumentalized strategies and sectarian mobilization but positively in favour of transformative dialogue and action. Post-civil society is a political condition marked by the inter-subjectivity of political movements, not around common class composition as a given structure or with a singular focus on and against the state, built on constant and continuous political mediation *within* and *between* the movements and arriving at terms of discourse that necessarily emerge in course of this interaction. 'Unity' between the movements is not a projected agenda to be aimed for but is realised as a lived practice. It is a reality marked by the seamlessness between *internality and externality*. Conflict, resistance, and self-critique are the conditions of solidarity, and the simultaneity and coexistence of these practices is the defining feature of the political. It is this simultaneity that ensures that the mediations between political movements entail politics beyond constituencies, which however do not dissolve into a singularity of a 'people' or the 'masses' that are constitutive of the project and politics of civil society.

Civil society is representative, and in fact, as we had noted in the chapter on the human rights struggle, renewed itself post-East European conflict around the binary between the all-encompassing 'we the people' or 'masses' as against the government. As Hardt and Negri note, '*The people* has traditionally been a unitary conception. The population, of course, is characterized by all kinds of differences, but the people reduces that diversity to a unity and makes of the population a single identity: "the people" is one'.[21] They further argue, 'the essence of the masses is indifference: all differences are submerged and drowned in the masses. All the colours of the population fade to gray. These masses are able to move in unison only because they form an indistinct, uniform conglomerate' (Hardt and Negri 2004: xiv). It is akin to the argument that Marx made in his commentary on the 'method of political economy' in *Grundrisse*. He pointed out that it would seem right to begin with population for the political economy, since it seems like a 'real and concrete' category. However, 'population is an abstraction if, for instance, one disregards the classes of which it is composed' (Marx and Engels 1986: 37).[22] Hardt and Negri therefore suggest the emerging 'multitude' as an alternative, to signify an actor who represents the *common* yet remains differentiated. They believe that the contemporary phase of globalization itself carries within it the possibility of allowing for various differentiated actors to 'discover the commonality that enables us to communicate and act together' (Hardt and Negri 2004: xiii). This process is integral to the growing lateral networks represented by the communication revolution of our times.

However, what this analysis seems to miss, as Laclau points out, is the idea of political mediation. The emancipator subject—the Multitude—seems to embody 'a spontaneous tendency to converge' the immanence-politics and political mediation disappear and actors seem to come together in a 'strategic void' (Laclau 2005). The practices of post-civil society are instead distinctly marked by the materiality of mediations between political movements. Such mediations are continuous and occur 'within' a movement—between its different segments—and between different political movements. It marks the moment when the agenda, strategies and modes of mobilization are mutually borrowed and fused with their 'own' idea of transformation. In the process, political movements begin to work in unison as much as in their differentiation. Each movement is distinct, yet continuously mutates under the impact of other political movements. It is these mutations that do not remain as distinct practices but become constitutive of the *self-representation* of various political movements. A world—'democratic space'—'of infinite multiplicity could also be said to affirm the *un*determined nature of anything and anybody' (Badiou 2006: xi).

As we noted in the previous chapters, each of the political movements we discussed engaged, transformed and in turn influenced other political movements. They remained and continue to remain distinct political movements—Dalit, Naxalite, human rights, feminist and collectives against pollution—yet a close reading will reveal the extent to which, they seem to also speak and also simultaneously work through the prisms provided by other political movements. The Dalit movement began with the caste–class approach and during the days of the struggles by the sub-castes they reiterated the class politics of the Naxalite movement in targeting the 'classes within caste groups'. Influence of the feminist politics on Dalit movement was discernible in new articulations by the Dalit feminists and also in the sub-caste movement growing sceptical about operating within the state-juridical categories and their debilitating effect on mobilization and collective struggles. Sub-caste movement raised similar concerns regarding state categories that feminist politics had reflected upon. Similarly, the Naxalite movement had its own internal 'dissent' by its Dalit and women cadre, both within its armed squads as well as in 'its' open organizations such as the civil liberties/democratic rights organizations. The HRM argued that violence has a political dimension not merely when it's against the state but it also needs to be approached politically in terms of its impact on Dalits and other vulnerable social groups. For instance, they raised the pertinent issue as to why a large number of those killed as informers by the Naxalite movement belonged to lower echelons of the society in terms of their caste and class background. 'Politics of recognition', initiated by the Dalit and feminist politics, when fused with political processes within organizations with class-based mobilization, they took a different turn beyond the identitarian emphasis and entailed various kinds of experiments at 'ideo-logical' and organizational levels. For instance, it 'compelled' radical left groups to forge 'independent' women's and Dalit organizations, which were in constant dialogue with 'the (revolutionary) party', and they learnt to forge anti-systemic struggles in consonance with the immediate experience of specific social groups; for instance they fought for reservations in the private sector, while waging a battle against privatization of the economy. Similarly, the women's movement the moment it expanded to include new classes and caste groups, it inaugurated new organizational mode of mobilizing without leaders. With the coming of new social constituencies as part of the anti-liquor movement, it was not 'merely' raising a women's question but critically exposing the nature and structure of the political economy on which the state was dependent—the nexus between legislators, police, mafia and the liquor contractors—by articulating the new hegemonic equivalence between citizen-consumer identities. They drew linkages between the culture of patriarchy and the 'development model' adopted by the state, and power relations in the family with the 'trucking and bartering' in the civil society.

It is these visible practices, yet non-events that mark the emergence of politics of post-civil society—the interstitial transformation. These varied and continuous internal–external mediations generate new political practices, actors and new kind of expanded agency. These mediations happen, not outside the context of specific groups and organised political movements but by thinking through them, and thinking with them. The new practices that emerge are 'in-against-and-beyond', while the modalities of a civil society are essentially presented in its binary approach. However, the change is not pre-figurative but figurative in the sense of the experiences of the past and the 'not-yet' dimension of future being 'presentified'. It is politics within constituencies that are taking the shape of politics beyond constituency. The later is not a distinct *moment* or a *movement* but integral to the way politics is playing out within the bounded constituencies. It is the deep sense of their 'own' histories that are being transformed into—leading up to, politics beyond constituencies.[23] It is these 'new' actors—without pure subjectivity—that are and will herald politics of post-civil society in India.

Notes

1. This lack of choice is somewhat akin to the way voters feel short-changed in having no choice between political parties they are asked to choose from.

2. It is intriguing, that policy makers, who work with precision and through planning and specific target goals that need to be laid out with utmost clarity and achieved within a specified time-frame, have fancied the nebulous and the 'neutral' zone of civil society as a site for their operations. Does this say something about the nature of the neutrality in civil society?

3. A good example of this is the recycling strategy that takes into account the needs of the future generations 'to come'; it draws continuity between the past and present and 'presentifies the future' (Brundtlard Report, World Commission on Environment and Development 1987).

4. Dominant structures and practices on their part have worked to incorporate values, ethics and politics that have emerged as a resistance against them, into their own fold. Recollect the instance of the way MNC chains such as McDonald's, among others, have collapsed consumerism with ecological concerns and philanthropy to help farmers and other deprived social groups (every burger you eat and coffee you consume contribute to their well-being!).

5. It needs to be reiterated here that the logic of circularity, as is generated through the points of intersection of practices in civil society, gets carried into and gets reproduced in and through the simultaneous strategies of political movements that emerge as a response to the circularity of the practices of civil society.

6. It is in this context that the recent spurge of spending exorbitant money on constructing parks and statues of Ambedkar by the Mayawati government in Uttar Pradesh sparked off a debate in India, as to what its consequences for Dalit politics are. One of the anxieties was that while it enables in Dalit symbols and icons occupying larger space in the public domain than what they were allowed to hitherto, however, this mode of pursuing the Dalit agenda is also shrouding the issues of land-redistribution and justice for Dalits that the state is unable to realize. Similar is the case in other states too. For an extensive field based analysis of this inability of the state in helping the Dalits to continue to have possession of land that was distributed by the state, for instance in Madhya Pradesh, due to the physical assaults from other powerful castes, including the emergent OBCs, see Pai 2010.

7. There are any number of narratives and instances in the popular memory of the nation where students from St. Stephen's College in Delhi, and Presidency College in Calcutta left their academic careers mid-way to join the Naxalite movement. The life of Arvind N. Das, writer and commentator, is a well known instance of a promising young man from a relatively affluent background, dropping out of his college to join the armed movement.

8. Ironically, as non-class movements were getting increasingly under the leadership and mediation of the middle class, the Naxalite movement seems to have travelled the other way round. It began in the 1970s with a middle class leadership and moved to have a social base among the peasants and the tribals and organic leaders from therein. As a news report in the Times of India observed 'It's a curious turn that Maoism has taken: Once a preserve of the educated youth, today it depends on the support of underprivileged tribals' (*TOI*, 12 August 2010: 11).

9. The campaign against untouchability and inclusion of caste in the Durban Conference, 2001, was spearheaded by the National Campaign on Dalit Human Rights (NCDHR),

composed of Dalit NGOs, academics and activists, most of who were professionals based in Delhi.

10. It is akin to the sympathy extended to the 'victim-subjects'—battered women, farmers who commit suicide, Muslims who lose their kith and kin in organized pogroms. However, this *sympathy* converts into *contempt* as soon as the same subjects choose to stand up and protest and refuse to be either sympathized with or willingly submit themselves to the patronage of the high and influential. This protest is then read as an uncivil act leading to breakdown of family, increasing casteism and communalism. In other words, as long as status quo is maintained, victimhood becomes a cause for concern and sympathy but if they wish to gain agency of their own, it becomes unacceptable. This is a typical form of what we could refer to as 'politics of charity'.

11. Some variants of recent scholarship celebrate the cult of the subaltern, and in the process undermine a critical engagement with such politics, in the name of recovering the agency of the subaltern, while in reality it only reimposes certain kinds of 'refracted patronage'. I have dealt with this argument in some detail in my 'Introduction: Why Interrogate Political Society?' (Gudavarthy 2012a).

12. This mode of privileging subaltern agency is central to much of contemporary post-colonial scholarship, and the subaltern studies project in India in particular. In the name of not 'imposing' normativity, or restricting it to theory, it moves ominously close to the kind of neutrality that civil society itself creates and operates on. (Chatterjee 2010; Gudavarthy 2012a).

13. This is the kind of narrative against centralization, legalization and modern governance, which James Scott builds in his recent work *The Art of Not Being Governed*. He argues that the geographical area that can be designated as *Zomia*—the uplands of Southeast Asia—is marked by 'strategic positioning' designed to keep the state at arm's length. He says, 'I argue that hill peoples are best understood as runaway, fugitive, maroon communities who have, over the course of two millennia, been fleeing the oppressions of state-making projects...' (Scott 2009: ix). What this analysis foregrounds is flight and mobility as a way to escape the state, and thereby narrowing its scope and control.

14. Deleuze and Guattari then cite the Autonomia movement of the early 1970s in Italy, which seemed on the verge of tearing the Italian political organism to pieces and replace it with the productivity and multiplicity of a desire for autonomy on all social levels.

15. As Petras and Veltmeyer point out, there is irony in the way the new assertions about statelessness are emerging in a context 'when the US is the only superpower, a hegemon, when almost 50 per cent of the 500 biggest multinational corporations (MNCs) are US-owned and headquartered, and Washington is leading a war of intervention against the peasants and workers of Afghanistan and Iraq...' (Petras and Veltmeyer 2005: 9). They therefore raise the pertinent question: How come, then, that the Empire is a post-imperialist phenomenon and a positive advance in history?

16. New modalities in state functioning at the global level according to Petras is best captured when 'the imperial state (the United States) combines protectionism at home, monopolies abroad, and free trade within the empire' (Petras 2000).

17. I use the term 'refolution' to refer to radical changes that combine peaceful, militant and strategies of resignification, and not those that inaugurate a new phase of capitalism, as Timothy Ash does, but those that block its spread. See Gudavarthy 2002. Timothy G. Ash uses this term in another context to explain the changes in Poland and Hungary referring to the collapse of the Communist party, elimination of military and economic ties to the former Soviet Union and transition to capitalism in Eastern Europe. For Ash these signify the peaceful character of revolutionary changes.

18. 'Refolutionary' strategy has to therefore capture the relation between institutions, and modalities of power through a 'non-reductive' analysis. Again, as Wendy Brown notes,

   ...Social workers, pentagon, and the police are not simply different faces of the state...but different kinds of power. Each works differently as power, produces different effects, engenders different kinds of possible resistance, and represents a different analytical frame, at the same time, each emerges and operates in specific historical, political, and economic relation with the others, and thus also demands an analysis that can non-reductively capture this relation. (Brown 1995: 175)

19. According to Mattei and Nader, 'We argue in this book that foreign-imposed privatization laws that facilitate unconscionable bargains at the expense of the people are vehicles of plunder, not legality' (Mattei and Nader 2008: 4). They include the international financial institutions such as the WTO, IMF and the World Bank, and other regional blocks such as the NAFTA as active partners in the ongoing process of 'plunder' of Asia, Africa and Latin America, apart from the Euro-American expansion through recent US aggression and occupation of Iraq. Finally, they caution that these systems of expansion and plunder are now being adopted by China and India.

20. Earlier too Marxist historians such as E. P. Thompson had argued that principles such as the rule of law can be more than a mere 'juridical illusion' and useful in 'the imposing of effective inhibitions upon power and the defence of the citizen from power's all-intrusive claims' (Thompson 1975: 266).

21. It is this singularity that makes 'the people' susceptible to mobilizations, as Gyan Prakash points out, by the current right-wing nationalists and other 'fascist organizations' in the past (Gyan Prakash, *The Hindu*, 24 January 2010). Also see Ajay Gudavarthy 2012b, 'In Defence of the Politician', *The Hindu*, 15 October 2012.

22. Marx therefore proposes a complex method of moving from the concrete back to the abstract:

   If one were to start with population, it would be a chaotic conception of the whole, and through closer definition one would arrive analytically at increasingly simple concepts...From there it would be return journey until one finally arrived once more at population, which this time would be not a chaotic conception of the whole, but a rich totality of many determinations and relations. (Marx and Engels 1986: 37)

23. Actors for the politics of post-civil society are located 'in-against-and-beyond' constituencies. Ideas and practices of specific movements mutate to spread across constituencies, and in that sense move beyond identifiable constituencies. However, movements, such as those for peace, disarmament, and environmental and ecological protection that are without national boundaries and 'natural' actors, have their future in being mutated with organised—constituency-based—political movements working 'in-against-and-beyond' constituencies, otherwise there would be an increasing possibility of such movements without natural constituencies getting further NGOized.

Desai, I. P. 1984. 'Should "Caste" be the Basis for Recognising Backwardness?' *Economic and Political Weekly*, 19(28) July 14: 1106–16.

Deshpande, Satish. 2003. *Contemporary India*. New Delhi: Penguin.

Devika, J. and A. K. Rajasree, 2012. 'Widow's Organizations in Kerala State, India: Seeking Citizenship Amidst the Decline of Political Society', in Ajay Gudavarthy (ed.), *Reframing Democracy and Agency in India: Interrogating Political Society*, pp. 201–232. London: Anthem.

Diamond, L. 1994. 'Rethinking Civil Society: Towards Democratic Consolidation', *Journal of Democracy*, 5(3): 5–17.

Drucker, P. 1994. *Post-Capitalist Society*. New York: Harper Paperbacks.

Dutta, N. 1998. 'From Subject to Citizens: Towards a History of the Indian Civil Rights Movement', in M. R. Anderson and Sumit Guha (eds) *Changing Concept of Rights and Justice in South Asia*. Delhi: Oxford University Press.

Edgley, C. and D. Brisset (ed.). 1990. *Life as Theatre: A Dramaturgical Source Book*. New York: Aldinede Gruyter.

Edwards, Michael and B. Foley. 2001. *Beyond Tocqueville*. Hanover: University Press of New England.

Edwards, Michael. 2009. 'Enthusiasts, Tacticians and Sceptics', The World Bank, Civil Society and Social Capital. www.alternativasociales.org (accessed in May 2010)

———. 2010. Civil Society, Polity (second edition), Cambridge.

Elliot, C. M. (ed.). 2004. *Civil Society and Democracy*. Oxford: Oxford University Press.

Escobar, Arturo. 1992. 'Planning' in W. Sachs (ed.) *Development Dictionary: A Guide to Knowledge*. London: Zed Books.

Feldman, L. 2002. 'Redistribution, Recognition, and the State', *Political Theory*, 30(3): 410–40.

Ferguson, J. 1990. *The Anti-Politics Machine: Development, Depoliticisation and Bureaucratic Power in Lesotho*. Cambridge: Cambridge University Press.

Fernandes, L. 2000. 'Restructuring the New Middle Class in Liberalizing India', *Comparative Studies of South Asia, Africa, Middle East*, 20(1/2): 88–112.

———. 2006. *India's New Middle Class: Democratic Politics in an Era of Economic Reform*. University of Minnesota Press.

Finn, G. 1996. *Why Althusser Killed his Wife?* New Jersey: Humanities Press.

Fisher, Frank. 1990. *Technocracy and the Politics of Expertise*. London: SAGE Publications.

Foley, M. and B. Edwards. 1996. 'Paradox of Civil Society', *Journal of Democracy*, 7(3): 38–52.

Fraser, Nancy. 2008. From Redistribution to Recognition? Dilemmas of Justice in a 'Post-Socialist Age', in Kevin Olson (ed.), Adding Insult to Injury, pp. 68–93. New York: Verso.

———. 1997a. 'Heterosexism, Misrecognition and Capitalism: A Response to Judith Butler' *Social Text* 15: 279–89.

———. 1997b. 'Against Pollyanna-ism: A Reply to Iris Young' in *New Left Review*, 1:223: 126–29.

———. 2000. 'Rethinking Recognition', *New Left Review*, 2(3): 107–20.

Fraser, Nancy. 2001. 'Recognition without Ethics', *Theory, Culture and Society*, 18(2–3): 21–42.

———. 2004. 'Rethinking the Public Sphere' in C. M. Elliot (ed.) *Civil Society and Democracy*.

———. 2005. 'Reframing Justice in a Globalizing World', *New Left Review*, 2(36): 69–88.

———. 'Against Pollyanna-ism: A Rejoinder to Iris Young' in Kevin Olson (ed.), pp. 107–112.

———. 2009. 'Feminism, Capitalism and the Cunning of History', *New Left Review*, 56: 97–117.

Fraser, Nancy and Axel Honneth. 2003. *Redistribution or Recognition: A Political-Philosophical Exchange*, London: Verso.

Frevert, Ute. 2005. 'Civil Society and Citizenship in Western Democracies: Historical Developments and Recent Challenges', in Rajeev Bhargava et al. (eds), *Civil Society, Public Sphere and Citizenship*, pp. 59–83. Delhi: SAGE Publications.

Friere, Paulo. 1972. *Pedagogy of the Oppressed*. Middlesex: Penguin Books.

Fukuyama, Francis. 1995. *Trust: The Social Virtues and the Creation of Prosperity*. New York: The Free Press.

Galanter, Marc. 1984. *Competing Equalities: Law and the Backward Classes in India*. New Delhi: Oxford University Press.

Gandhi, Nandita and Nandita Shah. 1992. *The Issues at Stake: Theory and Practice in the Contemporary Women's Movement in India*. New Delhi: Kali for Women.

Geras, Norman. 1990. *Discourses of Extremity*. London: Verso.

———. 1995. 'Democracy and the ends of Marxism', *New Left Review*, 203 (1): 92–106.

Geremak, Bronislaw. 1992. 'Civil Society Then and Now', *Journal of Democracy*, 3(2): 3–12.

Giri, Ananta. 2005. 'Civil Society and the Limits of Identity Politics', in N. Jayaram (ed.), *On Civil Society*, pp. 218–236. London: SAGE Publications.

Giddens, Anthony. 1984. *The Constitution of Society*, Polity Press, Cambridge.

Goonewarden, K. and K. N. Rankin. 2004. 'The Desire Called Civil Society: A Contribution to the Critique of a Bourgeoisie Category', *Political Theory*, 3(2): 117–49.

Gramsci, Antonio. 1971. *The Prison Notebooks*. New York: International Publishers.

Greenpeace. 2004. *State of Community Health at Medak District*. Bangalore: Greenpeace India.

Gudavarthy, Ajay. 1996. 'Marxism, Authoritarianism and Peoples Movements', *Economic and Political Weekly*, 31(13): 847–49.

———. 2002. 'Fragmentation and Solidarity: A Study of Caste, Class and Gender Movements in Andhra Pradesh, 1985–95'. Unpublished Ph.D. dissertation. Jawaharlal Nehru University.

———. 2004. 'Tailored for the Corporates?' *The Hindu*, 2 November.

———. 2005. 'Dalit and Naxalite Movements in Andhra Pradesh: Solidarity or Hegemony?' *Economic and Political Weekly*, 40(51): 5410–18.

Gudavarthy, Ajay. 2008. 'Gandhi, Dalits and Feminists: Recovering the Convergence', *Economic and Political Weekly*, 43(22): 83–90.

———. 2009. 'Globalisation and Regionalisation: Mapping the New Continental Drift', *Economic and Political Weekly*, 44(24): 93–101.

———. 2011a. 'The Anti-Graft Movement in India: Anna Hazare's Soap Opera', Working Paper Series No. 9, Institute for Global Law and Policy, Harvard University.

———. 2011b. 'Tangles of Telangana', *Indian Express*, July 11, 2011.

———. 2012a. *Re-Framing Democracy and Agency: Interrogating Political Society*. London: Anthem.

———. 2012b. 'In Defence of the Politician,' *The Hindu*, October 15.

Gudavarthy, A. and G. Vijay. 2000. 'Civil Society, State and Social Movements', *Economic and Political Weekly*, 35(12).

———. 2004. 'Andhra Pradesh: Some Contemporary Trends', *Economic and Political Weekly*, 39(16): 1571–74.

———. 2007. Antinomies of Political Society: Implications of Uncivil Development, *Economic and Political Weekly*, 52(28): 3051–60.

Gupta, Dipankar. 1985. 'On Altering the Ego in Peasant Histories: Paradoxes of the Ethnic Option', *Peasant Studies*, 13(1): 5–24.

———. 1997. 'Civil Society in the Indian Context: Letting the State off the Hook', *Contemporary Sociology*, 26(3): 305–307.

———. 2004. 'Civil Society or the State—What Happened to Citizenship?' in C. M. Elliot (ed.), *Civil Society and Democracy*, pp. 211–37. Oxford: Oxford University Press.

Guru, Gopal. 1995. 'Dalit Women Talk Differently', *Economic and Political Weekly*, 30(41–42): 2548–50.

———. 2001. 'The Language of Dalit-Bahujan Political Discourse' in Ghanshyam Shah (ed.), *Dalit Identity and Politics*, pp. 97–107. New Delhi: SAGE Publications.

———. 2002. 'How Egalitarian Are the Social Sciences in India?' *Economic and Political Weekly*, 37(50): 5003–5009.

———. 2005. 'Citizenship in Exile: A Dalit Case' in Rajeev Bhargava et al. (ed.), *Civil Society, Public Sphere and Citizenship*, pp. 260–272. New Delhi: SAGE Publications.

Guruvayya, V. 1999. Vempentta Maranakanda (Telugu), Diksuchi Prachuranalu, Srikakulam.

Habermas, Jurgen. 1987. *Theory of Communicative Action, Vol. II*. Cambridge: Polity Press.

Hanlon, R. 2000. 'Recovering the Subject: Subaltern Studies and History of Resistance in Colonial South Asia' in V. Chaturvedi (ed.) *Mapping Subaltern Studies and the Post-Colonial*, pp. 92–116. London: Verso.

Haragopal, G. and K. Balagopal. 1998. 'Civil Liberties Movement and the State in India' in M. Mohanty and Partha N. Mukherjee (eds), *Peoples Rights: Social Movements and the State in the Third World*, pp. 353–72. New Delhi: SAGE Publications.

Haragopal, G. 1993. 'The Koyyur Kidnap: Question of Human Rights', *Economic and Political Weekly*, 28(49): 2650–55.

Hardt, Michael and Negri, Antonio. 2001. *Empire*. Cambridge: Harvard University Press.

———. 2004. *Multitude: War and Democracy in the Age of Empire*. New York: Penguin.

Harriss, John, 'Civil Society: Universal Concept or Fab?' www.odi.org.ulc.

Harvey, David. 2008. *The Condition of Postmodernity*. Oxford: Blackwell.

Hawthorn, Geoffrey. 2001. 'The Promise of Civil Society in the South' in Sudipta Kaviraj and Sunil Khilnani (Eds), *Civil Society: History and Possibilities*, pp. 269–286. Cambridge: Cambridge University Press.

Hirschmann, Nancy. 1989. 'Freedom, Recognition and Obligation: A Feminist Approach to Political Theory', *American Political Science Review*, 83(4): 1227–44.

Holloway, John. 1991. 'The State and Everyday Struggle' in S. Clarke (ed.) *The State Debate*, pp. 201–31. London: Macmillan.

———. 2002. *Change the World without Taking Power*. London: Pluto Press.

———. 2005. 'No' in *Historical Materialism*, 13(4): 265–284.

Honneth, Axel. 2001. 'Recognition or Redistribution?' *Theory, Culture and Society*, 18(2–3): 43–55.

Human Rights Forum. 2000. Untitled Pamphlet. Hyderabad: HRF.

Hussain, Nasser. 2003. *The Jurisprudence on Emergency: Colonialism and the Rule of Law*, Ann Arbor: University of Michigan Press.

Illiah, Kancha. 1992. 'Andhra Pradesh's Anti-Liquor Movement', *Economic and Political Weekly*, 27(45): 2406–08.

———. 1995a. *Madduru Dalitha Streela Poratam: Peruguthunna Kula, Varga, Linga Chaitanyam*. Hyderabad: Sahachara Book Mark.

———. 1995b. 'Caste or Class or Caste-Class: A Study in Dalit Bahujan Consciousness and Struggles in Andhra Pradesh in the 1980s'. Research in Progress Papers. New Delhi: NMML.

———.1996. 'Why I Am Not a Hindu: A Sudra Critique of Hindutva Philosophy', *Culture and Political Economy*, Calcutta: Samya.

———. 2001. 'Dalitism vs Brahmanism: The Epistemological Conflict in History' in Ghanshyam Shah (ed.) *Dalit Identity and Politics*, pp. 108–128. New Delhi: SAGE.

———. 2004. 'Caste or Class or Caste-Class: A Study in Dalit Bahujan Consciousness and Struggles in AP in 1980s' in Manoranjan Mohanty (ed.), *Caste, Class and Gender*. New Delhi: SAGE.

———. 2009. *Post-Hindu India*. New Delhi: SAGE Publications.

Iyer, Raghavan. 1978. *The Moral and Political Thought of Gandhi*. Delhi: Oxford University Press.

Jameson, Frederic. 2000. 'Globalisation and Political Strategy', *New Left Review*, 4, July–August 2000: 49–68.

Janaki, K. 1999. *Role of Women in Freedom Struggle in Andhra Pradesh*. Hyderabad: Neelkamal Publishers.

Jayal, Niraja (ed). 2007. *Democracy in India*. Delhi: Oxford University Press.

Jayaram, N. 1999. *On Civil Society*: Issues and Perspectives. New Delhi: SAGE Publications.

Jenkins, Rob. 1999. *Democratic Politics and Economic Reforms in India*. Cambridge: Cambridge University Press.

Jessop, Bob. 1998. 'The Rise of Governance and the Risks of Failure: The Case of Economic Development', *International Social Sciences Journal*, 50(155): 29–45.

Joseph, Sarah. 2001. 'Democratic Governance: A New Agenda for Change' *Economic and Political Weekly*, 36(12) March 24: 24–30.

Kaiwar, Vasant. 2005. 'Silences in Post-Colonial Thought', *Economic and Political Weekly*, 40(34) August 20: 3732–38.

Kakarala, S. 1993. *Civil Rights Movement in India*. Ph.D. Dissertation, Centre for Social Studies, Surat.

Kamat, Sangeeta. 2002. *Development Hegemony: NGOs and the State in India*. Delhi: Oxford University Press.

Kannabiran, K. G. 1993. 'Koyyuru: Reflections on a Kidnap', *Economic and Political Weekly*, 28 (12–13): 495–98.

———. 2004. *The Wages of Impunity: Power, Justice and Human Rights*. New Delhi: Orient Longman.

Kannabiran, Kalpana. et al. (ed.). 1995. *Sarrihaddulu Leni Sandhyalu, Swecha Prachuranalu*. Hyderabad.

Kannabiran, Vasant and Kalpana Kannabiran. 1991. 'Caste and Gender: Understanding Dynamics of Power and Violence', *Economic and Political Weekly*, 26(37) September 14: 2130–34.

Kannabiran, Vasant and K. Lalitha. 1989. 'That Magic Time: Women in Telangana People's Struggle' in K. Sanghari (ed.) *Recasting Women*. New Delhi: Kali for Women.

Kapur, Ratna. 1996a. *Subversive Sites: Feminist Engagement with Law in India*. Delhi: SAGE Publications.

———. (ed.). 1996b. *Feminist Terrains in Legal Domains: Interdisciplinary Essays on Women and Law in India*. Delhi: Kali for Women.

———. 2005. *Erotic Justice: Law and New Politics of Post-Colonialism*. London: Glasshouse Press.

———. 2007. 'Challenging Liberal Subject: Law and Gender Justice in South Asia' in M. Mukhopadhyay (ed.), *Gender Justice, Citizenship, and Development*. Delhi: Zubaan.

Keith Michael Baker. 2001. 'Enlightenment and the Institution of Society: Notes for a Conceptual History', in Sudipta Kaviraj and Sunil Khilnani (eds), *Civil Society*, Cambridge, Cambridge University Press.

Khilnani, Sunil. 2001. 'The Development of Civil Society', in Sudipta Kaviraj and Sunil Khilnani (eds), *Civil Society: History and Possibilities*. Cambridge: Cambridge University Press.

Klein, Naomi. 2007. *The Shock Doctrine: The Rise of Disaster Capitalism*. New York: Picador.

Kothari, Rajini. 1988. *State Against Democracy*. Delhi: Ajanta Publishers.

———. 1989. 'The NGOs, The State and World Capitalism', *New Asian Visions*, 6(1).

———. 2005. *Rethinking Democracy*, Hyderabad: Orient Longman.

Kothari, S. and H. Sethi (eds). 1991. *Rethinking Human Rights*. Delhi: Lokayan Publications.

Kula Nirmulana (Telugu), Bulletin 2. June 2001. KNPS, Hyderabad.

Kula Nirmulana Porata Samithi, Pranalika—Nibandhanavali (Telugu). Undated. KNPS, Hyderabad.

Kumar, Krishna. 1993. 'Civil Society: An Inquiry into the Usefulness of an Historical Term', *British Journal of Sociology*, 44(3): 375–395.

Kumar, Radha. 1993. *The History of Doing: An Illustrated Account of Movements for Women's Rights and Feminism in India, 1800–1900*. Delhi: Zubaan.

Laclau, Ernesto. 1990. *New Reflections on the Revolution of Our Times*. London: Verso.

———. 2005. *On Populist Reason*. London: Verso.

Laclau, Ernesto and Chantall Mouffe. 1985. *Hegemony and Socialist Strategy: Towards a Radical Democratic Politics*. London: Verso.

———. 1987. 'Post-Marxism Without Apologies', *NLR* 166 (November–December): 79–107.

Lalitha, K. 1998. 'Women in Revolt: A Historical Analysis of the Progressive Organisation of Women in Andhra Pradesh', in S. Wieringa (ed.) *Women's Struggles and Strategies*. The Hague.

Locke, John. 2002. *The Second Treatise of Government*, ed. Tom Crawford, Mineola. New Jersey: Dover Publications.

Lokaneeta, Jinee. 2011. 'Truth Telling: Techniques in a Regime of Terror' in *Canada Watch*, Special Issue 'India: The World's Most Fragile of Democracies', Winter 2012: 35–38.

Lukes, Steven. 1985. *Marxism and Morality*. Oxford: Oxford University Press.

Luhmann, Niklas. 1982. *The Differentiation of Society*. New York: Columbia University Press.

Mackinnon, C. 1983. 'Feminism, Marxism, Method, and the State: Towards Feminist Jurisprudence', *Signs*. 8(4): 635–658.

Mackinon, C. A. 1987. *Feminism Unmodified: Discourse on Life and Law*. Cambridge: Harvard University Press.

Mahajan Front, 1999. Ummadi Ennikala Pranalika (Telugu), Mahajan Front, Hyderabad.

Mahajan, Gurpreet. 2004. 'Civil Society and its Avatars—What Happened to Freedom and Democracy', in C. M. Elliot (ed.), *Civil Society and Democracy*. Oxford: Oxford University Press.

Mahila Margam. The Official Organ of A.P. Chaitanya Mahila Samakhya, Hyderabad.

Mansbridge, J. (ed). 1990. 'The Rise and Fall of Self-Interest', in *Beyond Self-Interest*, pp. 3–22, Chicago: University of Chicago Press.

Marcuse, Herbert. 1965. 'Repressive Tolerance' in Robert Paul Wolff, Barrington Moore, jr., and Herbert Marcuse (eds), *A Critique of Pure Tolerance*, pp. 95–137. Boston: Beacon Press.

Markell, Patchen. 2000. 'The Recognition of Politics: A Comment on Emcke and Tully', *Constellations* 7(4): 496–506.

Martin Alcoff, Linda. 1995. 'Phenomenology, Post-Structuralism and Feminist Theory of the Concept of Experience' in Linda Fisher (ed.), *Feminist Phenomenology*, London: Klugn Academic Publishers.

Marx, Karl and Frederic Engels. 1986. *Collected Works*, Vols. 28 and 29. Moscow: Progress Publishers.

Mattei, U. and L. Nader. 2008. *Plunder: When the Rule of Law is Illegal*. Oxford: Blackwell.

McClain, L. and J. Fleming, 2000. 'Some Questions for Civil Society Revivalists', *Chicago-Kent Review*, 75 (2): 301–54.

Mcintosh, M. 1978. 'The State and the Oppression of Women', in *Feminism and Materialism* (ed.) A. Kuhn and A.M. Wolpe, London: Routledge.

Mehta, Uday Singh. 1999. *Liberalism and Empire: A Study in Nineteenth Century British Liberal Thought*. London: University of Chicago Press.

Melucci, Alberto. 1989. *Nomads of the Present*. Philadelphia: Temple University Press.

Menon, Nivedita. 2004. *Recovering Subversion*. Delhi: Permanent Black.

Meszaros, Istvan. 1985. *Philosophy, Ideology and Social Science*. New York: Prentice Hall.

Maria, Mies. 1976. 'The Sahada Movement: A Peasant Movement in Maharashtra, its Development and its Perspective', in *Journal of Peasant Studies*, 3(4) July: 472–82.

Mill, J. S. 1963. 'On Liberty', in *The Six Great Humanistic Essays of John Stuart Mill*, New York: Washington Square Press.

Mieville, C. 2006. *Between Equal Rights: A Marxist Theory of International Law*. New York: Haymarket Books.

Mitchell, Timothy. 1990. 'Everyday Metaphors of Power' *Theory and Society*, Vol. 19/5: 545–577.

Moore, Barrington. 1993. *Social Origins of Dictatorship and Democracy: Lord and Peasant in the Making of the Modern World*, Beacon Press.

Mouffe, Chantal. 1993. *The Return of the Political*, London: Verso.

———. 2005. *On the Political: Thinking in Action*. London: Routledge.

Mukhopadhya, Maitrayee. 2007. 'Situating Gender and Citizenship in Development Debates' in Mukhopadhya, M, et al. (ed.), *Gender Justice, Citizenship and Development*, pp. 171–222. New Delhi: Zubaan.

Muthaiah, P. 2004. 'Dandora: The Madiga Movement for Equal Identity and Social Justice in AP', *Social Action*, 54 (April–June).

———. 2007. 'SC-laku Vargeekarana Enduku?' AP Madiga Medhavula Forum, Hyderabad: Osmania University.

Nagaraj, D. R. 1993. *The Flaming Fleet: A Study of Dalit Movement in India*. Bangalore: South Forum Press.

Nalupu (ed.) B. Tarakam, 1991. Hyderabad Book Trust, Hyderabad. May 16–31 and June 1–15.

Nigam, Aditya. 2005. 'Civil Society and its Underground: Explorations in the Notions of Political Society' in Rajeev Bhargava et al. (eds), *Civil Society, Public Sphere and Citizenship*. Delhi: SAGE Publications.

Nigam, Aditya. 2008. 'The Implosion of "The Political"', *Journal of Contemporary Thought*, 27, Summer: 51–70.

Omvedt, Gail. 2001. 'Ambedkar and After: The Dalit Movement in India' in Ghanshyam Shah (ed.) *Dalit Identity and Politics*, pp. 143–159. New Delhi: SAGE Publications.

Pai, Sudha. 2010. *Developmental State and the Dalit Question in Madhya Pradesh: Congress Response*. New Delhi: Routledge.

Pamphlet on Attack by BCs on SCs, November 1999.

Pamphlet titled as 'Political Admirers of Janashakti', 1994.

Parekh, Bhikhu. 1993. 'Cultural Particularity of Liberal Democracy' in D. Held (ed.) *Prospects for Democracy*. Cambridge: Polity Press.

———. 1995. 'Jawaharlal Nehru and the Crisis of Modernisation' in U. Baxi and B. Parekh (eds), *Crisis and Change in Contemporary India*. Delhi: SAGE Publications.

———. 2008. *A New Politics of Identity*. New York: Palgrave Macmillan.

Pateman, Carole. 1992. 'Political Obligation, Freedom and Feminism', *American Political Science Review*, 86(1): 179–90.

Patnaik, A. K. 1995. 'Burden of Marx and Morals', *Economic and Political Weekly*, May 20 31(20): 202–04.

Perkins, John. 2004. *The Confessions of an Economic Hit Man*. New York: Plume.

Petras, James and Timothy F. Harding, 'Introduction', *Latin American Perspectives* 27(5), Radical Left Response to Global Impoverishment (Sep., 2000): 3–10.

Petras, James and H. Veltmeyer. 2005. *Empire with Imperialism: The Globalizing Dynamics of Neo-Liberal Capitalism*. London: Zed Books.

Phillips, Anne. 1995. *The Politics of Presence*. Oxford: Clarendon Press.

———. 2001. 'Feminism and Liberalism Revisited: Has Martha Nussbaum Got it Right? *Constellations*, 8/2: 249–66.

———. 2002. 'Does Feminism Need a Conception of Civil Society' in S. Chambers and W. Kymlicka (eds) *Alternative Conceptions of Civil Society*. Princeton: Princeton University Press.

Prakash, Gyan. 2010. 'In the Name of People', *The Hindu*, 24 January.

Prasad, Madhava. 1998. 'The State in/of Cinema.' in Partha Chatterjee (ed.), *Wages of Freedom: Fifty Years of the Indian Nation-State*, pp. 123–146. Delhi: Oxford Univeristy Press.

Purvis, T. and A. Hunt. 1999. 'Identity versus Citizenship: Transformations in the Discourses and Practices of Citizenship', *Social and Legal Studies*, 8(4): 457–482.

Putnam, Robert. D. 1995. 'Bowling Alone: America's Declining Social Capital', *Journal of Democracy*, 6(1): 65–78.

Ram, M. 1986. 'Civil Rights Situation in India', in A. R. Desai (ed.), *Violation of Democratic Rights in India*, Vol. 3. Bombay: Sangam Books.

Ramaswamy, Uma. 1984. 'Preference and Progress: The Scheduled Castes', *Economic and Political Weekly*, XIX(30) July 28: 12–14.

———. 1986. 'Protection and Inequality Among Backward Castes', *Economic and Political Weekly*, 21(9): 399–403.

claims—moral and epistemic—on the basis of asserting an integrated 'lived experience' that was only accessible to them. Such claims gave rise to a context where identity politics initially 'born of social critique invariably become conservative as they are forced to essentialize the identity and naturalize the boundaries of what they once grasped as a contingent effect of historically specific social power' (Brown 2001: 27). Recognition, from a legitimate claim, becomes a trap that disallows the 'not-yet' dimension of politics. Broader frames of combining caste–class give way to minimalist agendas that 'tends to preclude their addressing deep sources of injustice and to incite instead a politics that acts at the largely symbolic and gestural level, the level at which moralism runs rampant' (Ibid.: 39). The potential that identity and the symbolic have in framing material and economic demands is fractured and amputated, and converted into self-referential and self-contained dynamics—recognition against redistribution;[6] or with the Naxalite movement redistribution against recognition.

These claims of authenticity, as we had discussed in the chapter on Dalit politics, is the result of the way power is organized in civil society, which allows particularistic articulations but in the process also stigmatizes these very identities for their 'sectarian' claims, and thus initiating a process of what we called 'mobility without dignity'. The claims to authenticity in turn leads to the breakdown of inter-subjectivity, resulting in a phenomenon of arrested social base and exclusively privileging the voices and scripts audible and legible—legitimate—within the corridors of civil society. Thus, the interaction between multiple subjectivities, and their ensuing frameworks, is replaced by privileging singular voice of the most dominant social group within the Dalits, and the feminists, and this often turned out to be the voice of the urban middle class that the civil society itself privileged.

During the 1970s students and young radicals opted out of premier universities and colleges, and joined struggles in search of the route to de-class themselves.[7] However, by the 1990s, with the changing class composition among all social groups including that of the Dalits, there was a growth of a nascent but a strong component of middle class that assumed the leadership ranks of various political movements. Human rights movement had great discomfort in getting reconciled to the fact that it was 'merely' a movement with a social base almost exclusively amongst the middle class, which, as we noted, was one of the reasons that prompted a shift from initiating radical politicization to abstract moralism.[8] With regard to Dalit politics, the new middle class opened up a range of new issues, availed old institutional spaces and created new ones where necessary, and articulated new meanings and converted available categories into 'empty signifiers' when they, for instance, argued at a global level that 'caste is race'.[9] They sought new modes of mobilization and new venues to mount pressure on the state and to compel it to take action against caste based discrimination, by hitting where it hurts the most, in diluting its claim to sovereignty. However, on the other hand, the same class was at variance, distanced, and disconnected from the rest of segments of the same social group. While there was social and cultural similarity, there were marked differences in economic and class positionality. The new cracks that emerged were made good by taking recourse to a moral language that made it possible to represent all segments of the Dalits without necessitating a political negotiation of the new fragments and ensuing complexities that had emerged. Experiment was replaced with incommunicability and politics with morality. Agency of those struggling against was built *on* and *as* a *withdrawal* from political mediation—both internal and external. As with the feminist politics, while the restriction to urban middle classes brought in 'professional feminism'—subverting subversion—and a process of NGO-ization, and a marked decline in street protest politics as well as engagement with a wide array of social, political and economic issues at the points of their interaction. These were replaced by singular focus on legal reform, and exclusive celebration of cultural identities in the name of 'politics of difference' and plurality. It is the same middle class, classical representatives of civil society, which re-presents the politics of middlemen in the context of 'survival strategies' and 'contextual negotiations', adopted by the subaltern in the terrain referred to as 'political society'.

Thus, if identity politics—asserted since they were recognised and privileged by the civil society—lead to claims of authenticity, these claims in turn lead to breakdown of inter-subjectivity, and privileging of narrow social base that was often expressed through the exclusive articulations by the urban middle class, and a disengagement with other social constituencies, across caste, class and gender; this, in turn, entailed withdrawal from political mediation—between economic, political and cultural dimensions, this withdrawal, in the context of Dalit politics, was symptomatic of the process of internalization of the logic of 'racism at a distance', as Slovoj Zizek put it, of being ghettoized or framed as naturalized identities—claiming only Dalits speak for Dalits and that the Dalit is a self-enclosed (cultural)identity; and ghettoization through naturalized identities—as against historicization of identities—was in fact a mode of agency that took recourse to moralization—moralization of politics supplanted politicization of ethics—in creating the Dalit as a self-enclosed moral subject. In creating a self-enclosed moral subject, the Dalit movement gets disciplined within the contours of the *minimalism of civil society*—that includes distancing itself from a richer caste–class

References

Agamben, Giorgio. 1998. Heller-Roazen, trans. *Homo Sacer: Sovereign Power and Bare Life*. Stanford, CA: Stanford University Press.

Agnes, Flavia. 2009. 'Conjugality, Property, Morality and Maintenance', *Economic and Political Weekly*, 44: 58–64.

AILRC. 1993. 'Dandakaranya Adivasi Women`s Movement.' Hyderabad.

Alam, Javed. 1983. 'Peasantry, Politics and Historiography: Critique of the New Trend in Resistance to Marxism', *Social Scientist*, 11(2): 43–54.

Aloysius, G. 1998. *Nationalism without a Nation*. Delhi: Oxford University Press.

Anderson, Perry. 1980. *Arguments within English Marxism*. London: Verso.

Andhra Pradesh Civil Liberties Committee. 1985a. Fact Finding Team, Karamchedu, Salaha, Hyderabad.

———. 1985b. The State versus Civil Liberties Organisations—The case of APCLC, *Lokayan Bulletin* June.

———. 1991. The Chundur Carnage, APCLC, Vijayawada.

———. Undated. *Paura Hakkula Avagahana Charcha Patralu*. Hyderabad: APCLC.

Anveshi. 1993. 'Reworking Gender Relations, Redefining Politics', *Economic and Political Weekly*, 28(3–4): 87–90.

APDM (Andhra Pradesh Dalitha Mahasabha). 1985. *Pranalika*. Hyderabad: APDM.

Appadurai, Arjun. 1986. 'Theory of Anthropology: Centre and Periphery', *Comparative Studies in Society and History*, 28: 356–61.

Appiah, Kwame Anthony. 2006. 'The Politics of Identity', *Daedalus*, Fall, 135(4): 15–22.

Arendt, Hannah. 1970. *On Violence*. Mariner Books. New York.

Ash, Timothy. G. 1999. *The Uses of Adversity: Essays on the Fate of Central Europe*. London: Penguin Books.

Association for Protection of Democratic Rights. 1991. *Two Decades of APDR & Human Rights*. Calcutta: APDR.

Badiou, Alain. 2006. *Metapolitics*. London: Verso.

Balagopal, K. 1987. 'Our Democratic Future', *Lokayan Bulletin*, 5: 4–5.

———. 1992. 'Slaying of a Spirituous Demon', *Economic and Political Weekly*, November 14: 2457–61.

———. 1995. 'Democracy and the Fight against Communalism', *Economic and Political Weekly*, January 7: 57–60.

Balagopal, K. 1997. 'The Human Rights Movement: Its Context and Its Concerns', in *Indian Journal of Human Rights*, 1(1) (Jan–June): 82–106.

——— 2000. 'A Tangled Web', *Economic and Political Weekly*, March 25th: 1075–1081.

——— 2006. 'Chhattisgarh: Physiognomy of Violence', *Economic and Political Weekly*, 41(22), (June 03): 2183–2186.

———. Forthcoming Human Rights Movement in Andhra Pradesh: A Theoretical Reflection. In Ajay Gudavarthy and G. Vijay (eds) *Understanding Contemporary Andhra Pradesh*.

Banerjee, Sumanta. 1987. 'Tuning Our Ears to Discord: Response of the Democratic Rights Movement to the Question of Violence', *Lokayan Bulletin*, 5: 4/5.

Basu, A. 2001. 'The Dialectics of Hindu Nationalism', in A. Kohli (ed.) *The Success of India's Democracy*, pp. 163–89. Cambridge: Cambridge University Press.

Bauman, Zygmunt. 2001. 'The Great War of Recognition', *Theory, Culture and Society*, 18(2–3): 137–50.

Baxi, Upendra. 1998. 'The State and Human Rights Movements in India', in M. Mohanty et al (eds) *Peoples Rights*, pp. 335–52. New Delhi: SAGE Publications.

———. 2002. *The Future of Human Rights*. New Delhi: Oxford University Press.

Bayart, J. 1986. 'Civil Society in Africa' in Chabal, P. (ed.), *Political Domination in Africa*. Oxford University Press.

Beck, Ulrich. 1992. *Risk Society: Towards a New Modernity*. London: SAGE Publication.

Beetham, David. 1993. 'Liberal Democracy and the Limits of Democratization', in David Held (ed.), *Prospects for Democracy: North, South, East, West*, Cambridge: Polity Press.

Beteille, André. 1995. 'Universities as Institutions', *Economic and Political Weekly*, 30(11): 563–68.

———. 2004. 'Civil Society and its Institutions', in C. M. Elliot (ed.) *Civil Society and Democracy*.

Bevir, M. 1999. 'Foucault and Critique: Deploying Agency against Autonomy', *Political Theory*, 27(1): 65–84.

Bhargava, Rajeev. 2000. 'Ethical Insufficiency of Egoism and Altruism' in Rajendra Vohra et al. (eds) *Indian Democracy*, pp. 215–235. Delhi: SAGE Publications.

——— et al. (ed). 2005. *Citizenship, Civil Society and Public Sphere*. New Delhi: SAGE Publications.

Bilgrami, Akeel. 2003. 'Gandhi, the Philosopher', *Economic and Political Weekly*, 38(39): 4159–4165.

———. 2007. 'Secularism and the very Concept of Law', in Rajeshwari Sundar Rajan (ed.) *The Crisis of Secularism in India*, pp. 316–33. Duke: Duke University Press.

Brass, Paul. 2001. *Politics of India since Independence*. New Delhi: Cambridge University Press.

Breman, Jan. 2002. 'Communal Upheaval as Resurgence of Social Darwinism', *Economic and Political Weekly*, 37(16): 1485–88.

Rani, Jyothi and T. Vidmahe. 1999. 'Towards Women's Emanicipation: Three Decades of New Democratic Revolutionary Movement', *Indian Journal of Human Rights*, 3(1–2).

Rao, U.S. (ed.). 1991. *Edureeta*, May. Hyderabad: Marxist-Leninist Centre.

———. 1994. *Edureeta*. Hyderabad: Marxist-Leninist Centre.

Rao, Malleshwar. 2004. 'The Battle of the Bottle in Andhra Pradesh', *The Hindu*, 27 March.

Ratnam, K. Y. 1998. 'Dalit Movement in AP: A Study of Political Consciousness and Identity'. Unpublished Ph.D. thesis. Jawaharlal Nehru University, New Delhi.

Ravi, N. 1993. 'Democratic Movements and Dialectics', *Economic and Political Weekly*, 20(27–28) July 3–10: 1469–71.

Ray, Aswini. 2003. 'Human Rights Movement in India', *Economic and Political Weekly*, 38(32) August 9: 3409–15.

Reddi, S. 1950. 'Community-Conflict among the Depressed Castes of Andhra', *Man in India*, 31(4): 1–12.

Reddy, N. and Arun Patnaik. 1993. 'Anti-Arrack Agitation of Women in Andhra Pradesh', *Economic and Political Weekly*, 28(21) May 22: 1059–66.

Reddy, R. and G. Haragopal. 1985. 'The Pyraveekar: The "Fixer" in Rural India', *Asian Survey*, 25(11): 11148–162.

Report of the World Commission on Environment and Development: Our Common Future (Brundtland Report). Oxford: Oxford University Press, Published March 1987.

Rosenblum, N. 2002. 'Feminist Perspectives on Civil Society and Government', in Rosenblum et al. (eds) *Civil Society and Government*. Princeton: Princeton Univesity Press.

Rudoplh, L. and S. Rudoplh. 2004. 'The Coffee House and the Ashram' in C. M. Elliot (ed.) *Civil Society and Democracy*, pp. 377–404. Delhi: Oxford University Press.

———. 2006. *Postmodern Gandhi and Other Essays*. Oxford: Oxford University Press.

Rudoplh Lloyd and Sussane Hoeber Rudoplh. 2008. 'Explaining Indian Democracy: A Fifty-Year Perspective, 1956–2006'. Volume 1. *The Realm of Ideas: Inquiry and Theory*, Delhi: Oxford University Press.

Sainath, P. 1999. 'The Borderlines of Caste', *The Hindu*, 7 April.

Sader, Emir. 2002. 'Beyond Civil Society', *New Left Review*, 17 October, 87–99.

Samaddar, Ranabir. 2007. *The Materiality of Politics*. London: Anthem.

Sankaran, S. R. 1998. 'Development of Scheduled Castes in Andhra Pradesh', *Economic and Political Weekly*, 33(5): 208–211.

Sanyal, Kalyan. 2007. *Rethinking Capitalist Development*. Delhi: Routledge.

Sarukkai, Sundar. 2007. 'Dalit Experience and Theory', *Economic and Political Weekly*, 42 (40): 4043–4048.

Sayer, Andrew. 2005. *The Moral Significance of Class*. Cambridge: Cambridge University Press.

Schumpeter. 2011. 'Khaki Capitalism', *Indian Express*, 6 December.

Scott, James. 1986. 'Everyday Forms of Peasant Resistance', *Journal of Peasant Studies*, 13(2): 5–35.

———. 1998. *Seeing Like a State*. London: Yale University Press.

———. 2009. *The Art of Not Being Governed*. New Haven: Yale University Press.

Scott, Joan. 1992. 'Experience' in Joan W. Scott and Judith Butler (eds) *Feminists Theorize the Political*, pp. 22–40. New York: Routledge.

Sethi, J. D. 1975. *India in Crisis*. Delhi: Vikas Publications.

Shah, Ghanshyam. 2004. *Social Movements in India: A Review of Literature*. Delhi: SAGE Publications.

Shah, Nandita and Nandita Gandhi. 1992. *The Issues at Stake: Theory and Practice in the Contemporary Women's Movement in India*. Delhi: Kali for Women.

Shils, Edward, 1991. 'The Virtue of Civil Society,' *Government and Opposition*, 26(1) (Winter): 3–20.

Singh, Randhir. 1993. 'Terrorism, State Terrorism and Democratic Rights', in *Five Lectures in Marxist Mode*, pp. 60–90. Delhi: Ajanta Publications.

Singh, Ujjwal K. 2004. 'State and Emerging Interlocking Legal Systems', *Economic and Political Weekly*, 39: 149–54.

———. 2005. 'Democratising State and Society: Role of Civil Liberties and Democratic Rights Movements in India', *Contemporary India*, January—June.

Soper, Kate. 1987. 'Marxism and Morality', *New Left Review*, 1(163): 111–13.

Sreenivas, J. 2012. 'The Andhra Pradesh Liquor Scam', *Indian Express*, 12 April 2012.

Srinivas, S. V. 1999. 'Telugu Cinema, NTR and After: The Alluda Majaka Controversy Revisited', *Journal of Arts and Ideas*, 32–33.

Srinivasulu, K. 1994. 'Andhra Pradesh: BSP and Caste Politics', *Economic and Political Weekly*, 29(40): (October 1).

Stiglitz, Joseph. 2002. *Globalization and its Discontents*. New Delhi: Penguin.

Stree Shakti Sangathana. 1989. *We Were Making History: Life Stories Of Women in Telangana Peoples Struggle*. Delhi: Kali for Women.

Sudhakar. K. et. al (ed.) 1998. *Naxalbari Gamyam, Gamanam*. Hyderabad: Perspectives.

Sundarrayya, P. 1972. *Telangana People's Struggle and it's Lessons*. New Delhi: Foundation Books.

Sunder Rajan, Rajeshwari. 1999. *Signposts: Gender Issues in Post-Independence India*. Delhi: Kali for Women.

———. 2003. *The Scandal of the State*. London: Duke University Press.

Suneetha, A. 2003. *Institutional Response to Domestic Violence*. Hyderabad: Anveshi Research Centre for Women's Studies.

———. 2005. 'Adjudicating (Un) Domestic Battles', *Economic and Political Weekly*, XL(38) September 17: 4101–4103.

———. 2006. 'Women's Actions and Legal Institutions in the Face of Domestic Violence', *Economic and Political Weekly*, XLI(41) October 14: 4355–4362.

Suttner, R. 2001. *Inside Apartheids Prison*. Melbourne: Ocean Press.

Tarkunde, V. M. 1991. 'In Defence of Freedom', in A. R. Desai (ed.) *Governmental Lawlesness and Organised Struggles*. Bombay: Popular Prakashan.

Teltumbde, Anand. 2007. 'Divergence of the Left and Dalit Movements: Cause and Remedy' in M. Thangaraj (ed.), *Dalit Movements in South India*. Chennai: University of Madras.

Tharu, Susie and Tejaswini Niranjana. 1994. 'Problems for a Contemporary Theory of Gender', *Social Scientist*, 22(3–4): March–April: 93–118.

Thompson, E.P. 1975. *Whigs and Hunters: The Origin of the Black Act*. New York: Pantheon Books.

Thompson, E.P. 1985. 'Comment: Response to Arato and Cohen', *Praxis International*, 5(3): 75–85.

Times of India. August 12, 2010. 'How a Tribal Boy Becomes a Dreaded Naxalite'.

Uberoi, Patricia. 2003. 'Feminism and the Public-Private Distinction' in G. Mahajan (ed.) *The Public and the Private*, pp. 205–28. Delhi: SAGE Publications.

Verma, R. 2006. *Postcolonial Politics and Personal Law*. Delhi: Oxford University Press.

Vijay, G. 1999. 'Social Security of Labour in New Industrial Towns', *Economic and Political Weekly*, XXXIV(39) September 25: 10–18.

———. 2003. 'Other Side of New Industrialisation', *Economic and Political Weekly*, 38(48) Nov 29.

Vindhya, U. 1990. 'Women in Srikakulam Movement' in I. Sen (ed.) *A Space Within the Struggle: Women's Participation in People's Movements*. Delhi: Kali for Women.

———. 2000. 'Comrades-in-Arms: Sexuality and Identity in the Contemporary Revolutionary Movement in Andhra Pradesh and the Legacy of Chalam', in Mary E. John (ed.), *Question of Silence*. pp. 167–191.

Virasam, Postmortemku Migilina Mruthadehalu: Vempentta Ghatana Vasthavalu (Telugu), Navodaya Book House, Hyderabad, 1998.

Volga (ed.). Feminist Study Circle (Mimeo, undated).

———. 1994. *Nurella Chalam, Swechha Prachranalu*. Hyderabad.

Volga et al. 1995. *Saramsham*. (Report on the Anti-arrack Movement in Telugu). Asmita Resource Centre for Women, Hyderabad.

Walzer, M. 1984. 'Liberalism and the Art of Separation', *Political Theory*, 12(3): 315–330.

———. 1995. 'The Concept of Civil Society' in Michael Walzer (ed.), *Toward a Global Civil Society*, 7–28. Providence-Oxford: Berghahn Books.

———. 2002. 'Equality and Civil Society', in Simon Chambers and Will Kymlicka (eds) *Alternative Conceptions of Civil Society*, Princeton University Press, 34–49.

Wasserstrom, Richard A. 1971. *Morality and the Law*. California: Wardsworth Publishing Company.

Webber, David. 2001. *Good Budgeting, Better Justice: Modern Budget Practices for the Judicial Sector, Law and Development*, Working Paper Series, No. 3.

White, Gordon. 1994. 'Civil Society, Democratization and Development' in Democratization, 1(2): 375–390.

William, Patricia. 1991. *Alchemy of Race and Rights*. Cambridge: Harvard University Press.

Williams, Raymond. 1983. *Towards 2000*. London: Hogarth Press.

Winfield, R. D. 1995. *Law in Civil Society*. Kansas: University of Kansas.

Wood, E. M. 1990. 'The Uses and Abuses of Civil Society', in Ralph Miliband and John Saville (eds), *The Socialist Register*, pp. 60–84. Vol. 26.

———. 1995. 'Civil Society and the Politics of Identity' in (Chapter 8) *Democracy Against Capitalism: Renewing Historical Materialism*, pp. 238–263. Cambridge University Press.

Young, I. M. 2008. 'Unruly Categories: A Critique of Nancy Fraser's Dual Systems Theory' in Kevin Olson (ed.) pp. 89–111, *Adding Insult to Injury*, London: Verso.

Yudice, George. 1995. 'Civil Society, Consumption, and Governmentality in an Age of Global Restructuring: An Introduction', Social Text (Winter 45): 1–25.

Zizek, Slavoj. 1997. 'Multiculturalism, or, the Cultural Logic of Multinational Capitalism', *New Left Review* 225 (September–October): 28–51.

Index

About the Author

Ajay Gudavarthy is Assistant Professor at the Centre for Political Studies of Jawaharlal Nehru University, New Delhi. He was Charles Wallace Visiting Fellow for the year 2008 at the Centre for South Asian Studies, SOAS, University of London, Visiting Fellow at Goldsmiths, University of London, 2010 and Visiting Fellow, Centre for Citizenship, Civil Society and Rule of Law (CISRUL), University of Aberdeen, 2012. His areas of interest include political theory, human rights, civil society and political movements. He has edited a book titled *Re-framing Democracy and Agency in India: Interrogating Political Society* (2012). He is a regular columnist with *The Indian Express*, and has published in various national and international journals.

Brenkman, John. 1999. 'Extreme Criticism', Critical Inquiry, 26(1): 109–127.

Brown, Wendy. 1995. *The States of Injury*. Princeton: Princeton University Press.

———. 2001. *Politics Out of History*. Oxford: Princeton University Press.

———. 2006. *Regulating Aversion*. Princeton: Princeton University Press.

Butler, Judith. 1997. 'Merely Cultural' *Social Text*. 52.3 (Fall/Winter): 265–277.

———. 1992. 'Contingent Foundations: Feminism and the Question of Postmodernism in J. Scott (ed.) Feminists Theorize the Political*, Routledge: New York.

———. 2000. 'Subjection, Resistance, Resignification' in W. Brogan and J. Risser (eds) *American Continental Philosophy: A Reader*. Bloomington: Indiana University Press.

Callinicos, Alex. 2004. *Making History: Agency, Structure and Change in Social Theory*. London: BRILL.

———. 2006. *The Resources of Critique*. London: Polity Press.

Canclini, N. G. 2001. *Consumers and Citizens: Globalisation and Multicultural Conflicts*. Minneapolis: Minnesota Press.

Carothers, Thomas. 1998. 'The Rule of Law Revival', *Foreign Affairs*, March–April 77(2): 95–106.

Central Committee, CPI (ML) Peoples War, 'Fight against the Tendencies of Economism and Revisionism, *Peoples War*, October 1981.

Certeau, Michel De. 1988. *The Practices of Everyday Life*. Berkeley: University of California Press.

Chalam, G. V. 1926. *Man and Woman*. Vijayawada: Veni Press.

———. 1976. *Musings*. Hyderabad: Chalam Sahiti.

Chandhoke, Neera. 1995. *State and Civil Society: Explorations in Political Theory*. New Delhi: SAGE Publications.

———. 1998a. 'Thinking through Rights', *Economic and Political Weekly*, 33(5): 37–51.

———. 1998b. 'The Assertion of Civil Society against State' in M. Mohanty (ed.) *People's Rights*. Delhi: SAGE Publications.

———. 2001. 'The "Civil" and the "Political" in Civil Society, *Democratization*. 8(2): 1–24.

———. 2003. *The Conceits of Civil Society*. Delhi: Oxford University Press.

Chandra, Bipan et al. 1999. *India Since Independence*. New Delhi: Penguin.

———. 2003. *In the Name of Democracy: JP Movement and the Emergency*. New Delhi: Penguin.

Chatterjee, Partha. 1986. *Nationalist Thought and the Colonial World: A Derivative Discourse?* New Delhi: Oxford University Press.

———. 1993. *Nation and its Fragments: Colonial and Post Colonial Histories*. Princeton: Princeton University Press.

———. 1997. 'Beyond the Nation? Or Within?' *Economic and Political Weekly*, 33(5): 30–34.

———. 1998a. 'Community in the East', *Economic and Political Weekly*, 33(6): 277–82.

Chatterjee, Partha. 1998b. 'Development Planning and the Indian State', in Terence J. Byres (ed.) *The State and Development Planning in India*, 51–72. Delhi: Oxford University Press.

———. 2004. *Politics of the Governed*. Delhi: Permanent Black.

———. 2006. 'The Moment of Manoeuvre: Gandhi and the Critique of Civil Society' in A. Raghuram (ed.) *Debating Gandhi*. Delhi: Oxford University Press.

———. 2008. 'Democracy and Economic Transformation in India', *Economic and Political Weekly*, 43(16) April 19: 53–62.

———. 2010. *Empire and Nation*. New Delhi: Permanent Black.

Chen, Kuan Hsing. 2003. 'Civil Society and Min-Jian: On Political Society and Popular Democracy', *Cultural Studies*, 17(6): 877–896.

Chinnaiah, Jangam. 1998. 'Sub-Caste Consciousness and Challenges before Dalit Intellectuals', *Mainstream*, March 14: 7–8.

Churchich, N. 1994. *Marxism and Morality*. Cambridge: James Clarke.

COC, CPI (ML) Peoples War. 1995. 'Special Features of Indian Revolution'. Paper presented at International Seminar on 9–12 March, Hyderabad.

Cohen, J. and A. Arato. 1992. *Civil Society and Political Theory*. Cambridge: MIT Press.

Committee of Concerned Citizens. 1998. *In Search of Democratic Space*. Hyderabad: CCC.

———. 2006. *Negotiating Peace*. Hyderabad: CCC.

Connell, R. W. 1990. 'The State, Gender and Sexual Politics: Theory and Appraisal', *Theory and Society*, 19(5): 507–44.

Corbridge, Stuart, Glyn Williams, Manoj Srivastava and Rene Veron. 2005. *Seeing the State: Governance and Governmentality in India*. Cambridge: Cambridge University Press.

CPDR. 1991. 'The Civil Liberties Movement: A Perspective', in A. R. Desai, *Violation of Democratic Rights in India*, Vol. 3. Bombay: Sangam Books.

CPI (ML) Janashakti, 'Kulam Samasya' (Telugu), undated.

CPI (ML) PW Kendra Rajakeeya Nirmana Sameeksha, March 2001.

Dagger, Richard. 1997. *Civic Virtues: Rights, Citizenship, Republican Liberalism*. Oxford: Oxford University Press.

Dahlerup, D. 1994. 'Learning to Live with the State—State, Civil Society, and Market: Women's Need for State Interventions in East and West', *Women's Studies International Forum*, 17(2/3): 117–27.

Dalit Bahujan Mahasabha. 1998. 'Karamchedu Nundi Vempenttadhaka Dalitulapai Dhadulu Endhuku Jarugutunnai? Emi Cheyyali?' (Telugu). Hyderabad: DBMS.

Dalitha Pantherla Manifesto (Telugu). 1996. Navayuva Samakhya. Vijayawada.

Day, Richard J. F. 2005. *Gramsci is Dead*. Hyderabad: Orient Longman.

Dean, Jodi. 1992. 'Including Women: The Consequences and Side Effects of Feminist Critique of Civil Society', *Philosophy and Social Criticism*, 18(3–4): 379–406.

Deleuze, G. and F. Guatarri. 1988. *A Thousand Plateaus: Capitalism and Schizophrenia*. London: Athlove Press.